Fichte's *1804 Wissenschaftslehre*

SUNY series in Contemporary Continental Philosophy
———
Dennis J. Schmidt, editor

Fichte's *1804 Wissenschaftslehre*
Essays on the "Science of Knowing"

Edited by

Benjamin D. Crowe *and* Gabriel Gottlieb

Published by State University of New York Press, Albany

© 2024 State University of New York

All rights reserved

Printed in the United States of America

No part of this book may be used or reproduced in any manner whatsoever without written permission. No part of this book may be stored in a retrieval system or transmitted in any form or by any means including electronic, electrostatic, magnetic tape, mechanical, photocopying, recording, or otherwise without the prior permission in writing of the publisher.

For information, contact State University of New York Press, Albany, NY
www.sunypress.edu

Library of Congress Cataloging-in-Publication Data

Names: Crowe, Benjamin D., 1976– editor. | Gottlieb, Gabriel, editor.
Title: Fichte's 1804 Wissenschaftslehre : essays on the "Science of knowing" / edited by Benjamin Crowe and Gabriel Gottlieb.
Description: Albany : State University of New York Press, [2024] | Series: SUNY series in contemporary continental philosophy | Includes bibliographical references.
Identifiers: LCCN 2023015638 | ISBN 9781438495958 (hardcover : alk. paper) | ISBN 9781438495965 (ebook) | ISBN 9781438495941 (pbk. : alk. paper)
Subjects: LCSH: Fichte, Johann Gottlieb, 1762–1814. Wissenschaftslehre 1804 (1st version) | Fichte, Johann Gottlieb, 1762–1814. Wissenschaftslehre 1804 (2nd version) | Philosophy, German—19th century.
Classification: LCC B2848 .F565 2024 | DDC 193—dc23/eng/20231108
LC record available at https://lccn.loc.gov/2023015638

10 9 8 7 6 5 4 3 2 1

Contents

Acknowledgments ix

Abbreviations xi

Introduction 1
    Gabriel Gottlieb and Benjamin D. Crowe

Part 1. The Continuity Question

Chapter 1
The Absolute and the *1804 Wissenschaftslehre* 11
    C. Jeffery Kinlaw

Chapter 2
"You Can't Get There from Here": Fichte's (Unwritten)
1799 Review (*nach der Principien der Wissenschaftslehre*) of the
1804 Wissenschaftslehre 33
    Daniel Breazeale

Chapter 3
The First Principle in the Later Fichte: The (Not) "Surprising Insight"
in the Fifteenth Lecture of the *1804 Wissenschaftslehre* 61
    Michael Lewin

Chapter 4
Fichte's Reader and the Autopoiesis of the *Wissenschaftslehre*,
1794–1804 79
    Andrew J. Mitchell

Part 2. Key Concepts

Chapter 5
Into Death's Lair: Truth, Appearance, and the Irrational Gap in
Fichte's *1804 Wissenschaftslehre*   97
   Matthew Nini

Chapter 6
Nothing Remains: Notes on Fichte's "Irrational Gap" in the *1804*   119
Wissenschaftslehre
   F. Scott Scribner

Chapter 7
Pure Light and the Promethean Self of Fichte's *1804 Wissenschaftslehre*   131
   Kit Slover

Chapter 8
The Odyssey of the "Through" (*das Durch*)   145
   M. Jorge de Carvalho

Chapter 9
The "We" of Speculative Philosophy   173
   Benjamin D. Crowe

Part 3. System and Idealism

Chapter 10
The Quintuple Quintuplicity of Forms of (Self-)Consciousness in
Fichte's *1804 Wissenschaftslehre*   193
   Emiliano Acosta

Chapter 11
Immanent Thinking and the Activity of Philosophizing in
Fichte's *1804 Wissenschaftslehre*   215
   Angelica Nuzzo

Chapter 12
Fichte's *1804 Wissenschaftslehre*: A Possible Reply to Schelling's *Bruno*   235
   Michael Vater

Chapter 13
Fichte contra Idealism in the *1804 Wissenschaftslehre* 259
   Michael Steinberg

Chapter 14
The Self-Justification of Fichte's Philosophy 273
   Jacinto Rivera de Rosales†

Chapter 15
Blockchain as Fichtean Problem 291
   Adam Hankins

Chapter 16
Is Fichte a Kantian, a German Idealist, Both, or Neither? 313
   Tom Rockmore

Contributors 329

Index 331

Acknowledgments

This volume collects papers presented by an international group of scholars at the Fourteenth Biennial Meeting of the North American Fichte Society (May 22–25, 2019), which was dedicated to "The Wissenschaftslehre of 1804" and held at Xavier University in Cincinnati, Ohio. Approximately a year after the conference, while we were still at the beginning stages of putting this volume together, COVID-19 hit, and our lives, the lives of the contributors, and the lives of practically every Earthling were radically changed. Both of us were also raising newborns and toddlers during the pandemic, which challenged us in unexpected ways. Due to these circumstances, the volume took much longer than expected to organize and edit. We are truly grateful to our contributors as well as Michael Rinella and our collaborators at SUNY Press for their patience and support during these years.

We'd especially like to thank Dan Breazeale and Tom Rockmore for passing the torch to us as co-positors of the North American Fichte Society. We'd like to thank both Elizabeth Millán Brusslan for her support of this project and the anonymous reviewers who provided detailed and invaluable feedback on the manuscript. We are also grateful for the support of our wives (Kristen and Kristin) and our children who kindly put up with our Fichte fanaticism.

We dedicate this volume to the life and memory of Jacinto Rivera de Rosales, poet, philosopher, teacher, translator, muscian, and friend of Fichteans everywhere. Jacinto passed away October 15, 2021, and while he is greatly missed by the community of Fichteans worldwide, we will forever be indebted to his essential contributions. May his memory be a blessing.

Abbreviations

Throughout the volume we use the title *1804 Wissenschaftslehre* to refer to the second series of lectures on the *Wissenschaftslehre* delivered between April 16 and June 8, 1804. These lectures are collected in *J. G. Fichte-Gesamtausgabe der Bayerischen Akademie der Wissenschaften*, Reihe II, Band 8, and translated by Walter E. Wright as *The Science of Knowing: J. G. Fichte's 1804 Lectures on the Wissenschaftslehre*. This translation is used throughout, except where noted. We use superscripts to distinguish citations to the three-lecture series (1804^1, 1804^2, 1804^3), but the title *1804 Wissenschaftslehre*, for the purposes of this volume, is only used to refer to the 1804^2 series of lectures.

1804^2	*The Science of Knowing: J. G. Fichte's 1804 Lectures on the Wissenschaftslehre*, trans. Walter E. Wright (Albany: State University of New York Press, 2005).
AA	Immanuel Kant, *Gesammelte Schriften* (Berlin: de Gruyter, 1902ff).
EPW	*Fichte: Early Philosophical Writings*, ed. and trans. Daniel Breazeale (Ithaca, NY: Cornell University Press, 1988).
FNR	Fichte, *Foundations of Natural Right*, ed. Frederick Neuhouser, trans. Michael Baur (Cambridge: Cambridge University Press, 2000).
FEW	Fichte, *J. G. Fichte: Foundations of the Entire Wissenschaftslehre and Other Writings (1794–1795)*, ed. and trans. Daniel Breazeale (Oxford: Oxford University Press, 2021).
FTP	*Fichte: Foundations of Transcendental Philosophy (Wissenschaftslehre) nova methodo*, ed. and trans. Daniel Breazeale (Ithaca, NY: Cornell University Press, 1992).

GA   *J. G. Fichte-Gesamtausgabe der Bayerischen Akademie der Wissenschaften*, ed. Erich Fuchs, Reinhard Lauth†, and Hans Gliwitzky† (Stuttgart-Bad Cannstatt: Frommann-Holzboog, 1964–2012).

GWL   Fichte, *Grundlage der gesammten Wissenschaftslehre* (1794/1795).

IWL   Fichte, *Introductions to the Wissenschaftslehre and Other Writings*, ed. and trans. Daniel Breazeale (Indianapolis, IN: Hackett, 1994).

SE   Fichte, *System of Ethics,* ed. and trans. Daniel Breazeale and Günter Zöller (Cambridge: Cambridge University Press, 2005).

SK   *Science of Knowledge*, trans. Peter Heath and John Lachs (Cambridge: Cambridge University Press, 1970).

SS   Fichte, *System der Sittenlehre* (1798).

SW   *Johann Gottlieb Fichtes sämmtliche Werke*, ed. I. H. Fichte, 8 vols. (Berlin: Viet & Co., 1845–1846); rpt., along with the three vols. of *Johann Gottlieb Fichtes nachgelassene Werke* (Bonn: Adolphus-Marcus, 1834–1835), as *Fichtes Werke* (Berlin: de Gruyter, 1971).

WLnm[H]   Fichte, *Wissenschaftslehre nova methodo* ("Halle Nachshrift," 1796/1797).

WLnm[K]   Fichte, *Wissenschaftslehre nova methodo* ("Krause Nachschrift," 1798/1799).

Introduction

GABRIEL GOTTLIEB AND BENJAMIN CROWE

There is little doubt that Fichte's reputation as a philosopher is largely built upon the published writings of what is known as his Jena period, roughly 1793–1799. These were incredibly productive years for him, even if one cites only the three major works published while he was teaching and living in Jena: *Foundation of the Entire Wissenschaftslehre* (1794/1795), *Foundations of Natural Right* (1796/1797), and *The System of Ethics* (1798). When one considers his essays, lectures, and, particularly, his attempt to revise the *Wissenschaftslehre* according to a new method (the *Wissenschaftslehre nova methodo*), his time in Jena looks to be his most philosophically potent period, especially since it is these works that were available to students and his contemporaries and that shaped his reception during much of the nineteenth and twentieth centuries.

It is not surprising, then, to find that much of the scholarship on Fichte's philosophy, especially in the Anglo-American tradition, has focused on his Jena writings. Such a narrow focus is, however, unfortunate. After fleeing Jena due to the Atheism Controversy, Fichte did not stop expanding and revising the *Wissenschaftslehre* once he arrived in Berlin.[1] In fact, his productivity continued with the publication of "popular" philosophical works that stem from his time in Berlin: *The Characteristics of the Present Age* (1806), *The Way towards the Blessed Life, or on the Doctrine of Religion* (1806), and *Addresses to the German Nation* (1808). These works are not systematic elements of the *Wissenschaftslehre*, but they do, in their own unique ways, take for granted core elements of the *Wissenschaftslehre*. Yet, by the time these works were initially conceived and finally published, Fichte had reoriented his *Wissenschaftslehre* away from the idea that the entire science must be grounded in the self-activity of the pure I and toward a model of the *Wissenschaftslehre* where *absolute being* or *oneness* (rather than the absolute I) takes on a more prominent role.

Fichte's 1804 lectures on the *Wissenschaftslehre*, delivered in three different series, amount to one of his most thorough and radical reformulations of his philosophical system. The second series of lectures are the best known and were first translated into English as the *Science of Knowing* by Walter E. Wright in 2005. It is this series of lectures that serves as the primary work under investigation in the present volume.

The "Aphorisms on the Essence of Philosophy as a Science" (1804), a short unpublished piece of writing summarizing this second series of lectures he delivered between April 16 and June 8, 1804, the set of lectures examined herein, furnish a valuable perspective for understanding the lectures as a whole. Fichte explains that "the system" he names *Wissenschaftslehre*, what he also calls here *logologia* or simply "reason," proceeds by presenting the "primordial oneness of being and consciousness."[2] Traditionally, philosophers take *being*, he notes, as the relevant object of study. The aim is to address how knowledge of being's multiple determinations is possible. This is the case for classical philosophical doctrines, including Plato's forms, Descartes's thinking thing, or Spinoza's substance. Yet being, Fichte insists, arises only within consciousness and consciousness arises only with being, a point previous philosophers, except for Kant, failed to appreciate. The object of study for philosophy, then, ought to be not simply being or consciousness but their unity, or oneness. The task of philosophy, as Fichte notes, is to trace multiplicity back to absolute oneness, which is, at the same time, to present "the absolute."[3]

This second series of lectures (hereafter, the *1804 Wissenschaftslehre*) consists of two related parts: the First through Sixteenth Lectures provide an ascending analysis and construction of being, eventually arriving at the "fundamental principle": "*Being is entirely a self-enclosed singularity of immediately living being that can never go outside itself.*"[4] The goal, in presenting the absolute, is to present an absolute devoid of any disjunction, or a set of terms opposed to each other that are not resolved by some higher dialectical synthesis that discharges the disjunction in favor of oneness. The Seventeenth through Twenty-Eighth Lectures offer a construction of the appearing of being in its multiplicity. The difference between the multiplicity in the first half and the second is that the former is a factical multiplicity; once multiplicity is constructed as appearance or image, it has, in virtue of its construction from the absolute, shed its status as merely factical. In return, multiplicity is genetically constructed and grounded, rather merely given. Put differently, one might say that the given is conceived, once the ascent from absolute oneness is achieved (if it ever is), not as an assumed given that draws on what we might take to be obvious facts about the nature of experience but as a justified given required for the intelligibility of knowing itself.

Fichte delivered these lectures four times a week between April 16 and June 8, 1804. His audience included prominent members of the reformist administration that was in power in Prussia at that time. Men such as Altenstein, minister of education; Hardenburg, foreign minister and minister of finance; and Beyme, justice minister who eventually played a crucial role in the founding of Berlin's first university in 1809, all took a lively interest in Fichte and in his thought by conscientiously attending these and other lectures during this period. Fichte's audience also included around fifteen female attendees, including his wife Johanna and Henriette Herz (1764–1847), a prominent member of Berlin's Jewish cultural elite and the convener of a famous salon frequented by the likes of the Schlegel and Humboldt brothers, Schleiermacher, and other literati. On Sundays, Fichte convened "Conversatoria" for interested parties who wished to query him in a less formal setting about key concepts and arguments in the lectures. Despite his lack of a formal academic post, Fichte still called upon a devoted coterie of brilliant students.

Fichte's absolute oneness as presented in the *1804 Wissenschaftslehre* is an attempt, as listeners would have fully appreciated, to present a form of absolute idealism that responds to Schelling's identity philosophy, a transition in Schelling's philosophy that initiated a break or rupture between Fichte and Schelling; it additionally addresses Hegel's charge of subjectivism in his *Differenzschrift*.[5] Schelling was familiar with Fichte's absolute idealism as first developed in the 1804 lectures, but, it seems, primarily in the popular form they take in the *Blessed Life*, a work Schelling critically examines in his *Statement on the True Relationship of the Philosophy of Nature to the Revised Fichtean Doctrine*.[6] Hegel, however, appears largely indifferent to the post-Jena developments of Fichte's philosophy, as he continues throughout his career to take Fichte's Jena writings as the paradigmatic representation of Fichte's *Wissenschaftslehre*.

The *1804 Wissenschaftslehre* was not actually published until 1834 as part of the unpublished works included in the collected works (the *Sämmtlichen Werke*) edited by Fichte's son Immanuel Herman. Both Fichte's original manuscript, and the "clean copy" he prepared (as was his custom) following the conclusion of the lectures, are now lost. In the early twentieth century, a librarian in the city archives of Halle (which had boasted a reformist university until Prussia's defeat by Napoleon in 1806–1807) discovered a "*copia*" of the lectures in a hand other than Fichte's. The critical edition of Fichte's works reproduces both I. H. Fichte's version and the *copia* on facing pages, making it clear that (despite divergences) these derive from the same source (most likely Fichte's own copy). Since its publication, these lectures have increasingly influenced Fichte's European reception and, since their translation by Walter E. Wright as *The Science of Knowing*, his Anglo-American reception.

Since Fichte's *1804 Wissenschaftslehre* was not published during his lifetime, its influence was not immediate. One historically consequential engagement with these lectures is found in Emil Lask's *Fichtes Idealismus und die Geschichte* (1902), which examines and employs Fichte's neologism "facticity." Lask's engagement with Fichte importantly influenced Lukács and Heidegger, with the latter transforming the concept of facticity for the purpose of characterizing the thrownness of *Dasein*, a move that made the concept essential to phenomenology and continental philosophy more generally.[7] There is, it should be noted, an ever-growing literature in German on Fichte's *1804 Wissenschaftslehre*.[8] As scholarship in English explores Fichte's Berlin writings with greater attention, Fichte's 1804 lectures will prove essential to making sense of novel directions his work pursues. Walter Wright, the translator of *The Science of Knowing*, has rightly called Fichte's 1804 lectures "one of the masterworks in the European philosophical tradition," which represents the "pinnacle of Fichte's efforts to present his fundamental philosophical system."[9] After reading these essays in this volume, we hope you might find yourself agreeing with Wright's perhaps controversial claim.

This volume is organized, roughly, into three categories: (1) chapters that in one way or another address the relationship of the *1804 Wissenschaftslehre* to Fichte's Jena presentations of the *Wissenschaftslehre*, (2) chapters that focus on a key concept or set of concepts from the *1804 Wissenschaftslehre*, and (3) chapters that examine issues related to Fichte's conception of system and idealism. We recognize that some could fit easily in one or another category, but our hope is that this categorization will provide the reader with some general guidance regarding the central themes of each chapter.

In part 1, "The Continuity Question," fall the papers of C. Jeffrey Kinlaw, Daniel Breazeale, Andrew J. Mitchell, and Michael Lewin. Kinlaw's chapter nicely sets out the terms of the debate: Fichte's focus on absolute being or oneness looks to commit him not to the transcendental philosophy of his Jena writings but to a form of transcendent dogmatism. While Kinlaw is hesitant to provide a full-throated defense of the continuity view, the view that the absolute of the *1804 Wissenschaftslehre* is continuous with the absolute I of his Jena project, Kinlaw sketches one line of attack in support of the continuity view. In contrast, Daniel Breazeale, in what one might consider a work of creative nonfiction, imagines a review, composed by Fichte himself in 1799, of a recently discovered manuscript from 1804 (somehow it found its way back in time) that presents a new version of the *Wissenschaftslehre*. Here we have Fichte, in a sense, unwittingly reviewing his own work. On Breazeale's imaginative interpretation of Fichte's reading of the *1804 Wissenschaftslehre*, we see the ways in which the latter work departs from or is discontinuous with the Jena project. Michael Lewin offers a reading that bypasses the continuity view (absolute being is a version of the absolute I) and a version of the discontinuity view (the absolute is essentially God), the latter of which results in a form of transcendent dogmatism. Relying on the didactic resources of analogical thinking, Lewin offers a reading that accounts for Fichte's surprising identification in the Fifteenth Lecture of "being" with "absolute I." Finally, Andrew J. Mitchell also sees in the *1804 Wissenschaftslehre* a departure from Fichte's earlier writings, but here the lack of continuity is more narrowly circumscribed: the reader or listener is meant to enact the content of the *Wissenschaftslehre*, according to the Jena writings, while in the 1804 lectures she is meant to "host" the *Wissenschaftslehre*, thereby taking on at key moments a more passive position, one in which freedom is not a prerequisite for the construction of the *Wissenschaftslehre*.

Part 2 addresses "Key Concepts" developed in the *1804 Wissenschaftslehre*. Two chapters address what Fichte calls the "irrational gap," a gap that opens up between the absolute and appearance, or the movement from the absolute to the multiplicity of consciousness. Matthew Nini's interpretation of the *1804 Wissenschaftslehre* argues that the irrational gap is resolved by what he calls the "singularity thesis"—the absolute and consciousness are a singularity, outside of which nothing properly is, and the doctrine of appearances is developed on the basis of the singularity thesis, thereby allowing a move from singularity to a phenomenology of life. F. Scott Scribner, in contrast, takes a more skeptical approach to Fichte's attempts to address the problem of the irrational gap, as he sees each attempt to resolve the gap as arriving at a supplement that threatens to undermine the project of the *Wissenschaftslehre*. Kit Slover's chapter provides an interpretation of the structure and meaning of "pure light," M. Jorge de Carvalho addresses the meaning and role of Fichte's nominalization of the preposition *durch* as *das Durch*, and Benjamin D. Crowe takes Fichte's conception of the "We" as his primary object of study.

Part 3, "System and Idealism," includes essays that examine methodological themes and issues related to systematicity and Fichte's idealism. Emiliano Acosta examines Fichte's quintuplicity of quintuplicities or, as Fichte puts it: "[The] twenty-five main moments and fundamental determinations of knowledge in its origin," which the *1804 Wissenschaftslehre* establishes as a result of the five-fold synthesis. Angelica Nuzzo investigates methodological considerations relevant to thinking's performative immanence in the *1804 Wissenschaftslehre* and in Hegel's *Phenomenology of Spirit*. Michael Vater's analysis of Fichte's system of idealism and realism as developed in the *1804 Wissenschaftslehre* contrasts it to Schelling's contemporaneous identity philosophy and, in particular, his dialogue *Bruno*. Michael Steinberg similarly considers the relationship of idealism and realism in Fichte's 1804 system. He argues, contrary to what many might assume, that Fichte's *Wissenschaftslehre* offers a thorough defense of realism; additionally, the *1804 Wissenschaftslehre*'s critical stance toward idealism is not a repudiation of the Jena writings but a completion of that very project. Jacinto Rivera de Rosales provides an interpretation of the final lectures of the *1804 Wissenschaftslehre* where the system itself is justified in virtue of a self-justification. Adam Hankins reflects on the emergent technology of the blockchain in order to reconceptualize the problem of multiplicity, oneness, and certainty in Fichte's *1804 Wissenschaftslehre* for the purpose of revealing the ways in which a blockchain system offers a way to reconsider faith, trust, and certainty in theological contexts. Tom Rockmore offers an account of Fichte's position within the long history of idealism—is he, after all, really a German idealist? Appropriately, Rockmore concludes his essay with some reflections on the continuity question.

In his biography of Fichte, Manfred Kühn remarks that "it cannot be doubted that the [*1804 Wissenschaftslehre*] is much clearer than the *Grundlage* and the *Wissenschaftslehre nova methodo*, even though Fichte does not make it easy for his listeners here either."[10] We can certainly agree that Fichte does not make matters easy for his listeners; however, there is good reason to believe that, at least many students of Fichte's work who have cut their teeth on the Jena presentations of the *Wissenschaftslehre*, will find the *1804 Wissenschaftslehre* quite challenging, and perhaps, at times, impenetrable. Our hope is that the present volume will shine some "pure light" on Fichte's lectures and contribute to deepening our understanding of it by bridging the *hiatus* between impenetrability and intelligibility.

Notes

1. For an introduction and a collection of the relevant writings by Fichte and others, see Yolanda Estes and Curtis Bowman, *J. G. Fichte and the Atheism Dispute (1798–1800)* (New York: Routledge, 2016).

2. 1804², 205; *GA*, III/5, 246.
3. 1804², 24–25; *GA*, II/8, 9.
4. 1804², 121; *GA*, II/8, 242.
5. Fichte mentions "subjectivism" and offers critical remarks on Schelling's identify philosophy at the beginning of the Fourteenth Lecture. For Hegel's critique of Fichte see, Hegel's *The Difference Between Fichte and Schelling's System of Philosophy*, trans. H. S. Harris and Walter Cerf (Albany: State University of New York Press, 1977); for an account of Schelling's "identity philosophy," see Schelling, *Presentation of My System of Philosophy* in *The Philosophical Rupture between Fichte and Schelling: Selected Texts and Correspondence (1800–1802)*, eds. and trans. David W. Wood and Michael Vater (Albany: State University of New York Press, 2012).
6. Schelling, *Statement on the True Relationship of the Philosophy of Nature to the Revised Fichtean Doctrine*, trans. Dale E. Snow (Albany: State University of New York Press, 2018).
7. On the role of "facticity" in Fichte's Berlin writings, see G. Anthony Bruno, "Facticity and Genesis: Tracking Fichte's Method in the Berlin Wissenschaftslehre," in *The Enigma of Fichte's First Principles* (Brill, 2021), 177–97. For the connection to Lukács, see Tom Rockmore, "Fichte, Lask, and Lukács's Hegelian Marxism," *Journal of the History of Philosophy* 30, no. 4 (1992): 557–77. The Heidegger and Fichte connection, as mediated by Lask, has been explored much more. See, for instance, Theodore Kiesel, "Heidegger–Lask–Fichte," in *Heidegger, German Idealism, and Neo-Kantianism*, ed. Tom Rockmore (New York: Humanity Books, 2000); Alfred Denker, "The Young Heidegger and Fichte," in *Heidegger, German Idealism, and Neo-Kantianism*; M. Jorge de Carvalho, "Fichte, Heidegger, and the Concept of Facticity" in *Fichte and the Phenomenological Tradition*, eds. Violetta L. Waibel, Daniel Breazeale, and Tom Rockmore (New York: Walter de Gruyter, 2010); G. Anthony Bruno, "Hiatus Irrationalis: Lask's Fateful Misreading of Fichte," *European Journal of Philosophy* 30.3 (2022): 977–95.
8. For more recent German literature on Fichte's 1804 *Wissenschaftslehre*, see Ulrich Schlösser, *Das Erfassen des Einleuchtens: Fichtes Wissenschaftslehre von 1804 als Kritik an der Annahme entzogener Voraussetzungen unseres Wissens und als Phiosophie des Gewißseins* (Berlin: Phil-Verlag, 2001); Christian Danz, "Die Duplizität des Absoluten in der Wissenschaftslehre von 1804: Fichtes Auseinandersetzung mit Schellings identitätsphilosophischer Schrift 'Darstellung meines Systems,'" *Fichte-Studien* 12 (1997); Ludwig Siep, "Hegels Fichtekritik und die Wissenschaftslehre von 1804" (Freiburg: Alber, 1970).
9. Walter E. Wright, "Introduction," in *The Science of Knowing: J.G. Fichte's 1804 Lectures on the Wissenschaftslehre*, 4.
10. Manfred Kühn, *Johann Gottlieb Fichte: Ein deutscher Philosoph, 1762–1814* (C. H. Beck, 2012), 458.

Part 1

The Continuity Question

Chapter 1

The Absolute and the *1804 Wissenschaftslehre*

C. JEFFERY KINLAW

In the Fourth Lecture of the *1804 Wissenschaftslehre*, Fichte emphasizes that the task of the *Wissenschaftslehre* is to reconstruct the self-constituting act of absolute knowing with the expressed intent of linking that reconstruction to the Absolute itself. Executing that task, however, incurs a knotty problem: absolute knowing is, as Fichte describes it, a self-constituting act and thus self-enclosed, in itself and from itself, and accordingly inaccessible and even inconceivable. The Absolute's inaccessibility would appear to block any actual philosophical retrieval, or at least expose any reconstructive attempt to crushing skeptical objections. And yet Fichte argues that a proper understanding of the reconstructive task can solve this problem. Properly executed, philosophical reconstruction can succeed in retrieving the self-constituting act of absolute knowing from which the structure and content of consciousness can then be derived as the *Wissenschaftslehre* requires. This proper understanding informs both the nature of the *Wissenschaftlehre* and the self-conception of the philosopher.

Any solution to the problem must avoid at least two errors Fichte found annoyingly prominent in the decade-long reception of his *Wissenschaftslehre*: first, a reconstruction of the Absolute that is inordinately constructive—a product merely of pure thinking or sheer speculation, as he characterizes Schelling's philosophy of nature and philosophy of identity—which assumes that it can conceptually grasp the Absolute; second, that the Absolute, however conceived, is something factical, that is, something taken as given. The first and principle task to which Fichte devotes the bulk of the 1804 lectures is to resolve the distance between the Absolute's own self-constituting *act*—which Fichte describes in the Fifteenth Lecture as the pure act that is "the interpenetration of living and being"[1]—and the philosopher's *act* of reflective retrieval. What makes philosophical retrieval of the Absolute possible and what provides the essential propaedeutic for that retrieval is the thesis, to be confirmed in the execution of the (*Wissenschaftslehre*), that we are the image of the Absolute. Although Fichte identifies the Absolute with Being and thus presumably objectivity, which appears to expand the distance between ourselves and the Absolute, he connects us, as free, finite rational beings, directly to the Absolute itself in the Fifteenth Lecture: "But we live immediately in the act of living itself. For this reason, *we are* the one, undivided Being itself: in itself, from itself, through itself, which utterly cannot proceed outside itself into duality."[2] Put differently, we are, at least insipiently, the pure act of living, and living as absolute; in sum, we are free and absolutely self-determining rational beings. Put in these terms, one might read this passage and by extension the entire set of the 1804 lectures as a clarification and defense of the core nature of I-hood as developed and defended in the Jena *Wissenschaftslehre*, as well as identifying and explicating our self-knowledge as freely self-determining rational agents.

Fichte's conception of I-hood, as defended in the Jena *Wissenschaftslehre*, is metaphysically austere. The I is simply an act, specifically an act of free, absolute self-determination underlying and underwriting all consciousness though never appearing as an object within consciousness—and, moreover, an act of an embodied, rational organism. This metaphysical parsimony, of course, recedes significantly after Fichte arrives in Berlin, as he doesn't hesitate to engage in metaphysical analyses of various aspects of I-hood or to attribute metaphysical categories to what he calls the Absolute. And yet, these analyses and attributions serve, on one possible reading, primarily to reinforce and further explicate the conception of I-hood Fichte defends in the Jena writings. If this interpretation is accurate, then perhaps Fichte's so-called metaphysical turn is less pronounced and the continuity with his Jena writings stronger than conventionally assumed. The more specific interpretation I have in mind is this: whereas Fichte provides various metaphysical analyses of the Absolute, analyses structured as ascending levels of abstraction and which attribute metaphysical categories to the Absolute, his overall aim is to clarify and defend a conception of I-hood—that by

I-hood he means the act of free, absolute rational self-determination—which is largely consistent with his Jena view. Call this the continuity view (CV) whose central thesis can be express as follows: "The Central Thesis: By the Absolute, Fichte means (1) the act of free, absolute self-determination that is the necessary explanatory ground of consciousness, and (2) the animating spirit (*Geist*) of the community of free, rational, moral agents, that is, the moral world-order or normative world."[3]

Central to CV are passages, such as the one cited above, that link claims about the nature of the Absolute to a proper conception of ourselves as free, rational agents, a self-conception that then guides the philosopher's act of reflective retrieval of the Absolute. This means that we, especially when we fulfill our duty as moral agents to strive toward absolute independence as freely self-determining rational agents, are the image of the Absolute, and that, furthermore, what Fichte calls the Absolute is reducible to I-hood ostensibly supplemented, simply for clarification and justificatory purposes, by metaphysical attributions.

Any defense of CV faces a formidable challenge, specifically the criticism (which I outline below) that Fichte's identification of the Absolute with Being, and thus with objectivity, is an abandonment of transcendental philosophy for a position more closely associated with the transcendent dogmatism he criticized so vociferously in the Jena writings.[4] I do not claim that Fichte can meet this challenge successfully. Rather, I will outline how one might go about defending the first half of CV and specifically what that defense would need to accomplish. The chapter proceeds as follows. First, I explicate the main objection to CV and show why the objection is distinct from a reading of Fichte's identification of God with the divine world-order as consistent with CV. My defense of CV, or better, how one might (or should) defend CV, then proceeds as follows. First, I provide an account of the elusiveness of the Absolute, which arises from the disjunction between the Absolute itself and any philosophical reconstruction of the Absolute. A key question here, and especially for any defense of CV, will be to whom and to what sort of self-conception or epistemic standpoint is the Absolute fundamentally elusive. Second, I turn to Fichte's alternative view of reflective retrieval or reconstruction, which provides the proper epistemic standpoint from which to secure an actual insight (*Einsicht*) into the Absolute. Here Fichte's central claim that *we* are immediate Being provides the necessary insight for a philosophical retrieval of the Absolute and thus much of the heavy lifting to support CV.

14 | C. Jeffery Kinlaw

Fichte's Transcendent Turn and the Case against the Continuity View

Even though the Absolute, or its manifestation (*Evidenz*) as Light, is a self-constituting act, it nonetheless resides in the realm of objectivity (= Being) that is beyond consciousness, whereas the Jena *Wissenschaftslehre* maintains that all being lies within consciousness (Sein ist gesetzt Sein). If so, the *1804 Wissenschaftslehre* reverts to a transcendent dogmatism. Put differently, the I's original self-positing never appears immediately as an object within consciousness precisely because it is a necessary explanatory ground for any and all consciousness. As such, original self-positing transcends finite consciousness but not the I itself, since original self-positing *is* the I or I-hood. By affirming an Absolute (= Being or objectivity), the *1804 Wissenschaftslehre* abandons the transcendental standpoint and thereby transcendental philosophy. Specifically, Fichte violates the basic principle that one cannot exceed the boundaries of consciousness (a major transgression for the Jena *Wissenschaftslehre*), namely that one cannot go beyond the sheer fact that one encounters boundaries to consciousness. This, and not a transcendent Absolute, is the true basis for what is incomprehensible. The *1804 Wissenschaftslehre* thus mutates from a pragmatic history of the mind to a metaphysics of the Absolute. Call this the transcendence objection (TO).[5]

It is difficult to understate how devastating TO is for the overall consistency and coherence of Fichte's *1804 Wissenschaftslehre*. Consider a further objection that follows from TO. The *1804 Wissenschaftslehre* is, as evident to the most sympathetic reader, a purely theoretical undertaking, whereas Fichte's Jena insight into the nature of freedom is that reason is first and foremost practical—even theoretical reason is guided by practically rational concerns. Now recall that the insight into the Absolute, which philosophical reflection attempts to retrieve, is the Absolute's own insight. If the Absolute is independent Being, then how can the inner, self-constituting life of the Absolute be anything but inward necessity? How could it not thereby be the negation of all freedom? Where in Fichte's various descriptions of the Absolute in the 1804 lectures does one find distinct references to the will, freedom, and practical rationality? One cannot simply assert that the Absolute's freedom is its own self-constituting act. There would be more than a whiff of the a priori in that claim (if not a case of gross bootstrapping), and self-constitution doesn't entail freedom. More importantly, the distance between the Absolute's inner self-constituting act and the philosopher's reflective retrieval of that act, which is grounded in the philosopher's own practical self-determination, would be unbridgeable. The execution of the *1804 Wissenschaftslehre*, as a philosophical mission, would be precluded before it could begin. It is unsurprising, as a proponent of TO might add, that one finds hardly any references to practical self-determination in the 1804 lectures.

The project that is the *1804 Wissenschaftslehre* presupposes a continuity between the Absolute's self-constituting act and the philosopher's own act of reflective retrieval of the same. As noted, Fichte states unequivocally the "we" are Being itself or the Absolute. If TO is correct, however, the nature of the Absolute is inconsistent with any connection between the Absolute and ourselves as free, rational beings. To say that the Absolute and we are both self-constituting, even freely self-constituting, would not entail any connection between the Absolute's self-constituting act and our own. By its nature, the Absolute is pure objectivity and thus independent of the I's own acts. One possible response would be to interpret Fichte's overall strategy in the *1804 Wissenschaftslehre* as an analysis of the pure being of the I (or better, pure Being as the I) abstracted from the I's relation to anything external or foreign to the I. The focus, rather, would be on the inner structure of the I, that is, how one must think of the I as an act of self-determining, self-constitution. Since Being always refers to objectivity, Fichte's strategy then would be to start with consideration of the nature of the I as an object. In other words, adapt Allen Wood's reconstruction of Fichte's procedure with the will in the *System of Ethics* to an interpretation of Fichte's argumentative strategy in the *1804 Wissenschaftslehre*.[6] This interpretation, however, even if it were promising, presupposes precisely what the CV must establish, namely that the Absolute constitutes itself within the philosopher's reflective retrieval of it and does so precisely because the Absolute is the original self-constituting act of the I itself. Put succinctly, CV must establish that Fichte's move to transcendence is merely apparent, and by the Absolute Fichte means nothing more than I-hood itself, as defended in the Jena writings—or something grounded in I-hood, such as the moral world-order as developed in the essays that precipitated the atheism dispute (or both as CV maintains).

It is important to distinguish TO from Fichte's reference to the supersensible when by supersensible he means the moral world-order or the animating spirit of the community of moral agents. The moral world-order does refer to something transcendent but in an attenuated and unproblematic sense. I read Fichte's concept of the supersensible, though I cannot defend my interpretation here, to refer to what we might call the normative world, that is, a moral community of free rational beings standing in recognitive and communicative relations with one another, whose dutiful acts advance the development of that moral community and whose ultimate end is complete independence (from nature) in their free, moral self-determination. The normative world is transcendent in the sense that it is neither reducible to nor supervenient upon the natural world, though is surely part of an expanded—specifically something akin to a dual aspect—conception of the "natural" world. Just as the absolute, free self-determination of rational beings does not supervene on mechanical or biological processes, the normative world doesn't supervene on forces, processes, and laws of nature. Freely self-determining rational agents are embodied agents nonetheless, and the normative world is fundamentally a component of *this* world. Accordingly, had Fichte developed a comprehensive account of the normative world (or the divine world-order as he calls it in a late Jena essay[7]), which by his own admission would have been required to complete the *Wissenschaftslehre*, one would expect a consistent commitment to the metaphysical parsimony of his Jena period. The normative world transcends nature in the sense that it doesn't supervene on physical processes, just as free self-determining actions of rational human organisms transcends the physical world by not supervening on physical processes. But free, rational agency is the self-determination of human *organisms*, and the normative world consists of normative relations among those same organisms. Both are part of the basic furniture of *this* world. Furthermore, the normative world is derived from the I's absolute, free self-determination. Rather than being independent of I-hood, the normative world's explanatory ground is I-hood itself.

The proponent of CV cannot advance her case by attempting to interpret the Absolute of the *1804 Wissenschaftslehre* in terms of the supersensible world as I have described it. According to the TO objection, the Absolute is Being (= objectivity) and thus independent of all I-hood, whereas the supersensible world has its basis and animating principle precisely in the dynamics of I-hood. Were the Absolute simply the supersensible world, then the distance between the Absolute and finite, rational beings who attempt to reflectively retrieval the Absolute would be bridgeable. Unfortunately, this is not the case. Furthermore, Fichte's correspondence with Schelling after arriving in Berlin appears to support (though the evidence is admittedly ambiguous) TO.

In a dense letter to Schelling written the summer of 1801, Fichte objects to doing philosophy from the starting point of Being as opposed, as one would expect, to a "seeing." Consider, Fichte suggests, the self-evident cognition of a standard necessary truth of geometry (assuming Euclidean space)—the shortest distance between two fixed points is a straight line—and focus on one's own grasping of that proposition as a necessary, self-evident truth. One affirms that the proposition is valid for all possible lines and all possible rational beings and does this by positing the form of grasping something determined (one's own grasping of the proposition) and, at the same time, as something determinate (that the proposition is graspable by any rational being). The first involves, Fichte maintains, the positing of an individual finite being (the one who actually, in this instance, grasps the proposition), as well as the general, "empty form of egoity," which identifies the "spirit world."[8] Fichte continues: "Universal (finite) consciousness is therefore the union of the consciousness of the spirit world and that of the individual. The latter is the ideal ground of the former; the former ([which] can never, however, be *cognized* and *penetrated* by self-evidence) is the *real* ground of the latter."[9] What to make of this passage? The CV proponent might approach the passage in the following way. The foundational "seeing" to which Fichte refers anticipates the strategic starting point of the *1804 Wissenschaftslehre* by tying the general form of "egoity" that underlies and persists through all instances of knowing the geometric proposition in question to absolute knowing, which underlies and persists through all knowing. If absolute knowing is consistent with "egoity" in the letter, then, since Fichte connects the form of "egoity" to the "spirit" world, absolute knowing has its basis in the supersensible or normative world. And if so, absolute knowing is tied strictly to I-hood, or at least to something derivable from I-hood. This would enable the CV proponent then to make the case that by the Absolute Fichte means I-hood and thereby provide the point of contact necessary for the philosopher's successful reflective retrieval of the Absolute. Unfortunately, this strategy is not available to the CV advocate. First, the supporting textual evidence is missing from the *1804 Wissenschaftslehre*. Second, it leaves unexplicated the parenthetical clause in the ostensibly supporting passage: "the former [spirit world] which can never . . . be cognized and penetrated by self-evidence." What to make of this? In the next paragraph of the same letter, Fichte writes:

> I said, you yourself posit, i.e., you conceiving, your coincidence of subject-objectivity, as something *determined*. This takes place in absolute consciousness, which cannot be surpassed or reflected again in any consciousness. This determinacy is therefore an *absolute determinacy* that cannot be reflected or penetrated by any

> consciousness, which is = the former given actuality or reality, to *being*. Being is—a *seeing that is impenetrable to itself.* If however you posit this determinacy . . . as a quantum of opposing determinability, then the real ground lies outside all consciousness because precisely this quantum cannot be more or less separated. It is = X of self-evidence, the eternally impenetrable.[10]

I will forego any attempted exegesis of this dense passage and only point out that the "seeing" referenced in the passage appears to be something transcendent, independent of consciousness, and decidedly different from any allusion Fichte makes to the supersensible world. If "seeing" is Being, as the Absolute is Being, then seeing, which is the foundation of the *Wissenschaftslehre*, even if it is self-constituting activity (cf. the Absolute of the *1804 Wissenschaftslehre*), is something independent of consciousness. What initially appears as a transcendental starting point actually transforms the *Wissenschaftslehre* into a transcendent dogmatism—which becomes a defeater for CV.

The challenge facing CV is, as I've indicated, formidable. Without appealing to any of Fichte's discussions of the supersensible or normative world, much less his hints at how that world might be configured, the CV defender must provide compelling reasons for affirming that the Absolute is not something transcendent and must do so by arguing persuasively that by the Absolute Fichte means I-hood (or the general form of I-hood).

The Elusiveness of the Absolute

Any case for CV must defend the following claims. (1) Properly executed philosophical reflection can retrieve the self-constituting act that is the Absolute. What is at stake here is reflective retrieval of the grounding act from which all consciousness is then derived according to the principles of the *Wissenschaftslehre*. Most of the 1804 lectures are devoted to establishing precisely this claim. Specifically, Fichte's efforts are devoted primarily to identifying and explicating the proper starting point for the *Wissenschaftslehre* as well as the required epistemic standpoint from which one must think through the same. (2) The Absolute, despite the metaphysical categories Fichte ascribes to it, is reducible to I-hood. These two claims are interrelated, but without a strong case for the second, there is no possible defense of the first. Unless CV can establish a strong case for the claim that by the

Absolute Fichte means I-hood—that the Absolute is not independent of I-hood, and by I-hood Fichte means the self-constituting, absolute free act of self-determination in the Jena sense—the effort of reflective retrieval becomes impossible. The obvious obstacle to defending the second claim is that, as we have seen, Fichte equates the Absolute with Being (= objectivity), namely something independent of consciousness. CV's principal challenge and its most fundamental and requisite goal is to show that Fichte's conception of Being in this context has the narrow, technical meaning of *activity, vitality,* and *life* that, rather than designating something objective or independent of consciousness, ties the Absolute directly to I-hood and thereby provides the basis for Fichte's claim (already cited) that we free, self-determining rational agents are Being itself. The first step is to identity the problem of the Absolute's elusiveness for philosophical reflection in general and how that problem informs any attempt to retrieve the Absolute reflectively.

Fichte identifies the problem of the Absolute's elusiveness as early as the Fourth Lecture. The Absolute is self-constituting or self-constructing (*sich construiren*) whereas the *Wissenschaftslehre* is a reconstruction. By self-constituting, Fichte means that the Absolute is a self-constituting act, as noted in the Fifteenth Lecture where he describes the Absolute's "in-itselfness" as "pure act." Accordingly, reflective retrieval can never capture the originality and immediacy of the Absolute's (*Tatlichkeit*). Regardless of the level of abstraction to which the philosopher ascends, a disjunction remains between the Absolute's originality—the Absolute as essentially act—and the philosopher's reflective retrieval of that act. Consider the problem from the perspective of Breazeale's distinctions among forms of intellectual intuition.[11] Breazeale identifies four distinct types of intellectual intuition in Fichte's Jena period. His overall aim is to disambiguate intellectual intuition in general and provide a perspicuous explication of each type. What Breazeale calls **ii2** refers to the immediate, tacit awareness of the I's original self-constituting act of self-determination, the foundational act from which all consciousness is derived and thus the starting point of the *Wissenschaftslehre*. **ii1** and **ii3** are attempts to retrieve the content—the act of absolute, freely initiated self-determination—expressed in **ii2**. Fichte contends that when one acts dutifully—that is, independent and irrespective of one's desires and inclinations—and attends to act of free self-determination by which one acts, one can be aware of, at least analogously, the type of absolute self-determination expressed in **ii2**. This is **ii1**. The same content can be retrieved, though less perspicuously as Fichte admits, by his familiar admonition to think of yourself and observe what you do when you do so. The immediate awareness intrinsic to this reflective act is **ii3**. Both **ii1** and **ii3** retrieve, so Fichte maintains, the same content (absolute, free self-determination) as expressed in **ii2**, even though neither capture the originality and pure immediacy of **ii2**, which is more fundamental than either. And yet they are close enough approximations of **ii2** to provide the necessary insight into the freely self-determining act, which is the necessary explanatory ground of all consciousness, and thereby to motivate the *Wissenschaftslehre*. The insight emerges from **ii1** and **ii3** precisely because both are genuine iterations of the original act of self-determination expressed in **ii2**. Any conception of that original act emerges from an approximated repetition of the act. The elusiveness associated with **ii2** is one reason Fichte concedes that **ii2** is a necessary inference. The most that **ii1** and **ii3** can secure, though far from insignificant, is a glimpse of free, absolute self-determination robustly analogous to **ii2**. And this is as it should be since the original self-constituting act of self-determination expressed in **ii2** is the necessary ground of all the I's activity and all consciousness.

So far, the defender of CV might observe that this is consistent with the Jena *Wissenschaftslehre*. The Absolute is a self-constituting act just as the explanatory ground of all consciousness is an act and not something given as a sheer fact. The insight into one's original free self-determination (which, according to CV, is the Absolute) is not found but rather *produced* by the philosopher's act of reflective retrieval.[12] Second, the elusiveness of the Absolute arises primarily from its inferential status, just as the original self-positing act of the I does in the Jena writings. The elusiveness of the Absolute as presented in the *1804 Wissenschaftslehre* is more pronounced, however, notably in light of the forms of philosophical retrieval to which the Absolute is inaccessible. Fichte describes the problem in relation to what he calls "Light" (sometimes synonymous with the Absolute, but often referring to the manifestness (*Evidenz*) of the Absolute's self-constituting act) in the Eighth Lecture.[13] Any conceptualization of the Absolute self-constituting act will never grasp the act itself. Expressed in technical Jena terms, since a concept is activity at rest (i.e., the activity, not as such, but rather grasped in the form of a concept), a concept never captures an act's immediate (*tatlich*) quality. Put more strongly, the concept cannot incapsulate the act, and this exposes a cognate problem associated with the epistemic standpoint of the philosopher engaged in the work of reconstruction. Whatever can be brought under or encapsulated in a concept is subject to determination by the philosopher who posits the conceptualization. The Absolute, by contrast, is utterly self-sufficient, by which Fichte means that it eludes all conceptualization. Accordingly, any attempted conceptualization of the Absolute relativizes and thereby negates the Absolute (or its manifestness as Light). The type of conceptualization Fichte has in mind is the attempt, in his terms, to locate the Absolute within the concept itself, that is, to determine by abstractive analysis precisely what constitutes the Absolute. Even the refined concept of the Absolute secured by the highest abstractive analysis will not overcome the basic disjunction between the Absolute and the philosopher's reflective retrieval or reconstruction of the same. As Fichte notes, "the whole of reality according to its form is nothing more than the graveyard of the concept, which tries to find itself in the light."[14]

But there is a further, related problem. A standard reconstruction presupposes, as given and thus at least minimally objectivized, what it purports to reconstruct. The reconstruction begins with content that is taken as present and fixed—in Fichte's words, *dead*, precisely because givenness negates act. From this standpoint, the philosopher, from the start, is alienated from that which she attempts to capture in her reconstruction. Her reconstruction will be inordinately constructive and the insight obtained by her work guaranteed to miss the mark: "The insight, I say, is thoroughly negated in the living light. . . . The concept moves higher, [but] the true Light withdraws itself."[15] In sum, the Absolute's elusiveness exposes the two basic errors specified at the beginning of the chapter. When philosophical reconstruction attempts to situate the Absolute within its concept, reconstruction becomes inordinately constructive and inevitably reflects the bias (idealist or realist) of the philosopher. Relatedly, when the philosopher takes the Absolute as something fixed and given, she begins her reflections with a sharp disjunction between the Absolute and her own epistemic standpoint.

This is not to say, to be sure, that abstractive analyses fail to disclose something presumably intrinsic to the Absolute, namely that it is self-constituting and self-sufficient in itself, through itself, and from itself. Fichte contends that it is crucial for one to recognize that what the philosopher reflectively retrieves has the *same content* as the Absolute: "Should this indeed be the case, then an *absolute oneness* of content is manifest here and remains unaltered as oneness but that splits itself in the *vital fulfillment* of thinking into an inessential disjunction, which neither spoils the content in any way nor is grounded in it."[16] One might optimistically suggest that that problem of inordinate constructivism might be resolved by higher level of abstractive analysis, especially one that attempts to preserve the absoluteness, metaphysically construed (i.e., self-constituting, in itself), of the Absolute. The disjunction—perhaps more accurately, the hiatus—between the philosopher's reconstruction and the Absolute remains intact nonetheless and appears, moreover, to be intractable. As Fichte stresses in the opening lecture, any philosophical system that fails to eliminate all disjunctions from its foundational principle thereby refutes itself.[17] Additionally, how can philosophical reconstruction avoid the problem of givenness? As long as the disjunction—and, thereby, the distance—between the philosopher's reconstruction and what she attempts to retrieve reflectively remains, her reconstruction, even if it is a genuine reconstruction, will presuppose some degree of givenness, specifically something taken as objective. Fichte's solution is to suggest an alternative form of reflective retrieval, one that yields a content that is expressible in a concept without objectivizing that content. This is possible, however, only if the Absolute somehow constitutes itself in such a way that it is available for reflective retrieval, and on the further assumption that reflective retrieval will follow in its own attempted reconstruction the Absolute's own act of self-constitution—or in Hegel's terms, *die Sache selbst*. But this will not get Fichte what he needs. How could the Absolute constitute itself to make itself accessible to reflective retrieval when its self-constitution is the basis for its inaccessibility? How can the Absolute make itself accessible to philosophical reconstruction when it is, as Being (= objectivity), in principle external to consciousness? As Fichte summons his audience, "So . . . recall with me and consider the following: when we observe the light, the light is objectified, alienated from us, and killed as something primordial."[18]

Fichte makes his decisive move in the Fifteenth Lecture to the claim that *we* are absolute, that we bear within our subjectivity the image of the Absolute, thereby removing the distance—or rendering it inessential—between the Absolute and ourselves as philosophers willing to think through the *Wissenschaftslehre* and thereby underwriting the possibility for a properly construed reflective retrieval that captures the Absolute itself. If the Absolute is self-enclosed in its self-constituting act, the only way to bridge the gap between the Absolute and its reflective retrieval is, as we have seen, if the Absolute constitutes itself in a way that is available for philosophical retrieval. Any genuine philosophical retrieval is possible if and only if we ourselves are absolute in our self-constitution. Again, the question is, How so? The claim that we are absolute is to equate the Absolute's own self-constituting act with our own act of free, absolute self-determination. *We are absolute* means that the Absolute is reducible to I-hood, understood as consistent with the Fichte's Jena view. This is the core premise in the argument for CV and the way in which the defender of CV must interpret the key passage cited at the beginning of the chapter: "*We are* the one undivided Being itself, in itself, from itself, through itself, which cannot proceed outside of itself into duality."[19] As one commentator reminds us, this is not a claim that Fichte can prove.[20] Its proof, as the Jena *Wissenschaftslehre* emphasizes, depends upon the successful outcome of a philosophical experiment undertaken by anyone who has the reflective powers, intellectual openness, and willingness to perform it. Fichte, of course, is convinced that the underlying presupposition of the experiment—that we are absolute, freely self-determining rational agents—will be validated by the experiment, especially if one seeks to live her life accordingly. If, on the other hand, the CV advocate cannot eliminate the distance between the Absolute's self-constituting act and the philosopher's act of reflective retrieval of the Absolute's own act, the philosophical experiment that is the *Wissenschaftslehre* cannot even be undertaken.

In the Fifth Lecture in the context of an argument for the Absolute's (or Light's) elusiveness, Fichte writes:

> The concept of *reality*, of the inner material content of knowing, etc., which we have introduced is only the *negation* of insight and arises only from it; and this should not just be honestly admitted, rather, a philosophy which truly understands its own advantage should carefully enjoin this idea. In truth this is no negation, but rather the highest affirmation, which indeed is once again a concept but in truth we in no way *conceive* it, but rather we *have* it and *are* it.[21]

Only if we accept the finitude of any attempt to reconstruct the Absolute, so Fichte contends in the cited passage, will we be able to recognize that *we* bear the image of the Absolute in our own acts of absolute, free self-determination. Relinquishing the hubris of assuming that one, from her own finite epistemic standpoint, can conceptually comprehend the Absolute, along with an alternative view that the Absolute, in its self-subsistence or self-enclosure (*sich Entschlossenheit*), is *altogether* inaccessible, is necessarily propaedeutic for understanding the insight expressed in the passage. It is precisely for those who refuse to relinquish their philosophical pretentions that the Absolute remains elusive. Recognizing that we are self-constituting in our own acts of absolute self-determination doesn't eliminate, but only significantly mitigates the finitude of the alternative form of reflective retrieval that is necessarily connected to the insight into our own absoluteness. Again, **ii1** and **ii3** are only analogous to **ii2**, however strong the analogy is.

The Case for the Continuity View

I have argued that CV must establish that what Fichte means by the Absolute in the *1804 Wissenschaftslehre* is consistent with his conception of I-hood from the Jena writings. Once the defender of CV has made a strong case for this claim, she then can proceed to argue that the Absolute is accessible to a properly understood act of reflective retrieval. How best might she go about doing this? What further evidence can she provide for the far less baroque conception of the Absolute, from the perspective of readers of the Jena writings, she needs to defend? In what, more specifically, does this form of reflective retrieval, which she contends can access the self-constituting act of the Absolute, consist?

CV's defense of a reformulated reflective retrieval is based upon two core claims. (1) We are, at least incipiently, self-constituting and self-determining—self-constituting in our self-determination—rational agents. (2) The form of reflective retrieval capable of grasping the Absolute and communicating that insight in conceptual form is strictly correlated with claim 1. In fact, claims 1 and 2 form an organic unity: no proper self-conception, no reflective retrieval, and vice versa. The defender of CV must establish continuity between the Jena and 1804 conceptions of claims 1 and 2.

Fichte argues that there is an organic unity between the Absolute's self-constituting act and the philosopher's insight into that act. The organic unity is preserved if and only if claims 1 and 2 obtain, and 2 obtains if and only if the philosopher's reflective retrieval *re*constitutes the Absolute's own act of self-constitution. The organic unity, however, presupposes a certain form of reflective retrieval, not reflection in the standard sense that objectivizes that upon which one reflects—that is, not the form of philosophical reflection to which the Absolute remains elusive, as Fichte's critique of various forms of realism and idealism in the 1804 lectures reveals—but rather an act of self-determination that simultaneously focuses on one's immediate awareness of her self-determining act, which arises with and is intrinsic to the act itself. This act of **ii3** is familiar from the Jena writings, but it is the same act, so CV maintains, that Fichte targets in 1804. The organic unity between the Absolute's self-constituting act and the philosopher's reflective retrieval of the same presupposes, as a condition for its possibility, that the Absolute's self-constituting act is inseparable from its appearance.[22] Call this the inseparability thesis (IT). It is a vital premise in the CV defender's case for the Absolute's accessibility to philosophical retrieval.[23] Even if the proponent of CV can defend the reducibility of the Absolute to I-hood, the reducibility alone would not establish that the Absolute is thereby accessible to philosophical retrieval. IT bears much of the burden of establishing the claim that *we* are the image of the Absolute, which occupies most of Fichte's attention in part 2 (the Sixteenth through Twenty-Eighth Lectures) of the *1804 Wissenschaftslehre*. IT paves the way for the transition to the claim that *we* are absolute and that the Absolute appears precisely in our own acts of absolute self-determination. How might the CV advocate support this claim?

Fichte doesn't explicitly lay out the transition for his auditors (or readers), but the CV supporter should suggest that Fichte has in mind something like the following. Part 1 of the Fifth through Fifteenth Lectures takes the auditor/reader through a series of ascending levels of abstractive analyses of the Absolute culminating in the Fifteenth Lecture with the claim that we bear within ourselves the metaphysical attributions associated with the Absolute. The culmination, however, involves an alteration in the conception of the Absolute. As Fichte indicates, abstractive analyses treat the Absolute as what remains after all manifoldness has been abstracted.[24] Even the highest abstractive position, however, involves a disjunction between what one affirms of the Absolute—for instance, that it is from itself—and the epistemic standpoint of the philosopher, which is not "from itself." The disjunction creates an inconsistency, as Fichte states in the Nineteenth Lecture,[25] between what the philosopher affirms and the epistemic standpoint from which she affirms it—in Fichte's words, between what she says and what she does. Philosophical reflection purports to reconstitute the self-constituting act of the Absolute from epistemic standpoint that is not external to the Absolute. To accomplish this, the philosopher needs to *re*constitute the Absolute's own act (what she says or claims to do) in such a way that her act of *re*constitution is an iteration of the Absolute's act (what she does). What she needs is an epistemic standpoint from within the self-constituting act or "life" of the Absolute itself. That the Absolute's act *is* its appearance, that its *esse is its leben*,[26] which the CV defender would take to be the deeper meaning of IT, entails, assuming, as Fichte does, that the Absolute's self-constituting act is reflectively retrievable, that the Absolute is reflectively retrievable if and only if "we" can analogously recreate its act of self-constitution. And "we" can do so if and only if we are the image of the Absolute. Only then can the "life" of the Absolute be reconstituted and developed within us who attempt its reflective retrieval. One, therefore, does not engage in philosophical reflection from a standpoint entirely distinct from the Absolute, but rather from within the "life" of the Absolute itself. Again, this is possible because "we are Being itself": "But we live immediately in the act of living itself. For this reason, we are the one, undivided Being itself, in itself, from itself, through itself, which can never proceed outside itself."[27]

Fichte stresses that reflective retrieval of the Absolute is not a standard act of reflection. In fact, as the CV defender emphasizes, it is strictly *re*constructive, by which she means that the philosopher attempts to secure a thickly analogous iteration of the Absolute's own self-constituting act. In doing so, her act will be neither constructive nor a mere *Nachbild* of an act that takes place independent of her own act. She does not bring about the Absolute's self-constituting act; rather, *the Absolute constitutes itself within her act*, which becomes the source of the philosopher's insight. This is what Fichte means when he stresses in the Thirteenth Lecture that the insight itself is genetic.[28] The philosopher doesn't produce her insight. The insight produces itself within her.

> Here everything depends on this: that each person correctly identify with this insight, in this pure light; if each one does, then nothing will happen to extinguish this light again and to separate it from yourself. Each will see that the *light exists only insofar as it intuits vitally in him, even when it intuits what it has established*. The light exists only in living self-presentation as absolute insight, and whomever it does not grasp, hold, and fix in place where we now stand, that one never arrives at the living light, no matter what apparent substitute for it he may have.[29]

This passage is crucial for the CV defender's case for the reducibility of the Absolute to I-hood. If the Absolute self-constitutes itself within the philosopher's own reflective retrieval, then the Absolute would appear to *live* within the philosopher's (and, by extension, all rational beings') own free act of self-determination. If so, then the CV advocate would have a strong response to TO, that is, that not only is the Absolute not something transcendent (Being = objectivity) but also is not, in its inner life, the realm of freedom-negating necessity. The term "Being," as Fichte uses it in this context, is not a correlative or relational term. Being is the unity of *esse* and *leben*, and the metaphysical attributions to the Absolute serve to highlight that unity. Bracket the metaphysical ascriptions, so the CV defender will claim, and one has the unalloyed conception of I-hood from the Jena writings.

The cited passage also has important implications for the type of philosophical reflection Fichte defends, according to CV, in the *1804 Wissenschaftslehre*. The way in which the insight into the Absolute arises enables the philosopher to see that her own reflective retrieval simply puts her in the position of allowing the Absolute's self-constituting act to produce and manifest itself within her awareness.[30] This is the positive result of the philosopher's recognition of the finitude of her standpoint, that she cannot produce a concept of the Absolute itself, or, put differently, that the Absolute negates her concepts of it.[31] The CV proponent would contend that this is an illuminating clarification and defense of the basic Jena conception of philosophizing and philosophical insight. The philosophical experiment that yields **ii3** doesn't produce or construct the insight into self-positing that the act of **ii3** purportedly secures. When the philosopher thinks of herself and observes what she does when she does so (or, when she acts dutifully), she is aware immediately that her act is one of absolute, free self-determination. This, as noted earlier, is especially the case with **ii1** when an agent is directly aware of the freely initiated self-determination to act in accord with the moral law. The awareness arises within her simultaneously with and as intrinsic to her act. Whereas what she sees is only tightly analogous to **ii2** (the tacit awareness intrinsic to self-positing), she has placed herself in the most favorable position to see that deeper act of absolute, self-constituting self-determination, which initiates any and all actions and which is what she is as an I. In sum, her acts of self-reflection associated with **ii3 or ii1** (recall that both are acts of reflective retrieval) make possible her insight into the way in which I-hood constitutes itself in her immediate awareness. Put in approximate 1804 terms, her self-reflective acts of **ii3** and **ii1** are the appearance of the foundational act of free, absolute self-determination manifest in **ii2**, and our philosopher, when engaged in those acts, is the image of original, absolute self-determination that is the Absolute itself.

In the Sixteenth through Twenty-Eighth Lectures Fichte develops and defends his theory of image and the way in which *we* are the image of the Absolute. To be an image of the Absolute is to cultivate and expand one's capacity for absolute, free self-determination through rational action, especially when rational action answers to the normative requirements of the moral law. The CV advocate needs to provide an analysis of image and its relation to the Absolute and, specifically, to whom "we" refers when Fichte asserts that we are the image of the Absolute, that is consistent with the Jena (*Wissenschaftslehre*). My account of what CV needs will be quite formulaic, but I think that the general direction for further elucidation and defense should be apparent.

Fichte states explicitly that we finite, free rational beings are Being itself. According to CV, this means that the metaphysical qualities attributed to the Absolute (self-constituting, self-sufficient, in itself, etc.) also describe the absolute, free self-determination of finite rational beings—in sum, the core nature of I-hood. For most of us, however, these qualities are largely insipient and are never cultivated to anything like their fully developed potential, specifically for those of us whose rational agency extends no further than its service to our desires and inclinations or to the preserving of existing social and political structures. For his auditors and readers, Fichte is far more hopeful, even optimistic. By "we are Being itself" he means primarily those of us philosophically minded enough to think through the nature of I-hood as guided by the *Wissenschaftslehre* and to apply its insights to their everyday lives (or simply to do the latter), specifically to recognize and cultivate their capacity for free, absolute self-determination. The distinction between ourselves and the Absolute is basically the distance between ourselves as free, absolutely self-determining rational and moral agents who strive for absolute independence and the ultimate end of fully realized absoluteness or independence.[32] This is what it means, in Jena terms, to be the image of the Absolute. The Absolute manifests itself in its self-constituting act as absolute, self-determining activity, and, as Fichte maintains in his concluding lecture, the activity of self-formation, or literally self-making, (*Sichmachen*) is simply forming oneself into activity. "Here arise at one and the same time an absolute primordial activity, and also a making (or copying) of this primordial activity as its *image*. The former fundamentally explains the self-making and presenting manifestness that has grasped us in every investigation; that latter explains our reconstruction of this [manifestness] as it has also appeared in us."[33] This is an important passage for CV, since it appears to tie a rational agent's own self-formation to the original self-formative activity of the Absolute as manifested within a rational agent. According to CV, "absolute primordial activity" is foundational, self-constituting activity, or original self-positing. Our own acts of self-determination made explicit within and normative for our moral self-development cultivate our own core identity as absolute self-determining agents or as images of the Absolute. If, so the CV defender will insist, reflective retrieval of the Absolute takes place within the life of the Absolute itself whereby the distance between ourselves and the Absolute has been minimized or rendered, in Fichte's words "inessential," and if this claim is justified by the principle that the Absolute *is* in its self-manifestation in our free, absolute self-formative activity, then there is at least the beginning of a persuasive case for the claim that by the Absolute Fichte means I-hood. If so, this provides the basis for a persuasive defense of CV.

Fichte describes the Absolute's self-constituting act as a *groundless* self-projection, or, in his terms, a self-projection through a gap. The philosopher who attempts to ascertain the principle by which the Absolute projects itself comes to realize that the self-projection is *its own principle*. What Fichte means, according to CV, is that the Absolute's self-constituting act is an absolutely free act in the libertarian sense, namely, an act of free self-determination. This takes us, according to CV, to the core of I-hood, and provides further support for the claim that the Absolute is reducible to I-hood or absolute, free, self-determining and self-formative activity. In roughly Aristotelian terms, we are free beings to the extent that we cultivate that freedom. And the cultivation of that freedom arises from the insight we obtain from reflective retrieval of our original act of free, absolute self-determination, an insight acquired not by observing but rather by doing.

I have attempted in this chapter to outline how one might go about defending CV. To be sure, there is notable continuity between the Jena *Wissenschaftslehre* and the versions of the *Wissenschaftslehre* (in our case the 1804 lectures) Fichte presented after arriving in Berlin. CV affirms a significantly more expanded conception of that continuity. Although potential defeaters for CV are not insignificant (why orient the entire *Wissenschaftslehre* around the traditional metaphysical concept of the Absolute in the first place?), as I've noted, and although there are no doubt further unmentioned problems for CV, I hope to have shown how one might at least begin to defend CV, and that the case for CV might be stronger than commonly assumed.

Notes

1. 1804^2, 116; *GA*, II/8, 229.
2. 1804^2, 116; GA, II/8, 230. Translation altered and emphasis mine.
3. In the 1804 lectures Fichte focuses exclusively, according to CV, on claim 1. In fact, Fichte never undertook a full defense of 2, which would involve, as he insists in letters to Schelling in the years immediately preceding the 1804 lectures, a completion of the *Wissenschaftslehre*. What this would have involved is a complete derivation of the spiritual or intelligible world, or, as I would suggest, a derivation and development of the normative world. One way to respond to the objection that Fichte's Absolute identifies something transcendent—and is thus a betrayal of transcendental philosophy—is to argue that by the Absolute Fichte means the foundation and ultimate end of the normative world. That line of defense, if intended as a decisive defense, has its own serious difficulties, as will become evident

in what follows. A defense of 2, and thus a full defense of CV, is beyond the scope of this chapter. My concern is exclusively with 1. See Michael G. Vater and David W. Wood, *The Philosophical Rupture between Fichte and Schelling: Selected Texts and Correspondence (1800–1802)* (Albany: State University of New York Press, 2012), esp. 48–58. Hereafter cited as Vater and Wood.

    4. There is a hint of Fichte's criticism in his objection to Schelling's strategy, as Fichte reads it, to read I-hood as simply a higher potency within nature. As Fichte reads him, Schelling's approach comes close to endorsing a physicalist view of I-hood, as well as, here more importantly, taking its reality to be something given—"merely objective"—and thus to be found rather than produced by the I's own self-determining activity. See Vater and Wood, 44–45.

    5. My formulation and discussion of the transcendence objection is informed significantly by Daniel Breazeale's chapter in this volume: Daniel Breazeale, " 'You Can't Get There From Here': Fichte's (Unwritten) 1799 Review (*nach der Principien der Wissenschaftslehre*) of the *1804 Wissenschaftslehre*." I rely on Breazeale because his presentation of the problem is, in my judgment, especially perspicuous.

    6. See Allen Wood, *Fichte's Ethical Thought* (Oxford: Oxford University Press, 2016), 114. Also see *SS*, 23–29.

    7. Fichte, "On the Basis of Our Belief in a Divine Governance of the World," in *IWL*, 141–54; *GA*, I/5, 318–57.

    8. Vater and Wood, 56.

    9. Vater and Wood, 56. Emphasis Fichte.

    10. Vater and Wood, 56.

    11. See Daniel Breazeale, "Intellectual Intuition," in *Thinking Through the Wissenschaftlehre: Themes From Fichte's Early Philosophy* (Oxford: Oxford University Press, 2013), 197–229. Breazeale designates the four types of intellectual intuition with the symbolism **ii**. First, **ii1** is the immediate awareness an agent has of her own freedom whenever she acts specifically in accord with duty. Her awareness is of her own free, self-determining act irrespective of her inclinations and according to the normative authority of the moral law. For Fichte, this is the most accessible and convincing form of intellectual intuition. What Breazeale calls **ii2** is the way in which the I is present to itself in its own self-constituting act of free self-determination or (in Fichte's preferred term) self-positing. Ii3 refers to the immediate awareness of her I-hood when she engages in reflective retrieval of the self-constituting act of free, self-determination to which **ii2** points, thereby providing a second-order awareness of what is disclosed in **ii2**. This is precisely what Fichte references when he admonishes his students to observe what they do when they engage in some mental activity. **Ii3** is the starting point of thinking through the *Wissenschaftslehre*. Breazeale maintains that **ii4** is the central component of the *observational* method of genetic construction in which the transcendental philosopher engages when she thinks through *Wissenschaftslehre* constructively.

12. "And thus the standpoint of the [*Wissenschaftslehre*], which remains constant within consciousness, is in no way a synthesis *post factum*, but rather a synthesis *a priori*, finding neither division nor unity, but producing both in a single stroke." 1804², 42; *GA*, II/8, 56. Translation altered.

13. See 1804², 71; *GA*, II/8, 120–21.

14. *SK*, 71; *GA*, II/8, 121.

15. 1804², 81; *GA*, II/8, 146. Translation altered.

16. 1804², 63–64; *GA*, II/8, 102–3.

17. 1804², 23; *GA*, II/8, 6–8.

18. 1084², 62; *GA*, II/8, 101.

19. 1804², *GA*, II/8, 230–31. Translation altered and emphasis mine.

20. Hitoshe Minobe, "Das Absolute in der Wissenschaftslehre von 1804," *Fichte-Studien* 17 (2000): 167.

21. 1804², 81; *GA*, II/8, 143–44.

22. 1804², 144; *GA*, II/8, 294–95.

23. One could maintain that the Absolute is self-constituting in itself apart from its appearance. If so, one would be faced with two unacceptable alternatives. Either the Absolute is completely inaccessible, precisely because it is, as self-constituting, in principle independent of consciousness. This leads directly to the transcendence objection and the conclusion that reflective retrieval is blocked from the beginning. Or the Absolute constitutes itself apart from its appearance but somehow gives itself to reconstructive reflection. In this case, the Absolute would be taken as given, and assumed connection between itself and its appearance would be vulnerable to skeptical objections.

24. 1804², 143–44; *GA*, II/8, 293–95.

25. 1804², 142–43; *GA*, II/8, 291–93.

26. 1804², 116; *GA*, II/8, 230.

27. 1804², 116; *GA*, II/8, 230–31.

28. 1804², 103–4; *GA*, II/8, 195–97.

29. 1804², 60; *GA*, II/8, 96. Emphasis mine.

30. 1804², 53; *GA*, II/8, 81–82.

31. 1804², 42; *GA*, II/2, 56–57.

32. The CV advocate would need to provide an account of the Absolute as the ultimate end of all human striving toward absolute independence and fully developed moral agency, in sum, to completed humanity. Providing a fully adequate account (though probably not required for a persuasive case for CV) would require the CV advocate to do what Fichte refused to do—complete the *Wissenschaftslehre* by explicating what Fichte means by the supersensible world. This would involve a detailed explication and defense of claim 2 of CT.

33. 1804², 197; *GA*, II/8, 411–12.

Chapter 2

"You Can't Get There from Here"

Fichte's (Unwritten) 1799 Review (*nach der Principien der Wissenschaftslehre*) of the *1804 Wissenschaftslehre*

DANIEL BREAZEALE

I invite you to participate in an extravagant thought experiment and join me in a flight of *schaffende Einbildungskraft*—that is, "creative imagination." Imagine that the contents of volume II/10 of the Bayerische Akademie *Gesamtausgabe* of Fichte's works, the one containing the manuscript of the second series of private lectures on *Wissenschaftslehre* he delivered in Berlin in 1804, along with a complete student transcription of the same lectures, were somehow (thanks perhaps to a wrinkle in time, a worm hole, or a time-traveling DeLorean?) to have fallen into Fichte's possession in 1799 during his final months in Jena. Let us further suppose that the copy in question—like Fichte's own first book—were to have appeared anonymously, with no introduction nor title page. Imagine, finally, that Fichte was so stimulated and provoked by this unexpected discovery that he immediately drafted the following review of the mysteriously titled "*Wissenschaftslehre*, Presented in 1804."

In doing so, he could not have failed to notice the many striking similarities between his presentations of his own system over the course of his career at Jena and these similarly titled lectures, which even include passages referring to Fichte's own earlier writings and which claim to be fully compatible with the same. But still less could he have ignored what appear to be the main significant *differences* between his own *prima philosophia* and the one presented in these lectures. Here is the imaginary review in question.[1]

∼

A curious publication has recently come to my attention. It is an anonymously published work that claims to be a "presentation of the *Wissenschaftslehre*." The reader can imagine the pleasure with which I began reading the lectures of which this volume consists, since I have long maintained that "my philosophy [i.e., 'the *Wissenschaftslehre*' or *WL*] should be expounded in an infinite number of different ways," and I have frequently acknowledged that "everyone will have a different way of thinking it—and each person must think of it in a different way, in order to think it at all."[2] Accordingly, I have encouraged my readers and listeners to construct my system *for themselves* and to present it accordingly, and this would appear to be precisely what the author of this new *Wissenschaftslehre* considers himself to be doing.

As I continued to read, however, my enthusiasm was increasingly tempered: first, by the inherent difficulty of understanding precisely *what* our author is actually claiming and assessing his *evidence* for these claims, and second, by my growing awareness of the profound *differences* between his conception of the character and scope of the *Wissenschaftslehre* and my own. I am publishing this review in order to announce that I am *not* the author of this "new *Wissenschaftslehre*" and to warn anyone seeking a deeper understanding of my philosophy against this allegedly "new presentation" of the same. Despite the author's claim that these lectures are no more than a new and improved "presentation" of the system I have been developing over the past five years, it is, in fact, nothing of the kind.

Before examining the similarities and differences between my *Wissenschaftslehre* and this new one, however, a brief description of the latter is in order. It is divided into three major parts, beginning with a Prolegomenon (consisting of the first four lectures), in which the author outlines his conception of the task, method, and starting point of philosophy. In contrast to my own presentations, all of which begin with the concept of the I, this one begins with a claim about truth and knowledge—namely, that there *is* truth and that we, in fact, *possess* knowledge. In part 1, titled "Doctrine of Truth and Reason," our author traces what he describes as the "ascending path" from the factical (or a posteriori) unity of subject and object, which is allegedly present in every instance of genuine knowing, to a fully adequate conception of the absolute as an utterly self-sufficient and self-manifesting One, which reveals itself via "insight" to be the genetic ground of both knowing and being. This derivation of the absolute proceeds largely by means of an elaborate dialectic between ever more sophisticated forms of "idealism" and "realism," culminating in a supreme principle of absolute unity transcending both. (Here the author appears to be familiar with the similar dialectic expounded in parts 2 and 3 of my *Grundlage der gesamten Wissenschaftslehre*.) Part 2, the "Doctrine of Appearance and Illusion," traces the "descending path" from the incomprehensible absolute ground of knowing and being to the same manifold of experienced differences with which part 1 began. In the course of this derivation, our author offers provocative analyses of the initially "hypothetical" character of knowledge claims and of the critical function therein of the *durch* or "through," as well as of "the image" (*das Bild*) as the mediating link between subject and object, a discussion that would appear to have been directly inspired by my own examination of the same topic in my *Gründriss des Eigentümlichen der Wissenschaftslehre in Rücksicht auf das theoretische Vermögen.*[3]

Before evaluating the author's implicit claim to be presenting a new and improved version of my *Wissenschaftslehre,* I should make it clear that I do not claim to have understood everything contained in this volume. On the contrary, despite my best efforts, I often found myself rereading difficult passages over and over, trying—too often in vain—to discern their meaning. Hence, my comparison of this new *Wissenschaftslehre* with my own system will, perforce, be based up a less than ideal grasp of the former. Though I will have some harsh things to say about this new project and will firmly reject some of our author's conclusions, I must nevertheless express my gratitude to him for his positive insights and for his effort to improve upon my own—admittedly inadequate—presentations of the *Wissenschaftslehre.*

Similarities

Let me begin by mentioning a few of the more salient parallels between this "new" *Wissenschaftslehre* and my own.

Importance of the Wissenschaftslehre

The first point on which we are in agreement concerns the significance of the *Wissenschaftslehre.* As I have declared to my own students, "This is the philosophy that transforms man and lifts him to a new life. And I have claimed that with the discovery of this philosophy an entirely new epoch in the history of the human species has begun—or, if one prefers, an entirely new and different human species has arisen, one for which all previous forms of human nature and activity on earth are no more than preparatory, if they retain any value at all."[4] Our author appears to agree with this sentiment when he describes the *Wissenschaftslehre* as "a complete solution to the riddle of the world and of consciousness."[5] Indeed, at times he goes even further and asserts that "life is inseparably connected with the *Wissenschaftslehre* and with what it produces, and everyone must recognize that his entire life would be nothing and would be worthless and meaningless, and actually not exist at all, except insofar as one elevates oneself to absolute knowing."[6]

THE TASK OF PHILOSOPHY

We also share similar views concerning the general character and task of philosophy and hence of the *Wissenschaftslehre*. To be sure, we describe this task somewhat differently. I have described it as "displaying the foundation of all experience," and especially of "representations accompanied by a feeling of necessity."[7] The philosopher has to account for the "objective validity" of such representations and explain why we must think that things exist apart from them, even though, from the higher standpoint of transcendental philosophy, we can see that this is not really the case.[8]

Our author, in contrast, writes that the task of the *Wissenschaftslehre* is "*to trace all multiplicity* (which presses itself upon us in the usual view of life) *back to absolute oneness*,"[9] thereby overcoming the experienced divisions between thinking and being and between the supersensible and sensible realms. Broadly speaking, we agree that the task of philosophy is to overcome the experienced split between representations and things, subject and object, by tracing all such divisions back to a supreme principle, in which they are resolved. My name for this supreme principle is, of course, "I-hood" and his is "absolute being" or "what is absolutely One," though over the course of his treatise he appears to confer upon this same "absolute One," a rather bewildering variety of additional names, such as "pure knowing," "the essence of knowing," "substantial knowing," "self-sustaining substance," "pure light," "absolute light," "living being," and "pure reason," culminating in a definition of the absolute as "*a thoroughly self-enclosed singulum of immediately living being, which can never proceed outside itself.*"[10] In addition, at certain points in part 2, he identifies this same absolute with "the pure I" and, finally, with "God." Nevertheless, our projects appears to be similar: first to identify a source of absolute unity or self-identity and then to demonstrate its necessary relation to multiplicity and difference by deriving the latter from the former.

METHOD

We also agree on many points concerning the proper method for constructing such a system:

1. *Unity:* We both agree, for example, that the only way to overcome the division between subject and object is by *starting* with unity and then *deriving* multiplicity therefrom. The "unity" in question, moreover, must be a unity of unity and difference, since, as our author correctly observes, "true and proper oneness can only be the principle simultaneously of both the apparent oneness and the apparent multiplicity."[11] We are also in general agreement that there can only be one supreme principle from which everything else must be derived, a principle that is the ground not only of the *unity of experience* but also of the *systematic unity* of philosophy itself.

2. *Genesis:* We agree, moreover, that derivation of multiplicity from unity (or, in my case, of ordinary experience from the pure I) is not a matter of logical inference from a first principle or major premise but is instead a fundamentally descriptive enterprise. And what it describes is the *genesis* of ordinary experience from our systematic starting point. Just as I have consistently emphasized the "genetic" character of my own enterprise, so our author explicitly describes the goal of his *Wissenschaftslehre* as "to introduce entirely genetic self-evidence and then to deduce the factical therefrom,"[12] and he declares that "the fundamental maxim of our science is to apply the principle of genesis thoroughly and without exception."[13]

    Again like me, he also recognizes the all-important difference (ignored by, among others, Jacobi) between a philosophical reconstruction of the genetic acts he is describing and the original occurrence of the same—namely, that in any theoretical reconstruction (which is what philosophy offers) these acts must be carefully *distinguished* from one another and presented discursively in a certain, necessary sequence, even though they must all occur at once in order to occur at all. Thus he too recognizes the vast difference between the kind of a priori, genetic knowledge characteristic of the *Wissenschaftslehre* and the kind of a posteriori (or what he calls "factical") knowledge associated with the ordinary standpoint—though, like me as well, he concedes that philosophy must include an initially factical component, by means of which one raises oneself to that absolute standpoint from which genetic knowing first becomes possible. Indeed, the fundamental difference between *factical* and *genetic* knowing (and hence between "ordinary" and "philosophical" knowing) is one of the major themes of his treatise.

3. *Abstraction:* We also agree that the only way the philosopher can arrive at his first principle is by deliberate *abstraction* from the differences that characterize ordinary experience. As is well known, I have often instructed my students to turn their attention away from their experience of objects and to focus instead upon "he who is thinking them," thereby constructing for themselves the pure concept of I-hood, understood as a self-positing *Tathandlung* or subject-object. Similarly, our author instructs his readers to abstract from all concrete instances of knowing and to focus instead upon the pure form of "knowing as such," which, like the pure form of I-hood, is a unity that both generates and synthesizes the differences present in every instance of concrete knowing.

4. *Reflection:* We further agree that mere abstraction is not enough. One must also possess the talent and discipline required in order to focus one's attention upon what remains following such abstraction—and keep it there. In the words of our author, a student of the *Wissenschaftslehre* must possess "the talent for complete and full attentiveness."[14] Only then can one obtain the sort of "insight" required by the *Wissenschaftslehre*. I made a similar point in my own intro-

ductions to the *Wissenschaftslehre*, in which I emphasized that one must carefully observe the product of abstraction and maintain such attention. In short, abstraction must always be joined by *reflection*, which is an absolutely indispensable instrument in the toolbox of transcendental philosophy. Though he mentions reflection often enough, our author generally discusses it under the intriguing (if not entirely pellucid) name "energetic thinking."

5. *The law of thinking:* We also share a similar view of the basic character and fundamental law of thinking, inasmuch as we both understand thinking (*denken*) or comprehending (*begreifen*) to always involving *relation* and *difference*, in which one thing is always understood in terms of another, namely in terms of what it is not and in which things that are identified are always distinguishable. This, of course, is in accord with the Spinozistic principle that "all determination is negation," a principle that I, following the lead of the sharp-witted Maimon, call "the principle of determinability" and our author calls simply "the law of the 'through' or *Gesetz des Durch*."[15]

6. *Insight*: But reflection and energetic thinking are still not sufficient, for the philosopher must be able to recognize truth when he encounters it—or, as our author would prefer to express this: when it encounters him. I too have long insisted upon the importance of direct and immediate self-evidence for establishing a "real"—which is to say, a true—system of philosophy. I have described this by various names, the best known (as well as most widely misunderstood) of which is "intellectual intuition," a term which, in this context, refers to the philosopher's "immediate" awareness of the necessity of a certain act or relationship. Similarly, our author waxes positively purple in his enthusiasm for what he calls *Einsicht* or "insight" and exhorts his readers on nearly every page to develop and to deploy their own power of insight, which he sometimes refers to us "the transcendental sense,"[16] in order to "see into" (*einsehen*) whatever they are trying to grasp.

Though insight must always be the result of a freely initiated process of reflection (and hence of an *act*—which is why our author maintains that insight and "life" always go together), the consequence of this act is involuntary and immediate: something that *seizes one* and seems "to spring up without any assistance from us, *like a lightening flash*."[17] Indeed, as he likes to put it, it is more accurate to say that it is the insight that has produced itself in you and is, in this sense, "self-produced"—even though it is equally true that it could not have "produced itself" in this way without an act of free reflection on your part.[18] Nevertheless, our author insists that once you have actually obtained such insight, in which the distinction between subject and object vanishes completely, then it can equally well be said that "you yourself have become this insight and have been absorbed into it," which is why he claims that you cannot really doubt anything into which you have obtained insight.[19]

In other words, genuine insight wears its *Evidenz* on its sleeve—that into which one has obtained such insight is "self-evident" and beyond doubt. Though I do not deny that we indeed experience such "ah ha" moments of recognition and have, on occasion, made similar claims concerning the certainty of theoretical insight, I nevertheless find it impossible to endorse our author's claims concerning the self-evidence of some of his key assertions—a point to which I shall return.

7. *Making the Wissenschaftslehre one's own:* Taken together, all of these talents—abstraction, self-awareness, attentiveness, reflection, observation, energetic thinking, and intellectual intuition *cum* insight—constitute what our author correctly describes as "the art of philosophizing." Though we agree that certain individuals might be said to possess "philosophical genius," in the sense that they seem to possess a precocious ability and proclivity to engage in serious reflection and hence have an enhanced likelihood of obtaining philosophical insight, we also agree that the great majority of us must acquire this skill the old-fashioned way: by hard work and self-discipline, since, as our author and I agree, the requisite "insights" can occur only as a *result* of "energetic thinking."

Like me as well, our author recommends various exercises and techniques for acquiring the "art of philosophizing," but in the end we both conclude that everyone has the capacity to master this art and hence, if someone should fail to do so, then the fault is *his alone*. (Here, on the basis of personal experience, I should perhaps warn our author that many readers are nevertheless quite unwilling to accept such responsibility.)

A related point, to which we both return again and again, is that each person can and must grasp the *Wissenschaftslehre* entirely on his own, must make it his own, and must confirm its truth for himself, through his own insight. As I have written, "an inner act is required of the student of the *Wissenschaftslehre*," and "this science cannot do anything to convince anyone who does not wish to satisfy this condition, that is, who will not produce this intuition of his own I within himself, or who is unable to do so."[20] And this is why "the *Wissenschaftslehre* is the kind of philosophy that can be communicated only through the spirit and by no means through the mere letters. This is because its fundamental Ideas are ones that everyone who studies it must produce within himself by means of his own creative power of imagination."[21] So too, our author insists that his *Wissenschaftslehre* is not dependent upon "any specific modes of speech"[22] and insists upon the importance of making this philosophy *one's own* by "internally constructing it in a lucid and transparent manner," thereby creating for oneself "*a free, personal recreation of this presentation of the Wissenschaftslehre in its living profundity.*"[23]

8. *Incomprehensibility:* A controversial point on which we might at first seem to be in complete agreement concerns the limits of philosophical reflection, intuition, and insight. Some things, we agree, are simply incomprehensible, even for the *Wissenschaftslehre*. We both agree, e.g., that what is truly "absolute" and functions as the highest principle of the *Wissenschaftslehre*—whether we call this the pure I or pure knowing or pure being or God—lies, in an important sense, beyond our powers of comprehension. This is because

we can truly "comprehend" anything only by relating it to something else, to something that is supposed to be its *explanans* or explanatory ground. But what is "absolute" is, by definition, unconditioned and hence "groundless"—and therefore incomprehensible.

We further agree that we are nevertheless able to comprehend *why* this absolute is incomprehensible and, to this extent, obtain a certain insight into it after all. Thus, rather than being faced with an utter mystery, we are able to comprehend precisely *why* we have reached the limits of our powers of comprehension in this case and why such a limit is inevitable. Hence, even though our author says that the maxim of the *Wissenschaftslehre* is "to leave nothing uncomprehended," he is ultimately forced to admit that something (namely his "absolute One") is indeed incomprehensible, in which case we "will at least comprehend it as such, i.e., as absolutely incomprehensible, and as nothing more, and thereby we will also comprehend the point at which absolute comprehension can begin."[24] (As I will point out below, however, my *Wissenschaftslehre* acknowledges a much larger domain of incomprehensibility than his.)

9. *Idealism vs. realism:* Another interesting similarity between this new *Wissenschaftslehre* and my own is the heuristic, methodological use we make of the complex debate between "idealism" and "realism," by which we both understand certain persistent attitudes toward the relation of subject to object, and not primarily those philosophical systems that adopt these labels. As my readers will no doubt recall, part 2 of the *Grundlage der gesamten Wissenschaftslehre* advances in precisely this manner by means of a dialectical interplay between the claims of "idealism" and "realism," which become progressively more refined until these claims are synthetically united in a position that can be called "real-idealism"—which is just another name for "transcendental idealism," properly construed.[25] So too, in the first, "ascending" portion of his inquiry, our author deploys a very similar dialectic of idealism and realism for a similar purpose. Indeed, at some points he appears to be simply repeating what I wrote five years ago on this same topic.

10. *Ascending and descending paths:* With regard to the organization of this new *Wissenschaftslehre* into "ascending" and "descending" paths, this is precisely the organizational scheme I have been employing for years in my private lectures on *Wissenschaftslehre nova method*, which I am currently in the process of revising for serial publication. It could, I suppose, be a mere coincidence that our anonymous author adopts this same schema—or perhaps he was present during those lectures or had access to a transcription of the same? In any case, it is hard to believe that this obvious parallel is purely coincidental.

ACTIVITY AND LIFE

A final similarity worth noting between this new *Wissenschaftslehre* and my own, and one of the things that distinguishes us from many other systematic thinkers, is that we both insist that the "absolute"—however this is to be understood—must not be understood as any sort of static, enduring substance or being. Instead, it must be understood as fundamentally active, and all of its acts must be understood as acts of self-expression, through which alone it can appear. This is why it can be understood only genetically. As I wrote in the *Grundlage der gesamten Wissenschaftslehre*, "The concept of reality is first given through and along with the I. But the I *is* because it *posits itself*; and it *posits itself because* it *is*. *Self-positing* and *being* are therefore one and the same. But the concepts of *self-positing* and *activity* as such are also one and the same. All reality is therefore *active*, and everything that is *active* is reality."[26]

Instead of talking about "acting" and "the I," our author describes his absolute being or knowing as "living."[27] The point, however, is the same, and a very important point it is, since it is precisely this active or living character of our absolute that permits us to "derive" from it everything else as a manifestation or "appearance" of this absolute. In the case of my system, the "everything else" in question is the realm of finite, materially embodied consciousness, embedded in a social world and subject to a moral world order. In contrast, from the life of his absolute, our author proposes to derive not just the phenomenal realm of empirical cognition but also a still higher, but still subordinate, intermediate realm of "original appearance," of which ordinary experience is itself a further "appearance." Hence the "life" of his absolute embraces a much broader and more ambitious terrain than do the "acts" of mine.

Given these striking similarities, one might well conclude that there are no significant differences between this new *Wissenschaftslehre* and my own and thus view the former simply as a "new presentation of the latter." In order to explain why I cannot endorse this conclusion, I will first pose several questions concerning this new *Wissenschaftslehre* and then raise several objections to the same, all designed to display the profound and unbridgeable differences between our two projects.

Questions

First, three questions for the author of this new *Wissenschaftslehre*:

CAN PHILOSOPHY REALLY PROCEED BEYOND THE I?

One of the key inferences with which this treatise begins is the following: all genuine knowledge claims certainly do have as their object something (a thing, a state of affairs, a relation among propositions) that is taken to exist "in itself," independently of the knowing subject, even if the objects of our everyday knowledge claims are recognized by our author to be only "appearances"—more specifically, appearances of another, higher "original appearance" of the self-contained, living One. Our author defends this claim by appealing to his own self-evident insight into this matter, which supposedly reveals to him that whenever one "thinks energetically" about the meaning of any particular knowledge claim it is self-evident that, if knowledge is to be possible at all, then there must be an independently existing realm of objectivity. And he maintains that such knowledge is possible because it is actual, as (he claims) we can easily confirm for ourselves. It is, of course, undeniable that—*from the standpoint of everyday consciousness*—we all affirm the self-evident existence of an utterly external realm "beyond" consciousness. But our author claims that the existence of such a realm is equally self-evident *from the standpoint of transcendental philosophy*.

To be sure, he concedes that the ultimate ground of this apparently independent realm is "incomprehensible," yet it is nevertheless "absolutely real," and the source of the reality of our knowledge. Moreover, he contends that "the absolute springing forth of light and insight is directly bound up with this construction of the in-itself. It is obvious that *we* did not produce this insight, since it obviously produced itself and carried us along with it."[28] Though we are responsible for initiating the reflection that leads to such insight, we are not responsible for the insight itself. That is produced in us by something greater than any I—namely, by that absolute unity of being and knowing that expresses itself as "light" and thereby "illuminates" consciousness in the form of self-evident insight. But, he insists, "the light itself, at least in this, its absolute form, cannot exist in itself apart from the absolute, since nothing exists apart from the absolute, but instead has its source in the *in itself*."[29]

In contrast, as I put it in my *Naturrecht*, my claim is that "all *being*, that of the I as well as of the Not-I, is a determinate modification of consciousness, and without some consciousness there is no being."[30] In my view, the only kind of genuine "objectivity" is objectivity for consciousness, a point I tried to make in the following passage from the *Grundlage der gesamten Wissenschaftslehre*:

> Here we encounter crystal-clear evidence of what lies beyond the grasp of so many philosophers who, despite their alleged adherence to the Critical philosophy, have not yet freed themselves of their *transcendent dogmatism*: namely, evidence *that* and *how* the I is able to develop solely from itself everything that is ever supposed to be present in the I *and is able to do so without ever proceeding beyond the I or breaking out of its circle, which must necessarily be the case if the I is supposed to be an I.* . . . This way of proceeding nevertheless possesses objective validity, since it is the uniform procedure of all finite reason, and *there neither is nor can be any kind of objective validity other than the kind indicated. At the basis of the claim concerning some other type of objectivity there lies a demonstrably crude and palpable deception.*[31]

But is the latter not precisely the claim put forward by our author, who therefore appears if not to endorse then to be very friendly toward a "metaphysical" version of transcendent dogmatism? He is, of course, aware of my arguments against such dogmatism, which go back to my original announcement of my project, in the review of *Aenesidemus*, where I characterized transcendental philosophy as demonstrating the absolute impossibility of "going beyond the boundary of the human mind" and showing "that the thought of a thing possessing existence and specific properties *in itself* and apart from any faculty of representation is a piece of whimsy, a pipe-dream, a non-thought."[32] Yet this appears to be precisely what our author proposes to do. Nevertheless, he characterizes those—such as, presumably, myself—for whom the highest principle of philosophy is that of I-hood or "the pure I" as "trapped in the absolute I" and unable to raise themselves above it.[33] Hence my first question: Can we ever raise ourselves above the I, that is, the "standpoint of consciousness," and if so, how?

To his credit, our author recognizes that the *Wissenschaftslehre*—by which he here means *my Wissenschaftslehre*—has often been associated with such a "higher idealism," and he devotes a substantial portion of his Thirteenth Lecture to explaining why he thinks this is a misconception, at least as applied to *his Wissenschaftslehre*. He maintains that, since I begin not with the mere "fact" of consciousness, but with the concept of consciousness as a F/act or *Tathandlung* and hence with a *genetic* concept of pure I-hood, the latter cannot be the highest principle of philosophy after all, since it must be *produced*.[34] There must therefore be a still higher principle, since "the process of production lies *higher* than what is produced," and this supposedly justifies positing a still, higher absolute, one that explicitly transcends consciousness and can allegedly be shown to be the ground of the same. Consequently, he firmly rejects my claim that "the ground of truth qua truth lies in consciousness" and insists,

> The ground of truth qua truth by no means lies within consciousness, but lies entirely within truth itself. One must always subtract consciousness from truth, as in no way affecting the latter. Consciousness remains only the outer *appearance* of truth, from which you may very well be unable to extricate yourself, for reasons that will be explained. But if you believe that the reason why truth is truth lies within *consciousness,* then you are the victim of an illusion [*Schein*], and every time something seems to be true because you are conscious of it, you are, at root, [the victim of] idle illusion and error.[35]

Accordingly, the author of this new *Wissenschaftslehre* enjoins us—in our philosophizing—"to dismiss consciousness and to abstract from it,"[36] even if we are unable to do this, as a matter of fact, in our everyday lives. "Leaving consciousness totally out of play," according to him, is the only way "one obtains entrance into the *WL*,"[37] by which, of course, he means *his Wissenschaftslehre*, not mine. For me, however, this is not an option, since, as I recently wrote in my review of the unfortunate Mr. Werner's *Journal für Wahrheit*, "the fundamental principle of the Critical philosophy—namely, that we are unable to escape from the sphere of our own consciousness—

seems to us to be so self-evident that anyone who understands it at all must necessarily affirm it."[38]

In justification of his bold leap beyond consciousness, the author adduces the self-evidence of his own insight. So what is someone to say who does not share this insight, and indeed, whose own insight *contradicts* it? What if it is "self-evident" to me that what is "self-evident" to you is false?[39] I would invite our author to explain how such a fundamental disagreement is to be settled. And, if, like the dispute between "idealism" and "dogmatism," it cannot be settled theoretically, then is there any other way to settle it?

But first, a word about "incomprehensibility": consider the possibility that the domain of self-evidence is coextensive with that of the I. Perhaps all that can be theoretically self-evident to me, as a transcendental philosopher, are those acts that I am forced to reenact by and for myself as I engage in a laborious, a priori reconstruction of that original, spontaneous, and utterly nondiscursive *Tathundlung* through which alone both finite I-hood and its various realms of experience become possible. All that is required for such an account, in addition to this *Tathandlung*, is some notion of an *original limit* corresponding to those *original limitations* encountered by the original drive of every finite I to "fill up reality," the very limitations that occasion its spontaneous positing of its material, social, and moral worlds. For the truly transcendental philosopher, such limits are simply presupposed as conditions for the possibility of actual I-hood and cannot be further explained.

All we can know about these boundaries is what we posit in consequence of encountering them. Beyond this, they are incomprehensible, and we are forbidden, on solid transcendental grounds, from speculating about the possible ground or higher origin of these same boundaries—hard as it admittedly is to resist such speculation. (And here I publicly confess that I myself have not always been able to resist engaging in just such illicit speculations.)[40] But this is no real loss, since these same limits do not need to be comprehended as such in order to function within a rigorously transcendental account of the I and its experiences.

Not only do I see no need to go beyond these limits and posit a more remote but equally incomprehensible principle—one that is, in turn, supposed to "explain" the derivative, but no longer "incomprehensible" limits immediately encountered by finite I's—but I see good reasons *not* to do so, the same reasons adduced by Kant in his immortal demolition of speculative, dogmatic metaphysics. How, one wonders, would our author respond to the suspicion that what he is proposing amounts to a return to a pre–critical philosophical standpoint? He will protest that his "in itself" is unlike that of his pre-Kantian forebearers in that his "exists in the *concept*, and is therefore living,"⁴¹ which is to say, engaged in actively manifesting itself through appearance, including the apparent experience of thinking what appears to be objective being. Hence, "consciousness presupposes *light*, and is only one *determination* thereof."⁴² Indeed, there are not merely pre-Kantian but ancient anticipations of such a conception of the absolute—among, for example, neo-Platonists such as Plotinus and his followers. But does calling the transcendent One "active" really make it—or a doctrine of the same—any less transcendent?

CAN THEORETICAL INSIGHT STAND ON ITS OWN?

Here is how our author describes the "experience of knowing" in his Third Lecture: knowing "manifests itself" (*sich einleuchtete*) to us as existing for itself. Considered in abstraction from its concrete manifestations, pure knowing or "knowing in itself" always remains the same, the same unity of subject and object. It thereby manifests itself as "unchangeable or absolute, substantive and self-identical and thus as unity or oneness." Moreover, it presents itself to us in this way "with absolutely irresistible self-evidence. Whenever you obtain insight into anything, you assert that 'this is purely and simply how it is; I cannot see [*einsehen*] it any other way. . . . Knowing manifests itself to me as absolutely certain."⁴³ According to our author, the "insight" in question is simply a subjective manifestation of the absolute itself, in its guise as "pure light." Hence anyone in possession of such insight simply cannot help but "identify himself correctly with this insight, and thus with pure light, and if he does this, then this light will never again be extinguished or grow dim."⁴⁴

As our author readily concedes, such claims cannot persuade anyone who lacks firsthand experience of such insight and certainty. Nevertheless, he believes that he has refuted skepticism and that he has accomplished this by means of a purely theoretical insight concerning the nature of truth and knowing. He further believes that anyone capable of abstracting from concrete instances of knowing and thinking energetically about "knowing itself" will obtain "the factical insight" that we do indeed possess knowledge, that there really is truth.⁴⁵

To this, any skeptic worthy of the name would likely respond, How can you be sure that you are not deluded, that your vaunted "insight" is actually veridical and that you are fully competent to judge what is "self-evident"? For my part, I have publicly conceded that the *Wissenschaftslehre* is incapable of providing a purely theoretical refutation of skepticism. In this domain there is always room for one more question, Why?, and always the possibility of theoretical error. I may not have realized this as clearly five years ago as I do now, when my response to skeptical doubt concerning the possibility of certain knowledge would be similar to my response to doubt concerning the reality of freedom, namely:

> I am unable to doubt this freedom and this determination thereof without at the same time renouncing myself. I contend that this is something I cannot doubt; indeed, I maintain that I cannot even entertain the possibility that it is not so, the possibility that this inner voice [of conscience] deceives me and must first be authorized and established by something outside it. At this point, therefore, my reason is quiet unable to take me any further; I have reached the limit of all interpretation and explanation. This pronouncement is what is absolutely positive and categorical. I can go no further—so long, that is, as I do not wish to destroy my own inner self. Therefore, the sole reason why I cannot go any further is because I cannot *will* to go any further. Here lies that which sets a limit to the otherwise unbridled flight of argumentation and binds the mind because it binds the heart.[46]

As I expressed this same point in the "Second Introduction" in response to skeptical doubt concerning the true, active character of the I: I cannot be driven from my position, not because I possess theoretically indubitable insight into its certainty and truth, but "because I am not *permitted* to go beyond it."[47]

There is, in my view, no possibility of refuting skepticism by purely theoretical or intellectual means; it can be successfully challenged only *practically* by one who recognizes that the locus of *certainty* lies not in theory but in practice, specifically in conscientiously guided moral practice. As I concluded in my *Sittenlehre*, "Certainty is possible for me only as a moral being, since the criterion of all theoretical truth is not, in turn, a theoretical one.—The theoretical power of cognition cannot criticize and confirm itself. Instead, the criterion of all theoretical truth is a practical one, and it is our duty to stick to the latter."[48] In striking contrast, our author insists that "it is purely and simply the case that certainty rests purely and simply upon itself and is purely and simply from and through itself."[49]

What is the Relationship of Absolute Being to the I?

My final question for our author concerns his conception of the I, more specifically of the pure I. On several occasions he equates this I with his absolute One, though only after abstracting completely from the subject-object distinction—a distinction that would appear to be characteristic of I-hood. In his Third Lecture, for example, he asserts that "the I itself" is the paradigm of actual pure knowing, since I-hood involves not only the *difference* between subject and object but also the *unity* of the same. It is apparently only because of this structural isomorphism that he occasionally calls pure knowing the pure, absolute I.[50] This is, to say the least, obscure. What is the point of describing the I in this way? Apparently, what my "pure I" and his "absolute One" have in common is that both are active and self-expressive and are unconditionally and spontaneously so, and, of course, both involve an immediate union of subject and object.

But is this not a seriously deficient concept of I-hood? Just look at what is missing from his absolute—namely, freedom, will, choice, tendency, drive,[51] and real, efficacious action—not to *create*, as it were, the realm of appearances, but to *transform* it in accordance with freely posited goals. What is missing, in short, is any place for practical reason and action. This is lamentable, since, as I also noted in my *Sittenlehre*, "all the I's cognition is determined by its practical being—as indeed it must be, since this is what is highest in the I. The only firm and final foundation of all my cognitions is my duty. This is the intelligible 'in itself,' which transforms itself by means of the laws of sensible representation into a sensible world."[52] Needless to say, this is a very different notion of the in-itself and how it "transforms itself" into the sensible world than the one presented in this new *Wissenschaftslehre*. So, what, one wonders, are the possible advantages and disadvantages of replacing talk about "the I" with talk about "the absolute"? And what might have motivated our author, nevertheless, to identify his absolute with the pure I?

Objections

The Inherent Limits of Transcendental Philosop.hy

Here I will be restating in the form of an objection some of the same points I raised above in the form of questions concerning what is "comprehensible" by transcendental philosophy and the differences between my "pure I" and his "absolute One." Our author describes the all-important new standpoint of his *Wissenschaftslehre* as follows: "This is not philosophy from the standpoint of the We or the I; there is philosophy beyond the I. For this reason, the question concerning the possibility of philosophy depends on whether the I can perish and reason can appear in its pure form."⁵³ It would be difficult to imagine a clearer statement of the fundamental difference between his *Wissenschaftslehre* and my own. For all of its speculative ingenuity and ambition, this new *Wissenschaftslehre* utterly fails to recognize and to respect the inherent *limits* of all transcendental philosophy. Accordingly, his *Wissenschaftslehre* is an unstable mixture of transcendental modes of argument and transcendent claims concerning a reality beyond the scope of consciousness. To be sure, I agree with him that in order to accomplish a genetic derivation of ordinary experience, with its characteristic bifurcation of subject and object, the philosopher must begin with something that is exclusively neither one nor the other but is subject and object at once. Where we disagree is concerning the nature of this distinctive subject-object. In my view, the only subject-object to which we have immediate access (or, to use the language of our author), the only such principle concerning that we can obtain self-evident insight is that of I-hood itself. But we can *know* this absolute or pure I only because we *are* it. (To be sure that is by no means *all* that we are, but that hardly matters, since our first philosophical act is to abstract from everything but this pure I.)

Our author will, of course, insist that the same applies to his absolute knowing: we can obtain immediate insight into it only because we, in an important sense, *are* it. This, however, is a far more problematic claim than mine, since pure I-hood is nothing other than the fundamental structure and self-constituting *Tathandlung* that make *me* "an I" in the first place, which is why I enjoy such privileged access to it. As I noted in my lectures on *Wissenschaftslehre nova methodo*, the pure I is the *only* such subject-object or "absolute" that is "immediately given" to us, and it is for this reason "the fixed point beyond which philosophy cannot and may not go."⁵⁴

Surely, the same cannot be said of our author's "*thoroughly self-enclosed singulum of immediately living being*." Nowhere is this deficiency of this "new WL" more evident than in the author's blithe and repeated instruction for us to "abstract from consciousness" and that we do so in order to satisfy what he—citing Jacobi, of all people!—declares to be the true task of philosophy, namely "to reveal and to discover *being in and of itself*."⁵⁵

As I have explained numerous times, the limits of transcendental philosophy are coextensive with the limits of consciousness itself, and the task of this philosophy is not to know being itself, but rather to illuminate what—necessarily—lies within the domain of consciousness, while at the same time rigorously eschewing speculation concerning what—if anything—may lie outside this domain. In my *Sittenlehre* I described the boundaries in question as constituting the "original limitation" of every finite I, which discovers itself (and thereby discovers its world—inasmuch as "the world is nothing more than the I intuited in its original limits"[56]) to be constituted in a specific way, which "cannot be explained any further, since this constitutes our original limitation—which is something we cannot escape through our *acting*, and hence not through our *cognizing* either. To demand further explanation of this would be self-contradictory."[57] To be sure, from the ordinary standpoint we do "explain" these same limits to ourselves—namely, as products of our being affected by independently existing material objects; the transcendental philosopher then proceeds to "explain this explanation" in terms of the I's own necessary, law-governed actions in the face of its own original limitations. In my recent essay on our belief in a divine governance of the world I described the transcendental view of this matter as follows:

> The world is nothing but our own inner acting (qua pure intellect), made visible to the senses in accordance with comprehensible laws and limited by incomprehensible boundaries, within which we simply discover ourselves to be bound. . . . Granted, the origin of these boundaries is incomprehensible; but, replies practical philosophy, what is it that bothers you about this? Nothing is clearer or more certain than the *meaning* of these boundaries. They constitute your determinate place in the moral order of things. Whatever you perceive as a consequence of these boundaries possesses reality, the only kind of reality that pertains to you or exists for you. It is the ongoing interpretation of what your duty commands, the living expression of *what* you ought to do. Our world is the material of our duty made sensible. This is the only truly real element in things, the true, basic stuff of all appearance.[58]

With respect to these boundaries, my philosophy can do what our author claims to be able to do with respect to his transcendent absolute—that is, explain *why* we can go no further. This is why I announced from the start that the *Wissenschaftslehre* is nothing less—but also nothing more—than "an accurate portrayal of the system of the human mind" and described it as "a pragmatic history" of the same.⁵⁹ This is a stricture I wish our author had borne in mind, but instead, he has employed the general language and method of my philosophy to construct a metaphysics that neither Kant nor I would recognize as adhering to the transcendental spirit of the critical philosophy.

THE PRIMACY OF THE PRACTICAL

I have already alluded to this issue as well, when I contrasted the practical refutation of skepticism contained in my recent writings with the entirely theoretical refutation proposed in this new *Wissenschaftslehre*. This, however, is merely a symptom of a larger issue—namely, the nearly complete neglect by our author of what I have called the essential "practical activity" of the absolute. Whereas I have argued that there is no *knowing* without *willing* and *doing*, and have emphasized the necessary relation of both to the I's "original limitations," there is nothing comparable in this new *Wissenschaftslehre*. On this point as well, it appears to violate the spirit of Kant, who insisted upon the primacy of reason's practical over its theoretical interests. Instead, our author appears firmly committed to the self-sufficiency of theoretical (or "speculative") reason.

    To be sure, part 2 of his treatise includes an extended discussion of *das Soll* (the "should," or "ought"); however, this term seems to be here employed with a purely hypothetical or problematic—and hence purely theoretical—meaning, as in the phrase, "if x is *supposed to be* the case." This kind of hypothetical "should" has little in common with the very different kind of *categorical ought*, which I have demonstrated to a central condition for the very possibility of consciousness.⁶⁰ And, indeed, no such purely practical conditions are countenanced within this new *Wissenschaftslehre*. Though it includes numerous discussions of those acts by means of which the "living absolute" manifests itself, these all occur in a sterile, utterly theoretical context, where there can be no question of willing and choosing. On the contrary, we here seem to be in the realm of a thoroughgoing—and thoroughly incomprehensible—*system of necessity*.

    Our author also disagrees with the conclusions of my *Sittenlehre* regarding the role of conscientious feelings of duty in determining moral action, for he writes that "doing what is right from . . . the self-respect that arises from a categorical imperative produces only dead, cold fruit. . . . *Only when right action arises from clear insight does it occur with love and pleasure. Only then is the deed its own reward, self-sufficient and in need of nothing else.*"⁶¹

Such talk about the "love and pleasure" that should accompany a righteous deed is a clear indication of the spiritual gulf separating his *Wissenschaftslehre* from mine. This same gulf is glaringly evident in the following passage from this new *Wissenschaftslehre*:

> Here then is the entire result of our doctrine: Existence [*Dasein*] as such . . . does not possess its ground within itself, but in an absolute purpose [*Zweck*], *and this purpose is that absolute knowing is supposed to be*. Everything is posited and determined by this purpose, and only in achieving this purpose does it achieve and exhibit its actual determination or vocation [*Bestimmung*]. *There is value only in knowing, indeed, in absolute knowing, and everything else is worthless.*[62]

I am currently working on a book in which I intend to address this precise issue, and in it I intend to make it abundantly clear that the "absolute purpose" of our existence—"the vocation of humanity"—has nothing whatsoever to do with "absolute knowing." Instead, our highest goal is to act freely and confidently in accord with the demands of duty and to view the world and other human beings only from this perspective, a perspective I will describe as that of rational "belief" rather than of "knowledge"—absolute or otherwise.

The Spirit of the *Wissenschaftslehre*

When I originally conceived the project that became the *Wissenschaftslehre*, I described it privately as "a philosophy of striving [*StrebungsPhilosophie*],"[63] and shortly thereafter as "the first system of freedom."[64] After years of presenting and developing the *Wissenschaftslehre*, I still cannot think of any more appropriate way of designating the deepest *spirit* of my thought. And this is precisely the respect in which this new *Wissenschaftslehre* is most seriously wanting and why I am unable to hail it as a welcome new "presentation" of *the Wissenschaftslehre*. Just look at what is absent from this *prima philosophia* and contrast it with my own.

I have already called attention to the first and most obvious difference between my *Wissenschaftslehre* and this new one—namely, that the latter, by explicitly abstracting from consciousness, transcends what I take to be the necessary *limits* of any genuinely "transcendental" investigation. There is a vast difference between a "pragmatic history of the human mind" and a metaphysics of absolute genesis. Though the author at one point describes his new *Wissenschaftslehre* as "absolute idealism,"[65] I contend that is would be more properly described as a sophisticated, vaguely neo-Platonic variety of transcendent dogmatism.

In addition, no one would be tempted to describe this new *Wissenschaftslehre* as a "system of freedom." Though our author assigns human beings an indispensable role in his overall scheme (inasmuch as pure knowing can manifest and therefore "realize" itself only in finite knowers), there is no role for "freedom" in this process, appearances to the contrary notwithstanding. Even though we have an indispensable role to play in the "life" and "appearance" (and hence in the self-construction) of the absolute One, with which we may therefore even be said to coincide in moments of insight, our author explicitly notes that we do not accomplish this as "a *free* 'we,' *independent* of being."[66] Though he concedes that a certain "freedom of reflection" is presupposed along the ascending path of his project, he nevertheless concludes that, once we have obtained clear insight into the absolute and have come to understand that we are not, in fact, responsible for this "insight," we will then recognize that the freedom in question was no more than a factical appearance, and "all freedom is thereby annihilated [*vernichtet*]."[67]

Compare this with the following remark from my "Second Introduction": "For the idealist, nothing is positive but freedom, and, for him, being is nothing but a negation of freedom. It is only on this condition that idealism possesses a solid foundation and remains consistent with itself."[68] Our author, however, could not disagree with this statement more strongly, for he maintains that "insight into absolute inward necessity is the distinguishing mark of the *WL*" and any "freedom" or "contingency" that can be derived from this absolute can be no more than an *appearance*. This is a thesis that he (correctly) anticipates will be strongly resisted by those lacking the requisite insight, since, as he puts it, "freedom is the very last thing to go."[69] True enough! But our author seems oblivious to the fact that the reason why freedom is "the very last thing to go" is that our conviction that we are free was never grounded on any theoretical insight in the first place, but instead upon our *practical* awareness of our ability to obey or not to obey the dictates of conscience.

As for my final point, my characterization of the *Wissenschaftslehre* as a "philosophy of striving," this is one of the best-known features of my philosophy, which concludes that the "unity" that the *Wissenschaftslehre* begins by postulating is present for the finite I not as a *fact* or even as a *Tathandlung*, but only as something to be achieved, and to be achieved not by theoretical insight but by practical engagement with the Not-I. Since limitation of the I is a condition for any actual consciousness, the completion of the task of bringing the Not-I into complete harmony with the I, in accordance with our dutiful ends, would coincide with the complete abolition of I-hood as such. Consequently, our task is one that can never—even in principle—be completed but which we must never stop trying to complete. My system of freedom is not just a philosophy of striving; it is philosophy of *infinite* striving, and this is something that could never be said of the philosophy under review. I wish the anonymous author success in his endeavors, despite my grave reservations, but I beg him to relinquish the name "*Wissenschaftslehre*" and allow it to return to its rightful home.

Notes

1. Though page references are here provided to the published English translation of Fichte's writings, all the translations in this chapter are by the author.
2. "Fichte to Reinhold, March 21, 1797" (*EPW*, 417; *GA*, III/3, no. 354).
3. *EPW*, 278–84; *SW*, I, 374–81.
4. *EPW*, 208; *GA*, II/3, 333.
5. 1804^2, 151; *GA*, II/8, 308–9.
6. 1804^2, 181; *GA*, II/8, 378–79.
7. See § 1 of the "Second Introduction" to *Versuch einer neuen Darstellung der Wissenschaftslehre* (*IWL*, 7–9; *SW*, I, 422–24).
8. *FTP*, 78–79; *GA*, IV/3, 324.
9. 1804^2, 23; *GA*, II/8, 8–9.
10. 1804^2, 121; *GA*, II/8, 242–43.
11. 1804^2, 56; *GA*, II/8, 86–87.
12. 1804^2, 39; *GA*, II/8, 48–49.
13. 1804^2, 163; *GA*, II/8, 338–39.
14. 1804^2, 47; *GA*, II/8, 46–47.
15. See 1804^2, 85; *GA*, II/8, 156–57.
16. See 1804^2, 147, 155; *GA*, II/8, 300–01, 318–19.
17. 1804^2, 48; *GA*, II, 8, 68–69.
18. See 1804^2, 44; *GA*, II/8, 62–63.
19. 1804^2, 49; GA, II/8, 70–71.
20. *EPW*, 323–24; *SW*, II, 443.
21. *FEW*, 345; *SW*, I, 284. Compare this with the more recent admonition from my *System der Sittenlehre*: "In our system, one makes oneself into the ultimate basis [*Boden*] of one's philosophy, and that is why it must appear 'baseless' to any-

one unable to do this. . . . It is necessary that our philosophy confess this quite loudly, so that it might thereby finally be relieved of the unreasonable demand that it demonstrate to human beings from outside something that they have to create in themselves." *SE*, 31–32; *SW*, IV, 26.

22. 1804², 27; *GA*, II/8, 18–19.

23. 1804², 28–29; *GA*, II/8, 22–23.

24. 1804², 32; *GA*, II/8, 34–37. In this way, he boasts, we manage "to comprehend what is thoroughly incomprehensible *as incomprehensible*." 1804², 41; *GA*, II/8, 54–55.

25. "What then is the overall gist of the *WL*, summarized in a few words? It is this: Reason is absolutely self-sufficient; it exists only for itself. But nothing exists for reason except reason itself. It follows that everything reason is must have its foundation within reason itself and must be explicable solely on the basis of reason itself and not on the basis of anything outside reason, for reason could not get outside itself without renouncing itself. In short, the *WL* is transcendental idealism." *IWL*, 59; *SW*, I, 474.

26. *FEW*, 233; *SW*, I, 134.

27. "The sole being and life cannot exist nor be sought outside itself, nor can anything whatsoever exist outside it. . . . From a linguistic standpoint, 'being' is taken as a noun, but it cannot *be*, in the verbal sense—*esse in actu*—except immediately, in life itself." 1804², 116; *GA*, II/8, 230–31.

28. 1804², 98; *GA*, II/8, 186–87.

29. 1804², 99; *GA*, II/8, 186–88.

30. *FNR*, 4; *SW*, III, 2.

31. *FEW*, 349; *SW*, I, 289–90 (emphasis added). Hence, as noted in the second introduction to the *VWL*, "it would be completely absurd to consider the question concerning the existence of a being that has no relation to any consciousness." *IWL*, 39; *SW*, I, 456.

32. *EPW*, 71; *SW*, I, 16–17.

33. 1804², 105; *GA*, II/8, 200–01.

34. *Tathandlung* is compound word combining the words "deed" or "achievement" (*Tat*) with "action" (*Handlung*). The term *Tathandlung* had previously been employed in legal contexts to designate a violent or illegal act and in religious or theological contexts to refer to the original act of divine creation. For me, this term describes that act through which the I spontaneously becomes its own object and hence a "subject." Only the I is capable of such a *Tathandlung*. This is why I have emphasized the difference between a *Tathandlung* and a *Tatsache* ("fact" or "matter of fact"), which, unlike a fact/act, is something simply *discovered* rather than *actively accomplished* by the I.

35. 1804², 107; *GA*, II/8, 204–5.

36. 1804², 107; *GA*, II/8, 206–7.

37. 1804², 132; *GA*, II, 268–69.

38. *IWL*, 125; *GA*, I/4: 435.

39. On this point, too, I have sometimes been guilty myself, since, as I wrote to my esteemed predecessor K. L. Reinhold, "I always assume that many things are self-evident which hardly anyone else finds to be self-evident." *EPW*, 428; *GA*, III, no. 440.

40. For example, the "pure drive" to absolute spontaneity that features so prominently in my *System of Ethics* (*SE*, 134–36; *SW*, IV, 141–42) can surely be said to lie "beyond consciousness," but I was careful to note that even though this pure drive "is something that lies outside of all consciousness; it is nothing but a transcendental explanatory ground of something in consciousness." *SE*, 144; *SW*, IV, 152. Can the same be said about our author's "absolute One"?

41. See 1804², 99; *GA*, II/8, 188–89.

42. 1804², 103; *GA*, II/8, 194–95.

43. 1804², 35; *GA*, II/8, 38–39.

44. 1804², 60; *GA*, II/8, 96–97.

45. See, e.g., 1804², 166; GA, II/8, 344–45.

46. *IWL*, 147–48; *SW*, V, 182.

47. *IWL*, 49; *SW*, I, 466.

48. *SE*, 161; *SW*, I/4, 170.

49. 1804², 167; *GA*, II/8, 344–45.

50. See 1804², 35, 139; *GA*, II/8, 38–39, 184–85.

51. This treatise does include a single paragraph in which the "drive" (*Trieb*) of the absolute "to come out of itself" is mentioned (1804², 188; *GA*, II/8, 291–94). This, adds our author, is what underlies "the appearance of freedom," which, however, is for him just that: nothing but an *appearance*, which "does not enter into truth."

52. *SE*, 164; *SW*, IV, 172.

53. 1804², 139; *GA*, II/8, 284–85.

54. *FTP*, 144; *GA*, IV/3, 363. I reached a similar conclusion in *FNR*, were I wrote that "the I becomes conscious only of what emerges for it in this acting and through this acting (*simply and solely through this acting*) and this is the object of consciousness, or the thing. There is no other thing that exists for a rational being, and since one can talk of being and of a thing only in relation to a rational being, it follows that there is no other thing at all. Whoever talks about some other thing does not understand himself." *FNR*, 5; *SW*, III, 3.

55. 1804², 138; *GA*, II/8, 282–83.

56. *FNR*, 19; *SW*, III, 18.

57. *SE*, 97; *SW*, 101.

58. *IWL*, 150–51; *SW*, V, 184–86.

59. *EPW*, 130–31; *SW*, I, 177; *FEW*, 302; *SW*, I, 222.

60. "Categoricity" does eventually replace the problematic "*Soll*" in this new *Wissenschaftslehre* (see Seventeenth Lecture and following), but what replaces it as

categorical is not the *categorial ought* of the *Sittenlehre*. "Only in the insight into pure being and how we ourselves are absorbed into it does this *Soll* vanish completely, so that an absolute categoricity emerges, with no problematic presupposition." 1804², 130; *GA*, II/8, 264–65.

    61. 1804², 183; *GA*, II/8, 380–81.
    62. 1804², 182; *GA*, II/8, 378–79.
    63. *GA*, II/3, 265.
    64. *EPW*, 385; *GA*, III, no. 231.
    65. 1804², 135; *GA*, II/8, 272–73.
    66. 1804², 122; *GA*, II/8, 244–45.
    67. 1804², 149; *GA*, II/8, 304–6. The *existence* of our insight into the essence of reason (a.k.a. "the absolute") "appears to be possible only by means of freedom; and this is actually and in fact the case, which is to say that reason expresses itself as free. It is precisely the law and inner essence of reason that freedom should appear." 1804², 194; *GA*, II/8, 406–7.
    68. *IWL*, 84; *SW*, I, 499.
    69. 1804², 128–29; *GA*, II/8, 260–61.

Chapter 3

The First Principle in the Later Fichte

The (Not) "Surprising Insight" in the
Fifteenth Lecture of the *1804 Wissenschaftslehre*

MICHAEL LEWIN

Introduction

Several interpreters stress discontinuity in Fichte's development and believe that he abandons the critical path in his later works. Henrich and Gloy assume that the later Fichte transforms his "deficient" (circular) theory of self-consciousness by putting God as the primal unity and ground of self-consciousness on the top of his system.[1] God, the absolute being, is, as Rivera de Rosales writes, "the real condition or *ratio essendi*"[2] of knowledge in the *1804 Wissenschaftslehre*. These and similar views bring Fichte's later project close to mysticism and (neo-)Platonism: the absolute I and the world become merely a shadow of the highest principle. Numerous researchers try, however, "demystifying" his later works, claiming, like Ivaldo, that—although some passages may purport it—Fiche's later philosophy does not represent any "objectivistic metaphysics" or an "onto-theo-logic."[3] Ivaldo, Schmidt, Stolzenberg, Asmuth, Schlösser, Ivanenko, Traub, and Loock, to name a few, either equate the absolute being with the first principle of the Jena Fichte or recognize strong structural similarities to the absolute I and exclusively or prevalently transcendental forms of argumentation in Fichte's philosophy after 1800.⁴ The most promising demystification strategy is brought up by Schmidt, Stolzenberg, and—to some extent—Hoeltzel,⁵ who draw on Kant's concept of pure practical reason or reason in general to understand the highest principle in the Jena and Berlin Fichte. My alternative suggestion is Kant's theory of ideas, the theory of pure reason in the narrower sense as the starting point. The last decades of Kant research, especially—but not only—related to the *Transcendental Dialectic*,⁶ rediscovered the "other side," the nondestructive transcendental account of ideas and metaphysics. This helped to reveal the whole system of different kinds of ideas in Kant (postulates, transcendental, simple theoretical, practical [moral, religious, and political], aesthetical, architectonic ideas, and those ideas that represent the pure reason itself). According to Fichte's programmatic demand of a complete deduction of all main acts of consciousness, the system of ideas must be derived just as the system of categories and other results of the Kantian philosophy. The project must start with the self-positing of pure reason as the first and highest act in the *Wissenschaftslehre*. This is the key to understand different principles and their order in Fichte's works. I will not explain this view and Fichte's deduction of ideas in detail in this paper, but this is the background I will draw on.⁷

Following the "demystification agenda," I want to argue against the assumption that transcendental philosophy as a research program, which was introduced by Kant, is abandoned in the *1804 Wissenschaftslehre* or in general by the later Fichte. The concept of God—the absolute of the religious standpoint—is insofar (besides the practical implications) theoretically interesting and relevant for the scientific endeavor of the *Wissenschaftslehre*, as it is an important example of an idea that can be used to indicate existence of our *pure reason* (in the narrow sense) and to examine the functionality of pure reason. Fichte invites his audience in Berlin to create a pure concept of God, to investigate theoretical and practical dimensions, possibilities, and borders of our pure thinking. In the research program of transcendental philosophy, reason (in the narrow sense) is a faculty that operates with ideas as the purest form of representation. The common title for all ideas is, as Kant states in the *Transcendental Dialectic*, the unconditioned, or the *absolute*.⁸ To think the absolute means to use reason—a person who creates the idea of God proves herself to be capable of pure thinking, of freedom, or of the highest form of spontaneity. As God can be seen as *absolute*, of itself, in itself, and through itself, the reason, or the I, which "lives" in the activity of pure thinking or pure (self-) positing, can be regarded as absolute itself; it is as the *absolute* I. This is—in a few words—the basic "insight" in the Fifteenth Lecture of the *1804 Wissenschaftslehre*, which contains the "doctrine of *reason* and truth."[9]

What we find in the period between 1804 and 1806 in Fichte's works is not a mixture of purported transcendent cognitions and transcendental philosophy. Neither reason or self-consciousness nor the world is derived from God. But on the other side one also cannot simply equate the absolute with the absolute I. This would be unjustified considering the evolution of Fichte's thinking after 1800. In the following, I want to show how I have come to my interpretation of the "insight" Fichte speaks of in the Fifteenth Lecture, which must not necessarily be surprising for those familiar with the earlier versions of the *Wissenschaftslehre*. In the first section of this chapter, I want to argue that the thinking of different subject-object-relations, and the corresponding idealism-realism-dialectic, constitutes the structure of the *1804 Wissenschaftslehre*. This structure leaves no doubt that the absolute of the *Wissenschaftslehre* is the self-positing pure reason and that God cannot be the highest principle in Fichte's system. In the second section, I want to detect the duplicity of the *absolute* as God on the one hand and as reason (or I/We) on the other hand in this text and explain it in the sense of an analogy, which was—among other things—introduced for didactical purposes and productively used by the later Fichte.

Subject-Object-Relations (SOR)

The abstract terminology of subjects, objects, and their relation to each other is a basic tool used in the transcendental philosophy. Kant differentiates between subjective and objective deduction of categories and ideas, speaks of relations of representations to an absolute subject (soul) or to an absolute object (world),[10] describes self-consciousness in terms of a subject-object-relation, and so on. Karl Leonhard Reinhold recognized that subject-object relations underlie every epistemic act of consciousness, and that they are all mediated by different types of representation.[11] Thus he suggested the concept "representation" to be the central concept in transcendental philosophy and did it for a very good reason. Kant, namely, declared at the beginning of the *Transcendental Dialectic* "representation" as genus, under which stand all different types of representation analyzed in the *Critique of Pure Reason*: sensation, intuition, empirical and pure concepts, and ideas.[12] Subject, object, and their relation to each other via representation are therefore basic elements of all epistemic acts—Reinhold formulated this insight, as we know, as *principle of consciousness* (*Satz des Bewusstseins*), a fact that everyone should be able to prove as universally valid through personal introspection.

Fichte could not agree that the principle of consciousness is a solid ground for a system based on results of the Kantian philosophy. As he states in a letter to Reinhold: had Reinhold waited until all three *Critiques* appeared before starting to work on his system, he could have found the right first principle—it is the absolute I.[13] So, there are two basic modifications Fichte makes to Reinhold's model of subject-object-thinking that significantly change it. Firstly, subjects and objects are mediated not only by representation but also by all other acts of consciousness (*Bewusstseinshandlungen*) including pure acts of positing as well as feelings and acts of will, such as needs and conation (*Begehren* and *Streben*). Secondly, there is, in one single case—in the case of the absolute I—a unity of subject and object. This unity is established by means of a pure act of self-positing, a fact-act (*Tathandlung*) involving the *intellectual intuition*, which is not dependent on the subject-object-difference and therefore does not fall under the standard definition of a representation.

So what I want to point to is that Fichte creates a new transcendental apparatus and a new logic in working with abstract language of subjects, objects, and their interrelation, which goes beyond Kant's and Reinhold's usage of the same and becomes fully differentiated, especially in the year 1804. Subjects and objects play the role of abstract transcendental symbols used for difficult logical operations. One can also say they are *pictures* as well as, for instance, *light*, *life*, and other creative imaginations we encounter in the *1804 Wissenschaftslehre*. As Fichte stated in his essay *On the Linguistic Capacity and the Origin of Language* (1795),[14] he does not believe in the indispensability of written and spoken language for abstract thinking—one can also productively think in pictures created by our faculty of imagination. The advantage of thinking in abstract pictures like subject, object, the "through," pure being, absolute, the point of oneness, light, life, and so on lies in the possibility to eschew certain (empirical and nonempirical) content that could distract the philosopher from targeted logical operations. The problem is, however, that when it comes to a right interpretation of these imaginations, one can understand very different and even contrary concepts behind them, especially when some of the imaginations are used—depending on context—in many varying ways. In my opinion, the transcendental symbolism of subjects, objects, and their interrelations has five main functions in Fichte's philosophy. The abstract language of subjects and objects is used:

1. to indicate relations. Something can either relate to a subject or to an object, or something can be self-relating;
2. to articulate certain qualities and mental attitudes. "Subject" stands for activity, idealism, and thinking, whereas "object" stands for passivity, realism, and being;
3. to express standpoints. To do so, Fichte uses images of "enduring" (one can also say "standing" or "motionless" [S], [O]) as well as "moving" ("self-forming," "living" [S'], [O']) subjects and objects in the Twenty-Eighth Lecture 1804, II);
4. to illustrate objects of knowledge. "Subject-object" (S = O) stands, for example, for the absolute I or reason and "object," in the quality "enduring object" (O), for the world;
5. to express areas of science. Natural sciences, for example, primarily deal with nature; it is with "enduring object" (O). Jurisprudence deals with "enduring subject" (S).

The Unity of Subject and Object (S = O)

If I try to determine the unity of subject and object using these five points, I come to the following results:

1. A subject-object must be understood in terms of a *self-relation*, just like it was at the beginning of the first *Wissenschaftslehre* in Jena: I equals I, or, to put it in another way, I (respectively reason) is *for itself*; it posits its own being and therein lies its essence.[15] Any other possible relation to a subject or object is omitted in the act of self-positing: the I, with the predicate "absolute," is self-enclosed in a sphere in which it is only being for itself and not for the other.
2. As for the qualitative determination of a subject-object, it must be seen as *ideal-real* (respectively, *real-ideal*) or, which is the same, as *unity of thinking and being*. The Jena Fichte stated clearly that the *Wissenschaftslehre* is neither a mere idealism nor realism, but a combination of both. Its first principle expresses the unity of real and ideal elements: fact-

act means that I act (real activity) and that I have immediate consciousness of that act (ideal activity).[16] In other words, the self-positing is an expression of *being* of the absolute I, whereby "being" is to be understood in a higher sense, as pure real activity, which is inseparably accompanied by *thinking*; it is by intellectual intuition of the same.

3. "Subject-object" is a transcendental symbol that represents the standpoint of the *Wissenschaftslehre*. While every standpoint or worldview has its own absolute, the absolute of the *Wissenschaftslehre* is not an object or subject. Enduring or living and self-forming subjects and objects are—as Fichte demonstrates in the last lectures in 1804—just sides or appearances of the subject-object-unity.

4. This unity stands for what Fichte synonymously calls "absolute I," "reason," and "pure knowledge," which is the genuine object of knowledge of the *Wissenschaftslehre*.

5. The corresponding area of knowledge is *Wissenschaftslehre*, respectively, *critical metaphysics*.

The Structure of the *1804 Wissenschaftslehre*

The core thesis in the first section of my chapter is that subject-object-symbols are used by Fichte to structuralize the *Wissenschaftslehre*. If we find out that he assigned concrete and indisputable content to certain abstract operations with subjects and objects that constitute the structure of *Wissenschaftslehre*, it will shed light on what the first principle is or is not. There are at least four basic questions that are discussed in relation to the structure of Fichte's lectures 1804[2]: (1) At what point do the prolegomena end? (2) Where do we find the first principle?[17] (3) What is the concrete succession of bottom-up and top-down movements of deduction?[18] And (4) do Fichte's lectures in this period consist of a synthesis of twenty-five argumentation steps? This is a line of interpretation begun by Martial Gueroult, pursued by Joachim Widman, and recently revisited by Alexander Schnell.[19] What I am interested in and what has not been yet (as far as I know) discussed is a parallel between what I call the idealism-realism-dialectic,[20] which starts at the Eleventh and ends at the Fifteenth Lecture, and the deduction of five standpoints or areas, in which reason (pure knowledge) is active in the Twenty-Eighth Lecture.[21] I will illustrate this parallel with the help of the following intuitions and reflections:

a. The exceptional status of *1804 Wissenschaftslehre* is well known. It does not start with the first principle right away but with a bottom-up movement we also encounter in *The Vocation of Man* (1800) and in Fichte's late lectures on the *Facts of Consciousness* (1810–1813). This movement of ascent has the function to negate all constrained mental operations and points of view that are deficient and inappropriate to articulate the absolute principle. Perhaps one can also use the Hegelian term "sublate" (*aufheben*) in this context, as the abandoned standpoints are not discarded entirely but rather transformed into a higher unity of which they are all just certain sides. This higher unity or the absolute of the *Wissenschaftslehre* is an act of pure genesis, which differentiates itself inwardly into the same moments that were rejected and criticized as merely *factual*. In my reading of Fichte's lectures 1804^2, these moments are two different kinds of realism and idealism, which reappear as four standpoints below the self-positing of reason.

b. This statement can be supported by the thought that it is a not a mere coincidence that the reader of Fichte's *1804 Wissenschaftslehre* encounters exactly two realisms, a lower and a higher one, and two objects, an enduring (O) and living (O'), as well as two idealisms, a lower and a higher, and two subjects, an enduring (S) and living (S').

c. Furthermore, "realism" and "idealism" are, as Fichte states in the Fourteenth Lecture, just other words for *objectivism* and *subjectivism*.[22] So, if one considers the different functions of subject-object-symbols I have distinguished above, the following persistent meanings can be assigned to the moments of the idealism-realism-dialectic in correspondence to the five standpoints (I present first the realisms and then the idealisms and assign numbers from the hierarchical order in the doctrine of five standpoints to them).[23]

(1) Realism, or objectivism, is a mental attitude "of the thinking subject," which is characterized by passivity.[24] The subject gives itself up to an object and loses itself in the content without reflecting upon its own actions. This attitude appertains to sensuality and produces the enduring object (O), nature, the object of natural sciences.

(2) Higher realism, or objectivism, is characterized by the self-destruction of the subject. The object it relates to is seen as being self-constructing and therefore not, by any means, produced by it. "Hence, nothing at all remains here of a pregiven *us*."[25] The subject becomes engrossed in object in a higher sense, as a self-forming or living one (O'); it is God, the absolute of the religious standpoint and of theology.[26]

(3) Idealism, or subjectivism, is a mental attitude that relies heavily on the fact of reflection. This attitude leads to the standpoint of enduring subject (S), which determines the object and manifests itself in the standpoint of legality and morality.

(4) Higher idealism, or subjectivism, represents energy of thinking and creativity. Object is formed by the "living" subject (S'). This results in the standpoint of art and higher morality.

(5) Unity of realism and idealism, or of objectivism and subjectivism (O = S), is therefore reason or absolute I, the standpoint of the *Wissenschaftslehre* (see I [b]).[27] See table 3.1.

If I am right and this construction constitutes the structure of Fichte's lectures, there can be no doubt that the first principle of the *1804 Wissenschaftslehre* is not God, as it would be the position of *higher realism*, but pure

Table 3.1. The Structure of the *Wissenschaftslehre*

Idealism-Realism-Dialectic Lectures 11–14	Doctrine of Reason/Truth Lecture 15	5 Areas of Knowledge/Science/ 5 Spheres of Reason's Acting/ Appearance Lecture 28
(2) S (*idealism*)	O = S	(1) O (nature | sensuality | natural sciences)
(1) O (*realism*)	real = ideal	(2) S (person | right | jurisprudence)
(4) O' (higher *real*ism)	being = thinking	(3) S' (person | art | ethics & aesthetics)
(3) S' (higher *ideal*ism)		(4) O' (God | religion | theology)
(5) →		(5) S = O (reason | science | DoS)

Source: Author provided.

reason. Reason or the I is the only subject-object we have, which is real and ideal at the same time: it posits itself (being) and knows of it (thinking).[28]

There are, nonetheless, at least two points that may confuse a reader of Fichte's lectures 1804[2]. Firstly, Fichte sometimes speaks of a preference for realism (objectivism). This can lead to the belief that God is the real absolute of the *Wissenschaftslehre*. The relevant passages, however, furnish no proof for this assumption. In the Eleventh Lecture Fichte gives his listeners the main reason for the predilection for the realistic perspective: "Idealism renders impossible even the being of its opposite, and thus it is decidedly *one-sided*. On the other hand, realism at least leaves the being of its opposite undisputed."[29] In other words, radical idealism is more harmful to the *Wissenschaftslehre* than radical realism, which does not annihilate the thinking but just does not make use of it. This statement must be seen in the context of Jacobi's charge of nihilism against Fichte that pure systematic scientific knowledge leads to abandonment of reality.[30] Fichte countered this objection already in the end of the First Lecture: "Namely, as soon as one has heard that the science of knowing presents itself as idealism, one immediately infers that it locates the absolute in what I have been calling *thinking* or *consciousness* which stands over against being as its other half and which therefore can no more be the absolute than can its opposite."[31]

Pure knowledge is thus not merely an ideal but also a real acting. Self-positing is not only knowing of, but a real self-positing of reason. We perform this act and "live" in it; the knowledge has therefore reality for us. This reality does not come from the self-forming object; it is God, as this is the standpoint of higher realism, which, as Fichte said in the cited passage, "can no more be the absolute than can its opposite."

The second point, which can confuse the reader of Fichte's lectures even more, is his energetical and uncompromising appreciation of the absolute of the religious standpoint and of theology. It can even provoke the opinion that God is the actual absolute of the *Wissenschaftslehre*. The thesis of the second part of my chapter is that Fichte, being in conversation with his contemporaries, uses productively an analogy between the thinking of God on the one hand and the thinking of human pure reason on the other.

The Duplicity of the Absolute

If one consults relevant passages in the lectures 1804[2], one can notice a rivalry between two absolute principles, which may both claim to be the first principle of the *Wissenschaftslehre*. In the First Lecture it is stated clearly that the absolute of the *Wissenschaftslehre* is the pure unity of being and thinking, which can be called "pure knowledge" or "I."[32] In the Fifth Lecture, however, comes for the first time the idea of God on the scene, which Fichte, completely nonchalantly, proclaims as the real absolute in opposition to science as its mere expression: "Love of the absolute (or God) is the rational spirit's true element, in which alone it finds peace and blessedness; but science is the absolute's sweet expression; and, like the absolute, this can be loved only for its own sake."[33] It must be nonetheless remarked that Fichte calls God "absolute" in general, he does not declare it to be the absolute of the *Wissenschaftslehre*, which must be loved for its own sake. In the Eighth Lecture Fichte says: "If, as is customary, you want to call the absolutely independent One, the self consuming being, *God*, then [you could say that] all genuine existence is the intuition of God."[34] This is clearly a definition of the standpoint of religion that deals with the self-forming object in a higher sense (O'), and not with the subject-object.[35] In the following lectures, the idealism-realism-dialectic, we lose track of what the absolute really is. It is the absolute incognito, the real one, we are in search of, similarly to the method of dialectical movement in Hegel's *Phenomenology of Spirit* or *Encyclopedia*. In the doctrine of *reason and truth*, Fichte returns to the original statement of the First Lecture that reason, or "We," or "I," is the actual "one undivided being itself, in itself, of itself, through itself, which can never go outside itself to duality"—what he calls a "surprising insight" that he wanted to bring his audience to.[36] The object here is the same as the subject, which "lives" in the act of pure being—the I is for the I, completely enclosed in the act of self-making. In the Twenty-Eighth Lecture Fichte finally rectifies the order and hierarchy of absolute principles of sciences, leaving no doubt that God is the absolute of theology. The task of the *Wissenschaftslehre* to derive principles for other sciences by means of the reflection on the unity of being and thinking, on the act of self-positing of reason as object and subject at the same time, is herewith completed.

Why This Duplicity?

There are, however, good historical and systematic-philosophical reasons for what can cause the above-mentioned confusion. I want to name a few and concentrate on the latter. Firstly, what Fichte aims at with the esteem of the absolute of the religious standpoint is that it can be—together with the concept of self-positing pure reason—opposed to a mere realistic epistemology and empirical as well as noncritical metaphysical concept of world. God and reason are both examples for what Fichte calls the *higher* or *living being* contrary to the being in the sense of a *dead thing* as well as an objectivized thing-in-itself as in traditional metaphysics.[37] Secondly, this similarity can lead to fruitful parallels between God and pure reason. As I stated at the beginning, both principles can be designated by the term "absolute," not only in the sense of being the hard core of a standpoint, but also as the purest form of representation; it is idea. This has theoretical and practical implications that I want to discuss briefly in the last part of this chapter.

God and Pure Human Reason: Parallels

In the research program of transcendental philosophy, to create ideas of God and of the *absolute I* means to use the faculty of reason in the narrow sense. Whether Fichte's audience thinks of God or of the unity of being and thinking, they are using the purest form of spontaneity possible to us. These mental operations can be also described as acts of positing, of pure (self-)activity and pure thinking, which lead to pure knowledge. In the program of transcendental philosophy these operations do not result in the cognition of things-in-themselves. Instead, everyone who creates the idea of God or of the absolute I (of the pure reason itself) and reflects on it can notice the following: Firstly, both can be mentally represented as single, self-enclosed, and absolute entities in themselves, out of themselves, and through themselves. Secondly, we can grasp neither God nor the pure reason without objectifying them in the form of a concept. As Fichte states in the lectures 1804[2], in *The Way towards the Blessed Life* (1806), and in the *1812 Wissenschaftslehre*, God is a pure concept, and this is the way he appears in us; there is no emanation or becoming from God.[38] While the world follows from God in Spinoza, in the *Wissenschaftslehre* "God" appears merely as an "empty concept"—and the love of God, which is the primal affect (*Seinsaffekt*) of the religious world view, gives him reality.[39] Correspondingly, the self-positing reason is not a mere being but a thinking of this being, which has not only to be intuited intellectually but also to be fixated as a concept. These are the epistemological reasons why Fichte can begin his late versions of the *Wissenschaftslehre* with an analysis of the idea of God. What one learns from the creation of the idea of God can be also applied to the thinking of the idea of pure reason and vice versa.

For Fichte after 1800, in his vivid way of doing philosophy, it becomes a possible strategy to introduce the visitors of his lectures to the theory of self-positing pure reason.[40]

It is certainly also the religious thought of the *Image of God* (*Imago Dei*), in philosophical guise, that influences Fichte and makes parallels between divine and human reason—a merely "*symbolic* anthropomorphism"—possible.[41] As Kant stated in many passages in his work, it is allowed and is not a transcendent chain of reasoning to compare God and human reason under the condition of awareness that it is merely an *analogical thinking*—"cognition *according to analogy*."[42] For Kant it is very clear that we cannot think anything without categories. If we use categories to construct merely logically or formally a concept of God or of pure reason—for instance for the sake of critique—it does not mean that we automatically believe that we cognize real things-in-themselves.[43] This would be a mistake of the power of judgment, not of reason.[44] For the analogical thinking of divine and human reason, which, as Kant states, can be used for didactical reasons, for instance in religious practice and education, he uses the category of causality:

> I will say: *the causality of the highest cause* is that, with respect to the world, which *human reason* is with respect to its works of art. Thereby the nature of the highest cause itself remains unknown to me: I *compare* only its effect (*the order of the world*), which is known to me, and the conformity with reason of this effect, *with the effects of human reason that are known to me*, and in consequence I call the highest cause a reason, without thereby ascribing to it as its property the same thing I understand by this expression in humans, or in anything else known to me.[45]

The same way of thinking of pure reason as a faculty that has causality over (a) *the will* and (b) *the understanding*, and its picture and modification of the world, compared to God's reason, is something we encounter in the early Fichte:

(a):

> The categorical, the quality of the [moral, M.L.] law as simply unconditioned and incapable of being conditioned—this points to our higher origin, to our spiritual descent. It is a divine spark in us, and a pledge that We are of His race. Fichte 2010, 20.[46]

(b):
> Dogmatists who {consider the world to be something that exists by itself and who} nevertheless retain their moral and religious sentiments have to say that God created the world. {They cannot, however, explain this any further; for no understanding is produced, no matter how the dogmatist construes this claim.} The dogmatists consider God to be a pure intellect, the determinations of which can surely consist in nothing but concepts. This is also how the I has been considered here: it is a {pure} intellect, and its determinations are nothing but pure concepts. A material world is also present for the I, and therefore these pure concepts must transform themselves into a material world—though only into one that exists purely for the intellect. In the case of God, in contrast, these pure concepts must be transformed into a self-sufficient material world, one that also exists for another intellect {which is quite unintelligible}. The transcendental idealist has to explain only the former process; i.e., he has to show how the pure concepts {of a finite intellect}, considered in a certain way, transform themselves into material substances {[that is,] into a material world for this intellect—which is something that can and should be shown by the philosopher}.[47]

Before falling prey to later Fichte's vivid terminology and imaginary, the proponents of mystical interpretation of his works should give thought to this function of cognitions according to analogy that Fichte used from the early works on: the parallels encountered in thinking of God and reason, and the analogies between the "highest reason" and theoretical and practical sides of the human pure reason are perfect transcendental means—especially in the context of the past Atheism dispute—to give Fichte's audience a ladder to the standpoint of the *Wissenschaftslehre*.

Conclusion

So, is the insight in the Fifteenth Lecture surprising? It might feel so the first time one reads the *1804 Wissenschaftslehre*, and it certainly felt so for Fichte's audience in Berlin. But it should not be surprising after the systematic reconstruction of the structure of these lectures with the help of the five standpoints and the subject-object-symbolism. The *higher realism*, the giving oneself up to a self-forming, living object (O'), is something common to the fourth standpoint in the hierarchy of the five "absolutes," spheres of reason and knowledge, and world views. And it should also not be surprising after considering the epistemic thought experiments that lead to cognition of parallels in thinking of God and pure reason and the symbolic-anthropomorphic analogies between God's and human's pure reason. There is no better way for Fichte's audience to get into the *Wissenschaftslehre* and experience pure reason's activity than in thinking the absolute being (understanding it first as God and then as the absolute I; it is reason that creates the idea of God and of itself). There is, despite any technical, introductory, or other differences, a consistency in central determinations between the earlier and the later versions of the *Wissenschaftslehre*. The key concepts to notice and understand it—and with which I have worked—are *subject-object, idealism-realism,* and *pure reason*, the essence of which lies in the self-positing I, an alternative name for the absolute I, both in the earlier and later versions of the *Wissenschaftslehre*: "Reason is simply the I, and cannot be anything else than I."[48] Reason was, after all, since the beginning of Kant's transcendental project (as the faculty of pure reason in the narrow sense), responsible for ideas and absoluteness. Kant occasionally called it "pure activity" (*reine Tätigkeit*), "pure self-activity" (*reine Selbsttätigkeit*), "spontaneity," "causality," "freedom," and "the true I" (*das eigentliche Ich*) throughout his works. This, as Fichte would say, should be grasped *energetically* and examined systematically.

Notes

1. See Dieter Henrich, *Selbstverhältnisse: Gedanken und Auslegungen zu den Grundlagen der klassischen deutschen Philosophie* (Stuttgart: Reclam, 1982), 75–82; and Karen Gloy, *Bewusstseinstheorien: Zur Problematik und Geschichte des Bewusstseins und Selbstbewusstseins* (Freiburg: Alber, 1998), 226–37.

2. My translation of a sentence found in Jacinto Rivera de Rosales, "Die Welt als Bild," in *Johann Gottlieb Fichtes Wissenschaftslehre von 1812: Vermächtnis und Herausforderung des transzendentalen Idealismus*, ed. Thomas Sören Hoffmann (Berlin: Duncker & Humblot, 2016), 101.

3. My translation of expressions found in Marco Ivaldo, "Leben und Philosophie: Die *Anweisung zum seeligen Leben* als Antwort auf Jacobis Nihilismus-Vorwurf," *Fichte-Studien* 43 (2016): 182–83.

4. See Andreas Schmidt, *Der Grund des Wissens: Fichtes Wissenschaftslehre in den Versionen von 1794/95, 1804² und 1812* (Paderborn: Ferdinand Schöningh, 2004); Jürgen Stolzenberg, "Fichtes Deduktionen des Ich 1804 und 1794," *Fichte-Studien* 30 (2006): 1–13; Christoph Asmuth, "Transzendentalphilosophie oder absolute Metaphysik? Grundsätzliche Fragen an Fichtes Spätphilosophie," *Fichte-Studien* 31 (2007): 45–58; Ulrich Schlösser, *Das Erfassen des Einleuchtens: Fichtes Wissenschaftslehre von 1804 als Kritik an der Annahme entzogener Voraussetzungen unseres Wissens und als Philosophie des Gewisseins* (Berlin: Philo Fine Arts, 2001); Anton A. Ivanenko, *Философия как наукоучение: генезис научного метода в трудах И.Г. Фихте* (Saint Petersburg: Владимир Даль, 2012); Hartmut Traub, "Transzendentales Ich und absolutes Sein: Überlegungen zu Fichtes 'veränderten Lehre,'" *Fichte-Studien* 16 (1999): 39–56; Reinhard Loock, "Das Bild des absoluten Seins beim frühen und späten Fichte," *Fichte-Studien* 17 (2004): 83–102.

5. See Steven Hoeltzel, "The Unity of Reason in Kant and Fichte," in *Kant, Fichte, and the Legacy of Transcendental Idealism*, eds. Halla Kim and Steven Hoeltzel (Lanham, MD: Lexington Books, 2014), 129–52.

6. See, e.g., Nikolai F. Klimmek, *Kants System der transzendentalen Ideen* (Berlin: De Gruyter, 2005); Jannis Pissis, *Kants Transzendentale Dialektik: Zu ihrer systematischen Bedeutung* (Berlin: De Gruyter, 2012); Martin Bunte, *Erkenntnis und Funktion: Zur Vollständigkeit der Urteilstafel und Einheit des kantischen Systems* (Boston: De Gruyter, 2016); Marcus Willaschek, *Kant on the Sources of Metaphysics: The Dialectic of Pure Reason* (Cambridge: Cambridge University Press, 2018); and Rudolf Meer, *Der transzendentale Grundsatz der Vernunft. Funktion und Struktur des Anhangs zur Transzendentalen Dialektik der Kritik der reinen Vernunft* (Berlin: De Gruyter, 2019).

7. See Michael Lewin, *Das System der Ideen: Zur perspektivistisch-metaphilosophischen Begründung der Vernunft im Anschluss an Kant und Fichte* (Freiburg: Alber, 2021); and Michael Lewin, "The Faculty of Ideas: Kant's Concept of Reason in the Narrower Sense," *Open Philosophy* 5/1 (2022): 340–59.

8. KrV A324/B380.

9. 1804², 115; *GA*, II/8, 228–29, italics added.

10. See KrV A333–34/B390–91.

11. Reinhold's philosophy, a long time almost completely out of focus in the research on classical German philosophy, was rediscovered in the last decades. See especially *Krankheit des Zeitalters oder heilsame Provokation? Skeptizismus in der nachkantischen Philosophie*, eds. Martin Bondeli, Klaus Vieweg, and Jiri Chotas (Paderborn: Fink, 2016); George Giovanni, ed., *Karl Leonhard Reinhold and the Enlightenment* (Dordrecht: Springer, 2010); Wolfgang Kersting and Dirk Westerkamp, eds., *Am Rande des Idealismus: Studien zur Philosophie Karl Leonhard Reinholds* (Paderborn: Mentis, 2009); and Pierluigi Valenza, ed., *K. L. Reinhold: Am Vorhof des Idealismus* (Pisa: Istituti Editoriali e Poligrafici Internazionali, 2006).

12. See KrV A320/B376.

13. See the letter to Reinhold from July 2, 1795, *GA*, III/2, 346.

14. For the English translation, see Jerry Surber, "On the Linguistic Capacity and the Origin of Language," in *Language and German Idealism: Fichte's Linguistic Philosophy* (Atlantic Highlands, NJ: Humanities Press, 1996), 119–45. See *GA*, I/3, 103.

15. See *GWL*, *GA*, I/2, 259, and *WLnm[K]*, *GA*, IV/3, 328, 341.

16. See *WLnm[K]*, *GA*, IV/3, 361.

17. Do we really encounter it first in the Fifteenth Lecture—or even before? Or only and actually in the Twenty-Third Lecture. See Ulrich Schlösser, *Das Erfassen des Einleuchtens: Fichtes Wissenschaftslehre von 1804 als Kritik an der Annahme entzogener Voraussetzungen unseres Wissens und als Philosophie des Gewissseins* (Berlin: Philo Fine Arts, 2001).

18. See Jens Lemanski, *Summa und System: Historie und Systematik vollendeter bottom-up- und top-down-Theorien* (Paderborn: Mentis, 2013), 189–248.

19. See Martial Guéroult, *L'Évolution et la structure de la Doctrine de la science chez Fichte* (Paris: Les Belles Lettres, 1930); Joachim Widman, *Die Grundstruktur des transzendentalen Wissens: Nach Johann Gottlieb Fichtes Wissenschaftslehre 1804^2* (Hamburg: Meiner, 1977); Joachim Widman, "Zum Strukturverhältnis der W. L. 1804^1 und 1804^2," in *Johann Gottlieb Fichte, Erste Wissenschaftslehre von 1804*, ed. Hans Gliwitzky (Stuttgart: Kohlhammer, 1969); and Alexander Schnell, *Réflexion et Spéculation: L'idéalisme transcendantal chez Fichte et Schelling* (Grenoble: Millon, 2009), 31–42.

20. On the idealism-realism-relation in Fichte, see especially Valentin Pluder, *Die Vermittlung von Idealismus und Realismus in der Klassischen Deutschen Philosophie: Eine Studie zu Jacobi, Kant, Fichte, Schelling und Hegel* (Stuttgart: Frommann-Holzboog, 2013).

21. Fichte calls these five standpoints also spheres (*Wirkungssphären*), in which we operate with ideas (the spheres of pure reason's activity, if we keep in mind that this is the faculty that deals foremost with ideas in Kant and Fichte), in *On the Nature of the Scholar and Its Manifestations* (see *GA*, I, 8:79). See Johann Gottlieb Fichte, *Über Das Wesen Des Gelehrten*, eds. Alfred Denker, Jeffery Kinlaw, and Holger Zaborowski (Freiburg: Alber, 2020) for recent research on this text.

22. Fichte puts it very clearly: "Realism, or more accurately *objectivism*" and "idealism which, because of language's ambiguity, we might better call *subjectivism*." 1804^2, 109; *GA*, II/8, 214–15).

23. I will do it in no particular order, as my aim is not an interpretation of the dialectic, but simply the assignment of the S-O symbols to specific content from the Eleventh through Fourteenth Lectures and the summary in the second part of the Fifteenth Lecture.

24. 1804^2, 92; *GA*, II/8, 172–73.

25. 1804^2, 98; *GA*, II/8, 186–87.

26. This object in a higher sense was not yet present in the *Foundations of the Entire Wissenschaftslehre* (1794/1795).

27. This deduction of the sciences approximately corresponds to the deduction in the end of the *Wissenschaftslehre nova method*. WLnm[K], *GA*, IV/3, 520–23.

28. While in the case of God, there is a gap between the thinking reason and its object.

29. 1804^2, 92; *GA*, II/8, 172–73. In the Seventeenth and Twenty-First Lectures we encounter a preference for idealism. For the movement of descent, the idealistic aspects "of" and "through" are more relevant. Speaking of preferences, Fichte utters rather methodological remarks to explain and reflect on the procedure of bottom-up (preference for realism) and top-downdeductions (preference for idealism).

30. See for a broader context also Marco Ivaldo, "Leben und Philosophie: Die *Anweisung zum seeligen Leben* als Antwort auf Jacobis Nihilismus-Vorwurf," *Fichte-Studien* 43 (2016): 172–85.

31. 1804^2, 26; *GA*, II/8, 16–17.

32. 1804^2, 25–26; *GA*, II/8, 12–17.

33. 1804^2, 50–51; *GA*, II/8, 74–75.

34. 1804^2, 68; *GA*, II/8, 114–15.

35. One of the main tasks of the *Wissenschaftslehre* since its very beginning is to deduce from the only true first principle the principles of different areas of science. This includes their correction in the light of the enlightenment. Thus, Fichte wants us to understand the principle of theology in a right way. And this is something we learn from the first principle (of self-positing of reason)—God appears as a pure thought (idea of reason) as pure reason appears in a pure insight.

36. 1804^2, 116; *GA*, II/8, 230–31.

37. 1804^2, 25–26; *GA*, II/8, 12–17. The "pure" and "living being" is a conceptual abstraction that developed together with language, as Fichte explains in *On the Linguistic Capacity and the Origin of Language*, *GA*, I/3, 111–13.

38. "Weg mit jenem Phantasma, eines Werdens aus Gott, . . . einer Emanation" (*AzsL GA*, I/9, 119, cf. WL-1812-H *GA*, IV/4, 269). I abbreviate *The Way towards the Blessed Life* (1806) with *AzsL* and the 1812 *Wissenschaftslehre* (Halle-Nachschrift) with WL-1812-H.

39. In the *Wissenschaftslehre* "<finden> wir es nicht als das Seyn selbst, sondern als einen Gedanken" WL-1812 *GA*, II/13, 52. God is a "leere[r] Begriff[]] eines reinen Seyns" (AzsL GA, I/9, 167); "leere[r], über Gottes inneres Wesen schlechthin keinen Aufschluß gebende[r], Begriff" (AzsL GA, I/9, 110)—"die Liebe, ist die Quelle aller Gewißheit, und aller Wahrheit, und aller Realität" (AzsL GA, I/9, 167).

40. A motive for this strategy could have been given by Friedrich Karl Forberg, "Briefe über die neueste Philosophie," *Philosophisches Journal einer Gesellschaft teutscher Gelehrten* 6, no. 1 (1797): 44–88, who noticed that both ideas, the absolute I and God, seem ungraspable.

41. Kant, *Prolegomena to Any Future Metaphysics That Will Be Able to Come Forward as Science* in Immanuel Kant *Theoretical Philosophy after 1781*, eds. Henry. Allison and Peter Heath, trans. Gary. Hatfield (Cambridge: Cambridge University Press, 2004), 108; IV, 357.

42. See, e.g., Kant, *Prolegomena*, 108–11; IV, 357–60; Kant, *Critique of the Power of Judgment*, trans. Paul Guyer and Eric Matthews (Cambridge: Cambridge University Press, 2001), 321, 324; V, 456, 460; Kant, *Critique of Pure Reason*, trans. Paul Guyer and Allen Wood (Cambridge University Press, 1998, A762–73/B700–01, A678/B706.

43. For Kant's formal construction and determination of transcendental ideas with twelve categories see works on the "Transcendental Dialectic," especially Martin Bunte, *Erkenntnis und Funktion: Zur Vollständigkeit der Urteilstafel und Einheit des kantischen Systems* (Boston: De Gruyter, 2016); Jannis Pissis, *Kants Transzendentale Dialektik: Zu ihrer systematischen Bedeutung* (Berlin: De Gruyter, 2012); Nikolai F. Klimmek, *Kants System der transzendentalen Ideen* (Berlin: De Gruyter, 2005).

44. See KrV A642–43/B670–71.

45. Kant, *Prolegomena*, 49–169; IV, 360, emphasis added.

46. VCO, 20; *GA*, I/1, 145.

47. FTP, 418–19; *WLnm[K] GA*, IV/3, 496; see also *GWL GA*, I/2, 390–92.

48. 1804^2, 192; *GA*, II/8, 400.

Chapter 4

Fichte's Reader and the Autopoiesis of the *Wissenschaftslehre*, 1794–1804

ANDREW J. MITCHELL

One of the most distinctive elements of Fichte's thinking is his empowerment of the reader, or, in the case of his lectures, the auditor (I will use "reader" to refer to both). The reader who receives Fichte's teaching is no impartial party in the transmission of a doctrinal content. That reader is no indifferent onlooker able to objectively assess the advantages and disadvantages of the philosophical systems arrayed before its eyes. Rather, from the first full formulation of the *Foundation of the Entire Wissenschaftslehre* in 1794, the reader is implicated in what they are reading. This remains the case through the 1797 reformulation of the project *An Attempt at a New Presentation of the Wissenschaftslehre*. Looking at these two texts, we see that the reader's participation in and enactment of Fichte's philosophy is decisive for metaphysical, ethical, and social reasons.

But things are different in the *1804 Wissenschaftslehre*. The reader's role remains determinative, but now that role has shifted. Where once the reader was to think the *Wissenschaftslehre* and thereby lend it life, making it a truly living philosophical system, now that reader no longer thinks the system. The reader does not make connections or pursue the vicissitudes of transcendental argumentation. The reader is not needed *to think* the *Wissenschaftslehre* but *to host* it. By "host," I mean something between the way a computer platform runs or hosts a specific operating system, hardware hosting software, and the way in which a body may be host to a virus or disease. With this shift in the reader's role, there is a cascading shift in the metaphysical, ethical, and social dimensions of the *Wissenschaftslehre* project as a whole, as I hope to show.

Reader as Collaborator: The First Formulations of the *Wissenschaftslehre*, 1794–1797

Fichte's concern for the reader is evident from the outset of the *Foundations of the Entire Wissenschaftslehre*, where Fichte explains that the text before us is "extremely imperfect and defective."[1] Part of the reason for this, he explains, is "because I have sought to avoid, as much as possible, any fixed terminology—which provides the easiest means for literalists to rob any system of its spirit and transform it into a desiccated skeleton."[2] The unstated goal is thus an animated, living system, and insistence on fixed terminology is an obstacle to this. A fixed terminology implicitly asserts the authority of the writer. It monopolizes the language of ideas and thereby the understanding of them and ultimately sets conditions on their acceptance, that they be assumed in this language only. Fichte's refusal of fixed terminology is an opening to the reader. It rejects the image of the author as an all-knowing authority over the text. The verbatim text is not the important thing here, and the importance gained from authorship of that text diminishes accordingly, though it comes with an accompanying rise in the status of the reader, as we shall see.

A fixed terminology thus gives way before the thinking that the text is meant to provoke. This thinking experience can be articulated in many ways; there is no secret formula that captures it. And for this reason, no presentation of a system, however complete, will ever contain it. After Fichte reiterates that the *Wissenschaftslehre* will be "misunderstood by many people and not understood at all by even more," he immediately adds that "it will remain sorely in need of improvement in all its parts—not merely in its present, extremely incomplete presentation, but even following the most complete presentation that might be possible by any individual."[3] There is no fixed language for delivering the *Wissenschaftslehre* because the *Wissenschaftslehre* is not a content to be memorized; rather, it is a system to be constructed. As such it requires a constructor, and that constructor is the reader, who is here called on to act in the engagement of his or her I.

Fichte demonstrates in the *Wissenschaftslehre* that this I is no substantive or even steadily existing entity, but rather an act. Understanding the I in this way ultimately leads to an understanding of its practical activity in the world of negotiating with the not-I. Drives are introduced to explain behavior. This conception of the I is meant to have practical effect; it is meant to change our lives. Fichte can tell us about all the wonders we will achieve with this (as he basically did in "Concerning the Concept of the *Wissenschaftslehre*" prior to its publication), but for the system to get started it requires a reader, and not just one who dutifully drags their eyes across the pages. It requires a reader who acts, who acts on behalf of their I, and undertakes the task that is to be performed, understanding this thought and carrying it out in life. Fichte's philosophy takes the performance of this act as its point of departure. The reader is the one who performs the thought.

This means that the *Wissenschaftslehre*, like any prescribed performance, an athletic or aesthetic performance for instance, will require a certain ability in the performer. Not everyone will be able to perform it alike. For those readers who cannot, Fichte advises or rather "beseeches" them "not to waste their time on my writings."[4] This is because his philosophy has to presuppose an ability on the part of its reader; "it presupposes the free power of inner intuition."[5] A capable and free reader is needed to enact Fichte's thought.

This is not merely a matter of passively receiving intuitions, however. When Fichte presumes a "free power of inner intuition," the emphasis should fall on the freedom voiced here, and the participatory activity it makes possible. For we have more to do than passively watch intuitions flicker past. After Fichte dismisses those readers who cannot understand him, he explains that his text could have been made perfectly clear: "Were I to have enough time and space, I would be able to elevate each of my claims to any desired level of clarity."[6] This is not a failing for Fichte, but a feature:

> I consider it especially necessary to add that I do not say everything, but instead would like to leave something for my readers to think about as well. To be sure, I anticipate many misunderstandings, which I might have prevented with a few words. I have not added these few words, however, because I wished to encourage independent thinking. The *Wissenschaftslehre* should by no means force itself upon the reader, but should be a necessity for him, just as it was for its author.[7]

Fichte's text is explicitly written to offer the reader something "to think about," to activate his readers. That thinking reader is not just expected—he or she is presumed, presupposed, indeed, a necessity for the system itself.

The collaborative role that Fichte assigns to his reader has metaphysical, ethical, and even social consequences, which I would now like to detail before examining Fichte's 1804 formulation of the *Wissenschaftslehre* along the same lines.

METAPHYSICS: READER AS SYSTEM-COLLABORATOR

The *Foundations of the Entire Wissenschaftslehre* (1794) opens with Fichte's quest to find a fundamental first principle to use as the basis of his philosophical system. Even the most complete system to date, the Kantian system, for all its achievement, left much to be desired. It could not ground itself on a single fundamental principle while simultaneously maintaining an irresolvable separation between the sensible and the supersensible, the phenomenal and the noumenal, sense and intellect. Kant's successors would attempt to perfect and unify his system, maintaining that they held true to the "spirit" of Kant's work, if not strictly to the "letter." Chief among these was Reinhold. Reinhold had already pointed out that there was a lack of unity in Kant's system, that for all its architectonic breadth and detail, it still failed to ground itself on a single principle. Lacking this, it failed as a system. Reinhold attempted to solve this with his insistence on "representation," which he took as a blanket term covering intuitions, concepts, and ideas. Without such an attempt at unity, the split between sensibility and intellect remained fatal.

Fichte's breakthrough comes in his response to a critic of Reinhold's proposed solution, in Fichte's "Review of *Aenesidemus*." Here Fichte effectively realizes that no system can ever be complete as long as it is based on a principle as hitherto understood, observing, "The initial incorrect presupposition . . . was precisely the presupposition that one must begin with a fact. We certainly do require a first principle which is material and not merely formal. But such a principle does not have to express a *fact*; it can also express an *Act*—if I may risk asserting something which can be neither explained nor proven here."[8] Even assuming Reinhold was correct and that he did, in fact, unify Kant and create a completely unified system, it was still by means of such an outmoded principle. The resulting system was still something *objective*, a thought construct that one could take or leave as one wished. That system was a thought-object and this meant it necessarily had something outside of it, a thought-subject, the thinker of the system. So long as the thinker of the system remained outside the system, there was no way that a system could be said to be complete.

With this insight gleaned from the "Review of *Aenesidemus*," Fichte goes on to construct his *Wissenschaftslehre*, incorporating the thinker into the system itself. There is no principle at the base of Fichte's system, however fundamental we might claim it to be. Instead there is an act, and one that Fichte's reader must perform. Authorizing the reader to take up this act, Fichte includes the thinker of the system within it, the reader as system-collaborator.

Ethics: Respect and the Freedom of the Reader

In the 1797 *Attempt at a New Presentation of the Wissenschaftslehre* Fichte emphasizes the ethical dimension of readership. Noting that the self-consciousness presumed by his philosophy "does not simply occur without any assistance from us," Fichte calls on us to discover it: "This is something everyone has to discover immediately within himself; otherwise, he will never become acquainted with it at all."[9] To even intuit this requires us to act and perform, since the reader "can intuit the indicated act of the I only within himself; and in order to be able to intuit this act, he must perform it. He freely chooses to produce this act within himself."[10] This founding free act is the key to his system and its ethical import.

Initiating the *Wissenschaftslehre* in an act of freedom ensures that it will be a philosophical system that cannot be forced on a person. A person can be made by force to avow Platonism, tortured to the point of confessing Kantianism, but can never be compelled to avow the thought of Fichte. This is because these other systems are indifferent to their reader. To affirm such a system is the only choice the reader has. The reader can do nothing more than this and is not needed to do anything more than this. With Fichte, the philosophy is not a preexisting fact ready to be affirmed or not. Rather, it begins with an act. And no one can be compelled to perform this act. Indeed, for this reason we are always subject to fakers and poseurs who can claim to have done it without actually having done it: "If someone pretends to act in this manner, no one else can ever know whether he is proceeding correctly and in the manner requested. In a word: this type of consciousness cannot be proven to anyone."[11] Because it cannot be proven by simply avowing the words, Fichte's system cannot be imposed on another, and, conversely, one can never prove that one has in fact engaged it. The price of the reader's freedom and the break with fixed terminology is the loss of a particular kind of certainty, the desiccated certainty of the skeleton.

The *Wissenschaftslehre* is written with respect for this freedom of the reader. It requires a free reader to freely choose it. One cannot be forced into Fichteanism. One can certainly be forced into avowing it, but insofar as the philosophy is not a matter of fact, it is nothing that can simply be avowed. Indeed, it is the only such system of its kind: "For we have solemnly confessed on many occasions that we cannot force anyone to accept our system, since the acceptance of this system is something that depends upon freedom."[12] The *Wissenschaftslehre* is explicitly directed against coercion and domination.

Society: Reading as the Goal of Education Reform

Fichte requires a capable reader for the performance of his philosophy. That philosophy is one of freedom. To realize Fichte's system is to become more of oneself, to discover a new dimension of one's existence. For this reason, achieving the *Wissenschaftslehre* should be the goal of any government by and for independent, free beings. But Fichte cannot be everywhere to teach the *Wissenschaftslehre* on his own; he can, however, rely on the publication industry to disseminate his thought. The societal goal, then, becomes one of creating readers capable of realizing it. But education has been one-sided; people are specialized to the detriment of the whole person. In 1794, Fichte phrased it so:

> The *Wissenschaftslehre* is supposed to be exhaustive of the entire human being, and it can therefore be grasped only with the totality of one's powers. It can never become a universally endorsed philosophy so long as, in the case of so many human beings, the development of one of their mental powers is sacrificed to the advantage of another power, sacrificing the power of imagination to the advantage of the power of understanding or the power of understanding to the advantage of the power of imagination—or sacrificing both powers to the advantage of memory. For this reason, the *Wissenschaftslehre* will for a long time have to remain confined to a narrow circle, a truth that is as unpleasant to utter as it is to hear, but which is nevertheless the truth.[13]

Three years later, the issue has only grown in importance.

For Fichte, contemporary education is a matter of dominating the student and forcing doctrines upon him or her. People are being trained for their oppression, they "place more faith in some old book than they do in their own innermost consciousness."[14] Indeed, Fichte now realizes that they are intentionally educated for this. Education "only tries to produce people who are useful to others . . . and to accustom people to never initiating anything on their own, but always to expect the first stimulus to come from outside."[15] Against this, we need to "begin to educate human beings for their own purposes and as instruments of their own will and not as soulless instruments for the use of others."[16] The *Wissenschaftslehre* qua work of spirit would play a role in creating such people, creating its own audience of readers, indeed, creating informed, responsible citizens.

In all these ways, then, the reader is of crucial importance to Fichte's early system, where that reader metaphysically completes it by performing it, ethically justifies it as respectful of his or her freedom, and orients it toward the improvement of society.

Reader as Host: The *Wissenschaftslehre* of 1804

Ten years after the launch of the *Wissenschaftslehre*, much has changed. We might assign a large portion of that change to the name Schelling. Fichte's *1804 Wissenschaftslehre* is written in the light of Schelling's early adherence to and subsequent break with Fichte. The 1804 project is informed by Fichte's differences with Schellingian *Naturphilosophie* and its presumed "materialism," as well as his differences with Schelling's 1801 *Attempt at a Presentation of My System*, which Hegel basically adopted and praised explicitly against Fichte, in his 1801 work *The Difference Between the Fichtean and Schellingian Systems of Philosophy*. Fichte even calls Schelling "the hero of all passionate, and therefore empty and confused heads."[17] The name Schelling would thus come to stand for Fichte as the misunderstanding of his philosophy as a simple idealism. The *1804 Wissenschaftslehre* can be read as Fichte's corrective to this presumed misconception.

The reader (or auditor) is still critically important to this enterprise, for, as Fichte explains in the opening lecture regarding the basic truth that will form their subject-matter: "Not even the least spark of it can be grasped or communicated historically as an appropriation from someone else's mind. Rather, whomever would have it must produce it entirely out of himself."[18] Fichte can do his best to prepare the reader, but the goal is that "the insight will happen of itself without any further ado."[19] Even Fichte would vanish before this, "I wish to be considered silenced and erased, and you yourselves must come forward and stand in my place."[20] He adds at the outset of the next lecture, though, "If it were already completely clear to you, you would not need me any longer."[21] And need him, obviously, we do.

Fichte sets out in these lectures to do philosophy, which he provisionally defines as a quest for and presentation of the truth. Truth remains despite variance of opinions; truth is unchanging, and what is more, truth is a kind of unity or oneness. This leads Fichte to reformulate the task of philosophy in terms of this unity: "The essence of philosophy would consist in this: *to trace all multiplicity . . . back to absolute oneness.*"[22] Philosophy is not about empirical observation, that is the purview of history, rather philosophy always moves past these details, builds up from them, abstracts and generalizes from them, conceptualizes them. Philosophy climbs upward. As such, the quest for unity can be put another way: "The task of philosophy could be expressed as the presentation of the absolute."[23]

It is the presentation of this absolute that Fichte needs his readers to perform for themselves. The Third Lecture begins with such attempts: "I ask you to look sequentially at your own inner experience."[24] The reader might think of their morning, the individual moments and events of it. According to Fichte, we know each of these moments equally: "But now I ask you further: Do you not *know* in all these modifications; and is not your knowing, as knowing, the same self-identical knowing in all variations of the object?"[25] Fichte's point is that our knowledge is not tied to any particular object. The object varies and our knowledge remains the same. The conclusion: our knowledge is not dependent on anything objective. Or perhaps we should say: knowledge as such is not dependent on any particular object. Fichte will extend the point: knowledge is not dependent on any particular subject, either. We do not need to run through the variation of every possible determination of our morning (an infinite task) to attain this knowledge, as it is not dependent upon such subjective activity: "This knowing manifest itself independently of such experiments and completely a priori as self-sustaining and self-identical independent from all subjectivity and objectivity."[26] Otherwise put, knowing "is not subjective, is absolutely unalterable and self-identical not just independently from all variability of the object, but also independently from all variability of the subject without which the object doesn't exist."[27]

What we have arrived at is that the absolute is what unites being and thinking or is the unity of being and thinking. Now we might agree that when we think, we always think of something. We might agree consciousness is always intentional, or we might hold that for there to be thinking, there needs be a being who thinks—in all these ways we might understand there to be no thinking without being, but Fichte wants it the other way around as well: no being without thinking. "Absolutely all being posits a *thinking* or *consciousness* of itself."[28] The reason for this has to do with what Fichte calls "evidence" or "manifestness [*Evidenz*]" and how thinking and being both share in it.[29]

When I think of something, it appears to me. When I encounter a being, it appears to me. Thinking and being share in this appearing as manifest. Whatever particular thing becomes manifest, be it a being or a thought, it does so in this "space" or "field" of "manifestation," the space in which evidence shows itself. Fichte emphasizes the connection that consequently arises for being and thinking: "Nothing can occur in the manifest sphere of being without simultaneously occurring in the manifest sphere of thinking."[30] Manifestness is the space in which the various determinations and moments of our day are presented, but that manifestness is not identical with any definite manifest thing. This field of manifestation is the unchangeable that allows a plethora of constantly changing things to become manifest. Our knowledge depends on this field of manifestation, so much so that Fichte will even identify it with the a priori: "I would very much like to be spared the eternal struggle about whether in general there is manifestness or something a priori (for both are the same)."[31] We know in advance that both being and thought will make themselves manifest. For Fichte, "genuine transcendental philosophy" recognizes that "the dichotomy of B [being] and T [thought], which arises from A [the absolute], is mere appearance [*bloßer Erscheinung*]."[32]

The task of the science of knowledge, as the leading edge of philosophy, is to explore this oneness of manifestation: "'What is it in this qualitative oneness?' The true nature of the science of knowing resides in answering this question. In order to analyze this even further, it is clear that for this purpose one must inwardly construct this essence of knowing. Or, as in this case is exactly the same thing, *this essence must construct itself*."[33] The essence of knowing must construct itself. Any inward construction I do is merely to host that which constructs itself. My construction brings me to the place at which the insight might be received. I do not create it, it must live and grow on its own. It cannot be something static and dead like the factical; instead, it must be alive, genetic: "Manifestness [*Evidenz*] in itself is therefore genetic."[34] To highlight this active and living dimension, Fichte speaks of the space of manifestation in terms of light.

Light is both active and static. What remains constant about it, what allows it to sustain itself, is what we call "being" or "substance": "Substance is only the form of light as self-sufficient."[35] Otherwise, light is active, which is to say genetic, and this means that what shows itself in this light does so genetically: "All manifestness opens up into genetic manifestness, since pure light manifests itself implicitly as genesis."[36] Because both being and thought appear, we can now say that their union is in light: "Thus, pure light has prevailed as the one focus and the sole principle of both being and the concept."[37]

And here we arrive at the major difference in reader roles between the two texts. It hinges on the self-construction of the absolute. In 1794 we were collaborators in the mental construction and exhibition of it. In 1804, what is to be done? Our task is more to "see the light" than to contribute in any way. We are no longer needed to think or construct the absolute. Indeed, our task as reader now has nothing mental or intellectual about it, as Fichte acknowledges:

> Without any assistance from us, an insight will spring up by itself, like a lightning flash. The slowness or speed of one's mind has nothing more to do in this final event, *because the mind in general has no role in it.* For we do not create the truth, and things would be badly arranged if we had to do so; rather, truth creates itself by its own power, and it does so wherever the conditions of its creation are present, in the same way and at the same rate.[38]

We are not needed to "assist" in the presentation of the absolute. Any "inward construction" we are called upon to do merely sets the stage for what is to take place, the "epiphany."

The absolute originates, "springs up," by itself. Our minds play no role in this. It is not a mental event we participate in. Our only role is to be a "witness," as Fichte puts it later in the text: "We certainly actually and in fact *witness* the in-itself producing its construction."[39] Fichte describes the experience as an "epiphany [*Erscheinung*]."[40]

But does the *Wissenschaftlehre* need a reader simply to observe it? Here we have to understand the relation of observer and observed at a genetic level. The observer does not observe any static, outside, observable thing. The observer observes and thus inaugurates a genetic process. Fichte speaks of this in terms of a kind of consummation, even a "dissolution," of the subject into this moment of observation. The *Wissenschaftslehre* needs a space in which this genetic expression can play itself out. Fichte's concern with being becomes a concern for what is expressive in it, light. But expression is life, and the expressivity of light means it is alive. Such a life needs locating in a living being: "No expression or life of the light could arise unless we first unconditionally posit and see a life as a necessary determination of the light's being."[41] Fichte provisionally objects that "of course this life is not supposed to be our life, but rather the very life and self-construction of the in-itself."[42] But a few pages later he responds: "But *we live* immediately in the act of living itself, therefore we are the one undivided being itself, in itself, of itself, through itself, which can never go outside itself to duality."[43] Our life and the life of being's light are to merge.

If Fichte needed a mind to think A = A and thus I = I in 1794, ten years later he needs a living being. He needs a mind and a body, a life. This is the fleshy hardware needed to "run" the *Wissenschaftslehre* in 1804.[44] We are not needed to think it, only to stage it.

As the *Wissenschaftslehre* continues, all of this is examined and refined, ostensibly proceeding along genetic lines toward an understanding of ultimate oneness as the center of a complex of synthetic activity. This further teaching of the *Wissenschaftslehre* cannot come about if that prior understanding of the light has not been attained. In the *1804 Wissenschaftslehre*, the need for such light transforms the reader's role from one of collaborator to that of host. The reader's activity is to be spent preparing to receive the *Wissenschaftslehre*'s inconceivable experience. What follows from this?

Metaphysics: Reader as System-Witness

The reader's participation in the 1794 system allowed us to understand Fichte's reader as not standing outside of their particular philosophical system, but as actively participating in it. That system could not get off the ground without a reader who was capable of performing the simple acts of self-reflection that Fichte could prescribe but not presume. This made Fichte's reader an accomplice in the construction of the system. The 1794 *Wissenschaftslehre* begins from a point within the system. It begins with the refusal of any outside to the system, even on the part of its reader. That reader is already assimilated into the system as its performer.

The 1804 system does not require the same work of the reader. And thus we might wonder: Does this 1804 reader stand outside the system? Fichte's remarks averring that we are merely to witness the manifestational power of the light would seem to suggest just such an outside stance. But Fichte would point out that here we are presupposing a separation between subject and object, in accordance with which all that we experience would automatically be understood as "outside" of us. But from a higher perspective, Fichte could assure us, from that of the absolute, the subject/object split is preempted by a higher unity. The object can no longer be said to be something outside of me when it and I are united in a grander synthesis.

Be that as it may, the important point is not my location within the system, but my role. If I am merely assimilated into the system, I am just as much "outside" it, as if it never knew my name. Just as one can still be alone in a big city, one can be within a system and not yet be central to it. For me to be within the system, for the system to complete itself by encompassing everything within it, including its reader/performer, I must have a role in its construction; *the system must be part of me.* Without that investment, I am outside it. If I am to be a witness, I must remain outside it.

Fichte's emphasis on allowing the absolute to construct itself prohibits the consummation of the reader in the system. The reader remains exterior to it. At best, the reader provides the fleshy hardware for running the *Wissenschaftslehre* system software.

ETHICS: ANNULLING FREEDOM

In 1797, Fichte prided himself on how ethically advanced his system was. Because it depended on an internal act of consciousness, it could never be known whether one had actually performed the act or not. As such, one could not compel another into acceptance of the system. Or if one could, one could never rest assured that one's antagonist had meant what they avowed, or rather, that in merely avowing it, the system was brought into play. Fichte's system cannot be used as an instrument of violence or disrespect of another. They cannot be made to avow it. The system itself cannot be imposed. It is a free thinking inherently respectful of the freedom of others. Such a system of freedom is an ethical system.

In 1804, regardless of whether the reader is inside or outside of the system, the reader's freedom is no longer required. What is needed is acceptance, acquiescence, absorption. For Fichte, this is what it means to be rational: "We cannot create the conditions, they must emerge spontaneously. Reason must create itself, *independent from any volition or freedom, or self.*"[45] Freedom and volition are no longer of concern. Fichte repeats the point in describing his *Wissenschaftslehre* against the philosophical views of the day. The *Wissenschaftslehre* is "a science which brings all thinking without exception under the most stringent rules and *annuls all freedom of spirit* in the one, eternal, self-sustaining truth."[46] The concern with respecting the reader's freedom, much less the freedom of others, is nowhere to be found. Much of the ethical scaffolding of 1797 has fallen away.

SOCIETY: READING AS THE GOAL OF EDUCATION REFORM

The experience of the *Wissenschaftslehre* does not come about by the reader lending a hand. It happens when the reader sits back and cedes control or mastery. In 1794 and 1797, Fichte sketched a vision of education reform in light of the *Wissenschaftslehre*. Education was to be a cultivation of the whole person and for the purposes of augmenting freedom. Such free subjects were also considered the best subjects for a participatory political order.

In 1804, that global vision of education seems to have receded. This is not to say that education is not of concern any longer, but rather that it is now a matter of adopting techniques for improving the memory and focusing the attention so that the lectures may be better rehearsed outside of the auditorium. Education becomes training.

In keeping with this training, Fichte understands what he is doing as a kind of practice. His lectures and remarks "are designed to initiate you into the art which we will subsequently practice together, the art of philosophy."[47] Memory will be important for this, as Fichte does not fail to emphasize throughout the lectures. Points are introduced "in order to assist both your memories and repeated reproduction," restated "in case you find the following expression easier to remember," and summarized "briefly, clearly, and to fix the point easily in memory."[48]

But what is most crucial for the functioning of these lectures is something that Fichte cannot teach, something that "really cannot be imparted, namely the talent [*Talent*] for adopting them."[49] That talent is our attention: "The talent for adopting these lectures is the talent of full, complete attention."[50] The lectures will not serve their function of implanting the *Wissenschaftslehre* in a living host if that host is not first prepared for the adoption by entering a particular relaxed and focused state that Fichte calls "attention." The attentive mind best receives the uploaded system.

And where the implicit education platform of 1797 carried the promise of a deliberative democratic politics, this new focus on attention forebodes something else. For attention is inherently exclusive: "Full, complete attention, I have said, which throws itself into the present object with all its spiritual power, puts itself there and is completely absorbed in it, so that no other thought or fancy can occur."[51] But let us listen to Fichte when he details what is excluded: "There is no room for anything foreign [*das Fremde*] in a spirit totally absorbed in its object: full, complete attention as distinct from that partial attention which hears with half an ear and thinks with half its thinking power, interrupted and criss-crossed by all kinds of fugitive thoughts and fantasies."[52] The foreign and the fugitive must be excluded if there is to be attention. Whatever appeal these thoughts and fantasies might hope to raise with us is excluded from the outset. We make ourselves unreachable to their cries.

The focus on attention also allows Fichte to absolve himself of all blame for failures of the *Wissenschaftslehre* to take. If someone disagrees or if there is any dissent, there must have been a failure in application: "Those for whom things don't happen as we expect have not used these lectures as they should be used; and if things don't flow smoothly, they have only themselves to blame."[53] If you do not see what Fichte sees, the fault is entirely with you: "Whomever doesn't see it now must be lacking in the undivided attention required here."[54]

The broadly sketched educational plan of 1797 becomes a technique for the improvement of the attention in 1804, an attention that absolves Fichte of all responsibility for the adequacy of his teaching talent and ceases to require of the student any thought achieved on their own.

Conclusion

One of the enduring strengths of Fichte's thought is his understanding that philosophy is not an indifferent enterprise conducted by a mind with nothing at stake in the pursuit. Rather, philosophy claims us, and the truest philosophies claim us most deeply. In both the 1794 and 1804 versions of the *Wissenschaftslehre*, Fichte elevates his reader to serve a crucial role in the construction of the system. Philosophical worries lead Fichte to reformulate his system in 1804, provoking a slight shift in the role of the reader. Unfortunately, that same slight shift topples much of what made the 1794 text so profoundly engrossing in the first place. Metaphysically, the system seems incomplete; ethically, the reader is almost rendered passive with Fichte placing the blame for misunderstanding at the reader's feet; and even socially or politically, the gesture toward institutional change submerges in favor of techniques for isolated, individual self-betterment. Taken as a whole, it is hard to say the philosophical improvements to the system were worth the sacrifice of its reader.

Notes

1. *FEW*, 197; *GA*, I/2, 252.
2. *FEW*, 197; *GA*, I/2, 252.
3. *FEW*, 345; *GA*, I/2, 415–16.
4. *FEW*, 197; *GA*, I/2, 253.
5. *FEW*, 197; *GA*, I/2, 253.
6. *FEW*, 198; *GA*, I/2, 253.
7. *FEW*, 198; *GA*, I/2, 253.
8. *EPW*, 64; *GA*, I/2, 46.
9. *IWL*, 14, 46; *GA*, I/4, 191, 217.
10. *IWL*, 43; *GA*, I/4, 214.
11. *IWL*, 14; *GA*, I/4, 191.
12. *IWL*, 85; *GA*, I/4, 252.
13. *FEW*, 345n; *GA*, I/2, 415n.
14. *IWL*, 79; *GA*, I/4, 247.
15. *IWL*, 92; *GA*, I/4, 259.
16. *IWL*, 92; *GA*, I/4, 259.
17. 1804^2, 110; *GA*, II/8, 217.
18. 1804^2, 22; *GA*, II/8, 5.
19. 1804^2, 22; *GA*, II/8, 5.
20. 1804^2, 23; *GA*, II/8, 5.
21. 1804^2, 29; *GA*, II/8, 23.
22. 1804^2, 23; *GA*, II/8, 9.
23. 1804^2, 24; *GA*, II/8, 11.
24. 1804^2, 34; *GA*, II/8, 37.
25. 1804^2, 34–35; *GA*, II/8, 37.
26. 1804^2, 35; *GA*, II/8, 39.
27. 1804^2, 35; *GA*, II/8, 39.
28. 1804^2, 25; *GA*, II, 8, 13.
29. 1804^2, 35; *GA*, II/8, 39,
30. 1804^2, 30; *GA*, II/8, 25.
31. 1804^2, 36; *GA*, II/8, 41.
32. 1804^2, 30; *GA*, II/8, 27.
33. 1804^2, 37; *GA*, II/8, 43, emphasis mine.
34. 1804^2, 37; *GA*, II/8, 43.
35. 1804^2, 53; *GA*, II/8, 81.
36. 1804^2, 43; *GA*, II/8, 59.
37. 1804^2, 43; *GA*, II/8, 59.
38. 1804^2, 48; *GA*, II/8, 69, emphasis mine.
39. 1804^2, 103; *GA*, II/8, 195, emphasis mine.

40. 1804^2, 30; *GA*, II/8, 25.
41. 1804^2, 60–61; *GA*, II/8, 97.
42. 1804^2, 112; *GA*, II/8, 223.
43. 1804^2, 116; *GA*, II/8, 231.
44. Certainly the body was important in 1794, but thinking and being still remained separated, and this irreconcilable separation led to the asymptotic attempts at its closure, which formed the practical side of human existence for Fichte. In 1794, mind-body union was something to be attempted; in 1804, it became a fact, or rather, a genetic determination.
45. 1804^2, 45; *GA*, II/8, 63, emphasis mine.
46. 1804^2, 50; *GA*, II/8, 73, emphasis mine.
47. 1804^2, 23; *GA*, II/8, 7.
48. 1804^2, 59; *GA*, II/8, 93; 1804^2, 28; *GA*, II/8, 21; 1804^2, 36; *GA*, II/8, 43.
49. 1804^2, 47, tm; *GA*, II/8, 67.
50. 1804^2, 47, tm; *GA*, II/8, 67.
51. 1804^2, 47; *GA*, II/8, 67.
52. 1804^2, 47–48, tm; *GA*, II/8, 67.
53. 1804^2, 48; *GA*, II/8, 69.
54. 1804^2, 53; *GA*, II/8, 81.

Part 2
Key Concepts

Chapter 5

Into Death's Lair

Truth, Appearance, and the Irrational Gap in Fichte's *1804 Wissenschaftslehre*

MATTHEW NINI

During his Berlin exile, Fichte repeatedly reworked his *Wissenschaftslehre*. While insistent that his philosophy never changed, the radical transformation in presentation it continually underwent forces readers to approach each new version with fresh eyes. Perhaps Fichte intended it to be so: the new manner of expression devised during the Berlin period is meant, at least in part, to free philosophical practice from the drudgery of unreflective habit. The changes, then, are as much pedagogical as anything else. Now, Fichte was lecturing rather than writing, and his hearers were active participants who were meant to perform the system. Their aim was to become *Wissenschaftslehrers* whose attention to their own capacity for reflection would not only give them the means to think philosophically but allow for a truly philosophical life.

As such, *life* was the ultimate goal of this new iteration of the *Wissenschaftslehre*. As the ineffable totality in which we always already find ourselves, life (or "the One," or "Truth"—herein, we will simply use "Absolute") is the absolute principle of which conscious acts of judgment lose sight whenever they establish an object of experience. Reconciling life with discursive thought—or establishing the mutual interdependence of appearances and their conditions—lies at the heart this project. Fichte's solution is to develop an immanent system in which appearances are precisely appearances *of* life. The epistemological takeaway is that consciousness is always already immersed in this system: understanding is possible because intelligibility has been assumed. The entry point into such a system is attention to the compelling nature of objects. If the *Wissenschaftslehrers* will just pay attention to the fact *that* objects are intelligible, stresses Fichte, they will come to the conclusion that understanding and intelligibility mutually condition each other.

This chapter seeks to offer an interpretation of the second set of 1804 lectures on the *Wissenschaftslehre* by addressing the question it raises about an irrational gap or *hiatus irrationalis*. The *1804 Wissenschaftslehre* is made up of twenty-eight lectures. The first fifteen constitute a theory of Truth, a *Wahrheitslehre* that establishes the mutual interdependence of appearances and their conditions of thought (ultimately, the Absolute) by means of what we will be calling the "singularity thesis." The second half (Sixteenth Lecture to Twenty-Eighth Lecture) constitutes a *Bildlehre* or *Phänomenologie* that accounts for the appearing of particulars or "images" without making an appeal to a *tertium datur* that is neither appearance nor its conditions.[1] Where the two meet, in the transitional Fifteenth Lecture, one finds the articulation of a gap between the two, a hiatus between the Absolute and what appears in consciousness.

Fichte's strategy in resolving this gap is twofold, corresponding to the two main sections of the text. In the *Wahrheitslehre*, Fichte will resolve the problem of the irrational gap by proposing what we will call the "singularity thesis." In the *Bildlehre*, he will provide a theory of subjective experience in accord with what was established in the singularity thesis; moreover, it will be seamlessly integrated into what was established in the first part, such that the articulation of the Absolute at the center of the singularity thesis finds its full articulation only when the theory of appearances has been presented.

The *Wahrheitslehre:* Gap and Projection

The first part, the *Wahrheitslehre* or Theory of Truth, can be construed as an attempt at resolving the problem of the irrational gap through refining the transcendental method inherited from Kant. Fichte's quest for the integration of individual consciousness into a whole will take the form of a genetic deduction, tracing experience back to its foundations. The decisive move made here will be to posit a genetic deduction of experience that can in no way be derived from its conditions. The non-genetic, claims Fichte, can itself be genetically deduced *qua* non-genetic, a move that reveals the illusory nature of the gap. The theory of truth, then, establishes that "all Being is a self-enclosed singularity of immediately living being that can never get outside of itself."[2] In other words, when thinking being (what is), it is illegitimate to make an appeal to some third thing: appearances and their conditions constitute a homogeneity, a relational whole outside of which nothing *is*. I will be referring to this outcome as the *singularity thesis*. Its goal, then, is to think the Absolute and consciousness together, from within.

But what does Fichte mean by the terms "Absolute" and "consciousness"? In alternately naming the Absolute "Truth," he makes its meaning clear: it is what provides for the logical space in which a true judgment can be made, the overarching space of conditions in which experience occurs. Appearances appear *within* the Absolute as fish swim in water, or light provides for vision: it is the ineffable principle of intelligibility that allows for things to "make sense," this latter commonplace expression being nothing more than the admission *that* appearances do indeed appear. These appearances, moreover, do not refer to this or that object in the world. The *Wissenschaftslehre* is not a knowing of particulars, but a knowing of knowing, a manner of orienting oneself in thinking. The "appearances" we mean here are therefore the simple fact that different objects can and do appear in consciousness. In this way, the Absolute is not a set of particular conditions that procure an object, still less a table of categories for cognizing this or that object.

The central claim that grounds the singularity thesis is that Truth is One, and, to speak metaphorically, there is nothing outside the whole:[3] what appears, appears "in" the Absolute. Yet, whenever consciousness tries to grasp the condition of all-appearing that is the Absolute, it paradoxically moves further away from it. To determine an object, Fichte reasons, is to posit its truth outside of it, rendering the object "dead," disconnected from the context that provides for its Truth, and therefore "ungenetic."[4] Conditions, then, are the ever-disappearing goal beyond the horizon of appearances: the more one tries to traverse the space of conditions, the more it seems to expand.

Fichte seeks to rethink this paradox transcendentally, recasting it as a gap between consciousness and *Evidenz*.[5] While the former refers to the positing of an object's truth outside of it by means of operating a judgment about it, the latter describes the immediate "thereness" of what exists. The objects of knowledge present themselves to us with immediate certainty, and even if all the possible intellectual extrapolations of any given object of knowledge remain obscure, the object stands before us as something substantive. The *Wisseschaftslehrer* or initiate into Fichte's method can say, in examining it, "It is absolutely thus, I cannot conceive it differently."[6] *Evidenz* is therefore compelling, a witness to knowing that demands belief, and must be taken seriously.[7] In its utterly compelling immediate certainty, *Evidenz*—the starting point in Fichte's transcendental system—is identical to the end-point, the Absolute that provides for the broad unity of all experience. Both are expressions of the *thatness* of experience. The insight (*einsicht*) into this identity will constitute the unfolding of Fichte's system, the discursive construction that allows for one to intellectually differentiate between *Evidenz* as engrossing fact and *Evidenz* as ground for appearances. To return to the spatial metaphor of conditions as an untraversable horizon for experiences, Fichte's solution is to claim that one need not traverse it—one always already has and need only become aware of this. Hence the first step in articulating a singularity thesis is attention to *Evidenz*, a sort of contemplative act that first lets one recognize that discursive knowledge does not belong to Truth as One: it is opposed to the compellingness with which we are initially confronted. From *Evidenz* as fundamental experience, therefore, reflection leads us to a gap between it and the Truth of that experience as conscious product.

The fundamental expression of this gap is found in a diagram to which Fichte will return repeatedly:

$$A$$

$$x \ y \ z \bullet B-T^8$$

"A" stands for the Absolute but is in actuality an empty placeholder. The Absolute, after all, is life, and to conceptualize it is to separate it from its content. Key to understanding this is the equivalency between *Evidenz* and Absolute: if the Absolute is ineffable and is only known as pure *Thatness*—that Truth *is*—it presents itself according to two valences: ground and immediacy. Transcendentally speaking, if one begins with the immediately compelling nature of *Evidenz*, "A" is therefore a construction of consciousness, an empty space posited with the intent of bidding the Absolute to appear.[9] Insofar as it is a conceptual placeholder for the Absolute, "A" therefore represents Kant's thing in itself,[10] and Spinoza's substance.[11]

The long dashes stand for the transition points or breaks from the Absolute placeholder into particularity. While there are indeed two levels of particularization of Being, reading left-to-right in terms of logical precedence, these two breaks occur simultaneously and so are actually only one: in reality, then, there is only one dash and one point. The first separation into *Being* and *Thought* is the immediate requirement for judgments to come about: cognition is ultimately the separation of an object's existence from my perception of it. Yet if B-T is what provides for the subjective cognition of the many, it is not this downward movement that interests Fichte most: more importantly, they are the two elements of cognition whose foundation is an Absolute in which knowing and known are not conceived of separately. They are, then, the *a priori* and *a posteriori* of Kant's transcendental philosophy, the two kinds of mental expression whose root "A" is posited as being outside experience. Insofar as B-T can also be conceived as "thought" and "extension" such that they do not modify A, they also correspond to Spinoza's attributes.[12] The further, more determinate separation "x, y, z" describe the types of experience that play out in cognition, that is, A as mediated by B-T. Fichte describes these three types of experience as the sensible (or mutable), the intelligible (or immutable), and their unity.[13] These three types are inspired by Kant's three critiques but also refer to Spinoza's modes. Taken as a whole, B-T and x, y, z represent the world of discursive experience.

Crucial is the point (•) that separates the ineffable Absolute's placeholder "A" from the discursive world where one finds the products of consciousness. There is, as stated earlier, a necessary gap between these two. Yet the point does not represent the gap. The gap, rather, appears on its own whenever consciousness attempts to cognize the Absolute—that is, when one attempts to read the diagram from right to left. This is because cognition's modus operandi is judgment, and judgment separates rather than unifies. Instead, the point is a standpoint, a construction meant to provide a vantage point into the paradoxical nature of cognizing the Absolute. Its construction affirms the *thatness* of experience, or the bivalent nature of *Evidenz*, hovering between the discursive and the ineffable, "A" and the twofold break into experience. The point is a suspension that allows for a closer look at *Evidenz*, a look at appearance by means of separating oneself from what appears. Hence, "A" is considered to be an empty *thatness* lurking behind (or better still, within) experience, something that is evident but not itself conceptually accessible. Its role as ground of experience cannot be known until something actually appears. Switching metaphors, Fichte alternately describes this as light: light *enlightens* (*erleuchtet*) or creates a field of vision and cannot be observed as if it were an object. Something evident is something that is brought to light. Thereafter, the meta-philosophical exercise that is *Wissenschaftslehre* involves situating ourselves in the point. As such, it is the entryway into the system. "The science of knowing stands in the point,"[14] Fichte writes. The art of inhabiting the point consists in postponing the compelling nature of the appearance of particulars (their "coming to light"), while at the same time acknowledging *that* experience happens—hence a genetic rereading of Kant's injunction that we never leave experience. One situates oneself here by presupposing the *that* of an appearing, or the foundational character of "A,"[15] and then reconstructing the realm of experience within the point. The idea behind this move is that one cannot objectify the conditions of experience because one is always already *in* experience. Kant's error was to treat experience as if it were outside of and subsequent to the knowing subject—the very definition of *ungenetic*. In this sense, the singularity thesis of which we have been speaking is actually a logical consequence of genesis, the term Fichte himself preferred.

To make this presupposition (and subsequent reconstruction) requires *attention*. Of course, given Fichte's transcendental epistemology, knowledge itself is already a construction, and not one that can be willfully taken apart. The exercise here consists in the realization *that* knowing is a construction, a realization that allows for a reconstruction that can then be examined *as if* from without. If one can just hold fast to this *as if*, the rest of the process that is *Wissenschaftslehre* will necessarily ensue:

> As far as concerns the first item, the knack for grasping these lectures is the knack of full, complete attention [*das Talent der ganzen vollen Aufmerksamkeit*].... *Full, complete attention*, I have said, which throws itself into the present object with all its spiritual power, puts itself there and is completely absorbed in it, so that no other thought or fancy can occur.... [First] we are required to construct a specific concept internally. This is not difficult: anyone just paying attention to the description can do it [*Jeder, der nur auf die Beschreibung Acht hat, kann es*]; and we construct it in front of him. Next, hold together what has been constructed; and then, without any assistance from us, an insight will spring up by itself, like a lightning flash. The slowness or speed of one's mind has nothing more to do in this final event, because the mind in general has no role in it. For *we* do not create the truth, and things would be badly arranged if we had to do so; rather, truth creates itself by its own power.[16]

Paying attention, or thinking energetically (*energetisch*), as Fichte will often repeat, will allow one to place oneself in this *as if*, and come to "the insight into being," which is precisely the knowledge that "truth creates itself by its own power," and that we are already within this creative act, able to see it only through the contingent presupposing that is *Wissenschaftslehre*. Attention, then, is an active way of being passive and will later constitute the core of Fichte's phenomenology or theory of images. It fundamentally means that when one is conscious of something in particular, one is also aware of being conscious of anything at all. Said otherwise, thinking about something in particular and being conscious *that* one is thinking at all are inseparable.

Brought to its logical end, the insight into the *thatness* of the Absolute will lead to the conclusion that any gap between the Absolute-Truth and appearances (or, as just mentioned, between thinking and being-conscious-of-thinking) is illusory. This will come about through realizing that while consciousness cannot be escaped, it doesn't offer a speculative foundation for investigating the Absolute, since it sees it as an external, heterogeneous object rather than a horizon for true-appearing: "Although *factically* we could never negate consciousness, we will not really believe it when judging truth."[17] The fact that consciousness produces exactly the opposite of what it intends to when thinking the Absolute creates an "irrational gap" between appearances and their conditions. Seen from below, the gap is irrational, hiatus that cannot be bridged by thought, since the Absolute remains ineffable. But as we shall eventually see, from above—that is, the Absolute's standpoint (if one can speak of such perspective), there is no gap at all. Navigating this gap will require the sort of presuppositional thinking that attention exemplifies.

Understanding presuppositional thinking requires delving into the nature of subjective acts of knowing. Lurking behind any such act are two valences of subjectivity, one belonging to conditions of possibility and the other to determinate existence. Both valences are present in Kant's famous affirmation about knowing: "The *I think* must able to accompany all of my representations."[18] Here, what ought to be a unified subject is separated by two seemingly distinct expressions of subjectivity: first, an *I* expressed in the imperative and distanced from any concrete content; second, *my representations*, a determinacy that would seemingly be legitimized by the mere possibility of belonging to a concrete *I*. The former expresses subjectivity *tout court*, providing a space in which objects can present themselves (i.e., the subjective conditions of knowing), while the latter describes a more determinate subject, linked to some kind of content. These two affirmations are meant to coexist in a singular definition of transcendental philosophy that posits their necessary relationship to one another: the potential intelligibility of subjective appearances on the one hand, and their appearing *for me* on the other. Put simply, transcendental philosophy implies that appearance and intelligibility mutually condition each other. It is in this space of mutual conditioning that objects appear. But the reciprocity of appearance and intelligibly does not offer an account of the origins of objects, merely the conditions that make them possible. There is no accounting for the fact of their appearance as such.

Consciousness, however, wants precisely such an account, and seeks it in something external to itself and its object, a third thing to which it has no access. Ultimately, the object is an appearing whose origins are unknown, a thing "thrown" into consciousness seemingly out of nowhere.[19] In Fichte's terms, the object lacks genesis; it is in need of a conceptual link with the Absolute that prevents the disjunction between that object and its ground. This disjunction is nowhere more apparent than in Kant's philosophy and would seem to be constitutive of the transcendental method itself: in Kantian terms, "noumenal affection" or a causal relationship between condition and appearance is not only wrong, but it is the wrong question altogether, misunderstanding what a possibility-condition is. That the transcendental subject elaborates the objects in consciousness out of something given from nowhere means that it must project (*projiciert*) its object; it cannot account for the intelligible grounds that make objects possible, nor how those grounds somehow rendered objects of experience intelligible for consciousness. Objects are thus "projected through an absolute gap."[20] Objective knowledge means giving up on a genetic deduction of the object, since by definition it is non-genetic appearing. It comes through a gap from Truth (Being) to experience, described as "absolute" because the immediacy of its presence trumps its non-genetic source: from consciousness's point of view, what is *evident* should not appear, but it does.

If Truth or "the One" is life, something absolutely dynamic, with nothing existing outside of itself, then the object is that which is purely external, frozen into an image, and therefore "dead." The very act of thought *qua* consciousness involves projecting originary truth through an irrational gap and into "a place of death":

> This discontinuous projection is evidently the same one that we have previously called, and presently call, the form of outer

existence. . . . For what this means, as a projection, concerning which no further account can be given and which thus is discontinuous, is the same as what we called "death at the root" [*den Tod in der Wurzel*]. The gap, the rupture of intellectual activity in it, is just death's lair [*das Lager des Todes*]. Now we should not admit the validity of this projection, or form of outer existence, although we can never free ourselves from it factically; and we should know that it means nothing; we should know, wherever it arises, that it is indeed only the result and effect of mere consciousness (ignoring that this consciousness remains hidden in its roots) and therefore not let ourselves be led astray by it.[21]

Fichte's imagery here is at once ingenious and forceful: an object might be factical and hence undeniably "there," but its "thereness" is conditioned by its projection through a space of death, after which it becomes an inorganic, external product of consciousness. To explore this act of projection is to return the object to this place of transformation, the storehouse (*das Lager*) in which the inconceivable transition occurred. It is here that one finds the invisible root (*Wurzel*) of objective knowledge. The combined language of *Wurzel* and *Lager* evoke that of a *Höhle* or cave, a *Tierlager*, the place hidden in the ground where a wild beast comes and goes, dragging its prey and leaving behind the remains. Here, the point (•) takes on the valence of a place of death, an empty repository into which the constructs of consciousness are projected. The totality of reason's products—including the placeholder "A"—are in this way shown to be a mere precipitate, a *Todter Absatz*[22] or residual by-product. The language here is that of alchemy, the German *Absatz* translating the *caput mortuum* or neutralized remainder or precipitate of an alchemical experiment. If Truth is a self-contained whole, the objects of experience are mere leftovers.

The exploration of this place of death is a kind of alchemy of attention. The point (•) is the *Lager des Todes*, and in it, experience will be reconstructed. That the reconstruction follows the same pattern as construction leads to the insight that conceptual reflection itself cannot have an external foundation. *We* (the plural is used to denote the multiplicity of the factical) can reconstruct the formula above within the point *because* Being has initially constructed itself. The solitary "I" that is counterpart to our "we" is life, the Absolute. The non-genetic act of knowing objects is itself genetic precisely as a non-genetic act. This is the insight already mentioned above: the irrational gap only exists if one considers consciousness to be a closed totality that seeks its ground outside of itself. In the end, to realize that one is always already in experience is to acknowledge that, insofar as consciousness is concerned, the part and the whole are co-original: there is no experience without Truth, a "One," a field of intelligibility; on the other hand, the existence of this Truth likewise requires that something appears in it. The transcendental method gives no ontological precedence to subjectivity. Rather, a truly genetic transcendental exploration carves out a space for the subjective within the logical realm of Truth, the Absolute.

Objects, then, are really "empty repetitions" of the One, concretions that try to capture the ever-moving whole that is life, and which precedes reflection. For its part, consciousness is a "doubling,"[23] an image-of-an-image, nonrepresentational seeing of seeing. In Fichte's language, to exist is to be part of an in-, for-, and through-itself:

> Being is entirely of itself, in itself, and through itself; this self is not to be taken as an antithesis, but grasped with the requisite abstraction purely inwardly, as it very well can be grasped, and as I for example am most fervently conscious of grasping it. Therefore, to express ourselves scholastically, it has been constructed as a being in pure act [esse in mero actu], so that both being and living, and living and being completely interpenetrate, dissolve into one another, and are the same, and this self-same inwardness is the one completely unified being.[24]

At work here is not a refusal of particularity but of exteriority: in 1804, the *Wissenschaftslehre* is totally immanent, such that even traditional expressions of transcendence are integrated into seeing-of-seeing and imaging-of-imaging. Establishing immanence completes the argument grounding the Singularity thesis: the Absolute is a self-enclosed homogeneity, and objects are its precipitates or that which is genetically derived from the whole as non-genetic.

But the role of the subject here remains obscure. Until a space has been properly given to subjective experience within the whole that is the Absolute, Fichte will have got little further than Spinoza.[25] While one could identify a number of common structural points between Fichte and Spinoza's philosophy, the latter's worldview lacks a subjective dimension—it simply can't be inhabited. Fichte's system, on the other hand, is transcendental and must provide for subjective knowing. The solution to this comes in the second section, where Fichte provides a phenomenology of the (transcendental) subject who lives in the world described above. Moreover, he must do so without contravening the singularity thesis, lest the problem of the irrational gap return. These strictures will be navigated largely by means of attention; the subject's role in the whole will be to provide depth and not expansion—in other words, to show that the Absolute is *life*, something meaningful for those who experience it and belong to it.

The *Bildlehre*: Fichte's Transcendental Phenomenology

The first part of the *Wissenschaftslehre*, the theory of truth, established Fichte's singularity thesis, or the unity of experience via the interpenetration of appearances and conditions. Writes Fichte at the beginning of this second section, "Being is entirely a self-enclosed singularity {*Singulum*} of immediately living being that can never get outside itself."[26] Once this was established, an insight into the role of consciousness arose: in constituting objects, it removes us from the Absolute and consequently disconnects itself from its own origins. Its effect is "the absolute projection of an object whose origin is inexplicable, so that between the projective act and projected object everything is dark and bare."[27] This space between projective act and projective object is the *Lager des Todes*, the place of death in which we have tried to situate ourselves. This was done by a sort of meta-reflection on the nature on the inevitable gap between the Absolute and Consciousness, referred to by Fichte as the exercise of standing in the point. It is precisely a meta-standpoint, since the point is nothing at all; rather, it is a sort of schematism that allows one to focus on the *thatness* of experience and integrate consciousness into the whole. From this vantage point, it was determined that appearances are the opaque external layer of the Absolute, the visible outer shell of Truth. The next step in the argument consists in accounting for the Absolute as being the very principle of their appearing.

At the outset, it is clear that one cannot provide an account of the origins of consciousness discursively from within consciousness itself. The only viable means will be to offer an indirect proof, much in the spirit of the meta-standpoint (•) that provided for the insight into the singularity thesis. Bracketing what consciousness produces and shifting focus toward the very fact that consciousness occurs at all will therefore be the next step in Fichte's argument. In other words, if the objects of consciousness are compelling, or *evident*, this second half of the *1804 Wissenschaftslehre* will now have to bracket out the objects to focus on the compelling nature of the witness they provide. This focus on the evident nature of *Evidenz* (here, a deliberately tautological expression meant to pry apart the two valences of the word) will itself be a deduction of the condition of the possibility of singularity, a transcendental argument meant to show that the compellingness of experiences really belongs to the immediacy of the One Absolute. Because there is nothing "outside" the Absolute, this argument is secured by a meta-claim about *Evidenz*. The goal here is to move from an external mechanism, a mere conceptual singularity in which appearances presuppose an encounter in their very appearing, to a living Absolute in which a subject can feel at home, and whose participation in dynamic life qualitatively adds something to its self-constitution.

Fichte will arrive at this point through a closer analysis of the relationship between *Evidenz* and the Absolute. How, in other words, does one move from experience (*Evidenz* as compelling presence) to the Absolute as ground of experience, all the while affirming that there is nothing outside the Absolute? The task at hand therefore encompasses a threefold movement: (1) accepting the immediate credibility (or put speculatively: positing) of sense experience; (2) finding the conditions of the possibility for these experiences, or asking why they were found to be compelling in the first place; and (3) reflectively returning to experience, carrying with one the theoretical grounds found in the second step, but without losing any of the immediacy of experience. This, Fichte claims, is the very structure of a transcendental argument. Crucial is the third move, the return to experience after the examination of its conditions. It is here that all those who came before—Kant in particular—had failed, and where (or so Fichte claims) he will succeed.

This amendment and reparation of Kant is fundamentally an investigation into the two *I*'s found in Kant's *Ich denke*, the difference between the *Ich* of conditions and the "mine" of determinate existence. The Kantian claim is ultimately that whenever experience occurs in the subjective space of the *Ich*, a knowing subject manifests itself. The first two steps of Kant's argument (first, experience, and second, its conditions) would seem, on Fichte's terms, valid, but the third is problematic. While it does not add any new content, instead making a claim about the relations of step one and step two ("I am the subject that is the doing the thinking"), it does not secure a smooth transition back to immediate experience. Things are incognizable,[28] and we only have access to appearances. In the return movement, the credibility of experience is secured by a thing-in-itself. Yet the relationship between objects and this thing-in-itself remains obscure.[29] While it seems necessary for consciousness to carry out operations of objective knowledge, it cannot bridge the gap between lived experience and conceptual reflection.

Fichte's own account of the incompleteness of Kant's transcendental argument takes place at the beginning of the 1804 text, as a propaedeutic to his own transcendentalism. There, the problem is framed in terms of genesis: the sensible world "x" and the intelligible "z" have a shared "undiscoverable root."[30] Kant posits an external third thing as ground of both, a "*third* absolute, separate from the other two and self-sufficient, despite the fact that it is supposed to be the connection of both other terms."[31] Here, because experience is accounted for after the fact, the common ground is hypostatized. In terms of the three-step transcendental formula, Kant moves not from objects to their (intelligible) conditions and back to the objects but rather continues on to a third thing, a super-subjective presence, the thing-in-itself. For Fichte, a genetic argument is always a transcendental argument, and the necessary operation here is a tracing-back (*zurückführung*) rather than an infinite regress of objects. The singularity thesis, then, implying as it does that there is nothing outside of the Absolute, provides the impetus for the clarification of the transcendental method: in integrating experience into the Absolute, Fichte cannot make any appeals to some external third thing because the system does not provide for externality.[32]

Hence, if the theory of Truth followed a sort of *via negativa* whereby the products of everyday experience (including their subjective ground, consciousness) were negated in order to see that the gap separating them from Truth was in fact illusory, the corresponding movement now must be made; factical objects now have to be retrieved, but with the difference that we now know that they are indeed *factical* and that they need no external ground to justify their existence as such. What the presuppositional mode of thought, called *attention*, was able to bracket must now be retrieved, albeit without leaving this carefully cultivated state of attention. As Fichte repeatedly says, "Therefore, we let it all go as just a means of ascent, until it shows up again on our descent."[33]

Here, the language of descent is misleading. The path that the *Wissenschaftslehre* traces is not one that moves "upward" to an external absolute and then back down to the world of appearances. Fichte's own term for the "descent" is *absteigen*, its "ascending" counterpart being *aufsteigen*.[34] *Absteigen* is not meant to signify descent in a metaphysical sense but rather the point at which one stops off from a journey.[35] The word means, foremost, the interruption of movement. As such, its correlate is projection (*projiciert*), life itself or the Truth that is One, is described as a constant movement, a light that cannot be captured. The images that constitute factical existence are, by contrast, reified products of consciousness. The objects of experience are precisely where *Light* alights, the opaque surface that interrupts its trajectory. This space of alighting, the place where objects are projected, is of course the point (•) as *Lager des Todes*, empty but for having had the factical objects of consciousness projected into it. Practically speaking, it is purely through being attentive to the already present *Evidenz* of Being, its self-manifestation, that a genetic connection to the phenomenal becomes possible.

Here, attention once again becomes critical. As presuppositional thinking, it allows for a kind of imaginative self-insertion into this process, precisely in acknowledging that the point-of-view at which the *Wissenschaftslehrer* stands is not that of external, linear construction but part of what has already been constructed; not as the *I* of Kantian Critique, but rather as *We,* the empty repetition of a singular principle.[36] The *We*'s emptiness is precisely what gives existential traction to the *Lager* as place of a-lighting: "If this *We* . . . were to be deduced, it would be *in consciousness* that it could well remain."[37]

The shared emptiness of the *We* and the *Lager* is the grounding principle of phenomenal appearance. Hence both the appearing of the object in consciousness and the reflective act by which it appears have the same ground, a negative one. If we seek a ground, it could only be a non-principle, a negative ground wherein either side points to its other, and in their mutual outward orientation, to their unity. The search for a principle that explains either, then, points us back to the "act of being" that we have called life—the move from the conceptual to the Truth is spontaneous, non-genetic, and hence "comes out of nowhere"—and life can only manifest itself through the mutual conditioning of the *We* and the point. This interdependence of two "empty" things is a principled lack of principle, an ungrounded ground.[38]

This interdependence is the *Soll*, or to use Walter Wright's term, "imperative conditionality."[39] The *Soll*'s basic claim is that when a contingent fact is posited, certain necessary relations will ensue: "If [*Soll*] the absolute insight is to arise, that, etc., then such an ideal self-construction must be posited entirely factically. The explanation through immediate insight is conditioned by the absolutely factical presupposition of what is to be explained."[40] Whatever appears in consciousness must appear according to conditions. *That* something appears at all is therefore proof that its conditions are present. Yet if we are to take the singularity thesis seriously, it would seem that the Absolute is all that there is, and appearances are appearances of the Absolute. This Absolute, then, is the condition of the possibility of its own appearing. It is in this way that the Absolute's conditions and its appearing mutually inform each other: consciousness presumes *that* the absolute appears (it "projects") and then conducts an inquiry into the mutual conditioning of these two factors. That one *must* project in order to arrive at objective knowledge establishes the spontaneity of the act of knowing. Projecting is categorically necessary, even if it fundamentally separates us from Truth. This connection of the two is attention's work: it posits projection as necessary, and as *our* necessary act. Because neither has content, they yield to each other, and establish mutual interdependence.

In this way, the *Soll* contains the entirety of Fichte's transcendental theory of appearing *in nuce*. It is most clearly described according to a fivefold process:[41]

1. The first step is to establish the identity between the two valences of *Evidenz*. Before experience is reflected upon, it is immediately and compellingly present, an ineffable whole. The same can be said about the totality of intelligibility. I must therefore acknowledge *that* the world is intelligible to me and that the immediacy of what I understand in the world bears witness to this intelligibility. Here, the starting point and the end goal of the *Wissenschaftslehre* are identical, fused together in the fact *that* something is there.

2. The second step marks the introduction of consciousness's work of formal analysis of experience. Given that judgment separates, the content of consciousness can no longer be directly linked to its grounds; the *thatness* that unified *Evidenz* has been lost. This separation, which consciousness cannot cognize, is the gap, or *hiatus irrationalis*. It is attention that allows one to notice this gap. Paying attention to this separation then allows one to construct the point (•), the place from which the *Wissenschaftslehrer* can attentively observe the relationship between in-itself ("A") and for-consciousness (B-T; x, y, z).

3. The third step is the reconstruction of both experience (B-T; x, y, z) and the cognized placeholder "A" within the point. Now, one realizes that objects are not only ungenetic, but they

are *necessarily* ungenetic. As Fichte says, this is a "principled absence of principle."[42]

4. The fourth step consists in the realization that nothing is left outside of the point. All that remains, then, is projection itself, the act of projecting the cognizable into the artificially constructed point and holding it together by means of attention.

5. The fifth step is the reversibility of what was found to be on either side of the gap. That is, the mutual conditionality of both understanding and experience, of both valences of *Evidenz*, is grasped. Seen from experience, the gap is inevitable, and is the motivating factor in the act of projection. But seen from above, from the point of view of the Absolute (or of "thatness") there is no gap at all. It is an illusion produced by consciousness. Consciousness is here able to conceive of this reversibility by integrating itself into the system. Through attention, consciousness is able to deploy the whole process within the point. This is nothing more than attention to *thatness*, to a deliberated expansion and exploration of the *as if* that attention produced. In other words, attention to the unfolding of the *Soll* is itself an integral part of the *Soll*'s very unfolding.

In the end, attention freely posits the fivefold movement that is the *Soll* as a hypothesis. The hypothesis consists in the reconstructing of experience. The necessary relations of mutual conditioning that ensue from the assumed *thatness* of experience then function as a retroactive proof of what was initially posited. Fichte expresses this elegantly when he writes that "we are what we say, and we say what we are."[43] One could even go so far as to say that *attention*, the exploration of the *as if*, is itself the most important step of the argument, even if it is a meta-argumentative step, adding no new content or constructs. Through the *as if* of attention, the subject freely posits itself as part of the system, not as a mere object or Spinozist mode but as a free subject able to posit contingent facts. Attention ultimately shows that experience is not something external, but something integrated into the Absolute itself as the Absolute's self-appearing. The free subject is not a cog in a totalizing mechanism, but someone who is alive and at home in the Whole that is *life*.[44]

A properly transcendental argument cannot simply move from cause to *ex post facto* effects; to avoid this Kantian problem, Fichte accounts for his system genetically, from within, by means of the constructive powers of free subjective attention. The three steps of the transcendental argument that constitutes Fichte's phenomenology via the *Soll* could therefore be summarized as follows:

1. Experience is immediately compelling. But why is the testimony of states of affairs in the world that it provides found to be compelling in the first place?

2. Answering this question leads to searching for the conditions of the possibility of experience. The answer that this investigation yields is that the immediacy of experience is one with the ineffable totality of its grounds: *Evidenz* is both compelling immediacy in experience and a grounding *Singulum* that provides for the truth of what is.

3. The third step provides no new content but constitutes an indirect proof of numbers 1 and 2: when a contingent fact has been posited, necessary internal relations ensue—conditions provide for intelligibility, and intelligibility, for conditions. The Absolute is itself the condition of the possibility of its own appearing.

Conclusion: From Gap to Standpoint

The final steps of Fichte's transcendental argument seem far away from our initial problem—that of an irrational gap between an Absolute as condition of appearances and those appearances themselves—moving into a phenomenological discussion of what it means to feel at home. Yet both questions belong to the broad transcendental argument that Fichte is making, one that tries to redeem lived subjectivity as an integral part of the fabric of reality. Taken in its entirety, Fichte's argument is meant to address a fundamental problem as old as epistemology itself: the intractability of experience. Whenever a particular experience steps into the foreground *as mine*, the very things that make it intelligible to me disappear. It is precisely this paradox that the *hiatus irrationalis* seeks to capture, focusing on the logical space between foreground and background. In articulating the problem thus, Fichte shifts the focus that its classical iteration gave it, that of Kantian intuition, which foists the problematic nature of its claims onto a thing-in-itself, ignoring the question of intractability. By moving from a singularity thesis to a phenomenology of life, Fichte shows not only that the gap between the Absolute and Experience is illusory but that intuition's very modus operandi is what generates this illusion. One overcomes this not by renouncing the work of consciousness but rather by bracketing its content to contemplate *that* it happens at all. Contemplation cannot replace the basic functionalities of consciousness, but it can provide it with self-understanding. And the form of contemplation that Fichte proposes, attention, is ultimately a passive act expressed in the active mood, a way being attentive to what already is that grounds one's own participation in that state of affairs. Its real achievement lies in cultivating the realization that one is engrossed in one's own mode of existence, a change in attitude that makes a constitutive difference. For Fichte, this piety of attention is precisely what transforms mere existence into something more—life.

Notes

1. Fichte writes: "So then, on a particular occasion I divided the science of knowing into two main parts; one, that it is a doctrine of reason and truth, and second, that it is a doctrine of appearance and illusion, but one that is indeed true and is grounded in truth." (1804^2, 115; *GA*, II/8, 229).

2. 1804^2, 121; *GA*, II/8, 243.

3. Using spatial constructions to define the unity of appearance and condition is perilous. Since Fichte intends his philosophy to be a transcendental one, describing conditions as merely the sum of appearances would be to reify and quantify both. At best, one could say that the singularity thesis will establish a whole with fluid borders. Much better is Fichte's own light metaphor, which will be made explicit later.

4. The "concept of being" *qua* concept is "dead in itself," 1804^2, 54; *GA*, II/8, 83.

5. Walter Wright translates it as "manifestness." While his definition, "the clarity of an immediate mental grasp, certain of its contents," is correct, "manifestness" is a gloss: what is immediately *evident* is not the same as what is manifest, which implies a sort of revelatory unveiling. Here, I will retain the German to highlight its status as a technical term.

6. 1804^2, 35; *GA*, II/8, 39.

7. Here, Fichte continues the protracted legal metaphor inherited from Kant. A *Deduktion* refers to contingent arguments for property claims. *Compelling evidence*

works in a similar way: witness is provided, and at the same time, arguments are made that concur with the witness.

8. The diagram is first introduced on 1804^2, 30; *GA*, II/8, 25, and is expressed in various forms throughout the lectures. The two manuscripts available to us, *SW* and *Copia*, reproduce them differently. My version is based on the one found at the beginning of 1804^2, 40; *GA*, II/8, 52–53.

9. Initially, writes Fichte, it would seem that consciousness's mere positing of A furnishes an absolute principle. But it is merely a working principle and must be recognized as such in order to function: "We only seem to have [posited an Absolute], but it is an empty seeming. We see merely *that* it is so, but we but we have no insight into what this qualitive oneness in fact is" (1804^2, 36; *GA*, II/8, 41; trans. modified).

10. Fichte writes: "All transcendental philosophy, such as Kant's (and in this respect the science of knowing is not yet different from his philosophy), posits the absolute neither in being nor in consciousness but in the union of both." 1804^2, 30; *GA*, II/8, 25.

11. Fichte writes: "[A] must actually be a *purely self-sustaining substance.*" 1804^2, 34; *GA*, II/8, 37. Also, "I claim that this much is evident from all philosophies prior to Kant, the absolute was located in being, that is, in the dead thing as thing." 1804^2, 25; *GA*, II/8, 11. The connection between Spinoza, death, and the Absolute is also inferentially present in remarks made about Jacobi in 1804^2, 138–40; *GA*, II/8, 283–87. Fichte's Singularity thesis could be seen as a transcendental revisiting of Spinozist ontology.

12. I follow George di Giovanni for the Spinoza connection in the diagram; for the role of absolute, modes, and attributes in Fichte, see George di Giovanni, "The Spinozism of Fichte's Transcendental Argument in the Lecture Notes of 1804," in *Fichte und seine Zeit*, eds. Matteo d'Alfonso, Carla De Pascale, Erich Fuchs, and Marco Ivaldo. *Fichte-Studien*, 44 (2016): 49–63. The Kant allusions are made quite explicitly and at some length by Fichte himself at 1804^2, 31–33; *GA*, II/8, 29–35.

13. "The way his decisive and only truly meaningful works, the three critiques, come before us, Kant has made three starts. In the *Critique of Pure Reason*, his absolute (x) is *sensible experience*. . . . In [the *Critique of Practical* Reason] the I comes to light as something in itself through the inherent categorical concept as it could not possibly do in the *Critique of Pure Reason*, which is solely based on, and drawn from, what is empirically; and thus we get the second absolute, a moral world = z. . . . And so the *Critique of Judgment* appears, and in its Introduction, the most important part of this very important book, we find the confession that the sensible and supersensible worlds must come together in a common but wholly unknown root, which would be the third absolute = y." 1804^2, 31–32; *GA*, II/8, 28–31.

14. 1804^2, 40; *GA*, II/8, 53.

15. Fichte writes: "Thus, the basic character of the ideal perspective is that it originates from the presupposition of a being which is only hypothetical and

therefore based wholly on itself; and it is very natural that it finds just this same being, which it presupposes as absolute, to be absolute again in its genetic deduction, since it certainly does not begin there in order to negate itself, but to produce itself genetically." 1804^2, 89; *GA*, II/8, 165. The presupposition and what it supposes will prove to be mutually conditioning through the *Soll* in the Ninth Lecture.

16. 1804^2, 47–48; *GA*, II/8, 67–68.
17. 1804^2, 110; *GA*, II, 217.
18. *AA*, 3, 108 (KrV B131).
19. "Or, la caractéristique *ontologique* de l'objet, c'est-à-dire de l'objet-*Projektum* est précisément d'être sans origine assignable, d'avoir, dans l'éloignement de la projection, effacé, pour ainsi dire, son propre trajet, bref, d'être proprement jeté à la face en venant de nulle part." Jean-Christophe Goddard, *Fichte (1801–1813): L'émancipation philosophique* (Paris: Presses Universitaires de France, 1993), 45. Goddard also proposes, following a suggestion made by Pierre François Moreau, that the object here is a not a *Gegenstand*, as traditional metaphysics might call it, but a *Gegenwurf*, something thrown into consciousness. Goddard, 44.
20. 1804^2, 111; *GA*, II/8, 219.
21. 1804^2, 111–12; *GA*, II/8, 221.
22. 1804^2, 43; *GA*, II/8, 59.
23. 1804^2, 117; *GA*, II/8, 235.
24. 1804^2, 116; *GA*, II/8, 229.
25. Cf. 1804^2, 68–69; *GA*, II/8, 112–16.
26. 1804^2, 121; *GA*, II/8, 243.
27. 1804^2, 119; *GA*, II/8, 237.
28. *AA*, 3, 56–57 (KrV A30/B45).
29. Cf. *AA*, 3, 50 (KrV A19/B34). Fichte previously addressed this problem of "noumenal affection" in the second introduction to the *Wissenschaftslehre*. *SW*, I, 488.
30. 1804^2, 36; *GA*, II/8, 41.
31. 1804^2, 32; *GA*, II/8, 31.
32. Martial Gueroult sees the passage from Truth to image (phenomena) as a kind of ontological argument, analogous to the passage from Essence to Existence in classical metaphysics. "Ainsi, nous sommes *ipso facto* Raison pure, et la Lumière a un concept originaire de son essence propre. Ce concept se confirme par le fait de son accomplissement immédiat dans la *Visiblité*." Gueroult, II, 124, cf. Twentieth Lecture. Descartes's ontological argument is indeed a transcendental argument, but even more explicity than Kant, moves from conditions to a super-subject, God. In this sense, Gueroult's Fichte fails to accomplish the task set before him: the passage back to experience remains incomplete.
33. 1804^2,156; *GA*, II/8, 320. See also, 1804^2, 61; *GA*, II/8, 98; 1804^2, 100; *GA*, II/8, 189; 1804^2, 141, 142; *GA*, II/8, 289, 291; 1804^2, 147, 150; *GA*, II/8, 300, 307.

34. Hence the above is "wir lassen es daher, als bloßes Mittel des Heraufsteigens fallen, bis es im Herabsteigen sich wieder findet." *GA*, II/8, 320.

35. *Absteigen* can signify both "coming down" or "getting off," as in dismounting a horse or getting off a train. More pointedly, one "puts down" (*Absteigen*) from a long journey the same way that, in English, one is "put up" in a hotel.

36. Fichte writes: "[If] being cannot ever get outside of itself and nothing can be apart from it, then it must be being itself which thus constructs itself, to the extent that this construction is to occur. Or, as is completely synonymous: We certainly are the agents who carry out this construction." 1804^2, 122; *GA*, II/8, 245.

37. 1804^2, 123; *GA*, II/8, 249.

38. Fichte writes: "Being's ideal self-construction is projected through an absolute gap, and is thereby made into an absolutely factical and external existence. Now this existence, as absolute existence, can have no higher principle at all in the sphere of existence, and in this sense is precisely lacking a principle. Its 'principle' in this unprincipledness is just the projection itself." 1804^2, 124; *GA*, II/8, 251.

39. Cf. Translator's note to the Twenty-Sixth Lecture, 1804^2, 224.

40. 1804^2, 125; *GA*, II/8, 250.

41. It is, then, the expression of what Fichte calls "quintuplicity" (*Fünffachkeit*), cf. 1804^2, 45–46; *GA*, II/8, 65; 1804^2, 200; *GA*, II/8, 418. While Fichte never offers a concrete definition of the term, one can posit that it is linked to the elaboration of the *Soll* in the Seventeenth Lecture. Helpfully, Martial Gueroult describes it according to the following formula: [(a + b), (b + a)]. Gueroult, II, 120.

42. 1804^2, 124; *GA*, II/8, 251.

43. 1804^2, 168; *GA*, II/8, 348.

44. This is argued for at length in the Twenty-Seventh Lecture. Here, Fichte reminds his listeners that the Absolute an in-itself, and that if this can be grasped, it is because we must be ourselves within the absolute. Yet "we are not just the bare fact [that we can grasp the Absolute as internal to it] but instead we are simultaneously the insight that this fact is reason's pure original expression and life; that the fact is origin, and the origin, fact." 1804^2, 194; *GA*, II/8, 404. *That* we are consciousness means that we are the (genetic) product of the Absolute. This insight (or meta-insight, as it were, since it says nothing about consciousness per se) is itself the performance of *WL*, "reason's immediate expression and life." 1804^2,194; *GA*, II/8, 406. That consciousness can freely posit a contingent rational fact by reconstructing experience, which eventually proves its validity via the mutual interdependence of intelligibility and understanding (i.e., the *Soll*) is proof that freedom is an integral part of the self-constituting system: "In its existence, the insight appears to be possible only by means of freedom . . . reason shows itself as freely self-expressing." 1804^2,194; *GA*, II/8, 406. Reason appears as inwardly free.

Chapter 6

Nothing Remains

Notes on Fichte's "Irrational Gap" in the *1804 Wissenschaftslehre*

F. SCOTT SCRIBNER

In the *1804 Wissenschaftslehre,* Fichte's attempt to move from an ordinary consciousness to a recognition of transcendental consciousness as absolute necessarily encounters various structural illusions endemic to the finite mind. Bridging this difference between finite and infinite consciousness therefore requires a number of often illusory conceptual lynch pins named variously as disjunctions, projections, and gaps.

In the *1804 Wissenschaftslehre,* Fichte names the central illusion of finite consciousness the "irrational gap." And it operates with a nebulous centrality not unlike the Kantian thing-in-itself. Fichte will describe this "projection through an irrational gap [*proiectio per hiatum irrationale*]" as follows: "Between the projective act and the projective object everything is dark and bare."[1]

I take him to mean that modes of both idealist and realist epistemologies are inadequate given that both projective acts and projective objects, respectively, are partial truths. This *proiectum per hiatum* is an illusion constitutive of consciousness itself, much like the illusions that Kant himself outlined in *The Critique of Pure Reason.* It is a factical and unavoidable aspect of ordinary consciousness.[2] While one could try, intellectually, to destroy one element then another, the respective illusions of realism then idealism, it is a difficult, exhausting, and a not altogether fruitful path. Like a Zen master trying to clear consciousness, Fichte's recommendation is not to fight these illusions but simply to recognize them or what they are and, ultimately, to ignore them.[3]

Fichte is then left with the radical post-epistemological claim that, even at the highest levels, there is nothing outside of the illusory act of projection itself—and this itself, of course, is an illusion. He writes, "Therefore *nothing remains . . . except the principle of projection itself and this is an act.*"[4] The principle of projection, then, is the founding act, the fundamental principle—even if what this act posits is "something unprincipled."[5] In a play on the English translation *Tathandlung*, perhaps we might say that rather than a "fact-act," what Fichte is proposing is a "gap-act": a pure act, a pure projection arising out of the "irrational gap" in which, in effect, nothing remains.

My argument is as follows. I begin by outlining the manner in which Fichte's philosophy of genesis in the *1804 Wissenschaftslehre* is a continuation and expansion of his earlier account of the *Tathandlung*. In addition, this dynamic of producer and product, being and appearance, is, at core, a disjunction—a dynamic disjunction that seeks to move beyond the mere partial truths or illusions of idealism and realism, respectively. I argue, through a close textual reading of Fichte's account of the "irrational gap," that this central illusion for finite thinking threatens a kind of contagion to the central disjunctive motor of Fichte's entire philosophy of genesis. The unnamable anarchic absolute threatens even Fichte's architectonic of a transformed critical philosophy. He fortifies a bulwark against such threats primarily through the distinction between *legitimate* and so-called *illegitimate* disjunctions by naming the illegitimate one an "irrational gap." Nevertheless, I suggest that it is Fichte's own analysis of the irrational gap that threatens the undoing of his entire system in two main ways. First, I show that his attempt to contain the irrational gap's radical "absence of principle" by means of making even its very unprincipledness into a principle is a not altogether successful linguistic sleight of hand. And second, I show that Fichte's own critical dismissal of the irrational gap leads him initially to affirm the true absolute in-itself as a fundamental "remainder" or "supplement," which despite his immediate backtracking already suggests a kind of contagion of infinite supplementation and, in short, a dangerous point of undoing for the very distinction between legitimate and illegitimate disjunctions and consequently the system itself.

The *Tathandlung*

As is well known, Fichte developed his revolutionary account of the *Tathandlung* as a creative revision of Reinhold's notion of the *Tatsache*. Reinhold sought to articulate a systematic account of critical philosophy as a rigorous science, famously naming the reflective principle of consciousness as a fact of consciousness, a *Tatsache*. Inspired by Schulze's critique of Reinhold's *Tatsache* as an unconvincing and flawed first principle, Fichte sought a new foundation for critical philosophy. Fichte begins to articulate his account of the *Tathundlung* in his review of Schulze's *Aenesidemus*. Here he affirms Reinhold's account of a first principle of consciousness as a fact, a *Tatsache*, but significantly transforms it by highlighting it primarily as an activity, a fact-act or *Tathandlung*. This transformation of the Kantian-I that accompanies all representations, from a mere fact into an activity, or fact-act, highlights a positing in which being and activity arise simultaneously. Fichtean positing (*setzen*) then is not a creation ex nihilo but the activity of self-awareness or consciousness in which being co-emerges by means of activity. It is significant to recognize that knowing and doing, idealism and realism, the theoretical and the practical, all remain co-emergent and interdependent from the very start with the *Tathandlung* as first principle. The fact of our originating activity of self-conscious is more like a phenomenological dynamic process of founding and founded acts in which we engage in a continuous interpretation of ourselves and world in a codependent, emergent process.

It is little surprise, then, that such an emergent dynamic process, which lies at the heart of the project of *Wissenschaftslehre*, has on the one hand been resistant to conceptual determination (like an easy systematization of idealism or realism) and on the other hand is carried-over and recast by Fichte in the *1804 Wissenschaftslehre* as move away from a philosophy grounded in transcendental subjectivity. While Fichte marshals a wide range of concepts to account for this dynamic of constituted and constituting activity of the *Tathandlung*, this dynamic force named variously in the *1804 Wissenschaftslehre* from his notion of "Life" or his account of the formerly transcendental subject as a "through" (*das Durch*), I argue that his notion of the projective-gap stands both as his most elusive and most sustained articulation of what I argue is his revised account of the *Tathandlung*.

In the *1804 Wissenschaftslehre*, Fichte's broader account of philosophy itself as a philosophy of genesis continues the project of the *Tathandlung* and arises in part out of the dynamic difference or gap of producer and product, activity and appearance. Fichte states in the *1804 Wissenschaftslehre* that even in his "Review of *Anesidemus*" he offered "a maxim identical with the principle of absolute genesis."[6] For Fichte, the principle of disjunction is the principle of appearance.[7] Disjunction marks the fundamental gap between the unmanifest energy of genesis itself and its manifest appearance. Disjunction is the fundamental architecture of the *Wissenschaftslehre* and most two-worlds theory philosophy. Disjunction appears in his early Jena period accounts of the impasse between idealism and realism (dogmatism)—resolvable only by the choice of one's character—and here, in the *1804 Wissenschaftslehre*, in his exposition of the absolute and its appearance.

The *Yin* and *Yang* of Fichtean Disjunctions

The *1804 Wissenschaftslehre* offers a fascinating look into Fichte's initial attempt to preserve a Kantian-inspired vocabulary of rules, principles, and deductions in the face of a subject (the absolute) that absolutely resists, if not outright refuses, such conceptual distinctness. Fichte's innovative spirit leads him to rework some of his own earlier pioneering work on the concept of the self. And he recognizes that every system, every epistemology, every architectonic of knowing is structured with constitutive blind spots. From within the perspective of finite knowing, each view is riddled with illusions. Fichte exclaims with typical bombast: "In every case the rule is this: tell me exactly what you do not know and do not understand, and I will list with total precision all errors and illusions which you believe, and it will prove correct."[8] Every epistemological strategy is structured with illusions.

Such illusions are indeed endemic to both realism and idealism. Fichte thus encourages "that one not stubbornly hold onto the principle of idealism, the energy of reflection, but rather yield patiently to its opposite: The realistic perspective."[9] He explains, idealism and realism are not "artificial philosophical systems" but rather are "wholly natural disjunctions and partialities of common knowing."[10]

Moreover, Fichte recognizes that the disjunction of idealism and realism cannot be resolved head-on through the impasse of its opposition. But rather "we must fight against" each "on its own grounds" by means of its own "self-contradiction."[11] As Fichte explains: "Through this very contradiction . . . realism's empirical principle would become genetic, and in this genesis, perhaps it will become the principle of a higher realism and idealism united into one."[12] Here what was previously understood factically is now understood genetically. Each harbors within it the potential to become its opposite. And we must not forget that, at base, the original idea of the *Tathandlung* stands as a dynamic process that sets otherwise sedimented notions into dynamic co-emergent development. And so while Fichte can write, "Thus idealism, which posits an absolute intuition of life, is refuted at its root by a still deeper founding of realism," we must not forget that the inverse is also true.[13]

Fichte explicitly describes his method as "a descent into phenomenology": the demand for a kind *epoche* or suspension of the respective truth claims of both idealism and realism, made necessary by the illusory or limited claims of each respective outlook, thereby allows a free exploration of "this empty repetition and doubling."[14] Thus he will assert, "The higher maxim presented in this reasoning would be just this: to give no credence to the assertions of simple immediate consciousness, even if one cannot free oneself from them, but rather to abstract from them."[15]

Admittedly, Fichte seems to waffle between affirming idealism and fully embracing his own recognition of the mutual limitations of realism and idealism that would allow him to move beyond both. For instance, he writes: "Thus, our science . . . would at last become idealist while still pursuing some higher idealism that would seem to seek a third way beyond the realism/idealism.[16]

In the Eleventh Lecture, Fichte offers us a transcendental account of the manifestation of the absolute by means of two central terms: life and the through (*das Durch*). The notion of life stands as a non-manifest, indeterminable potential energy, while the through appears as a prism or image-screen through which life is to be made manifest. The problem with this or any interpretation, however, is legion. First, all such terminology is not merely codependent (like the producer/product of the *Tathandlung*) but is self-acknowledged by Fichte as self-consciously tentative, inadequate, and self-effacing.[17] As Fichte notes at one point of conclusion, "Everything has dissolved into one = 0."[18] A second complexity is Fichte's methodological predilection to offer an analysis from both idealistic and realistic perspectives. And while Fichte has long engaged in such an approach, I would argue that he now uses such a methodology as a device of mutual self-annulment to catapult his work towards a kind of post-epistemology.

These two highest disjunctions of idealism and realism inevitably doom us to a perspectivalism of partial truth and we are left with a fundamental "conflict of maxims," which Fichte circles through several times in a spiraling ascension in an apparent effort to search out a still further meta-perspective he names a "law of maxims" and will later seem to align with the principle of disjunction itself.[19]

The ready potential collapse of realism and idealism into one another is not a "night in which all cows are black," but rather signals a circling or spiraling around the more fundamental and unnamable disjunction that each pole structurally makes possible. Fichte makes clear that each term has the potentiality of the other within it, whose center-point and deepest principle is disjunction itself. He writes: "If one embraces a 'through' just a little energetically, it can be seen as the same principle as disjunction."[20] Yet how or why is this possible?

Since each respective pole of the idealism/realism dyad is contingent, codependent, and illusory, it harbors its opposite within itself. And more radically still, since even collectively we are left with the poles of mutually buttressed illusions, the foreground/background schema itself tends to invert, and the principle of disjunction itself moves to center stage. The truth of the Through is disjunction itself.

Disjunctions: Legitimate and Illegitimate

While the legacy of critical philosophy has certainly expanded to accommodate the absolute within its straining architecture, Fichte must still seek to protect his explanatory apparatus against the threat of breaches by the unnamable void. It is with this in mind that we should consider both Fichte's stated reasons for the demarcation of legitimate and illegitimate disjunctions and other motivations left unsaid.

Fichte's own articulation of the legitimate disjunction is bound up with both his attempt to move beyond the limited epistemologies of realism and idealism and his recasting of the ends of philosophy itself. The function of the real or legitimate disjunction then is as follows: he writes, "There is a necessary gap in the continuity of genesis, and a *proiectum per hiatum*—here presumably not an irrational one. Rather it is [a projection] which separates reason in its pure oneness from all appearance."[21] The legitimate disjunction is the work of philosophical genesis itself.

Fichte names the so-called illegitimate disjunction the "irrational gap." The irrational gap is the fundamental illusion of finite factical consciousness. It appears as a genetic oneness or source, but Fichte ultimately claims it is a non-genesis: it is the work of death.[22] The central problem is this: like

Kantian transcendental illusion, the irrational gap illegitimately posits a kind of sedimented oneness in lieu of the sheer genesis of the absolute.

The original disjunction of pure oneness and appearance marks the very cauldron of philosophical genesis itself, or rather philosophy as genesis. Far from the Hegelian characterization of philosophy as a writing of "grey on grey," Fichte rails against and dismisses any philosophy parading as reconstruction as a work of death. And this too is the central problem with the irrational gap: as a non-genesis, or mere pretender or illusion of genesis, it is at best a mere reconstruction. Fichte asserts: "We, the we who can only reconstruct, cannot do philosophy . . . instead philosophy must just be, but this is possible only to the extent we can perish . . . the question of about the possibility of philosophy depends on whether the I can perish and reason can come purely to manifestation."[23] Since the power of activity or genesis has now been displaced to the absolute, any move other than yielding in openness to the fulguration of creative energy is but a shallow and thus illusory reconstruction. He implores us then, that "we must become aware of something beyond a reconstruction."[24] But is this the real problem the irrational gap poses for Fichte and his system?

The Irrational Gap and the Principle of Unprincipledness

The irrational gap for Fichte operates as a projection without principle. He writes, being "is projected absolutely onto the form of outer existence, in a provisional way, without any ground or principle for this projection, thus through an irrational gap."[25] And although the irrational gap is defined then as a projection without principle, what Fichte now seeks is precisely a principle for the irrational gap, a principle for this very instance of unprincipledness. He explains, "The principle for the irrational gap as such, i.e., for the absolute absence of principle, as such should be demonstrated."[26] But how, then, would one demonstrate an "absolute absence of principle"? Realizing the stakes and consequences, Fichte quickly amends this call for a demonstration, recognizing that a demonstration of an "absolute absence of principle" would amount to a de facto annulment. He explains his preference or call for a new principle or meta-principle in lieu of demonstration as follows: "Obviously, not insofar as it is an absence of principle, because then it would negate and destroy itself, a very different thing from it being provided with a principle."[27]

With this paradox in mind, let's first follow out Fichte's preference for the principle of unprincipledness. He writes, "Being's ideal self-construction is projected through an absolute gap and is thereby made into an absolutely factical and external existence."[28] The self-generative disjunction, an amalgam of self-enclosed energy and its appearance, emerges as external existence. He continues, "Now this existence, as absolute existence, can have no higher principle . . . and in this sense is precisely lacking a principle." Not surprisingly, Fichte describes the irrational gap as a non-genesis because here existence, as "absolute existence," appears cut off from its deeper genetic roots or principles. Like the self-enclosed, unnamable energy called life that remains bound to its disjunctive other for appearance, here too, with the irrational gap, we are confronted with an unbridgeable chasm in which external existence operates in a self-enclosed manner, cut off from a deeper principle that would unite it to its genetic source. After all, Fichte seems to create a distinction between something like real being and its projection. He writes, "Hence too it is not claimed, and cannot be claimed, that being in-itself constructs itself ideally, but rather only that it is projected as constructing itself so."[29] The irrational gap defines an absolute unbridgeable disjunction, one cut off from its genetic source. There is absolute (external) existence and its projective act, but one without a deeper principle or source. Fichte concludes, "Therefore nothing remains—except projection itself."[30] Of course "nothing remains—once this factical being has been annulled as absolute by the demonstration that the projection is its principle," or, in other words, that its principle is precisely unprincipledness.[31] Yet, as we noted earlier, if Fichte turned to call for a "principle of unprincipledness" as a way to amend his initial demand for a demonstration of the "absence of principle" out of fear that it would "negate and destroy itself," what have we really gained in this revision? And what is at stake in this distinction if indeed in the end existence too has been "annulled"?

To transform the anarchic "absolute absence of principle" into a "principle of unprincipledness" is surely a linguistic sleight of hand that seeks to shackle and contain the unruly fulguration of the absolute within a conceptual frame. And this, no doubt, is what distinguishes a rational gap from an irrational one. Fichte explains: "To say that a principle must be provided for it means therefore that a principle must be provided for it solely as an act in general, and as this act in itself posits something unprincipled."[32] The projective act posits something unprincipled, namely existence, and itself stands as a principle of unprincipledness. The irrational gap presents a multifaceted danger to Fichte's architectonic.

First, it stands as an unavoidable illusion for finite, factical thinking; it cannot be defeated, only ignored. Second, Fichte's frighteningly nihilistic claim that in the end "nothing remains" leaves us with an uncontained projective act that seems to leave it untethered from both product and genetic source, a thinly veiled anarchic activity, that is contained primarily by making its unprincipledness itself into a meta-principle. And while these so-called normal or natural disjunctions—which find their source grounded in a deeper genetic principle (by partaking of the philosophy of genesis)—would seem immune, Fichte's very distinction between legitimate and illegitimate disjunctions and his will to make a principle of unprincipledness, I would suggest, indicates a perhaps justified worry of a contagion, of an absolute uncontainable by constraints of critical philosophy.

The Irrational Gap and the Paradox of the Supplement

The irrational gap arises as a projected "oneness," as an illusion that has not been determined genetically.[33] The truth of our realism is a projection of factical consciousness that must be abstracted from to achieve a higher insight. Now, although thinking and consciousness remain bound and codependent in factical life, Fichte is explicitly asking us to abstract from consciousness to produce a pure thinking.[34] He explains, "Immediate consciousness is in no way sufficient and that hence it does not suffice in its basic law of *proiectum per hiatum*."[35] Factical consciousness projects a oneness, but its "inconceivability and inexplicability" leave it as illegitimate.[36] Clearly, much is at stake here for Fichte. His entire system depends upon this proper demarcation between legitimate and illegitimate disjunctions. He asks, "Why should it be given-up?" His answer: "Being in-itself [was dissolved] as a negation and relational term. Hence we must let that go, if it, or our entire system, is to survive."[37]

Fichte's effort to save his system, ironically, may well be the point of its own undoing. He critiques the so-called irrational gap as providing a mere illusory, relational in-itself and asserts that proof of a true in-itself is that it exists as a supplement or remainder (*Zusatz*). Of course, what is even more confounding, as we will soon see, is that Fichte will also disparagingly refer to the irrational gap as a supplement as well.

Fichte tries to solidify the status of the true in-itself by imploring us to partake in his performative method. In effect, he is asking us to perform our own first-person philosophical experiment to confirm the reality of the absolute in-itself as a supplement or remainder. He exclaims: "But something is still left over for us. I affirm this and instruct you to find it with me: being and existing and resting, taken as absolute remains."[38] Being is the ultimate remainder. Fichte, of course, having grounded his refutation of the irrational gap, in defining the true in-itself (in distinction from mere pretenders) as itself a remainder, quickly recognizes that structural and systemic dangers of such supplementation and proceeds to qualify such talk as a mere pedagogical heuristic "for clarification and illustration."[39] Yet the length to which Fichte goes to ameliorate and reverse his initial refutation of the irrational gap by means of characterizing the absolute in-itself as a supplement or remainder may well be an index of its danger. The cure, it turns out, in the wrong dose, may well be a poison.

Fichte launches into what can best be called an anti-supplement diatribe, in a barely containable discourse of "not-needing," whose proliferation seems to mirror the uncontainable contagion of an endless supplementation that Fichte needs to avoid at all costs if his system is to survive. He starts off reaffirming that "'Being in-itself' means a being that indeed needs no other for its existence."[40] He affirms: "Precisely through this not-needing it becomes intrinsically more and more real than it was before; and this not-needing does not belong to its absolute not-needing, and so too with the not-needing of this not-needing, of not-needing—and so this supplement in its endless repeatability remains always the same." And Fichte concludes to affirm a final dismissive (even if rhetorically it proves too late), exhorting that the foregoing "always means nothing in relation to the essence taken seriously and inwardly."[41]

While the danger of supplementation is now clear, more confusing still is that Fichte also identifies the irrational gap itself as a supplement. He writes: "To be sure, in another shape this projection is the in-itself's supplement (*Zusatz*), whose nothingness has already been realized. . . . If it does deceive us . . . we will never arrive at origin {Genesis}."[42] Far from a refutation, isn't this the problem with all supplements and all origins for that matter: that the true origin is forever deferred and displaced, operating in a kind of infinite regress? And how different is this from Fichte's absolute in-itself really? After all, in the *1804 Wissenschaftslehre*, aren't we really on a fascinating but never-ending ride of prepositional displacements? Of froms (*von*) and throughs (*das Durch*) in which, in effect, it is disjunctions all the way down? An infinite remainder of supplementation that leaves little light, whether metaphorical or rational, in the collapsing distinction between so-called rational and irrational gaps? And if there is an ever dwindling and collapsing difference between so-called legitimate and illegitimate gaps, then we may well conclude that what holds for the irrational gap can be said of Fichte's entire architectonic of the *1804 Wissenschaftslehre*: nothing remains.

Notes

1. 1804^2, 119; *GA*, II/8, 238.
2. 1804^2, 119; *GA*, II/8, 238.
3. 1804^2, 119; *GA*, II/8, 238.
4. 1804^2, 124; *GA*, II/8, 250.
5. 1804^2, 124; *GA*, II/8, 250.
6. 1804^2, 119; *GA*, II/8, 239.
7. 1804^2, 160; *GA*, II/8, 330–31.
8. 1804^2, 93; *GA*, II/8, 174–75.
9. 1804^2, 95; *GA*, II/8, 178–79.
10. 1804^2, 95; *GA*, II/8, 178–79.
11. 1804^2, 97; *GA*, II/8, 182–83.
12. 1804^2, 97; GA, II/8, 182–83.
13. 1804^2, 98; *GA*, II/8, 186–87.
14. 1804^2, 118; *GA*, II/8, 236–37.
15. 1804^2, 119; *GA*, II/8, 236–37.
16. 1804^2, 135, 157; *GA*, II/8, 236–37, 322–23.
17. Jacques Derrida might say under "erasure" as a way to express the same kind of semiotic and conceptual instability that Fichte confronts. And what both are wrestling with is the epistemological problem of anti-foundationalism. For a penetrating analysis of the problem of foundations in German Idealism, situated in reference to the work of Derrida, see Gasché's work. Rudolph Gasché, *The Tain in the Mirror: Derrida and the Philosophy of Reflection* (Boston: Harvard University Press, 1988).
18. 1804^2, 91; *GA*, II/8, 170–71.
19. 1804^2, 92; *GA*, II/8, 172–73.
20. 1804^2, 84; *GA*, II/8, 153–54.
21. 1804^2, 158; *GA*, II/8, 324–25.
22. 1804^2, 119; *GA*, II/8, 237–38.
23. 1804^2, 139; *GA*, II/8, 284–85.
24. 1804^2, 139; *GA*, II/8, 284–85.
25. 1804^2, 124; *GA*, II/8, 248–49.
26. 1804^2, 124; *GA*, II/8, 250–51.
27. 1804^2, 124; *GA*, II/8, 250–51.
28. 1804^2, 124; *GA*, II/8, 251–52.
29. 1804^2, 124; *GA*, II/8, 251–52.
30. 1804^2, 124; *GA*, II/8, 251–52.
31. 1804^2, 124; *GA*, II/8, 251–52.
32. 1804^2, 124; *GA*, II/8, 251–52.
33. 1804^2, 120; *GA*, II/8, 240–41.
34. 1804^2, 111; *GA*, II/8, 218–19.
35. 1804^2, 119; *GA*, II/8, 237–38.

36. 1804², 113; *GA*, II/8, 222–23.
37. 1804², 114; *GA*, II/8, 226–27.
38. 1804², 114; *GA*, II/8, 226–27.
39. 1804², 114; *GA*, II/8, 226–27.
40. 1804², 114; *GA*, II/8, 226–27.
41. 1804², 114; *GA*, II/8, 226–27.
42. 1804², 114; *GA*, II/8, 226–27.

Chapter 7

Pure Light and the Promethean Self of Fichte's *1804 Wissenschaftslehre*

Kit Slover

J. G. Fichte first introduces the term "pure light" to his *1804 Wissenschaftslehre* during the course of an extended criticism of Kant's entire system of philosophy. He writes:

> Kantian speculation ends at its highest point with factical manifestness: the insight *that* at the basis of both the sensible and supersensible worlds, there must be a principle of connection, thus a thoroughly genetic principle which creates and determines both worlds absolutely.... This basic law of oneness remains only factical for [Kant], and therefore its object is unexamined, because he allows it to work on him only mechanically; but he does not bring this action itself and its law into his highest awareness anew. If he did so, *pure light would dawn on him and he would come to the science of knowing.*[1]

In this passage, Fichte presents the recognition of "pure light" as the specific difference between his own science of knowing and Kant's critical philosophy. Both Kant and Fichte recognize the necessary unity of the sensible and supersensible worlds, but Kant, Fichte claims, is driven to this recognition only by reason's mechanical desire for thoroughgoing systematicity. Thus, Kant has no *genetic* understanding of *how* the sensible unites with the supersensible; he has only the *factical* understanding *that* this unity must take place. If Kant were to attain a genetic insight into this unity—that is, insight into precisely *how* it is enacted—then "pure light" would dawn on him and his system would merge with Fichte's. To understand pure light, then, is to understand the genetic unity of the sensible and the supersensible worlds.

This chapter will interrogate the structure of pure light and attempt to explain how it brings genetic unity to the sensible and supersensible worlds. First, I will elucidate the problem that pure light is meant to solve, showing it to constitute Fichte's attempt to unify being and thinking without introducing a secondary division between the sensible and supersensible worlds. Second, I will interrogate the structure of "pure knowing" from which pure light is supposed to emerge, showing knowing to consist in nothing other than the unchangeable self-identity of the absolutely changeable. Third, I will show pure knowing to constitute both the self-positing and the self-negation of the absolute concept and argue that, as such, pure knowing already constitutes the unity of being and thinking, or *pure light*. Finally, I will argue that Fichte's unification of being and thinking in the principle of pure light avoids producing a secondary division between the sensible and supersensible worlds only by introducing *death* to the transcendental structure of subjectivity. A promethean subject who dies and is reborn *through* its death, I will show, is the *blood price* of an actual genetic unity of being and thinking.

Kant, Pure Light, and the Transcendental Deduction

Fichte's derivation of the principle of pure light, as the block quote above suggests, is born from his simultaneous respect and criticism of Kant. Fichte respects Kant because, as the only other "transcendental" philosopher, Kant conceives the absolute not as being but as "the indivisible union of being and thinking."[2] But, as we saw, he criticizes Kant for failing to properly account for a corresponding unity of the sensible and the supersensible. Fichte not only recognizes this latter unity alongside the former one, but he even conceives these two unities to be one and the same. Referring to being and thinking as "B and T" and the sensible and supersensible worlds as well as their unity as "x, y, z," Fichte writes:

> A [the absolute] is admitted; it divides itself both into B and T and simultaneously into x, y, z. Both divisions are equally

absolute; one is not possible without the other. Therefore, the insight with which the science of knowing begins and which constitutes its distinction from Kantianism is not at all to be found in the insight into the division into B and T . . . nor in the insight into the division of x, y, z . . . rather it is to be found in the insight into the immediate *inseparability* of these two modes of division.[3]

According to this passage, Kant fails on two counts: (1) he fails to explain the *unity of the sensible and the supersensible* (henceforth, SU), and (2) he fails to explain how SU is already entailed by the *transcendental unity of being and thinking* (henceforth, TU). What distinguishes the science of knowing from Kantianism, then, is its ability to posit the absolute as the determinate *unity* of SU and TU. And, as we saw above, Fichte's name for the difference between his and Kant's philosophies is "pure light." Thus, the principle of pure light is simply what embodies the determinate unity of SU and TU.

To get a sense of how this determinate unity needs to work for Fichte, I will offer a brief explanation of why Kant's commitment to TU precludes, rather than entails, a concomitant commitment to SU. This will allow us to understand why Fichte is so determined to give a "genetic" explanation of the absolute.

Kant defends the legitimacy of TU primarily in the first *Critique*'s "Transcendental Deduction," which proves that the logical forms of judgment (i.e., of *thought*) condition the possibility of the *objects* of thought (i.e., *beings*) so that "objective experience" (the *absolute*) shows itself as the product of both thought and being. To establish this, Kant argues that our capacity to represent a sensible manifold (i.e., our capacity to represent *being*) implies that this manifold is conditioned by certain meta-sensible representations that we deploy to represent ourselves. I must be able to represent myself through any representations that appear in my experience, since by definition *I* am the one who represents those appearances. These meta-sensible, or self-recognitive, representations must be concepts, it turns out, because Kant allows us only two representational types, concepts and sensible intuitions, and a meta-sensible representation clearly cannot be sensible. Hence, objective experience, the absolute, must be the union of concepts and intuitions, thought and being.

Now, this defense of TU—that is, of the claim that the absolute is the union of thought and being—paradoxically relies on a radical *disunity* of thought and being, which ultimately gives rise to the sensible/supersensible divide. For we are only able to employ concepts for the self-recognition to which all sensible appearances entitle us because we take concepts as *non*-sensible representations. The moment we collapse the distinction between concepts and sensible intuitions, we lose our right to apply concepts, as meta-sensible representations, to the sensible manifold at all. Hence, our continued commitment to TU, according to Kant's line of argumentation, requires us to represent an unbridgeable divide between concepts and intuitions, thought and being, and this unbridgeable divide, as Henry Allison points out, leads to the necessary idea of a pure understanding with a perspective on a supersensible world distinct from the sensible one.[4]

What Kant's transcendental deduction teaches us is that any attempt to affirm *both* TU *and* SU cannot ground TU in any sort of constitutive divide between concepts and intuitions. This divide, while enabling the affirmation of TU, will invariably require the denial of SU. Hence, Fichte's derivation of pure light must somehow posit the absolute in the union of thought and being *without* relying on any irreducible difference between these two representational types. It must, rather, show both thought and being to *co-emerge* from the same source. Such a genetic affirmation of TU will enable us to endorse SU simultaneously because it will prevent the sensible/supersensible divide from ever arising in the first place. Hence, going forward, Fichte's entire task must be to show being and thinking to co-emerge from the same genetic source.

Pure Knowing and Pure Light

The derivation of pure light, we have just seen, consists entirely in the articulation of the absolute as the genetic union of being and thinking. We will have derived the principle of pure light when we have shown being and thinking to emerge from, and return to, the same absolute source. Thus, Fichte begins this genetic derivation by elucidating the factical unity of being and thinking that occurs in every act of "knowing." Knowledge, Fichte reasons, is nothing other than the correspondence of a concept, or thought, with its object, or being. This means that knowledge, sufficiently understood, already constitutes a certain union of being and thinking, and for this reason Fichte fixates upon it as the first *factical* manifestation of the absolute: "Surely everyone who is willing to reflect can perceive that absolutely all being posits a *thinking* or *consciousness* of itself; and that therefore mere being is always only one half of a whole together with the thought of it. . . . Thus, absolute oneness . . . resides in the principle . . . of the absolute *oneness* and *indivisibility* of [being and thinking], which is equally . . . the principle of their disjunction. We will name this principle *pure knowing*."[5]

The task is to show "pure knowing," or the mere *correspondence* of thought and being, to develop itself into "pure light," or the *genetic unity* of these terms.

Fichte continues this development by identifying being and conceptual thought with the absolutely changeable, and their correspondence (i.e., knowing) with the absolutely unchangeable. Fichte writes:

> We can demonstrate immediately that knowing can actually appear as something standing on its own. I ask you to look sequentially at your own inner experience: if you remember it accurately, you will find the object and its representation, with all their modifications. But now I ask further: Do you not *know* in all these modifications; and is not your knowing, as knowing, the same self-identical knowing in all variations of the object? As surely as you say, "Yes," to this inquiry . . . so surely will knowledge manifest and present itself to you . . . as a substantive, as staying the same as itself through all change in its object; and thus as a oneness, qualitatively changeless in itself.[6]

When we attend to the basic character of our experience as it elapses, Fichte claims, we observe a twofold process. On the one hand, we observe the constant change of our conceptual thought as it struggles to continuously correspond to an object that is itself changing in time. If the object of my knowledge is the "sun," for example, then, as it travels continuously across the sky, I must perpetually adjust my *concept* of it in order to consistently represent it correctly. On the other hand, since "knowing" denotes nothing other than the correct correspondence of being and thinking, and this correspondence is continuously maintained through, and as a result of, the continuous changes in conceptual thought, it is clear that the "knowledge" of any object remains self-identical across all that object's changes. While the corresponding terms (i.e., being and thinking) are continuously changing in time, the correspondence itself (i.e., knowing) remains self-identical throughout and perpetually unchanged.

This exercise allows us to apply contrary properties to "knowing" and "conceptual thought," respectively. As the correspondence between concept and object that remains self-identical throughout all change in the corresponding terms, knowing is *self-sufficient, autonomous,* and *independent.* It does not rely on any particular concept or any particular being to be itself but rather persists as itself no matter what concept/being pair presently instantiates it. Conceptual thought, by contrast, suffers from a double dependence on both being and knowing. It is always a mediate "construction," depending in each case upon the particular being that it represents. It is a vanishing point of stability that defines the law of change that applies to a given species of being and makes it suitable for knowledge. Thus, conceptual thought is always constructed and mediated through being. We seem to emerge from Fichte's factical exercise with two unproblematically opposed terms: self-identical knowing on the one hand and constantly different consciousness on the other.

But a closer look shows our definition of knowing as the correspondence of being and thinking to in fact predicate contrary properties of knowing itself. For, on the one hand, as we have seen, this definition shows knowing to remain unchanged throughout the constant variations in concept and object. As the correspondence between terms that are perpetually changing together and in answer to one another, knowing itself is self-identical throughout all change, self-sufficient and substantial. But, on the other hand, this same definition shows knowing to be self-identical and self-sufficient only insofar as constant change afflicts the terms of which it is the correspondence. The correspondence of concept and object stands apart from its corresponding terms as a substance of its own only insofar as these terms are always already different from themselves in every instant. If concept and object were not undergoing constant change, then their "correspondence" would never have the opportunity to remain identical to itself through change. The constant change in concept and object, then, is the background against which the self-identicality and unchangeability of knowing can first appear. This means that while knowing itself certainly is unchangeable, it also implies and, in a way, depends upon change.

To express this internally conflicted definition of knowing in more systematic language, Fichte presents us with a figure that employs his shorthand[7] for the absolute, being, thinking, and so on and attempts to represent the contradiction at the heart of knowing:

$$A$$

$$x\ y\ z \bullet B–T$$

The key terms in this figure are "A" and the point. "A" represents something like pure, immediate substantiality—A is like an Aristotelian substance that not only *persists* through all change but also makes no necessary reference to change in its definition. It remains itself regardless of whether change takes place. The point (•), by contrast, is pure, absolutely mediate immersion in change—it is nothing other than the relation that change expresses, constantly different from itself, perhaps comparable to Aristotelian *activity*. To capture the conflicted essence of knowing that I have been discussing, Fichte argues that knowing (or the science of knowing) belongs in neither A nor the point, "but rather in the oneness of both."[8] As the unity of A and the point (henceforth, AP), knowing is neither an indifferent substance, self-identical with *no* relation to change, nor a mere change, constantly different from itself. Rather, knowing is a substance whose substantiality consists in nothing other than its constant difference from itself and, vice versa, a constant difference from itself that constitutes a substantiality. As the correspondence of constantly and necessarily changing terms, knowing is itself—is constantly *identical* with itself—exclusively through the change in those terms. Knowing is a self-identical substance that consists in nothing but constant change and a constant change that constitutes a self-identical substance. By constantly *differing from itself* (as the point dictates) knowing, or AP, adequates its essence and remains eternally *identical* to itself (as A dictates).

Hence, an adequate understanding of the definition of "knowing" shows it to be nothing other than the pure self-identicality of AP. The pure correspondence of being and thinking is eternally itself *through* the constant difference in the corresponding terms. Pure light, I will show, is the imminent product of the dialectic between these two opposing aspects of pure knowing itself.

The Genesis of Pure Light

In this section, I will show AP—or pure knowing, adequately understood—to produce "pure light" simply by developing the dialectic that defines its essence. First, it will reveal itself as the *absolute concept*, thereby developing the first term of pure light's genetic unity. Second, the absoluteness of the absolute concept will show AP to in fact be inconceivable. Finally, this very inconceivability will prove itself to be a remnant of conceptuality and will, accordingly, vacate the essence of AP on its own terms, leaving only *being* behind, the second term of pure light's unity. In this way, I will show, pure light expresses both the *absolute concept* and the *double negation* of that concept.

Fichte begins his derivation of pure light by discovering the absolute concept, or the origin of thinking, lurking within the definition of pure knowing that we already have before us. He writes: "Once again to adduce an even higher perspective what is the science of knowing? Neither A nor the point, but instead the inner *organic oneness* of both. . . . The organic oneness of both is a construction or a concept, and indeed the single absolute concept, abstracted from nothing existing, since even its own separate existence is denied."[9] In this passage, Fichte defines AP as the *single absolute concept*. This is initially surprising because, according to our analysis, AP is not a concept, but rather the articulation of the fully developed *correspondence* of concept and being. Thus, calling AP a *concept* seems to beg the question. But what Fichte seems to be doing here is calling our attention to the fact that AP, as the incarnation of the correspondence between concept and being, also exhibits all the core traits of a concept and therefore qualifies as one. For, as we saw above, a concept in general is a mediate representation of a certain change. It represents the common law that organizes a given manifold of mutually distinct and perpetually transforming elements. It is nothing other than unity that subsists through a change.

Similarly, AP—that is, the unity of the absolutely self-identical "A" and the absolutely changing "point"—is nothing other than a pure unity that subsists through pure change. It is a substance that maintains its self-identicality only by persisting through an ongoing and continuous change. Thus, as such a unity of self-identicality and change, Fichte suggests, AP qualifies as a *concept*: it is the conceptual unity that defines the ongoing alteration of conceptuality as such. It qualifies further as the *absolute* concept because, while most concepts supervene upon changing beings from which they remain distinct, AP's self-identicality *is* the constant change that it determines, and the constant change that it determines is the change of the conceptual itself. The unity of AP fully merges with the change that it determines because the constancy of this change *is* the unity that determines it. This elliptical, fractalizing sequence—which shows AP, the deeper principle of conceptuality to itself *be* a concept—completes the genesis of *thought*, providing the first term of pure light's unity.

Defining AP in this way, however, produces two successive negations that will ultimately make thought give way to *being*. The first negation shows the absoluteness of AP's conceptuality to actually render it inconceivable. We have just seen that AP qualifies as a concept because, like all concepts, it is a unity that norms a changeable manifold, itself remaining unchanged, and it stands apart from all other concepts as the "single *absolute*" one because it alone *is* the changeable manifold that it itself norms and unifies. Fichte shows next, however, that this very absoluteness of AP's conceptuality in fact disqualifies it from being a concept at all. He writes: "Now to be sure this point of oneness [viz., AP] can be realized *immediately, oscillating and expending itself* in this point. . . . But this point can neither be expressed nor reconstructed in its immediacy, since all expression or reconstruction is conceiving and is intrinsically *mediated*. . . . Thus, since reconstruction is conceiving, and since this very conceiving explicitly abandons its own *intrinsic validity*, this is precisely a case of conceiving the inconceivable *as inconceivable*."[10] Concepts are, by definition, *mediate* representations of changing manifolds. According to Kant's definition, which I take Fichte to have in mind here, concepts institute unity in the sensible manifold only because they meta-sensibly represent that same manifold in a way that enables an act of self-recognition or apperception. Their authority lies entirely in their *mediacy*—their ability to represent the very same appearances that we've already apprehended sensibly but in a different way. Any concept that loses its mediacy, then, effectively loses its conceptuality. The unity of the concept must remain thoroughly distinct from the variations of the manifold that it unifies. But we have just seen that, in the case of AP, the unity of the concept does not remain distinct from the change that it unifies, but rather *is* that change (this was the condition of its absoluteness). This means that the very condition that confers absolute conceptuality on AP also strips AP of that conceptuality. The conceptuality of the concept is negated by its very absoluteness. Or, as Fichte puts it: "Inconceivability itself originates in the concept and in pure immediate manifestness."[11] Hence, the first negation reveals AP as the *inconceivable*.

The second negation both counteracts and amplifies this result, exorcising "inconceivability" from the essence of AP and releasing pure knowing into its pure self-sufficiency. The negation proceeds by recognizing that inconceivability is still a property of pure knowing, predicated by the absolute concept, viz., by means of its self-negation, so that inconceivability must turn out to be its own negation. Fichte writes: "Now to be sure inconceivability is only the negation of the concept, an expression of its annulment. Therefore it is something which originates from both the concept and knowing themselves; it is a quality transferred by means of absolute manifestness. Noting this, and therefore abstracting from this quality, nothing remains for oneness except absoluteness or pure self-sufficiency."[12] Since the content of the property of "inconceivability" states that the entity of which it is a property (viz., knowing, or AP) must be alienated from everything conceptual, while the form of inconceivability is that it is the result of conceptual predication (by means of the negation of the absolute concept), it follows that inconceivability must negate itself, stripping itself from the essence of pure knowing, and, as Fichte states, leaving only "absoluteness" or pure self-sufficiency behind. This second negation counteracts the previous one because it results in the negation of the sole conclusion that the first negation achieves. But it also amplifies the previous negation because it completes the project of alienating AP from everything conceptual. The key to this step is to recognize that, just as the absolute concept, qua absolute, was already its own negation, so the property of inconceivability, qua property, is likewise already its own negation.

The completion of this second negation of the absolute concept purifies AP of the last remnants of anything conceptual and, simultaneously, generates *intuition*, or the realm of being, the second term of pure light's genetic unity. Fichte explains: "Having recognized this inconceivability as an alien quality introduced by knowing, I said before, only pure self-sufficiency, or substantiality, remains in the absolute; and it is quite true that at best this self-sufficiency does not originate in the concept, since it enters only with the latter's annulling. But it is clear that [self-sufficiency] enters only within immediate manifestness, within intuition."[13] Because the second negation has purified AP of even a negative relation to conceptuality, leaving only pure self-sufficiency behind, this self-sufficiency cannot be hosted by anything conceptual. It must rather be hosted by the faculty of *immediate manifestness*, and this, following Kant, is none other than intuition, or the faculty that relates immediately to being. Hence, the complete destruction of the absolute concept is simultaneously the generation of being.

With this, the genesis of pure light has been completed. The self-development of AP has produced both terms of the unity and returned them to the common source of the light. Fichte writes:

> Secondly, the previously presented relation of concept to being and vice versa is further determined as follows: If there is to be an expression and realization of the absolute light, then the concept must be posited so that it can be negated by the immediate light, since the expression of pure light consists just

in this negation. But the result of this expression is being in itself, period. [This result] is inconceivable precisely because pure light is simultaneously destruction of the concept. Thus, pure light has prevailed as the one focus and the sole principle of both being and the concept.[14]

Pure light is the self-development of the pure concept, the self-destruction of that concept, and the bursting forth of being from that self-destruction. As a principle, pure light holds together both the birth and death of the concept, preserving them as moments of its own genesis. Hence, to return to the language of the first section, the affirmation of pure light is the affirmation of TU, or of the transcendental unity of thought and being.

Two Worlds Unity and the Constant Death of the Self-Recognitive Subject

The principle of pure light, in addition to unifying thought and being, I argue, also brings unity to the sensible and the supersensible world, cleaving the spatiotemporal world of natural law together with the purely ideal world of moral imperatives. For, we saw that Kant is forced to introduce a distinction between these two worlds only because his transcendental deduction of the categories relies fundamentally on the representation of a distinction between concepts and intuitions. Concepts and intuitions must stand apart from one another for Kant, joining only within a common but constitutively unknowable root. If they did not, then the key move in the deduction, the appeal to self-recognitive, meta-sensible representation, would not retrieve concepts as the agents of this meta-sensible self-recognition. But because Kant must maintain this irreducible distinction between concepts and intuitions, he is forced to give concepts a role to play beyond the conditions of intuition, and this ultimately gives birth to a supersensible world of ideas that, by definition, can never unite with the sensible or objective one. Thus, the way Kant closes the being/thinking divide is what generates the sensible/supersensible dissension.

We can see, then, that Fichte is able to resolve the conflict between the sensible and the supersensible simply by closing the being/thinking divide in a way that never gives rise to it. By showing being and thinking to co-emerge from and subsist only within the genetic principle of pure light, Fichte is able to posit the absolute in the unity of thinking (concepts) and being (intuitions) *without* representing an irreducible divide between these two representational types. He therefore never encounters the difficulty that afflicts Kant's entire critical philosophy, forcing him to posit two irreconcilable worlds. In short, because Kant's deduction posits the absolute only in the *factical* unity of concepts and intuitions, he is required to found the cleavage between the sensible and the supersensible on the irreducible distinction of the these two representational types; by contrast, since Fichte posits the absolute in the genetic unity of concepts and intuitions, he never encounters the sensible/supersensible problem at all.

However, the complete genetic unity that the principle of pure light enacts comes at a price. Pure light manages to introduce genetic unity to concepts and intuitions, the sensible and the supersensible, only through an act of destruction. The concept is posited so that it can be annihilated. But concepts, as I explored in the first section of this chapter, are nothing other than agents of the subject's own self-recognition. And moreover, the subject itself *is* this act of self-recognition, or apperception. For Fichte and Kant, the subject is not *first of all* a Cartesian substance that may or may not recognize itself; it is rather *nothing other than* its self-recognition. This means that the destruction of the absolute concept that the pure light enacts is likewise the destruction, or *death*, of the subject itself. Fichte explains:

> One term is *being*, the other—the negated concept—is without doubt *subjective* thought, or consciousness. Therefore we now have one of the two basic disjunctions, that into B and T (being and thinking), we have grasped this . . . as proceeding completely and simply from oneness, (L = light); and thereby . . . we would simultaneously have the schema for the negation of the I in the pure light and even have it *intuitively*. For if . . . one posits that the principle of the negated concept is just the I . . . then its destruction in the face of what is valid in itself is simultaneously *my* destruction in the same moment, since I as its principle no longer exist. My being grasped and torn apart by the manifestness which *I* did not make, but which creates itself, is the phenomenal image of my being negated and extinguished in the pure light.[15]

Pure light grasps and tears us apart. It is nothing other than the extinction of the I, the negation of the absolute concept by which the I fundamentally is. But it also retains the I through this destruction, preserves it, depends on it, and effectively recreates it *in* the act of destruction. The light both needs and destroys the concept, requires and annihilates the I. Hence, pure light, or the principle of real genetic unity in being and thinking, sensible and supersensible, is nothing other than the cycle of Promethean death and rebirth that defines and destroys subjectivity itself.

Notes

1. 1804^2, 37; *GA*, II/8, 44, emphasis added.
2. 1804^2, 31; *GA*, II/8, 28.
3. 1804^2, 32–33; *GA*, II/8, 34.
4. See Henry E. Allison, *Kant's Transcendental Idealism* (New Haven, CT: Yale University Press, 2004), 16–17.
5. 1804^2, 25; *GA*, II/8, 14.
6. 1804^2, 34–35; *GA*, II/8, 37–38.
7. A = absolute; x = sensible world; z = supersensible world; y = the unity of x and y. B = being; T = thinking.
8. 1804^2, 41; *GA*, II/8, 54.
9. 1804^2, 42; *GA*, II/8, 57.
10. 1804^2, 42; *GA*, II/8, 59, emphasis added.
11. 1804^2, 43; *GA*, II/8, 59.
12. 1804^2, 43; *GA*, II/8, 59.
13. 1804^2, 43; *GA*, II/8, 59.
14. 1804^2, 43; *GA*, II/8, 59.
15. 1804^2, 69; *GA*, II/8, 117.

Chapter 8

The Odyssey of the "Through" (*das Durch*)

M. Jorge de Carvalho

The *1804 Wissenschaftslehre* is a complex maze and requires something like an Ariadne's thread to help us find a way through its intricacies. But the problem is that the thread is itself intricate and cannot be drawn in one move. We must therefore confine ourselves to a more modest task. We focus our attention on one small part of the maze and try to provide an Ariadne's thread to get through it.

The part of the maze we want to focus on in this chapter is what might be termed the "odyssey of the Through" (or the "metamorphoses of the Through") in Fichte's *1804 Wissenschaftslehre*. The odyssey we are talking about begins with a grammatical oddity: Fichte makes a noun out of a preposition (*durch*: through) and speaks of *das Durch* ("the through"). Simple and modest *durch* is forced to go beyond its usual responsibilities, to leave its grammatical home and sail into the high seas of philosophical inquiry. This grammatical metamorphosis of a preposition into a noun comes into play in the seventh session, and then again in the Tenth, Eleventh, Twelfth, Thirteenth, Fourteenth, Eighteenth, and Nineteenth Lectures. Fichte uses it without any explanation or discussion, as if to suggest that its meaning is self-evident. And the fact is that this grammatical anomaly becomes one of the key notions not only in the sessions just mentioned but, indeed, in the whole framework of the 1804 lectures.

But the question is, What does this morphological and semantic oddity stand for? *Prima facie*, everything seems to suggest that Fichte is speaking neither of the many connections that can be expressed by the preposition in question nor of a particular instance (a particular *durch*—a particular "through") among many others.[1] He is apparently speaking of *DAS Durch* (*the* through). That is, he seems to have in mind *das Durch* as a *singulare tantum*: *das Durch* ("the through") as such viz. the "through *itself*"—what might be described as an *absolutized through* so that there is only one "through" viz. that the through he is referring to is, as it were, an overarching or all-encompassing "through."

But then again, this does not seem particularly helpful, for it raises this question: In what sense can one speak of an absolute—an overarching and all-encompassing—"through"? In other words, the grammatically odd *das Durch* seems to denote an equally odd and puzzling philosophical notion—and we could say with Churchill, "It is a riddle, wrapped in a mystery . . . but perhaps there is a key."

On second thought, we could have quoted Churchill's whole sentence, instead of mutilating it: "It is a riddle, wrapped in a mystery, inside an enigma." For Fichte's *das Durch* does not make its appearance at an early stage of the 1804 lectures. As pointed out above, it does not come into play before the seventh lesson, after much has been done. And, what is more, Fichte's *das Durch* is devised as a metamorphosis of what precedes (as a further continuation of the odyssey that has been taking place since the First Lecture), but also as a staging post on the way to subsequent developments (i.e., to the continuation of the said odyssey and metamorphosis). This means that in order to fully understand what Fichte's *das Durch* is all about, we should follow the Homeric formula and look ἅμα πρόσσω καὶ ὀπίσω ("both forward and backward at the same time").[2] But this is precisely what the framework of this chapter does not allow us to do: we must leave out the overarching odyssey of the *1804 Wissenschaftslehre* (both the whole chain of preceding metamorphoses and the whole chain of subsequent metamorphoses until the end of the 1804 lectures). The result is that we must deal with the grammatical mystery, and the conceptual riddle of *das Durch*, without being able to tackle the enigma of Fichte's "complete statement" as laid out in his 1804 lectures.

But this is not all. There is still something else that gives a special character to the connection between *das Durch* and everything else in the 1804 lectures. One of the intriguing things about these lectures is the fact that they stage a series of metamorphoses of the very same thing: what Fichte terms the *Einheitspunkt* (the all-encompassing *Mittelpunkt*). In a way, it is always about the same thing: the "absolute *Einheit*," the all-encompassing connection or absolute connection between everything and everything. The whole operation amounts to a gradual revision of the same thing (to the gradual deepening of the very same fundamental insight). Plato's imaginary etymology of ἄνθρωπος in his *Cratylus* (ἀναθρῶν ἃ ὄπωπε, "one who observes closely and reconsiders what he has seen") finds a particularly rich illustration here.[3] From the very beginning everything revolves around the said universal *Einheitspunkt* or *Mittelpunkt*. And this *Einheitspunkt* or *Mittelpunkt* undergoes wave after wave of analysis and is reconsidered again and again. Most texts (and, for that matter, most philosophical texts) move from one thing to another. They tackle a variety of topics so that different objects are examined one after another. Not so in the case of the *1804 Wissenschaftslehre*. Most of it amounts to an insistent examination of the very same key point. Fichte comes back to it from ever-new angles; he goes into detail and explores all the ins and outs of the key point in question.

We can also express this by saying that the 1804 lectures stage what might be described as a cognitive drama whose dramatis personae have precious little to do with separate entities or separate notions, added to one another and interacting with one another in such a way that they are completely independent from each other. The whole point is that the dramatis personae in question (the cognitive dramatis personae that the *1804 Wissenschaftslehre* is all about) are *protean variations* of the very same fundamental dramatis persona—they stand for an ever-closer awareness viz. for increasingly deep knowledge of the same thing (of its complexity and intricacy). To be sure, the *1804 Wissenschaftslehre* unfolds as a landscape of contrasts (and indeed of radical contrasts)—the plethora of cognitive dramatis personae we have referred to. But the point is that they are all contrasts within the same thing. And it is also true that Fichte's 1804 lectures present a tangled web of unexpected turns and surprises. The lectures are anything but uneventful. But the point is that, paradoxically enough, all unexpected turns and surprises take *place within the very same* fundamental insight or key point. It is always about the latter, and what we are dealing with here is a very particular kind of surprise and otherness—namely, the surprise and otherness (the radical otherness) of the same thing.

But how can this be? Contrary to what may seem to be the case, the fact that one has already caught sight of the key point (the *Einheitspunkt* or *Mittelpunkt*) in question—and this means the fact that one has caught sight of *everything* in the light of the *Einheitspunkt* or *Mittelpunkt* (the fundamental insight in question)—does not preclude the possibility that one is still missing the point and failing to grasp what the fundamental insight is really all about. As a matter of fact, the "mesh" can be still too coarse to capture the most decisive nuances. And here, too, God and the devil are in the details. If the mesh is coarse, nothing prevents the finer nuances upon which everything depends from slipping through one's fingers. Hence, the byword must be "tighten the mesh" or "tighten the grip"—"fine-tune the understanding of the key point." And that is what the *1804 Wissenschaftslehre* is all about. In other words, Fichte is striving to get rid of what might be described as pockets of remaining unawareness (or remaining shallowness) undermining our initial understanding of the *Einheitspunkt*—and indeed the understanding we are able to acquire in each of the intermediate stages that come into play one after the other in the 1804 lectures. It is all a question of increasingly detailed and differentiated insight into the said *Einheitspunkt* or *Mittelpunkt*. As Fichte put it, it is all about "*dasselbe von einer anderen Seite und Tiefe*,"[4] "*weiter bestimmt und tiefer gefasst*"[5] ("the same point, from another side and depth," "further determined and grasped more deeply than before"). And the point is that the heightened degree of reflexivity that the *1804 Wissenschaftslehre* is all about gives the *Einheitspunkt* (the key point viz. the fundamental insight in question) a whole new complexion: it appears in a very different light; it redefines itself again and again. In short, the spiral of reflectivity/reflection presented in these lectures turns out to be a spiral of increasing understanding of the *Einheitspunkt* or *Mittelpunkt* and therefore of everything that depends on it—that is, of everything *tout court*.

Now, this brief outline reveals two important points. The first has to do with the connection between *das Durch* and the *Einheitspunkt* or *Mittelpunkt* around which everything revolves. As pointed out previously, *das Durch* stands for an overarching, all-encompassing connection (i.e., for some kind of connection between everything and everything). But, as it turns out, it is far from being the first mention of something like this in the 1804 lectures; for a universal connection between everything and everything is what these lectures are all about from the very beginning. *Das Durch* is rather intended to denote a *metamorphosis* of the all-encompassing *Einheitpunkt* viz. *Milttelpunkt*: a further determination of it (viz. of one of the cognitive dramatis personae in which it unfolds). In short, *das Durch* is a further step in the spiral of reflectivity, in which the all-encompassing *Einheitspunkt* viz. *Mittelpunkt* redefines itself again and again.

This brings us to the second point. As just mentioned, Fichte's *das Durch* is a staging post in the long spiral of reflection conducted by Fichte in his *1804 Wissenschaftslehre*. On the one hand, it redefines the previous stages. On the other hand, it is to be further redefined by the views presented till the end of the 1804 lectures. All this means that, taken by itself, with no regard for the whole line of development (i.e., for all the other lectures, for the whole of which it is a part), *das Durch* is uprooted from its proper context like a fish out of water. Or, put another way, we are trying to get a microscopic image of a small part of an organism (this living creature: the *1804 Wissenschaftslehre*), while the corresponding microscopic image of the whole organism in question (the whole 1804 lectures on the same scale) is still missing and must be left for another day. And this in turn means that this chapter deals with an isolated piece of a very complex puzzle—the result being that the puzzle piece in question can change its complexion when everything is put together and it resumes its place among all the other pieces (i.e., in the framework of a thorough examination and cross-checking of them all). However, we have no choice but to accept this risk and plunge in medias res.

We turn our attention to the Seventh Lecture, where *das Durch* comes into the picture for the first time. As a matter of fact, the whole chapter will concentrate on the Seventh Lecture. To be sure, the latter is but the first of a series of developments concerning *das Durch*; it is, as it were, the opening book of the Odyssey we are talking about. But, on the one hand, even a complete account of the *Durch* and its odyssey would go far beyond the scope of this chapter. On the other hand, we should not forget that the beginning is, as the ancient saying goes, ἥμισυ παντός—the half of every work ("well begun is half done")—and that the Athenian from Plato's *Laws* does not exaggerate when he goes a step further and states that "it is truly more than the half" (πλέον ἢ τὸ ἥμισυ).[6]

The Antithesis between *Durch* and *Und:* Hiatuses and Empty Fillers

The context in which Fichte speaks of *das Durch* in the Seventh Lecture is defined by two main determining factors. Firstly, *das Durch* seems to be the very opposite of "das leere Flickwort *und*" ("the empty filler *and*") and what it stands for. Secondly, das *Durch* is closely associated with what Fichte terms "the image" ("*das Bild*")—a notion he discussed in the Fourth, Fifth, and Sixth Lectures in connection with his analysis of *Begriff* (Stellvertreter und Abbild des Lichts). In other words, there is some kind of essential connection between *das Durch* and "*das Bild*" so that either *das Durch* is key to understanding the image as such or the latter is key to understanding the former—or both.

Let us take a closer look at the two "plates" of this diptych. The first determining factor has to do with a *contrast medium* against which *das Durch* (or at least some essential features of it) stands out and can be readily seen. As just mentioned, Fichte focuses on the contrast between *das Durch* and what he terms "das leere Flickwort *und*" ("the empty filler word *and*"). The passage we are referring to reads as follows: "Do we want to divide the true into two parts and then conflate these parts with the empty filler word '*and*' (das leere Flickwort *und*), a word which we scarcely understand and which is the least understandable word in all language, a word which is not explicated by any previous philosophy (it is indeed the *synthesis post factum*)?"[7]

But what does this mean?

First, Fichte is referring to *filler words* (fillers, gap fillers, or stopgaps—buffering words used to pad out sentences without adding any useful information or to disguise syntactic discontinuity by producing the illusion of real syntactic connection where there is nothing but a loose paratactic structure). In his *Anthropology from a Pragmatic Point of View*, Kant describes *Flickwörter* in the following terms: "*Phrasen zu bloßer Ausfüllung der Leere an Gedanken* ("Clichés [or catch-phrases]—used merely to stuff the emptiness of thought.")[8]

Secondly, Fichte is focusing on a particular word, the *Bindewort* "*und*" (the coordinating conjunction "and," commonly used to connect words, phrases, clauses, or prefixes). But the point is not that this connective word can be occasionally used as a filler. It is rather the claim that it is *intrinsically* a filler—that it is always a filler and nothing but a filler. But this is not all: Fichte's claim has a still wider scope. On closer inspection it emerges that the "*und*" he is referring to does not take place only when the connective word is used. The point is that there is such a thing as a silent "*und*," and that this silent "*und*" is constantly intervening as a filler in the way things appear to us. That is, in this case too, a simple and modest word is forced to go beyond its usual responsibilities, leave its grammatical home, and sail into the high seas of philosophical inquiry.

Fichte is drawing our attention to the fact that if we check how various representational contents are connected with each other, we will see that the connective link (the separation and apposition of many and indeed most representational contents) is a *formal* operator (the same for many different cases) and, as if this were not enough, the formal operator in question does not withstand critical scrutiny, for it lacks any really *intelligible* content.

In other words, Fichte alludes to a complex state of affairs consisting of two main components. On the one hand, his point is that our representational manifold is riddled with a very dense network of scotomata, as it were: blind spots of diminished acuity (n.b., intelligibility-related blind spots). More often than not, the transition from a given A to a given B is just a leap from one to the other. In the final analysis, there is simple juxtaposition: a hiatus between A and B; no real thread of connection between them, no really intelligible content leading from one to the other. As Fichte puts it, the thread of understanding does not run continuously from A to B without any break. The thread of real insight is interrupted by all sorts of gaps, hiatuses, or cognitive blanks (one could also say lacunae viz. blind spots).

But, on the other hand, the cognitive holes or blind spots (the intelligibility-related lacunae or hiatuses) we are talking about are bridged by formal connectors acting as gap fillers or stopgaps. Or rather they are automatically bridged by what might be termed the *Ur-füller* (the *original* stopgap or *primordial* stopgap), namely the representational "*Und*" as such. The point is that though the latter amounts to nothing more than pure addition (blind addition, empty addition) or pure juxtaposition (blind juxtaposition, empty juxtaposition), it acts as a full cognitive content. In other words, although the representational "*Und*" amounts to nothing but a blind leap from A to B (i.e., pure representational parataxis), it manages to masquerade as real representational syntax (i.e., as a really intelligible connection between A and B). In short, the "*Und*" plays the role of a cognitive fig leaf concealing the cognitive gaps or hiatuses.

In order to be effective, this gap filler must do its work discretely and indeed in such a way that it manages at the same time to hide the cognitive gaps and to hide its own presence, namely its own intervention as a gap filler. Or, put another way, in order to do its work properly the particular kind of cognitive fig leaf we are talking about must *cover its tracks* and be there without attracting attention.

In short, complete unawareness of the gaps or lacunae and complete unawareness of the "*Und*" (the cognitive gap filler) as such is what Fichte's "*Und*" is all about. As is also the case with scotomata and blind spots, Fichte's cognitive gaps and the corresponding gap filler go hand in hand with significantly diminished acuity. Fichte's primordial filler (the representational "*Und*" he refers to) performs its functions by drawing attention from the transition from A to B (i.e., by making us skip the transition)—and this also means by drawing our attention from itself (by making us skip itself and perceive itself less acutely).

Now, this seems to be what Fichte has in mind when he speaks of "das leere Flickwort *und*" as an important component of our usual representational world—and indeed as the very form or structure of what he terms the *synthesis post factum*. The point seems to be that the latter is not just characterized by its empirical origin and by its lack of universal validity, but just as much by the fact that it is undermined by its inability to provide anything but empty and blind connections. Fichte's wording when he speaks of "das leere Flickwort *und*" seems intended to suggest that our usual representational world is riddled both with cognitive gaps and with cognitive stopgaps or gap fillers (and notably with the primordial filler or proto-filler "*Und*") so that on closer inspection it turns out to be nothing but *Flickwerk* (i.e., sheer *patchwork*), or rather a particular kind of patchwork, namely one that gives the illusion of being absolutely seamless (of continuity where there is none, and the whole thing is held together by blind and empty fillers). In short, Fichte's point is that our usual representational world is nothing but *discontinuity in the guise of continuity* (n.b., intelligibility-related discontinuity in the guise of intelligibility-related continuity).[9]

The Opposite of the "*Und*": Das Durch and its Cognitive Program

This provides the basis for understanding one of the main aspects of Fichte's *das Durch*: the fact that it has to do with the exact opposite of all this—that is, with real continuity, an uninterrupted thread of intelligibility from each A to each B. In other words, *das Durch* stands for a philosophical task, viz. a cognitive program: nothing less than the complete elimination of every *aggregatum*, of all such *rhapsodistical* manifold, and this means both of all discontinuity (the complete elimination of all hiatuses) and of all discontinuity in the guise of continuity (the complete elimination of all fillers). The connection between every A and every B must be grasped in such a way that we are able to find in A (in A as such) something leading to B (and vice versa). Put another way: A must show itself in such a way that it entails in itself the thread leading to B, and B must show itself in such a way that it entails in itself the thread leading to A. And so in all other cases.

We can also express this cognitive program by saying that B must cease to be something *supervenient* to A, and A must cease to be something supervenient to B. There must be an essential connection between them, and knowledge of A and B must also be knowledge of an essential connection between them. Fichte's *das Durch* designates this thread of real continuity—that is, an insight into this entirely intelligible connection—between A and B.

Hence, *das Durch* reverses the emphasis: while the hiatuses and the filler-riddled manifold of our usual representational world skips the transition from A to B or does not pay attention to it, Fichte's *das Durch* puts the main focus on the transition from A to B (viz. from B to A). In this new approach, the key is (1) what might be termed the "transition-what," (2) the fact that the latter must be rooted both in A and B, and (3) the fact that the "transition-what" must be as fully a *content* (and as fully a definite and intelligible content) as A or B. In the Tenth Lecture, Fichte puts this in a nutshell when he speaks of *Durchheit* ("throughness") and paraphrases the latter in the following terms: "Durchheit, des *Fortgehens von einem zum andern*" ("throughness of [continuous] progression from one to another").[10]

But we are going too fast. As a matter of fact, the above could mislead one into believing that Fichte's *das Durch* reverses the emphasis in the sense that it concentrates on what we have termed the "transition what" or the "transition content" at the expense of A and B (viz. of their own contents). But on closer inspection it emerges that this is not what Fichte's *das Durch* is all about. On the contrary, as mentioned before, the point is that the transition between A and B must be rooted both in A and in B; the point is a continuous thread of intelligibility and insight between A and B. In short, the point is that we cannot deal with cognitive contents like independent Lego pieces; the point is the need for what might be described as one and the same intrinsically complex content, encompassing both A and B and their intrinsic connection with each other. To sum up, Fichte's *das Durch* has to do with the very opposite of any Lego content, be that A, B, or the transition from A to B, and so on. As Fichte puts it, it is all about a *thread* of continuous intelligibility running throughout all cognitive contents in question.

But this is not all. Even if he does not say why *das Durch* is so important, Fichte is not just claiming that there are two possible ways of conceiving the connection between various cognitive contents. His point is rather that the first does not meet essential requirements intrinsic to the very idea of knowledge. It is not a question of excessive ambition (of cognitive megalomania or cognitive "nitpicking"); regardless of whether Fichte's desideratum is or is not attainable, it is not a question of *desider-*

ium inane. It is something entailed in the very idea of knowledge, and in what knowledge is all about. In other words, the point is that if a cognitive manifold is dotted with cognitive gaps and with the kind of empty gap filler Fichte's "das leere Flickwort *und*" stands for (if it is nothing but the said cognitive discontinuity in the guise of continuity), it collides with the work description of knowledge as such—with the set of specifications proper to it (viz. with what must be attained if there is to be any real knowledge at all). In short, the realm of "das leere Flickwort *und*" is undermined and compromised as knowledge: it simply will not do. As such, knowledge must take the shape of the *Durch*.

Finally, this brings us to the "odyssey of the *Durch*." It is no exaggeration to speak of an *odyssey* because what is at stake here is nothing less than a radical change of perspective. In the final analysis, the cognitive task or the cognitive program Fichte's *das Durch* stands for has a very wide scope: it has to do with a radical and massive change. It is not just a question of a particular A and a particular B (or, for that matter, a particular C and D, etc.). The change Fichte is referring to concerns the whole field of knowledge (and the connection between all its contents, without exception). In short, the claim is that in order to meet the formal requirements intrinsic to the very idea of knowledge, nothing less than the whole field of knowledge must take the form of an overarching *Durch*. And it is almost needless to say that pretty much the same applies to the whole cognitive drama the *1804 Wissenschaftslehre* is all about.

To be sure, as mentioned above, there is no explicit mention of *das Durch* before the Seventh Lecture. But it should be noted that what we are dealing with here is the very opposite of an encapsulated insight that does not concern or affect the other dramatis personae of the 1804 lectures. Quite the reverse is actually the case: everything else must meet this essential cognitive requirement. The distinctive awareness of "das leere Flickwort *und*" and that something like a *Durch* is absolutely essential to real knowledge draws our attention to the fact that the "new wine" of the *Wissenschaftslehre* should not be put in the "old skins" (namely in the old skin of "das leere Flickwort *und*," i.e., of the *synthesis post factum*). In every case, the old skin must be replaced by something new—namely, *das Durch*. In fact, if it is to provide real knowledge and be true to its own principle, the whole cognitive drama the *1804 Wissenschaftslehre* is all about must take this new form. And this, in turn, means that the dramatis personae (the cognitive dramatis personae playing a role in the 1804 lectures) must be related to each other in a very specific way. As pointed out above, they are not insulated from each other:

they affect and transform each other (so that the spiral of reflection we have spoken about amounts to something like A × B × C × D). But this is not all. The point now is that there must be some kind of essential inclusion of each of them in all the others. In other words, there must be a continuous thread of intelligibility leading from one cognitive dramatis persona to the other (they cannot be linked by an empty "*Und*": there must be a *Durch* between them—or they must be part and parcel of the very same *Durch*). Or else they must fall and give way to other dramatis personae precisely because they fail to meet this requirement.

In short, this new development raises the bar so that the *Durch* is part of the very demanding set of specifications the *1804 Wissenschaftslehre* is supposed to meet and by which it should be judged.

"*Und*" and *Durch* in Other Fichtean Texts from the Same Period

Contrary to what may seem to be the case, this passage on "das leere Flickwort *und*" from the Seventh Lecture is not an isolated reference. There are parallel references to this topic both in the *1804 Wissenschaftslehre* and in other texts from this period, notably in *Zur Ausarbeitung der Wissenschaftslehre*, in the *Propädeutik Erlangen*, in the so-called *erster Vortrag*, in the *1805 Wissenschaftslehre*, and in *Die Principien der Gottes-, Sitten- und Rechtslehre*. Let us take a brief look at them.

First, in many different contexts Fichte insists on the key idea that in our usual representational world many (and indeed most) terms are connected *per hiatum* (he speaks of *Hiatus, Lücke, Kluft*, etc.). This notion does not play a pivotal role just in a certain context (notably when Fichte focuses on the *projectio per hiatum absolutum* viz. per *hiatum irrationalem*).[11] As a matter of fact, it has to do with a general problem concerning the connection between any two terms. In the *Propädeutik Erlangen* he writes: "*There is no continuous progress between A and B, but a hiatus.*"[12] In *Zur Ausarbeitung der Wissenschaftslehre* we can read: "*In the transition from one form of thought to the other there is no continuity, no line, but an absolute leap through the void, two points placed in a sequence.*"[13] In the *1804 Wissenschaftslehre* (Fourteenth Lecture) he speaks of an *Abbrechen des Intelligierens*,[14] that is, of the rupture of intellectual insight or the interruption of intellection—and therefore of a gap in understanding, and he reminds us that the gap he is referring to is "unable to give a proper account of itself" (*ohne gehörige*

Rechenschaft von sich ablegen zu können). In the *1805 Wissenschaftslehre* he calls it an *unbegreiflicher Zusammenhang* ("incomprehensible connection")[15] and a *Hiatus in der Continuität des Ersehens*[16] ("hiatus in the continuity of one's grasp or understanding").

Secondly, this notion that there is something like an interrupted thread of intellection or insight is associated with both an analysis of the "*und*" as such (not the grammatical "*und*" but what we have termed the *representational* "*und*") and the idea that the latter is, as it were, a *representational Flickwort*—the result being the claim that our usual representational world is largely nothing but *Flickwerk* or patchwork.

The *1805 Wissenschaftslehre* is particularly clear in this regard. Fichte contrasts what he terms the *logical* "*und*" viz. the logical "both" (the one he is referring to in the *1804 Wissenschaftslehre*) and the *transcendental* "*und*" (the *transcendental* "both"). He describes the former in the following terms: "A logical 'both' and logical 'and,' stapling together and, if I may say so, mending [patching, cobbling] different things."[17] All emphasis is thus put on the fact that the various terms in question are *sewn* or *patched* together, but in such a way that there remains a *leap* or *discontinuity* between them so that the tissue of our representations is anything but seamless. This idea is enhanced by the contrast with what Fichte terms the *transcendental* "*und*": "Neither without the other: both not only in *external* but in internal and organic unity. A transcendental 'And, making opposites flow into each other to the point of interpenetration (*Ein transcendentales, entgegengesetzte bis zur Durchdringung in einander überfliessendes und*)."[18] This is of course, a very acute and lively description of *das Durch*.

The same idea is expressed in *Die Principien der Gottes-, Sitten- und Rechtslehre*, when Fichte describes the basic structure of our usual representation as follows: "Beide Bestandtheile bloß zu einander hinzu zählen, und sie durch einen dritten in ihnen nicht liegenden, bloß an einander heften lassen, sondern wir mussen sie innerlich, u. organisch sich durchdringen lassen."[19] Once again, the point is that various elements are stitched together, and that the presence of a connecting operator does not change the fact that there is no continuous intelligible connection between the terms in question so that, at the end of the day, there is nothing but a blind leap between them.

In the *erster Vortrag* (*1804 Wissenschaftslehre*[1]) Latin's characteristic conciseness enables Fichte to sum up his view in a very clear and compelling manner: "*Zusammenfliken der Wahrheit. Oculi plus quam oculus.* ("Patching-together [mending-together] of truth. [Multiple] eyes instead of [just] one eye.")[20] It is not that difficult to see what he has in mind. On the one hand, once again the idea of *Flicken, Zusammenflicken*, and the like; on the other hand, this intriguing formulation: "oculi plus quam oculus" (*multiple eyes rather than one*). That is, Fichte is conveying the idea that whether we are aware of it or not, the manifold of our usual representation is like a cubist picture: the connection between A and B (the connection between our A's and B's, between the *oculus* seeing A and the *oculus* seeing B) resembles a *mosaic of fragments*—viz. the cubist juxtaposition of disassembled planes not linked by the flow of uninterrupted surface transitions. Put another way, just as in a cubist painting, here too the various components of our usual representation are *side by side*, but they are not really *integrated*; there is no real transition from the sight of A to the sight of B, and so on. In sum, the *oculi* between the *oculi* (the eyes between the eyes: the "intermediate eyes" needed to make one single *oculus* out of the fragmentary *oculi* Fichte refers to) are missing. The main difference is that whereas in the case of a cubist picture we immediately notice that there is no uninterrupted flow and that the transitions are missing, in the case of our usual representational world what Fichte terms "das leere *Flickwort und*" creates the illusion of integration and uninterrupted flow (i.e., the illusion of one continuous *oculus*), where in fact there is none, and all disparate and fragmentary *oculi* are connected by nothing but blind spots: leaps and the cognitive fig leaf (the empty filler "*und*") concealing them.[21]

Thirdly, other passages confirm that in Fichte's view the task is to ensure the complete elimination of all such hiatuses and fillers. This is not the place to review all the passages in question, and we must limit ourselves to considering just one from the *erster Vortrag*. Fichte writes: "So there is a hiatus between the two. This need not be the case. . . . So what should be placed between the two? Just continuity, so that one could see immediately how both are connected, the eye could follow the genesis of the connection, and be itself the genetic connection . . . immediate merging of unity into the sequence, and vice versa (*Verschmelzen der Einheit in die Folge, u. umgekehrt*). Let oneness be a sequence, and sequence itself oneness . . . (*unmittelbares Verschmelzen der Einheit in die Folge, u. umgekehrt. Die Einheit sey Folge, u. die Folge selber sey Einheit.*"[22] One of the reasons for choosing this passage is the fact that it provides a clear identikit picture, as it were, of what *das Durch* is all about. Fichte speaks of "Einheit und Folge"—that is, of unit/ unity and sequence (succession viz. string). *Einheit* stands here for A, B, C, etc., for their respective content (namely the identity of each of them with itself). *Folge* stands for the transition from A to B, from B to C, viz. for the manifold as such. And according to this passage, the aim is nothing less than complete *Verschmelzen der Einheit in die Folge, u. umgekehrt*. In other words, the task is to achieve complete fusion of one into the other, so that (1) each term entails in itself the transition to the other and (2) the transition entails in itself both its *terminus a quo* and its *terminus ad quem*. As a result, *Einheit* and *Folge* become exactly the same (*Die Einheit sey Folge, u. die Folge selber sey Einheit*), and there is nothing but a continual flow. Some lines further down, Fichte insists on this by saying: "It is therefore unity and sequence (principle of the sequence of two entailed in it) and, if one is to understand this correctly: stationary and flowing, immanent and emanent, itself unity and disuniting [or disjunting], in absolute unity of essence (*stehend und ausfliessend, immanent und emanent, Einheit und disjungierend selbst in absoluter WesensEinheit*)."[23] That is, the *Wissenschaftslehre* aims at achieving complete interpenetration, absolute essential unity or rather oneness (absolute *WesensEinheit*) between the stationary (each A being itself and remaining in itself: *stehend*) and the flowing or effluent (each A being the *terminus a quo* of a transition to something else: *ausfliessend*), between the immanent and the emanent (*immanent u. emanent*), and between conjunction and disjunction (*Einheit u. disjungierend*). And the point is that, at the end of the day, these are just different ways of expressing the same thing—namely, *das Durch*.

Finally, let us take into account the methodological remarks made by Fichte in the Ninth Lecture. He writes:

> This observation provides exactly the right task for our further procedure; and I wish that we could come to know this procedure in its unity right now in advance, so that we would not go astray among the various forms and changes which it may assume as we go along, would easily recognize the very same procedure in every possible circumstance only with this or that modification, and would know which modification it was and from whence it comes. The genetic relation whose interruption has come to light must be established. This cannot simply be done by inserting new terms and thereby filling the gap, for where would we get them? We are scarcely capable of adding something in thought where nothing exists. Therefore, the genetic relation which is currently missing must be found in the terms already available; we have not yet considered them correctly, i.e., completely genetically, but so far still only considered them in part factically.[24]

But what does this mean?

First, Fichte highlights the fact that his modus operandi is always the same. According to him, it is always a question of identifying the gaps or interruptions and trying to fill them (we might add that it is always a question of debunking and exposing the empty fillers, thereby paving the way for identifying the gaps or interruptions and filling them). He could hardly be more explicit about his claim that the *Wissenschaftslehre* is, from start to finish, an "odyssey of the *Durch*." Secondly, he points out that this cannot simply be done by inserting new terms. The crux of the matter is that the real transitions or connections Fichte is looking for—that is, the *Durch*—must be found in the terms already available. In other words, it is never a question of *Hinzudenken* (*Hinzudenken Etwas, wo Nichts ist*: of "adding something in thought where nothing exists"). Hence the key for attaining the kind of continuous insight Fichte's *Durch* stands for is a thorough reconsideration of the terms already available, viz. of the interrupted lines one is dealing with.

A Bridgehead in the Realm of *das Durch*: The *Durch* between Image and the Imaged

Having said that, it is time now to turn our attention to the fact that the Seventh Lecture does not limit itself to focus on the "*Durch*" as a cognitive requirement. As pointed out above, there is a second aspect to it, and this second aspect is no less important. We can even say that that, in a way, it is the key point. The second aspect we are referring to has to do with a *deformalization*, as it were, of the *Durch*—with a concrete instance of it, namely image, viz. with the intrinsic link between image (*das Bild*) and the imaged (*das Abgebildete*) and with the fact that this intrinsic link illustrates and therefore enables us to see what the "*Durch*" is all about.

But in what sense is what Fichte terms "*das Bild*," "the image" (viz. the link between the image and the imaged) of such a nature that it illustrates *das Durch*? In order to answer this question, we will take a quick glance at the context.

It all begins with a renewed discussion of *Begriff*, viz. of the *Objektivierung* by means of which pure light (*das reine Licht* in the Fichtean sense of the word) becomes an object. For anything to become an object there must be a concept (*Begriff*) of it so that the relation to it is, as it were, mediated by the concept in question: "The light is in us (that is, in what we ourselves are and do in observing it) not *immediately* but rather through a *representative* or *proxy* (durch einen *Repräsentanten* und *Stellverteter*), which objectifies it as such, and so kills it."[25] Fichte focuses on "*das betrachtete Licht*" (light witnessed from an observation point, as it were, so that it is observed and considered as light and therefore becomes *observed* light: light seized or grasped as light).

At this point he is trying to carry out a twofold task. In a way, he is describing what might be termed the *Ur-objektivierung* or the *Ur-Betrachtung* (the primordial-objectification or primordial-consideration/observation)—namely, the *Objektivierung des Lichts*: the objectification of light in the sense this word has in the 1804 lectures. And that is why he says he is speaking of the *Ur-begriff*[26] (the primordial concept). But this is only part of the picture. For at the same time he is also trying to get an insight into *Objectivierung* or *Betrachtung* (objectification or consideration/observation) as such. As he puts it, his remarks focus on "this observing (or considering) itself, in its inner form."[27] In this regard, his point is that, at the end of the day, *Betrachtung* or *Objektivierung* is essentially an image: a *Stellvertreter* and *Abbild* (i.e., something constituted in such a way that it sets up a relation to an object and does so by presenting itself as a *Stellvertreter* and *Abbild*—as a representant or proxy and copy or likeness—of the object in question, i.e., of what it images).

In this regard Fichte contrasts three different layers:

1. Das *Aufgehen*, in this case the *Aufgehen im Licht* (being completely absorbed in it and merged into it, in which case the light he is referring to does not even appear as such or as an object, for one is too close to see it);

2. *Objektivierung* (objectifying or objectification), that is, image (*Bild*) or *Begriff*. In other words, the *Stellvertreter und Abbild*: a representant or proxy and copy or likeness that brings about a mediated relation to something and thereby creates the conditions for it to appear—in this case the copy or likeness of light in the Fichtean sense of the word;

3. The essential link between image and the imaged—i.e., between the representant (proxy, copy or likeness) and whatever it stands for.

The difference between this third layer and the second lies in the fact that the essential link Fichte is now referring to transcends or goes beyond the image as such (i.e., the representant or proxy, the copy or likeness as such)—and indeed so much so that the image as such is just a *moment* of the complex unity in question.

And this is precisely the point. Fichte stresses the fact that once the image comes into the picture, the *Einheitspunkt* or *Mittelpunkt* is transferred from the pure light, viz. the *Aufgehen* in it (being completely *absorbed* in it), and indeed from the *Stellvertreter* und *Repräsentant* or *Bild* (i.e., the *image* itself), to the essential link between the *image* and the *imaged*. Put another way: the protagonist—the "torch-bearer" (the "wick" of it all: *der Träger aller Realität im Wissen*)—is now the essential connection between the image and the imaged (*das Bild* and *das Abgebildete*) viz. representation and what is represented in it (*Repräsentation* and *das darin Repräsentierte*):

> So then, where does the highest oneness and the true principle now rest? No longer, as above, in the light itself, since we, as living, are absorbed in the light (merged into it). Neither [is it] in the representative and image of the light which is to be identified now: because it is clear that a representative without the representation of what is represented or an image without the imaging of what it images, is nothing. In short, an image as such, according to its nature, has no intrinsic self-sufficiency, but rather points toward some external, primordial source (*auf ein ursprüngliches außer ihm*).[28]

Here we reach the key point, namely the connection between image and *das Durch* (the answer to the question as to how the image is of such a nature that it illustrates *das Durch* in the Fichtean sense of the word). On the one hand, Fichte highlights the fact that the image and the imaged are by no means the same, that there is disjunction between them (that they are *Disjunktionsglieder*). On the other hand, he points out that the two *Disjunktionsglieder* in question differ from each other in such a manner that none of them can be without the other (n.b., none of them can be itself— can be what it is—without the other). The image (*das Bild*) cannot be an image without the imaged (*das Abbgebildete*). And, conversely, the imaged (*das Abgebildete*) cannot be something imaged without the image (*das Bild*). "Here, therefore, we have not only, as above, factical manifestness, as with

A and the 'point'; instead [we even have] conceptual manifestness: oneness only with disjunction, and vice versa. 'Even conceptual manifestness,' I say: something imaged—like the light, in this case—is not conceivable without an image, nor likewise an image, qua image, without something imaged."[29]

As Fichte points out, there is what might be described as an intrinsic and comprehensible transition from each *Disjunktionsglied* (image or the imaged, *das Bild* and *das Abgebildete*) to the other. None of them suffices itself: each of them requires the other. As a result, the absolute minimum cannot be just one of them. The absolute minimum requires both; for the very identity of each of them requires and brings into play the other. And what we are dealing with here is an intrinsically complex identity that illustrates what Fichte's *das Durch* is all about.

It is therefore no accident that we can express the link between image and the imaged in the terms used by Fichte in the *erster Vortrag* to characterize *das Durch*: the link between image and the imaged illustrates a complete *Verschmelzen der Einheit in die Folge, u. umgekehrt* ("complete fusion or merging of one into the other and vice versa"), so that each term entails in itself the transition to the other and the transition entails in itself both its *terminus a quo* and its *terminus ad quem*. The link between image and the imaged is such that *Einheit* and *Folge* become exactly the same (as Fichte puts it in the *erster Vortrag*: *Die Einheit sey Folge, u. die Folge selber sey Einheit*)—and there is nothing but a continual flow. In short, the link between image and the imaged shows what complete interpenetration or absolute essential unity (absolute *WesensEinheit*) between the stationary (each A being itself and remaining in itself: *stehend*) and the flowing or effluent (each A being the *terminus a quo* of a transition to something else: *ausfliessend*), between the immanent and the emanent (*immanent u. emanent*), and between conjunction and disjunction (*Einheit u. disjungierend*) is all about. The description fits like a glove.

We can also express this by saying that as far as image and the imaged is concerned, unity—oneness—is intrinsically twofold and duality intrinsically onefold.

Much of the Seventh Lecture is a more thorough analysis of this topic or a deeper reflection on this fundamental insight.

Fichte asks his listeners (viz. his readers) to contemplate what happens when one realizes that the image and the imaged have the kind of connection with each other just outlined:

> Notice this important fact, which will take one deep into the
> subject matter, if it is properly grasped here. In this case you

carry out an act of thinking, which has essence . . . and is fully and completely self-identical and unchangeable in relation to this essence. I cannot share this with you directly, nor can you share it with me; but we can construct it, either from the concept of something imaged which then posits an image, or from the image which then posits something imaged. I ask: apart from the arrangement of the terms, which is irrelevant here—[that is,] as far as the inner content of thinking is concerned—have we then thought two different things in the two concepts thus fulfilled, or is it not rather that we have thought exactly the same thing in both?[30]

He then highlights several points.

Firstly, he insists on the difference between what he terms "the arrangement or the order of the terms" (*die zur Sache gar nicht gehörige Stellung der Glieder*)—namely, the fact that they can be considered "either from the concept of something imaged which then posits an image, or from the image which then posits something imaged"—and the *inner content* of thinking (*den eigentlichen innern Inhalt des Denkens*), or the said essential interrelation or "oneness" between image and the imaged. He then stresses that the former does not prevent the latter and is in fact secondary to the latter:

> The listener must be able to elevate himself so as to abstract, in the manner required here, from the inessential matter of the arrangement or order, and [to elevate himself] to the essential matter, namely the content . . . , and then the insight which is intended will immediately manifest itself to him. Should this indeed be the case, then an *absolute oneness* of content is manifest here that remains unaltered as oneness but that splits itself only in the *vital fulfillment* of thinking into an inessential disjunction, which neither spoils the content in any way nor is grounded in it. Either [there] is an *objective* disjunction into *something imaged* and its *image*, or, if you prefer, [there is] a *subjective-objective* disjunction into a *conception* of something imaged on the basis of the directly posited image, and a *conception* of the image on the basis of the directly posited imaged something.[31]

In other words, Fichte draws our attention to the complex interplay of elements involved in the insight he is talking about. The absolute oneness between image and the imaged is such that the said *either/or* between these two possible ways of looking at it is as rooted in the very nature of the connection between image and the imaged as the essential oneness between them. But the emphasis is on the "relation of forces" between these two aspects, viz. on the difference between the *essential* and the *inessential* (*das Wesentliche* and *das Außerwesentliche*). Or to be more precise, the emphasis is on the claim that the *oneness—das Durch—*between image and the imaged provides the basis for the twofoldness (i.e., for the either/or), and indeed in such a manner that the latter is but a secondary feature of the former.

Secondly, Fichte draws our attention to the absolute validity of the insight he is referring to—that is, to the fact that it attributes to itself nothing less than *unlimited* validity, and indeed so much so that we are incapable of conceiving any real restriction to its validity and the insight in question claims to grasp "truth in itself, which we recognize as being and remaining true even if no one saw it."[32] In other words, the essential oneness—*das Durch*—between image and the imaged is "self-subsistent, totally unchangeable and indestructible."[33]

Thirdly, Fichte contrasts the link between the image and the imaged (i.e., the *Durch*-connection between them) and the very different kind of interaction or reciprocal influence (*gegenseitige Bedingtheit*) that was at stake in previous developments—namely, the *gegenseitige Bedingtheit* in which each term is subject to the influence of the other (A subject to the influence of B and vice versa), but in such a manner that each of them can still be itself (be what it is) without the other (apart of the other):

> "Previously, the concept qualified both life and the appearance of light, and these conversely qualified the concept's being. Therefore, it was a reciprocal influence, and every [act of] thinking the two terms was qualified externally. Now the same single concept grounds its appearance through its own essential being; therefore, in this concept the image and what it images are posited absolutely, things which are constructed organically only through one another. And, hence, its appearance announces, and is the exponent of, its inner being, as an organic unity of the *through-one-another*, which must be presupposed. Its being for itself, permanent and unchanging, and as an inner organization of the *through-one-another*—essential, but in no way externally constructed—are completely one: therefore, in this case, *absolute oneness* is grounded and explained through itself.[34]

Now, this enables us to grasp the main point: Fichte's *das Durch* takes on a concrete shape in the "*innerliche, wesentliche*" "*organische Einheit des Durcheinander*"³⁵ ("inner and essential," "organic unity of the *through-one-another*") between image and the imaged (*Bild und Abgebildetes*). The insight into this *Durcheinander* establishes, as it were, "a first bridgehead" in the realm of *das Durch*.

The *Und* within the *Durch* (the Odyssey Continues)

But this is not all. In a way, it is just half of the picture, for the Seventh Lecture ends with what might be described as a *peripeteia* or reversal of the situation. Fichte reconsiders the fundamental insight in question and presents it in a different light: "In this regard I ask: Does the image, as image, completely and unconditionally posit something imaged? And if you answer 'Yes,' does not the something imaged likewise posit such an image? Now without further ado I admit that both can be seen (by you) as posited immediately by the other, but only if you posit one of the two as prior."³⁶

And he insists on this new aspect:

> That is, I ask about the truth in itself, which we recognize as being and remaining true even if no one saw it, and we ask: Is it not true in itself that the image entails something imaged and vice versa? And, in this case, what exactly is true in itself? Just reduce what remains as a pure truth to the briefest expression. Perhaps that a posits b and b, a? Do we want to divide the true into two parts and then conflate (*allegieren*) these parts with the empty filler "*and*," a word which we scarcely understand and which is the least understandable word in all language, a word which is not explicated by any previous philosophy (it is indeed the synthesis *post factum*)?³⁷

Fichte focuses on a disjunction within the *Durch*-connection between image and the imaged—namely, the disjunction between *b.a* and *a.b*, that is, between positing the image as prior to the imaged or the latter as prior to the former. As he points out, the very insight (the very "truth") he is talking about must take one of the two as prior to the other. It is intrinsically divided into two parts and can—indeed must—take two different forms, depending on whether *a.b* comes before *b.a* or the other way around.[38] To be sure, this whole *either/or* seems to be counterbalanced by the fact that the *Durch*-connection between image and the imaged is a *Durch-einander*—and therefore all about reciprocal implication (*a* entails *b* just as much as *b* entails *a*). But this does not change the fact that the insight in question comprises two parts that are different from one another—and indeed so much so that on closer inspection it emerges that we are not dealing with one but with two insights and that the latter are connected by a "leeres Flickwort *und*"—and not by a *Durch*. Or, as Fichte puts it, we limit ourselves to conflating (*alligieren*) the two.[39]

But there is more. As Fichte points out, it is not just a question of priority. For the two possibilities he is referring to—namely *a* positing *b* (image is prior to the imaged) and *b* positing *a* (the imaged is prior to the image)—stand for two very different *meanings* of *a* and *b*. He writes:

> How could we, since beyond this it is certainly clear that the determination of the terms derives solely from their place in the sequence—for example, that image is the consequent because something imaged is the antecedent, and vice versa.—Furthermore, if one enters more deeply into the meaning and sense of both terms, it is clear that their meaning simply changes itself into the expression "antecedent" and "consequent," while something imaged is really antecedent (*realiter antecedens*) and ideally etc. (*idealiter pp*): thus, all this, in turn, dissolves into appearance. So then, what common element remains behind as the condition for the whole exchange? Obviously only the through-one-another (*nur das eine Durch einander*) that initially holds together every consequence[-relation] however it might have been grasped, and which, as through-one-another (*als Durch einander*), leaves the consequence[-relation] exactly as free in all directions (*allseitig*) as it has appeared to be.[40]

In other words, everything depends on whether image plays the role of the *antecedens*, and the imaged plays the role of the *consequens*, or it is the other way around. And what is more, the very meaning of image and the imaged is at stake. For image as *antecedens* is one thing, as *consequens* it is quite another. And pretty much the same holds true for the imaged. As a matter of fact, the either/or we are dealing with here concerns nothing less than the difference between the *terminus a quo* and the *terminus ad quem* of

Kant's so-called Copernican revolution.⁴¹ So that the difference could hardly be more pronounced. And this in turn means that, in the final analysis, what is at stake here is not just a particular arrangement within the *Durch* between the image and the imaged, but the very nature of the *Durch* in question (i.e., the very nature of the link between image and the imaged).

Hence, what at first seemed to be a *Durch* and nothing but a *Durch* turns out to be undermined by the presence of "das leere Flickwort *und*" viz. of *synthesis post factum*.

Firstly, there is a "leeres Flickwort *und*" between the two said possibilities: the priority of *a.b* versus the priority of *b.a*.

Secondly, there is a "leeres Flickwort *und*" between the *Durch* itself (the *Durch*-connection between image and the imaged) and the two possible arrangements in question: they are both loosely rooted in the said "*Durch*-connection," but in such a manner that the latter seems to be completely neutral with regard to this specific either/or.

Thirdly, the two opposite priorities in question amount to an either/or—a "leeres Flickwort *und*"—between two completely different meanings of the *relata* (image and the imaged).

Fourthly, as a result, the two opposite priorities in question amount to nothing less than an either/or (a "leeres Flickwort *und*") between two completely different meanings of the whole insight in question—that is, an either/or (and a "leeres Flickwort *und*") between two completely different meanings of the *Durch* Fichte is referring to.⁴²

To sum up, it is not exaggerated to say that the seventh session ends by showing that the *Durch* it is all about is permeated with the exact opposite: with "das leere Flickwort *und*" viz. with *synthesis post factum*. The link between image and the imaged seemed to be a bridgehead in the realm of the *Durch*. And in a way it is so. But it turns out to be riddled with hiatuses and fillers (and therefore undermined by a fifth column, as it were, of emptiness and lack of intelligibility). Pretty much like the hero of the Odyssey, when he seems to be already reaching Ithaca but then, all of a sudden, finds himself still with a long way to go.

Notes

1. That is, A through B, C through D, E through F, and so on.
2. *Iliad*, I, 343.
3. *Cratylus*, 399c.

4. 1804², 57; *GA*, II/8, 89.
5. 1804², 64; *GA*, II/8, 105.
6. Cf. Plato, *Laws* 753e, 765e, 775e; and *Republic* 377a.
7. 1804², 65; *GA*, II/8, 107.
8. Kant, *AA*, V/II, 149. For the translation, cf. V. L. Dowdell and H. H. Rudnick, eds., *Kant Anthropology from a Pragmatic Point of View* (Carbondale: Southern Illinois University Press, 1996), 35; and R. B. Louden, ed., *Kant Anthropology from a Pragmatic Point of View* (Cambridge: Cambridge University Press, 2006), 40. On Kant's use of "Flickwort," see notably S. L. Kowalewski and W. Stark, eds., *Königsberger Kantiana* (Hamburg: Meiner, 2000), 297; and F. C. Starke, ed., *I. Kants Menschenkunde*, im Anhang I. Kants Anweisung zur Menschen- und Weltkenntniß nach dessen Vorlesungen im Winterhalbjahre 1790–1791 (Hildesheim, NY: Olms, 1976), 80; and *Refl.* 1482; *AA*, XV, 681. On Flickwörter, see also J. C. Adelung, *Ueber den Deutschen Styl*: Zweiter Band, Besondere Arten des Styles, 3. vermehrte und verbesserte Auflage (Berlin: Voß & Sohn, 1790), 276: "Wörter, welche nicht nur keine anschauliche Vorstellung enthalten, sondern auch in der Reihe der Vorstellungen völlig überflüßig sind, und nur zur Erfüllung des Sylbenmaßes, oder um des Reimes willen gebraucht werden. Solche Wörter werden Flickwörter, und mit einem edlern Ausdrucke Füllwörter genannt. Da sie zugleich wider die Präcision sündigen, so sind sie doppelt fehlerhaft."
9. In a way, Fichte follows in the footsteps of Hume and Kant when they point out that causal connections are based on a *formal connecting operator* so that this connecting operator is in fact *always the same* and provides *no real insight* into its own meaning and, in fact, turns out to be blind. Fichte radicalizes this claim by evincing that, in our usual representational world, pretty much the same holds true for all synthesis. To be sure, there are various synthetic operators (spatial juxtaposition, temporal succession, diachronic identity, substance/accident, causality, subject/object, etc.). But Fichte's point is that each one of them revolves around a central "*und*" so that the latter is, as it were, the *Ur-connecting operator*, and indeed one that is blind and undermined by a hiatus. Hence, our usual representational world turns out to be "*und*"-infested and therefore peppered with a plethora of blind spots, gaps, and leaps. And the only reason why it does not look so is the fact that our usual representational world is anything but accurate, thorough, or sharp-sighted and we have much in common with Mr. Magoo.
10. 1804², 84; *GA*, II/8, 155, emphasis added.
11. See notably *GA*, II/8, 219–21, 225, 231, 249–51, 263, 269, 295, 355, 359–61, and 385.
12. *Propädeutik. Erlangen* (1805), *GA*, II/9, 55.
13. *Zur Ausarbeitung der Wissenschaftslehre*, *GA*, II/6, 57.
14. 1804², 112; *GA*, II/ 8, 221.
15. *WL 1805*, *GA*, II/9, 187.
16. *WL 1805*, *GA*, II/9, 222.

17. *WL*, 1805; *GA*, II/9, 193.
18. *WL*, 1805; *GA*, II/9, 193.
19. *Die Principien der Gottes-Sitten-u. Rechtlehre*; *GA*, II/7, 426.
20. *WL*, 1804[1]; *GA*, II/7, 77.
21. Bear in mind that the lack of flow (the disassembled planes) we are talking about is by no means specific to Cubism, as though the latter were something artificial and had nothing whatsoever to do with "normal" perception. As a matter of fact, Cubism touches on a weak spot of "normal" perception. It draws our attention to a fundamental feature of our usual representational world, which is continuously going on in it whether we are aware of it or not. It all has to do with what Husserl termed *Abschattungen* or *adumbrations*: the fact that any given three-dimensional object is split into a series of disassembled adumbrations (at one time from this side, then from another, etc. in such a manner that there is always a geometrical ratio between the surfaces or planes acting as adumbrations and the whole adumbrated three-dimensional object they stand for). If you take a closer look at this phenomenon, you will find that each particular *Abschattung* refers to all the others (that is why you can speak of an *Abschattung* in the first place) but in such a way that what you really have in each case is just the single *Abschattung* in question + a merely symbolical reference to all the others, and when you change what Leibniz termed the *intuentis situs* and look at the same three-dimensional object from another angle you have another particular *Abschattung*, and once again everything else—including the previous *Abschattung(en)*—in a purely symbolic manner (in the Leibnizean sense of the word). In short, each *Abschattung* is constituted in such a way that the surfaces or planes acting as adumbrations are its sole really intuitive component: everything else (the reference to other adumbrations) might be described as purely symbolic "suspension marks" that refer to concrete contents but without providing any real intuition or perception of them. As a result, each *Abschattung* loses sight of almost all the others, and more importantly it has no idea of how any two different *Abschattungen* are connected and flow into each other. What is more, in our usual perception of the world, all different *Abschattungen* or adumbrations of the same three-dimensional object are linked by a synthesis of succession, not by a *synthesis of simultaneity*—when simultaneity between its parts is what any three-dimensional object is all about. At the end of the day, we have absolutely no idea of what the simultaneous integration of two different *Abschattungen* or adumbrations—let alone the simultaneous synthesis of all *Abschattungen* (from all possible, interior, and exterior angles)—really looks like.

To sum up, all our usual perception of three-dimensional objects is intrinsically fragmentary: everything is given in instalments, as it were; there is no real transition, no real connection—no simultaneous transition-content—between any different *Abschattungen*; and the ensuing gaps are filled by a representational "leeres Flickwort *und*," which makes us perceive the synthesis of succession between all different *Abschattungen* as a synthesis of simultaneity so that we constantly mistake scattered puzzle pieces for the missing whole. Cubism has the merit of highlighting this phenomenon.

22. *WL*, 1804[1], *GA*, II/7, 129.
23. *WL*, 1804/I, *GA*, II/7, 130.
24. 1804[2], 75; *GA*, II/8, 131.
25. 1804[2], 63; *GA*, II/8, 101. Cf. 1804[2], 80; *GA*, II/8, 143, 147.
26. 1804[2], 63; *GA*, II/8, 103.
27. 1804[2], 63; *GA*, II/8, 101.
28. 1804[2], 63; *GA*, II/8, 101.
29. 1804[2], 63; *GA*, II/8, 101–3.
30. 1804[2], 63; *GA*, II/8, 103.
31. 1804[2], 63; *GA*, II/8, 103.
32. 1804[2], 65; *GA*, II/8, 107.
33. 1804[2], 64; *GA*, II/8, 105.
34. 1804[2], 64; *GA*, II/8, 105.

35. 1804[2], 64; *GA*, II/8, 105. See also *GA*, II/8, 107 ("das reine Durch einander"); and, in the ninth session, *GA*, II/8, 129, 131.

36. 1804[2], 64–65; *GA*, II/8, 105–7.
37. 1804[2], 65; *GA*, II/8, 105–7.

38. This is why in the Tenth Lecture (1804[2], 84; *GA*, II/8, 155) Fichte expresses this by saying that the insight into the *Durch* has a factical support, viz. a factical "carrier" (*einen faktischen Träger*): "The concept's inward and completely immutable essence has already been acknowledged in an earlier lecture as a '*through*.' Although in its content this insight is in no way factical but grasped purely by the intellect, nevertheless it has a factical support [or "carrier"] (*einen faktischen Träger*): the construction of the image and the thing imaged, and the indifference of the consequence[-relation] between them."

39. Wright's translation is flawed, for he renders "alligieren" with "link"—and thereby misses the whole point. As a matter of fact, "alligieren" and "Alligation" are used by Fichte to convey not the general idea of connection, link and the like, but the specific idea of *conflation*: of a "patchwork"-conjunction (of what Kant used to term *aggregatum, farrago, coacervatio*, etc.). See notably *System der Sittenlehre* 1798; *GA*, I/5, 116; Darstellung *WL*, 1801/2; *GA*, II/6, 289.

40. 1804[2], 65; *GA*, II/8, 107.

41. Both in the Seventh and in the Tenth Lecture Fichte expresses this by the contrast between "idealiter" and "realiter"—that is, between what might be termed the *idealiter-version* and the *realiter-version* of the *Durch* between image and the imaged. Cf. *GA*, II/8, 107–9 and note 52 below. But in order to fully understand this point, it should be borne in mind that Fichte is not just referring to the contrast between the imaged as something *existing beyond representational life* and image as an *essential component of the latter*. His point is that the contrast in question also

applies to what he terms *Objektivierung*, i.e., to the connection between *Begriff* on the one hand and its object on the other—even when the latter, too, is an inner component of (viz. something essentially belonging to) one's "representational life." In other words, what is at stake here is an overarching either/or so that there is room for what might be described as a repetition or reenactment of Kant's so-called Copernican revolution within the framework of one's representational life—i.e., with regard to its various components. And in particular, the point is that there is room for a repetition or reenactment of Kant's so-called Copernican revolution between (1) *Objektivierung* or *Begriff* as the image and (2) the object of *Objektivierung* as the imaged. The result being an either/or between what might be termed the *realiter-version* and the *idealiter-version* of *Begriff*.

42. In the Ninth Lecture (1804², 73; *GA*, II/8, 127) Fichte expresses this with a formula:

B. L. S. (or, B. S. L.)

In this formula "B" stands for *Bild*, "L" for *Licht*—that is, for *das Abgebildete* (so that the formula could also read: B. A. S.). "S" stands for *Succession*—that is, for *Succession* und *Consequenz*. This means for the aforementioned either/or between *a.b* and *b.a* (i.e., {*a* as *antecedens*/*b* as *consequens*} versus {*a* as *consequens*/*b* as antecedens}). This means that "S" also stands for "das leere Flickwort *und*" (the *synthesis post factum*) between *das Durch* itself and the two alternatives in question, as well as for the either/or ("das leere Flickwort *und*") between two *completely different meanings* of *a* and *b*, and, last but not least, for two completely different meanings of the *Durch* between *a* and *b* (i.e., for the two completely different meanings of *Begriff*).

In other words, the formula "B. L. S." expresses (1) the *Durch* between image and the imaged (B. L.)—or, as Fichte puts it in the ninth session "ein blosses Durch einander, ohne alle Consequenz d. i. ohne antecedens und Consequens" (1804², 74; *GA*, II/8, 129) and (2) "S" (Succession), that is, the said either/or (*antecedens und consequens*): the *asymmetrical* element within the *Durch* and the fact that this asymmetrical element spells out nothing less than what might be described as two very different versions of the *Durch* (and in this sense nothing less than two very different *Durch*'s between image and the imaged). To sum up, "S" expresses the fact that the *Durch* between image and the imaged is riddled with the opposite: with "das leere Flickwort Durch."

The latter aspect is highlighted at the end of the seventh session, when Fichte speaks of the *either/or* between what he terms "das abgebildete realiter antecedens, und idealiter pp" (1804², 65; *GA*, II/8, 107) viz. "Akt und Consequenz entweder *idealiter*, oder *realiter*" (1804², 65; *GA*, II/8, 107–9) and then presents the following diagram:

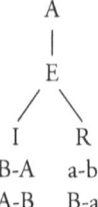

In this diagram "I" stands for *idealiter*, "R" for *realiter*. "$\frac{B\text{-}A}{A\text{-}B}$" stands for b.a (image as *antecedens* and the imaged as *consequens*—that is, the *I-version* of the reciprocal implication viz. of the Durch), while "$\frac{a\text{-}b}{B\text{-}a}$" stands for a.b, that is, for the R-version of the reciprocal implication viz. of the *Durch*.

Chapter 9

The "We" of Speculative Philosophy

BENJAMIN D. CROWE

While few doubt the importance of Fichte's 1804 lecture cycle on the *Wissenschaftslehre*, fewer still would challenge the observation that it is among the more difficult and enigmatic products of the classical era in German philosophy.[1] There are different ways to go about unraveling some of the interpretive mysteries this material presents; here, I follow up some clues from Fichte himself. In the manuscript for the *1804 Wissenschaftslehre*, Fichte warns against approaching his philosophy in a "*bloße historisch*" manner. What he means is that, despite its title, one should not approach his philosophy as a doctrine (*Lehre*) alongside others. Fichte does, however, situate his philosophical project historically in another sense, by joining in the debates of the era and by contextualizing his ideas in the larger sweep of the history of thought. Fichte also liked to say that each presentation of the *Wissenschaftslehre*, whether written or oral, was uniquely dissimilar from all the others, while his system as such is a single *geistige Einheit*, an organic whole of reciprocally determining principles, each of which is essential for all the rest.

From early in his career, Fichte stressed the importance of adopting the *perspective* that grounds the distinctive knowledge claims of philosophy. The conceptual and methodological bonds between a free act of reflection whereby one steps out of the immediacy of the empirical domain and the self-positing I that is the principle of the "first system of freedom" are deep indeed. The philosophical perspective is, as Fichte stresses again and again, not a *Lehre* but an activity, a self-activity that discloses the structure of self-activity as such. In the 1804 lectures, Fichte thematizes this bond between perspective and principle as the "We." The "We" is a perspective in which individuals *actively* participate that brings with it insight into its own necessary structure. Fichte here frames the adoption of the "We" as rejoinder to Jacobi's skepticism about speculative philosophy. The "We" is a self-certifying point of view that defines rationality in the theoretical, practical, religious, and aesthetic domains. Comparing Fichte's discussions of the "We" in the *1804 Wissenschaftslehre* with those found in other texts from his Berlin years both demonstrates its systematic significance and determines the contours of the idea more precisely.

In the Eighteenth Lecture of the *1804 Wissenschaftslehre*, Fichte compares his current "system" with the view of F. H. Jacobi, who, in contrast with Reinhold and Schelling, comes out fairly well. What Fichte here labels Jacobi's "system" is the *Unphilosophie* that Jacobi had proclaimed in his open letter to Fichte of 1799. Fichte describes the main claim this way: "With great philosophical talent Jacobi tries to jettison philosophy itself."[2] Unfortunately, in so doing Jacobi thereby "flatters the prevailing indolence and denial toward philosophy."[3] According to Jacobi, from the "right-side-up" point of view, taking things to be the way they seem is the natural stance. To claim to grasp "being in itself" behind or beyond the appearances is to abandon common sense and natural reflection (*Besinnung*) and to enter a domain of lifeless abstractions, fictions, and nonentities.[4] What Jacobi tries to "jettison" is the very possibility of speculative knowledge.

Fichte takes Jacobi's argument to begin with the observation that philosophical concepts concern abstractions. From there, Jacobi charges speculative philosophers with hypostasizing these abstractions and substituting the constructed "explanation" for the thing itself. Fichte grants Jacobi the point that philosophical theorizing is undetermined by the givens of experience and that it relies on a constructive method. Moreover, he claims to agree wholeheartedly with Jacobi's claim that "philosophy should reveal and discover *being in and of itself*."[5] Fichte therefore ranks Jacobi higher than those "who just fool around with nature and with reason." Hence, the seriousness of Jacobi's challenge to the kind of philosophy Fichte pursues; it cannot discover "being in and of itself" but only provide a "display of our productive imagination." For Fichte, this would mean that where once the completed system of reason beckoned, we must now be contented with "edifying remarks for every day of the year."[6]

In the *1804 Wissenschaftslehre* Fichte is thus partly concerned to show that philosophical knowledge of "being in and of itself" *is* possible; indeed, the burden of the lectures is to show in a very direct way that it exists, by "providing the terms for insight," which "each individual must fulfill . . . in himself," thereby coming to have the very knowledge the possibility of which Jacobi has denied. The *Wissenschaftslehre* stakes a claim to knowledge of the "supersensible substrate" of nature and freedom, the unconditioned or Absolute, that Kant had left as something undeterminable.[7] Fichte maintains that the *Wissenschaftslehre* can succeed in tracing the factical back to its genesis, in fulfilling the ancient philosophical quest to resolve the many into the one, but only if philosophical or a priori knowledge is actually possible. So, Fichte's first move is to grant the truth of Jacobi's skepticism, but only *to a limited extent*. He writes: "*We*, the we who can only reconstruct, cannot do philosophy: equally, there is no philosophy individually and personally; instead philosophy must just be, but this is possible only to the extent that we perish, along with all reconstruction, and pure reason emerges pure and alone; since the latter in its purity is philosophy itself. From the perspective of 'we' or 'I' there is non-philosophy; there is only one [once one has gone] beyond the I."[8]

Fichte is using "philosophy" in this passage in a normative register, or as he would say, as designating a "task" (*Aufgabe*). There is an activity called "philosophy" that people engage in, but it is bound to fail to discover "being in and of itself." But, viewed "from above," as it were, there remains the possibility of philosophy in the *proper* sense. Put another way: Fichte grants that Jacobi is quite right that philosophy is impossible for *us*, but there is the suggestion of more than one "we," such that only the ordinary "we"—a collection of individuals—is incapable of discovering "being in and of itself." There is another *we* that does not simply "reconstruct" reality. This other "we"—only dubbed as such elsewhere—*is* what Fichte calls in this passage "pure reason." Fichte agrees with Jacobi that speculative knowledge cannot rest on the reconstruction of the given by means of abstractions. But he disagrees with Jacobi in maintaining that "being in and of itself" just *is* knowing, which is something that *we* can ourselves know, because we *are* it.

Back upstream, however, Fichte's initial point is just that Jacobi's own position implies a higher point of view. For "when he *says*: we can only reconstruct, he achieves ipso facto in that very moment something more than re-construction, and has at least drawn himself happily out of the 'We' of which we have spoken."[9] Otherwise, how could he be so confident in the universal judgment that "we can only reconstruct"? That is, Jacobi's skepticism assumes a distinction between being and a mere reconstruction of being in thought that requires already having a grasp on "something original, independent prior to all construction" in order to ground the distinction.[10] Jacobi can only assert things about "us" because he has a priori knowledge of the difference between "our" point of view and "being in and of itself."

There is a promissory note at the core of the *1804 Wissenschaftslehre*. As he later notes, a system that remains merely "hypothetical" at the end of the day has failed to overcome the specter of "absolute skepticism."[11] Fichte has only shown that Jacobi's objection to the possibility of speculative knowledge is inconsistent. What is required is what he later describes as an "ascent . . . undertaken . . . for clearing our vision and opening it to the absolute by abstracting from all relations."[12] This "ascent" is itself premised on skepticism—or rather on the kernel of truth in Jacobi's own skepticism, once properly understood to apply to "mere consciousness" and its illusion of an irrational *hiatus* or gap between subject and object.[13] That is, coming to doubt the apparent validity of the empirical point of view by reflecting upon it constitutes a step toward truth.

Readers of some of Fichte's other principal works will find a parallel between his remarks here about going "beyond the I" and his characterization of moral striving, for instance in the *System of Ethics* of 1798. There, to take just one example, Fichte writes that "it is precisely by means of this disappearance and annihilation of one's entire *individuality* that everyone becomes a pure presentation of the moral law in the world of sense and thus becomes a 'pure I.'"[14] This vision of the progressive overcoming of individuality and the emergence of a unified *Geist* can be found in Fichte's later lectures on ethics (1812) and, elaborated in "popular" form, in *The Way towards the Blessed Life* (1806). The trajectory of the moral life and the path of scientific inquiry turn out to both involve the overcoming of our given or "factical" individuality and transposition into a different condition, one that is essentially common. We become the "We." The *1804 Wissenschaftslehre* is an exercise in this very self-overcoming, in transcending our conditioned, empirical selves for the sake of a higher unity grounded in reason.

At the start of his 1804 lectures, Fichte spends several sessions providing a general characterization of the *Wissenschaftslehre* and setting forth some of the preconditions understanding his system. He says there that his ideal listener is really a co-investigator, that is, "one who is able to reproduce the lecture for himself at home, not literally {*unmittelbar*} for that would be mechanical memory, but by pondering and reflection."[15] This, in turn, means that one must possess a "living *image of this oneness*," that is, a non-objectifying insight into the unitary genetic ground of factical experience, which can then serve as a criterion *and* aim for reflection.[16] All "philosophy," says Fichte, ultimately involves tracing back the multiplicity (*Mannigfaltigkeit*) of the given back to the "One." Philosophical systems differ in terms of how they characterize this unitary ground. The "oneness" in the *Wissenschaftslehre* is "inwardly living, active and powerful."[17] It is not an object or an "in itself," however, but rather is "what *we* are, and pursue, and live" (loc. cit.; emphasis added). The key question for Fichte's *philosophia prima*, then, is how one can have scientific insight into this ground—variously called the absolute, being, light, and reason, all interchangeable designations that bear little on the argument itself according to Fichte—without objectifying it and thus canceling any hope of knowledge.

Such access first involves the overcoming of individual obstacles to inquiry, such as inattention, prior to embarking on the "constructive" task, which involves the careful construction of concepts and then the juxtaposition or "holding together" of what has been constructed. In this way "without any assistance from us, an insight will spring up *by itself*, like a lightning flash."[18] Fichte's presentation of his system has the advantage that the "*same thing* is constantly repeated in the most various terms," providing many alternate occasions for the sought after insight.

But, at the end of the day, Fichte's presentation also puts a demand on those who would try to understand it. This demand falls upon "minds *as such*," abstracting away from differences in mental capacity such as speed of thought. It is the demand to escape the illusion "that you yourself are the very thing that objectively posits {*objectiviert*} this one knowing, that you therefore are the subject with it as your object."[19] This "illusion" is precisely what afflicts the ordinary "us," upon whose philosophical ambitions Jacobi rightly casts doubt according to Fichte. Adopting my habitual, individual point of view gives the impression that the concepts I construct are *mine* in some superlative sense and are somehow indexed to my own subjectivity; Jacobi's point, which Fichte endorses here, is that a system composed of them is at best a kind of projection of my own mind, revealing a lot more about me than about any "reality." But again, the responsibility rests on individual minds "as such," and the return of this illusion reflects the fact that you "only entered half way, you never threw yourself into, and rooted yourself in, this insight."[20]

Fichte's discussion of the conditions or occasions of philosophical insight then takes a moralizing direction, perhaps already prefigured in his strident insistence on a universal demand devolved to each individual.

He abruptly ascribes many of the obstacles to understanding to a "lack in one's love of science," which turns out to be an expression of the same "ruling passions" that ultimately preclude "love of the absolute (or God)," which "is the rational spirit's true element, in which alone it finds peace and blessedness."[21] At its nadir, this lack of love turns into positive hatred, itself rooted in selfishness and reflected in the dogmatist's being "unwilling to admit that anything could occur in the domain of knowing that [he] had not itself discovered, and long been aware of."[22] Also to be guarded against is a way of thinking that "loves the free play of its mental capacities with the objects of knowing (which it in the same manner partially becomes)."[23] "Making something up" is mistaken for thinking. In either case, the *Wissenschaftslehre* is presented in such a way so as to "humiliate" the self-love at the root of these forms of intellectual dishonesty. Speaking of the lover of "free play," Fichte notes that a "science which brings all thinking without exception under the most stringent rules and annuls all freedom of spirit in the one, eternal, self-sustaining truth can hardly please such a disposition."[24] Fichte's final word on the subject is that "there is no room for anything common or ignoble in the soul given over to this love [of God], and that its purification and healing are intrinsic to it."[25]

What is striking about this discussion is that "love of science" and "love of God" have something in common. They both involve the exercise of *reason*, over against unregulated phantasy and dogmatic empiricism. In fact, in *The Way towards the Blessed Life* of 1806, Fichte will identify the scientific point of view (*Ansicht*) as the fulfillment of the spirit's drive to be the "image of God." In the *1804 Wissenschaftslehre*, philosophical knowledge requires transcendence of personal subjectivity for the sake of becoming a sort of participant-observer in the "self-construction" of the Absolute. Philosophy, we're told, engages in the "living self-construction of the in itself within the light." The ordinary "us" has to have disappeared somewhere along the way for this participation to be possible. In this absolute self-construction "nothing at all remains here of a pregiven *us*: and this is the *higher* realistic perspective.[26] Fichte calls this perspective "realistic" not because it regards something as unproblematically given but because the insight is not different from that about which it is an insight. Considered from the philosophical perspective, the unifying principle that is sought after, the "in itself," "deposits" itself (Fichte's language suggests a crystalline form precipitating out of a solution) "in your knowing and *as* your knowing."[27] This makes higher realism into "higher *idealism*," since speculative knowledge is the knowledge *of knowledge*, knowledge's knowledge of itself.

This "higher idealism" is carefully distinguished from what we would call "subjective idealism," which "makes immediate consciousness into the absolute."[28] Fichte complains about how most people have mistakenly understood the idealism of his *Wissenschaftslehre* to be just this sort of view. This "lower" idealism, however, treats consciousness as a given "fact" whereas the *Wissenschaftslehre* "lays as its ground and has given evidence for, an *enactment*, which in these lectures I have called by the Greek term *genesis*."[29] That is, consciousness is not taken as a given but rather is *brought forth* reflectively in a way that establishes its necessity. Contrary to the impressions of many readers, says Fichte, the first principle of the *Wissenschaftslehre* is in fact *not* the I "as found and perceived," the "individual personal being of each one." This I is a "given" of experience, and from the point of view of Fichte's *genetic* idealism, it is actually derivative of what he elsewhere describes of the originary "reflection [*Reflex*]" that knowing has of itself. In other words, philosophical knowledge is possible—*pace* Jacobi—for we can come to adopt the point of view that knowing as such has on itself, which discloses knowing to be that which is "in and of itself." Crucially, as Fichte goes on to say, this reflexive point of view is not the awareness we have of our individual minds, but rather the awareness that *mind as such* has of itself is mirrored by the former. What Fichte is describing is a kind of unity of apperception, one that is not individuated but apprehends a unity of every individual subject's self-awareness—not the unity of an *I*, but of a *We*. In the first lecture cycle of 1804, Fichte explains how the "We" becomes a "unity of spirit" through the *Wissenschaftslehre*, that is, becomes self-aware as the necessary structure of all knowing: "I have expressly explained that this is basic error regarding the *Wissenschaftslehre* that must be canceled, [viz.,] that I have somehow thought an *I*; but I have established the *We* as the investigating subject that within the unity of the *Wissenschaftslehre* fuses into a unity of spirit."[30] This crucial shift of perspective is elaborated elsewhere in the first lecture series, where Fichte describes various senses in which the *Wissenschaftslehre* is "constrained," "bound," or "subjected to [*gebunden an*]" various conditions. One of these is the "*subjective identity*" of each member of a "manifold of objective I's or persons."[31] In other words, philosophy starts where we are, individuals capable of apperceiving the unified stream of our own conscious lives—a capacity that does not extend to the subjective unity of other people's conscious lives. Reverting to almost Leibnizian language, Fichte allows that each empirical individual can be looked at as a distinctive "view" or "perspective" (*Ansicht*) on the absolute, different from all the rest. He characterizes the *Ansicht* of the *Wissenschaftslehre*, on the other hand, as a "*collective consciousness* [*Gesamtbewußtseyn*]" that each individual participates in to the extent that he or she "has arrived at absolute inner self-sufficiency [*Selbständigkeit*] of consciousness."[32] Fichte later on provides an elliptical discussion of the need for this ascent from the subjective point of view to a "co-consciousness [*Mitbewußtseyn*]," which he later tries to capture as a transformation of one's "eye" or way of seeing.[33]

What is clear is that, beyond the "immediate personal being of each one," there is the "We"—the one, unified life that is shared by all rational agents, which is not some object that we have to discover in the world, but rather it is ourselves—only, as Fichte has said already, it is not our empirical selves, but a higher unity that is discovered to us by adopting the transcendental point of view. As Fichte says later on in the 1804 lectures, "*we live* immediately in the act of living itself, therefore we are the one undivided being itself, in itself, of itself, through itself, which can never go outside itself to duality."[34] Since we ourselves are members of this undivided "being" it cannot properly speaking be an "in itself" that we can only "reconstruct." Likewise, Fichte emphasizes: "Surely we know that we are not talking about this We-in-itself, separated by an irrational discontinuity from the other We which ought to be conscious [or better "is supposed to be conscious"]; rather, [we are talking] purely about the one We-in-itself, living purely in itself, which we conceive merely through our own energetic negation of the conceiving which obtrudes on us empirically here. This We, is *immediate* living itself."[35] The act whereby "we" overcome our limited, empirically conditioned point of view is the very act whereby "we" grasp a different, higher "We," which is not a collection of individuals by a unitary structure in which we all participate. Indeed, as Fichte makes clear in the 1804[1] cycle, the empirical I disappears, and the distinction between persons as concrete individuals is, as it were, "suspended" from this point of view.[36] This "We" cannot even be "characterized" from an external point of view; all that can be said of it is that it is "actual life itself" in its immediacy. Moreover, coming to have a share in this "actual life itself" is not matter of empirically perceiving our own lives but of "the genetic insight into life and the I, which emerges from the construction of the one being, and vice versa."[37] That is, the "life" that characterizes this "We" is not a class concept (e.g., the class of all living things of which we can see we are members); it is a *transcendental concept*, a way of designating something that is always already there, which we can have knowledge of in the form of "genetic insight."

The "We" is also not a generalization based on the observation of shared properties across individuals. Instead, it is a *subject*; it is something that we are, and it can be characterized in subjective terms as a point of view. And so, rather than being the public presentation of the private content of Fichte's thoughts, the *Wissenschaftslehre* proceeds necessarily as a joint enterprise. Its own unity is secured by non-objectifying philosophical insight into the unitary ground of the factical and by sharing or participating in this insight. In the process of generating it, those who undertake the philosophical investigation are themselves somehow *unified*. Fichte's language, here from the 1804[1] series, suggests however more than the kind of unity that results from sharing in a common enterprise or having a common goal. A unity of *perspective* (*Ansicht*) like this is different from a unity of intention, a unity of principles, or even a shared methodology. Yet each of these more familiar kinds of unity is an achievement on Fichte's view, for people tend to take their given individuality as their "principle," that is, to assume the objective reality of how things seem from this point of view. It is in fact "We"—"You and I"—as a "spiritual unity of consciousness" that share insight into the nature of knowing as such.[38]

The "higher" We must "coincide" with "being itself" for philosophical knowledge to be more than a mere projection of our subjectivity. "We certainly are the agents who carry out this construction, but we do it insofar as we are being itself, as has been seen, and we coincide with it; but by no means as a 'we' which is *free* and *independent* from being, as could possible [sic] seem to be the case, and as it actually appears to be, if we give ourselves over to appearance."[39] Fichte here introduces the qualification that a "we" independent of being is an *appearance*, the genesis of which is precisely what the *Wissenschaftslehre* is meant to explain. To "give ourselves over" to it is to take the appearance of simple givenness at face value and to accept our everyday conscious experience of ourselves as distinct individuals each distinct from the rest of the objects of experience as the final word. Fichte urges that his philosophical system "is not in any way based in the vain 'I' of consciousness that emptily objectifies *being*; rather it is grounded in being itself."[40] The absolute, or "knowing [*Wissen*]" in a superlative sense, is always "in itself" and "it is *us*," something that can be seen once one has overcome the empirical "we" for a higher spiritual unity.

Only on these premises can there be any insight into the absolute, contrary to what he labels in 1804[1] as an "alien-objective theory."[41] The absolute, to adopt the Schellingian term that Fichte appropriates during this period in his career, is not an *object* that we intuit together, but a shared intuition of our common rationality or spontaneity. The "We" that is constituted in this way is obviously not our everyday "I's" collected together, since as Fichte points out time and again we do not perceive our *spontaneity* in our ordinary consciousness. In another passage from 1804[1], Fichte argues that the only true sense in which the absolute can exist "outside of itself" is "in its image [*Bilde*], which we ourselves are in our inner nature [*Wesen*]."[42] A purely "immanent unity" cannot go outside of itself—instead its own inner "energy" just is its image—a "*bildendes* Bild"; this is the "We" that arises in transcendental insight."[43]

With the centrality of the We for Fichte's project in the *1804 Wissenschaftslehre* thus established, it is worthwhile returning at this point to the parallel shown earlier between the exercise of self-transcendence in *prima philosophia* and the disappearance of individuality in moral striving. By the by, this helps to illuminate some of Fichte's otherwise puzzling remarks, found throughout his writings from the final decade of his career, that absolute idealists like Schelling and Hegel cannot adequately reconstruct moral life because of their conception of the absolute as "dead." For Fichte, his erstwhile comrades in arms neglected the key moment in the synthetic ascent whereby the limited empirical I is overcome and the perspective of a higher "We" is adopted. Without some sense of this higher "We," one has more or less acquiesced in the unphilosophical point of view that accepts the givens of experience. These include one's sense of oneself as a private subject charged with somehow overcoming the "gap" between self and others and self and world. Thus, in the Twenty-Fifth Lecture of the *1804 Wissenschaftslehre*, Fichte says, "We know very well that we have not always been the one insight that we now are and live, but that we have ascended to it by means of all our previous considerations."[44] This recognition also indicates a new task, namely that of explaining how "our *transformation* [*Werden*] into absolute knowing" takes place.

I have established above that, for Fichte, this transformation into a higher "We" is central both to accomplishing genetic insight and to differentiating the *Wissenschaftslehre* from other attempts at determining the "supersensible substrate" of appearance. But, in Twenty-Fifth Lecture, Fichte raises the stakes. "Everyone must confess that, apart from the extent to which he elevates himself to absolute knowing, his entire life would be nothing, would lack worth and meaning, and would truly not even exist."[45] Notably, "absolute knowing" isn't the same thing as the *Wissenschaftslehre in specie* "because the latter is only a means, and has only instrumental value, by no means intrinsic value. Whoever has arrived no longer worries about the latter."[46]

The important point here is not that people's lives are worthless if they have failed to master Fichte's system. It turns out that there are other ways of elevating oneself to absolute knowing (i.e., morality and religion), which require philosophical grounding to be sure but suffice in and of themselves to lend a life "worth and meaning." Here, Fichte draws a parallel between his own assertion that it is the life of wisdom that is highest and the perspective of the Johannine corpus in the New Testament, a point Fichte will make more stridently in his *The Way towards the Blessed Life*, which received a much wider public reception than did the 1804 lectures. Arriving at "the one insight that we now are and live," that is, the trans-personal perspective of the "We" is, for Fichte, essentially what religion is all about. For this reason, he lambastes eighteenth-century deists who have "changed Christianity into a doctrine and ethics of prudence," for treating God as a peculiar sort of extramundane object that must be worshiped for the sake of supernal blessedness. In reality, as both Fichte and the Johannine tradition agree, "even if he wishes to do so, the one in whom the light has inwardly dawned cannot fail to shine outwardly. . . . Only when right action arises from clear insight does it occur with love and pleasure. Only then does the act, self-sufficient and requiring nothing else, reward itself."[47] Fichte is an avowed pluralist when it comes to ways in which one might arrive at the dawning of this "inward light." For example, in his 1812 lectures on ethics, Fichte picks up on Lessing's conception of revelation as the "education of the human species," exploring how such insight can be mediated historically having once dawned upon inspired individuals. But the 1804 lecture series points to another path as well. Fichte's presentation of the *Wissenschaftslehre*, whose success is made contingent on the insight of the listeners, can by now be seen as attempting to bring about just this insight, which involves identification with a higher "We" and the eclipse of the self-interested perspective that lays prudence at the basis of religious ethics.

Another thing to note about this discussion: Fichte's comments echo his criticisms of what he had once called "stoicism" (with a lower-case *s*) in *Attempt at a Critique of All Revelation*, namely, a one-sided morality based on an opposition between reason and natural inclination. Like Jacobi, Fichte was deeply dissatisfied with Kant's argument for the postulates of pure practical reason for introducing plainly heteronomous motives into moral life as if to soothe a flesh that has been thoroughly mortified. While the connection is not obvious in the *1804 Wissenschaftslehre*, Fichte's claim is that the *Wissenschaftslehre* can ground what he calls a "higher morality" on which action flows from a unified character and in which substantive values replace the mere form of the will are the touchstone of moral life. This is because philosophy shows how it is possible to transcend individuality for the point of view of the "We," which is a *normative* point of view.

Other texts surrounding the 1804 lectures on *philosophia prima* fill in some of Fichte's thoughts on the relationship between the higher We of the *Wissenschaftslehre* and the moral life. Thus, in the lectures on "principles," presented in early 1805, Fichte draws a distinction between an *empirical* and an *a priori* or *philosophical* conception of morality. The former identifies morality with social custom, as the German "*Sitte*" readily allows.[48] The "absolute morals of r.[eason] as such," on the other hand, rests on the "concept of the one I, carried over [to others] without any division" and concerns "simply what all, as if they were a single [person] and so had only a single will and single power [*Kraft*], ought to do."[49] Philosophical ethics is grounded in the perspective of the higher "We."

In the Twenty-Seventh Lecture of the *1804 Wissenschaftslehre*, Fichte's description of the nature of philosophical insight tracks the very same outlook. He writes: "This very insight, or the science of knowing, is reason's immediate expression and life: the single life of reason unfolded immediately in itself and permeated by itself. Precisely because, just as one lives in it there as seeing, or it appears, thus reason itself lives and appears."[50] The "insight" described here as "reason's immediate expression and life" is what constitutes the higher "We" *for us*, and it is *as* this We that people are supposed to pursue philosophical inquiry *and* deliberate about their lives. The higher We is a "collective consciousness" or a "co-consciousness." But what does it mean to be or to become this "We"? This question presses itself, first of all by the textual issue of Fichte's direct denial of the existence of any "collective consciousness" per se.[51] Second, this is because other philosophers do have accounts of how one comes to take up a trans-personal, *impartial*, point of view for the sake of thinking through a philosophical or practical problem. In Fichte's lifetime, for instance, one could cite Adam Smith's discussions the sense of duty and the "impartial spectator," the "man within" and "substitute to the Deity" in part 3 of *The Theory of Moral Sentiments*. Or, closer to home, the device of the "original position" from John Rawls's *Theory of Justice* is familiar.

Fichte's comments on collective or shared consciousness in 1804 do not clarify things much. Among the few passages to be found is the following, from the 1804³ series. "My mind [*Geist*] disappeared and yours took its place. From now on, whatever is supposed to be mentally accomplished and thought in this assembly [*Versammlung*] will be thought by you as an assembly. For only in this way will we become an assembly that communicates with itself [*sich mittheilende Versammlung*]. Were I to think of this all by myself, it would be just as well for me to stay alone in my room."⁵² What could it mean to replace one person's mind with another? What does it mean to think *as* an "assembly" of people? On the one hand, it could mean that each person has the same thought—after all, Fichte insists that each participant have a "living image" of the genetic ground of experience. But one could perfectly well have such a "living image" all alone, which makes the shared enterprise no longer essential to the achievement of philosophical insight. This result plainly conflicts with Fichte's insistence that it is only as a certain "We" that philosophical insight is possible at all.

Several sections of the 1812 lectures on ethics provide some, but by no means the only, clues as to what it might mean to become this "higher" We. The Twentieth Lecture is a transitional point in that series. It is here that Fichte arrives at the apex of his deduction of both the "purely formal" and "qualitatively formal" concepts of duty, beyond which philosophy cannot go in order to derive a true "doctrine of duty" (*Pflichtlehre*). First, Fichte says that the argument to that point has established that the I is only aware of itself as "real"—by which he means as a genuine moral actor—when "it appears to itself as a member of the community, of a totality [*eines Ganzen*] of which it is an integral part."⁵³ He then has this to say about this totality:

> {The individual as a real consciousness thus appears [to himself]} as something in himself, yet as a part of the whole and within the order of the whole, for only the whole exists in itself. Hence, when it comes to *concepts*, [the individual] exhibits himself as real only in those that are purely and simply [*schlechthin*] directed toward the community as a whole and that he can only think to the extent that he grasps himself as an image of the whole. Are there such [concepts]? Every scientific insight, to the extent that it is articulated *in a way that obtains universally or is universally valid*, posits reason as something universal that is identical to itself; and no one understands such a proposition who has not established this identity of reason in itself and cast off all individuality.⁵⁴

What is particularly striking here is that Fichte's go-to example of what it is like to occupy the moral point of view is *scientific insight*. This is not unlike the way in which morality and religion were employed in our series of the 1804 lecture cycle in order to explicate the nature of the scientific "We." By scientific insight, Fichte means the comprehension of rational necessity, which inherently involves being cognizant of a lawfulness that is binding on all individual minds. In more practical or concrete terms, these concepts are embedded in a shared activity of communication.[55] An anonymous transcript records a formal schema provided by Fichte in his efforts to clarify the nature of this higher communal consciousness; it shows how a common "mind" or "spirit"—G for *Geist*—achieves a "breakthrough" in one of its "individual shapes" (i.e., one of *us*, schematized by Fichte as A, B, C, etc.) in the form of some communicable content that is of universal validity rather than being merely peculiar to an individual.

This seems to be all we get from Fichte about what it might be to be a higher "We": "{The individual as a real consciousness thus appears [to himself]} as something in himself, yet as a part of the whole and within the order of the whole, for only the whole exists in itself." By itself, I don't find this to be ultimately satisfying, though it does suggest some useful parallels in the views of the later British Idealists, particularly T. H. Green, and the point of view represented in F. H. Bradley's "My Station and Its Duties." I'm going to avoid the temptation to explain the obscure by the more obscure, however, and get back to Fichte.

This discussion leads into his first characterization of the "qualitatively formal" concept of duty: "The task is laid upon each [individual] to make all others equal or equivalent [*gleich*] to himself and to become equal or equivalent to them. At some point they cross the threshold [*In einiger Zeit sind sie es darüber*]."[56] This "qualitatively formal"—that is, slightly less abstract and unhelpful—version of the concept of duty is just the familiar admonition to regard oneself and others as in some sense the same or to regard oneself and others in the same way. This is still formal, since what it means to do this in any given case is a matter for each individual, who must therefore "inspect his own breast regarding what he ought to do."[57]

While keeping it formal, Fichte expands on the idea a bit further on:

> In the first instance, the task is laid upon each individual to communicate his perspective [*Ansicht*] to all and to make those of others his own [*sich anzueignen*], to form [*bilden*] himself until the point of harmony with what obtains universally [*gemeingültigen*] within others' [perspectives], while these should do likewise

regarding what obtains universally in his. Each [individual] has his own spiritual character in this scenario, but the task is for all to mingle these characters into one, {so that} the whole community is of a single mind [*Sinne*].[58]

This task, as he puts it later, comprises the one and only "form of the will" that "negates the division of life into individual worlds."[59] Now, to describe "collective consciousness" as a "task" or as the normative "form of the will" is one thing. It is something else to say that there is in fact a higher unity of reason of which we can become directly aware, whether through scientific insight or moral character. This point brings me back to where I started from—namely, Fichte's attempt to overcome Jacobi's skepticism about speculative philosophy. Recall that it is not enough for Fichte to simply point out Jacobi's assumption of something like the speculative stance in his very argument against its possibility. Fichte undertakes to show ultimately that philosophical knowledge must be possible because it actually exists—or rather, we must be brought to see that it exists by actually having it. Doing so requires, however, that we become different, that we come to self-consciously instantiate the higher unity of reason. I was wondering about what it might mean to do this, and I found some help in what Fichte has to say about morality. One surprising result of looking down this trail is that the 1804 cycle of lectures on *prima philosophia* can be partly read as an exercise in self-overcoming leading to the very insight that, Fichte says, leads to morality all by itself. This is so because both science (in Fichte's sense of "science") and morality occupy the perspective of a higher We, a totality of individuals viewed apart from their sensible particularities. When we're this "We," we do not identify with "our" natural or social individual "selves," and we comprehend rational necessities rather than private fancies.

But does all this successfully refute Jacobi's skepticism? On one level it is a somewhat inspired move, for Fichte grants Jacobi some important points and appeals to a distinction that Jacobi would surely endorse—that is, between a selfish and a virtuous character. Further, the idea that rationality and the pursuit of truth are shared achievements and communal activities would doubtless have resonated for Jacobi, who took up a deeply dialogical approach to philosophy. The problem would instead be precisely the key element of Fichte's solution, that is, the very idea of a higher "We" that abstracts from all particularity. Perhaps, having given Fichte his due, we should let Jacobi's *Edward Allwill* get the final say on this idea:

Only our *philosophers* can make their abode among the cliffs in the proximity of heaven, unpolluted by any haze, with the endless *brightness* and endless *void* all around. I would lose my breath there. The air is already too thin for me where I am; so I am constantly scheming how to come down gradually just a bit more. There is also no denying that in a narrower horizon objects come to us with much more warmth for the eye and heart. Boundless boundaries, space without measure or end—wherever I get a glimpse of this, I sink into a hell of dread. For this reason I like to restrict myself a bit—indulge in terrestrial beginnings, where I see an end to what I am doing, yet must commit all my forces to it.[60]

Notes

1. To speak more accurately, Fichte presented three cycles of lectures spanning from early 1804 until about the same time the following year. His important *popular* addressee followed these more technical lectures in quick succession and were intended by Fichte as parts of the first comprehensive, public presentation of his system of philosophy since the debacle of the "atheism controversy" in 1799.

2. 1804^2, 139; *GA*, II/8, 283.

3. 1804^2, 139; *GA*, II/8, 283.

4. I have looked at the debate between Fichte and Jacobi, as well as the text of the open letter, from other angles elsewhere. See "Idealism and Nihilism," in *Kant, Fichte, and the Legacy of Transcendental Idealism*, eds. Halla Kim and Steve Hoeltzl (Lanham, MD: Lexington Books, 2015): 153–68; and "Jacobi on Practical Nihilism," in *Practical Philosophy from Kant to Hegel: Freedom, Right, and Revolution*, eds. James Clarke and Gabriel Gottlieb (Cambridge: Cambridge University Press, 2021), 157–73.

5. In his correspondence with Thomas Wizenmann, and then with Hamann and Mendelssohn, Jacobi proclaimed as his principle the demand that philosophy must "discover existence [*Dasein zu enthüllen*]" and that a philosopher must be "loyal" to her own finite nature. Jacobi reiterated this commitment in the 1799 "To Fichte," the principal text from Jacobi to which Fichte is responding in 1804^2.

6. 1804^2, 139; *GA*, II/8, 283.

7. 1804^2, 22; *GA*, II/8, 5; 1804^2, 31–32; *GA*, II/8, 28.

8. 1804^2, 139; *GA*, II/8, 285.

9. 1804^2, 139; *GA*, II/8, 285.

10. 1804^2, 139; *GA*, II/8, 285.

11. 1804^2, 149; *GA*, II/8, 304.

12. 1804², 154; *GA*, II/8, 316.
13. 1804², 107; *GA*, II/8, 206; 1804², 110; *GA*, II/8, 216.
14. SE, 245; *GA*, I/5, 231, emphasis added.
15. 1804², 27; *GA*, II/8, 19.
16. Cf. this comment from the Second Lecture of 1804¹: "This [image] of the W[issenschaftslehre] is thus *your own*, which you will produce, that will be represented ahead of time by you in an image." *GA*, II/7, 75.
17. 1804², 56; *GA*, II/8, 87.
18. 1804², 48; *GA*, II/8, 68–69.
19. 1804², 49; *GA*, II/8, 70.
20. 1804², 49; *GA*, II/8, 70.
21. 1804², 50–51; *GA*, II/8, 72.
22. 1804², 49; *GA*, II/8, 71.
23. 1804², 50; *GA*, II/8, 73.
24. 1804², 50; *GA*, II/8, 73.
25. 1804², 51; *GA*, II/8, 77.
26. 1804², 98; *GA*, II/8, 186.
27. 1804², 99; *GA*, II/8, 188.
28. 1804², 105; *GA*, II/8, 200.
29. 1804², 105; *GA*, II/8, 200.
30. *GA*, II/7, 123.
31. *GA*, II/7, 77.
32. *GA*, II/7, 77.
33. *GA*, II/7, 92–93, 99.
34. 1804², 116; *GA*, II/8, 231.
35. 1804², 116; *GA*, II/8, 231.
36. *GA*, II/7, 123.
37. 1804², 117; *GA*, II/8, 232.
38. *GA*, II/7, 123–24.
39. 1804², 122; *GA*, II/8, 244–45.
40. *GA*, II/7, 128.
41. *GA*, II/7, 123.
42. *GA*, II/7, 152.
43. GA, II/7, 154, 161.
44. 1804², 181; *GA*, II/8, 377.
45. 1804², 181; *GA*, II/8, 378.
46. 1804², 182; *GA*, II/8, 378–79.
47. 1804², 183; *GA*, II/8, 381.
48. *GA*, II/7, 379.
49. *GA*, II/7, 379.
50. 1804², 194; *GA*, II/8, 406.
51. *GA*, II/13, 357–59.

52. *GA*, II/7, 301–2.
53. *GA*, II/13, 357.
54. *GA*, II/13, 357.
55. *GA*, II/13, 357–58.
56. *GA*, II/13, 358.
57. *GA*, IV/6, 126.
58. *GA*, II/13, 359.
59. *GA*, II/13, 363.
60. Friedrich Heinrich Jacobi, *Werke, Vol. 6/1*, eds. Carmen Götz and Walter Jaeschke (Stuttgart: Frommann-Holzboog, 2006), 135.

Part 3

System and Idealism

Chapter 10

The Quintuple Quintuplicity of Forms of (Self-)Consciousness in Fichte's *1804 Wissenschaftslehre*

EMILIANO ACOSTA

One of the new developments of the doctrine of science in 1804 is the a priori concept of the existent I (i.e., of the absolute knowledge in the appearance) as a quintuplicity of forms of (self-)consciousness, wherein each form is structured in a new quintuplicity: the well-know quintuplicity of quintuplicities, or in Fichte's terms: "[the] twenty-five main moments and fundamental determinations of knowledge in its origin."[1] The main five I-forms that exhaust the concept of the existent rational and free being are the sensualist, the legal, the moral, the religious, and the philosophical (self-)consciousness. They all have to be understood as manifestations of the absolute unity of reason (i.e., of the unity of truth and certainty without any mediation).[2] They are the result of thinking the one reason as spontaneously emerging in the realm of multiplicity. Because they all are *reason* (i.e., unity of subject and object) in the phenomenal realm, they also spontaneously generate themselves and their worlds. In doing so, they separately develop into new quintuplicities following a different unifying principle. They form their own worlds, legal and moral systems, religions, and philosophies.

Nevertheless, there is a fundamental difference between the first four forms and the fifth one: the philosophical form of (self-)consciousness, which is according to Fichte the doctrine of science *in actu*, is the only one, wherein the one reason completely achieves the knowledge about itself as generative activity. Whereas the first four forms are characterized by a not-knowing of the real truth about reason, the philosophical self-consciousness is existent self-knowledge of reason *as* reason. So, only the philosophical (self-)consciousness truthfully represents the absolute knowledge in the phenomenal world. Although all the five I-forms are reason in the existential form, namely free generative activity in the phenomenal realm, they are not effectively self-conscious as manifestations of reason. In Hegelian terms, one could say that these forms are still not *for themselves*. Put in Fichte's Jena terms: the I of the first four main fundamental determinations of knowledge has still not posed itself consciously *as an I*.

From this fundamental difference, however, Fichte does not deduce a distinction between necessary and accidental forms of (self-)consciousness. All five forms are necessary, since according to Fichte the first four forms of the phenomenal existence of reason are the condition of possibility of the fifth one. In other words, without the presupposition of the existence of the first four non-philosophical I-forms, Fichte cannot genetically deduce the possibility of the emergence of absolute knowledge in phenomenal reality, namely in the form of the doctrine of science.

Before 1804, there is no such thematization of the phenomenal multiplicity of existent self-consciousness. The doctrine of science *nova methodo*, for instance, deduces a quintuple structure of the individual (self-)consciousness; however, this (self-)consciousness is not the mentioned a priori concept of an existent multiplicity but rather the a priori universal form of all possible existent self-consciousness.[3] The novelty of the concept of the existence of five *quintuple* forms of (self-)consciousness in 1804 resides not only in the fact that the existent I is conceived in its absolute multiplicity but also in the fact that the 1804 I-quintuplicity *positively* integrates forms of self-knowledge and knowledge of reality that lack the insight in the absolute nature of reason and therefore produce according to Fichte a distorted image of reality and subjectivity—for instance, the idea of God as a person, of civil society as material for the exercise of moral virtues, of morality as nothing but a correlate of positive law, and of being as essentially matter. Moreover, by genetically deducing this fivefold fivefoldness that exhausts the realm of possible forms of appearance of (self-)consciousness and their respective worlds, the doctrine of science returns to its principle, and so it fulfills what Fichte considers the task of philosophy: the leading back of multiplicity to unity.[4]

The quintuplicity of quintuple forms of (self-)consciousness is the last issue Fichte discusses in the *1804 Wissenschaftslehre*. Since the *1804 Wissenschaftslehre* is basically a reiteration of the first course Fichte gave that year in Berlin,[5] one must not be surprised that this quintuplicity has also been the last concept deduced in 1804[1] lectures. In both cases, despite the above-mentioned systematical significance of this quintuplicity, Fichte does not dedicate too much time for the explanation of the elements involved in it: almost three of the 122 pages of the manuscript of 1804[1] lectures, and in the case of the *1804 Wissenschaftslehre*, only six of the 424 pages of the manuscript.[6] Whereas the quintuplicity of (self-)consciousness appears in the 1804[1] lectures and the *1804 Wissenschaftslehre* only in the last lecture, in the third and last Berliner course on the doctrine of science, this quintuplicity is the central concept of the last four lectures (twelve of the forty-four pages of the manuscript).[7] Nevertheless, in 1804[3] lectures, Fichte presents the quintuplicity of (self-)consciousness in a less systematic way. There are only sporadic mentions of the five fundamental I-forms and the quintuple structure of each form of (self-)consciousness is not discussed at all.

Quintuplicity as Method

Already in de doctrine of science *nova methodo* (1796/1799) Fichte is aware that a "complete synthesis has 5 members."[8] However, it is only after 1804 that he begins to systematically apply the schema of the quintuplicity as a methodological tool in order to exhaustively analyze or genetically reconstruct a concept. Between 1804 and 1806 Fichte intensively makes use of the quintuplicity device, not only in his lectures about the doctrine of science in Berlin and Erlangen[9] but also in the three works he publishes in 1806: *On the Essence of the Scholar*, *The Fundamental Characteristics of the Present Age*, and *The Way towards the Blessed Life*.

In his writing on the scholar, Fichte gives an exhaustive account of the concept of "the righteous scholar" (*der rechtschaffene Gelehrte*) by presenting it in its fundamental five specifications: (1) the aspiring scholar, or the student; (2) the scholar who supervises, conduces, and improves the relation of civil society to nature; (3) the scholar who administers, improves, and legislates about social and political life; (4) the scholar who teaches and forms the new generations of scholars; and (5) the scholar who communicates in books his knowledge to the scientific community.[10] In his work on philosophy of history, Fichte explains the concept of "Humanity's life on earth" by deducing the five necessary epochs of the history of the progress of humanity toward the absolute reign of reason: (1) the age of the reign of instincts, (2) the age of the reign of coercive law, (3) the age of absolute indifference toward truth in general and of total anarchy, (4) the age of the reign of science, and (5) the age of the reign of productive and creative reason, in which freedom acts effectively as the principle for all human actions.[11] Lastly, in his so-called doctrine of religion, Fichte describes five worldviews as the five elementary forms that exhaust all possible lived experiences of the world: the standpoint of (1) the senses, (2) legal and moral deontology, (3) free and creative morality, (4) religion, and (5) science or philosophy.[12]

In the three cases, the methodological tool of quintuplicity serves to systematize the multiplicity a concept refers to, or as Kant says, makes recognizable.[13] In these quintuplicities, however, the relation of the five elements to each other and to the whole is not the same. In the case of the scholar, there is a distinction between the student and the other four forms of phenomenally being a scholar. Nevertheless, they complement each other. None of the last four forms represents the most accurate or the highest manifestation of the scholar in the realm of phenomenality. There is also the possibility of moving from the one form to the other. In different moments of his or her life, the same scholar can fulfill different scholar-functions. Moreover, being a righteous scholar means, according to Fichte, being capable of executing all possible tasks mentioned. In the case of the quintuplicity in humanity's history, there is a clear hierarchy among the five elements. The last historical period is the only one that completely represents the goal of humanity. All ages, however, complement each other since they all are necessary moments of the same historical process. In order to arrive at the fifth age, humanity has to pass through the other four ages. In the case of the worldviews, there is also a hierarchy, but this can be read in different ways. There is a distinction between worldviews that conceive the rational being as subjected to an external power (the first two) and worldviews wherein the individual is self-conscious as incarnation of the absolute freedom of reason and knows that this freedom is internal (the last three). Within this distinction, the third worldview can be considered the highest one, since the activity needed for transforming the world and so fulfilling the principal duty of all rational being is to be found in this third standpoint, whereas the last two standpoints are basically two different forms of interpreting the free self-consciousness and transforming power that appeared in the third level of the worldviews.[14] The five worldviews do not complement each other. The lower forms of self-consciousness are not a condition of possibility of the higher ones. In order to get a higher worldview, individuals do not have to necessarily pass through the other ones. The individual's passing from one form to the other is not generated by an immanent cause. It is like a miracle, as Fichte explains, it just happens.[15]

In all these examples of quintuplicity, multiplicity represents the moment of alterability or becoming of the mere concept. The concept, exclusively considered in its general formulation (the righteous scholar, the history of humanity, the subjective standpoint of the world), appears in relation to its content as a steady unity. Fichte solves the opposition between unity and multiplicity and between unchangeable and changeable by deducing the quintuplicity that makes visible both the existence of the unity of a concept in the multiplicity as well as the necessary connection of the multiplicity with its concept. Fichte's concept of quintuplicity shows that the concept is empty without its multiplicity and the multiplicity is invisible without the concept. The quintuplicity makes both sides of the relation necessary. Hence, quintuplicity is unity conceived as multiplicity as well as multiplicity conceived as unity.

Furthermore, the quintuplicity sets in motion the steadiness of the mere concept by showing the necessary dispersion of the concept in five main specifications, namely that the complete meaning of the concept necessarily is its quintuple specification. The definition of the scholar as the individual who has seen the "divine idea,"[16] for instance, is not the real concept of scholar. Besides, the quintuplicity fixes the infinite movement of multiplicity—what Hegel calls the bad/simple or negative infinity[17]—by bringing it to its main determinations.[18] Quintuplicity consists in fact of the concept's returning to itself from its dispersion in multiplicity, but this coming back to the origin accomplishes itself in and through a positively appropriation of the particularity inherent to multiplicity. For instance, the return of the concept of humanity to its origin consists of the whole historical process of humanity.[19]

On the Quintuple Quintuplicity of (Self-)Consciousness

Concerning the quintuplicity-tool applied to the concept of the I, Fichte, as mentioned previously, offers at the end of his doctrine of science *nova methodo* a quintuple synthesis of the I as the concept of the embodied self-consciousness. This (self-)consciousness is the I that has been individualized by the summons to freely act.[20] So, it is an individual embedded in the multiplicity of moral beings, which according to Fichte is only a numerical and not a qualitative multiplicity. All moral individuals are actually nothing but actions of the one moral subject to whom the categorical imperative is addressed.[21] Although the quintuple synthesis of the I of the doctrine of science *nova methodo* seems to be closer to the a priori form of the phenomenal I than the first fivefold description of the I in the *1804 Wissenschaftslehre* (consisting of being, thinking, and the three realms discovered by Kant's critiques),[22] the fivefold consideration of the I in the *nova methodo* is not representative of the a priori concept of a real effective multiplicity of rational and free beings Fichte systematically presents and genetically connects with pure knowledge at the end of the *1804 Wissenschaftslehre*. The quintuple (self-)consciousness of the *nova methodo* seems to corresponds rather with the fifth form of (self-)consciousness of 1804, the philosophical I.

According to the *1804 Wissenschaftslehre*, the phenomenal manifestation of the absolute unity of reason (i.e., of the pure concept of [self-]consciousness) necessarily consists of a multiplicity of existing self-conscious and free beings that can be systematized in a quintuplicity of forms of (self-)consciousness. These forms are, as mentioned, the sensualist, the legal, the moral, the religious, and the philosophical I. So, when the I becomes effectively real, namely when (self-)consciousness generates itself in phenomenal reality, the I necessarily results in a fivefold differentiation of itself.

That the absolute unity of reason—that is, "reason *as absolutely unified*" ("die Vernunft *als absolute Eins*")[23]—necessarily transits from the realm of pure and intern activity and life to the phenomenal realm in terms of objectivizing visibility and effective existence is due to the internal law of the one reason, which, since it is categorical, cannot be explained. So, like in the *nova methodo*, there is in the *1804 Wissenschaftslehre* a categorical imperative requiring the exteriorization of freedom. However, this freedom is the spontaneity of the one reason that as such encompasses the theoretical and the practical realms and has to be conceived as beyond the divide subject-object. So, the fundamental imperative of reason is not specifically moral, it is rather more basic or, as Fichte would say, more originary than Kant's categorical imperative.[24]

This imperative, which Fichte in 1804 calls the ought (*Soll*) or the law (*Gesetz*), reads as follows: reason ought to know itself. Reason, namely, ought to become its own object. At the beginning of the last lecture of the *1804 Wissenschaftslehre*, Fichte says that "reason is simply the cause of its own existence and own objectivity for itself; and its original or fundamental life consists precisely of this."[25] The spontaneous passing of reason as subject to reason as object reveals not only that reason is absolutely free but that reason essentially consists of this freedom to become its own object. Fichte conceives reason as the spontaneous activity of passing from itself as resting in itself (i.e., the *singulum* at the end of the first part of these lectures[26])—to itself in the form of being-in-an-other—and so becoming-an-other-to-itself. Fichte formulates reason's process of spontaneously becoming its own object in terms of a passing from the subject to the predicate in the proposition "reason ought to objectivize itself."[27] In the notion of spontaneously following the internal law, it can be seen that freedom and necessity are in the case of reason the same. This freedom is as absolute as the internal law of reason. This means it is not conditioned by an external cause and hence cannot be explained—it merely happens without any motive.[28]

On the side of the existing individual reason (i.e., the phenomenal I as empirical singularity) freedom appears, on the contrary, as free will in the sense of arbitrariness. The freedom that characterizes the individual existent self-consciousness is not directly connected with necessity. It is rather the freedom of deciding whether or not to know what the one reason actually is, namely, to know that reason's exteriorization in the phenomenal realm, that is, its original disjunction in thinking (subject) and being (object), is inherent to its nature. Although the manifestation of the one reason in the realm of phenomenality under the form of a multiplicity of rational beings is an act both of freedom and of necessity, the individual self-consciousness in terms of the individual's knowledge of being a manifestation of the one reason—that is, the individual's becoming doctrine of science *in actu*—is according to Fichte essentially contingent. It totally depends on the arbitrariness of each rational being.[29]

According to Fichte, however, there are not two but three possible ways of dealing with the drive every rational individual has to authentic philosophical knowledge,[30] since the denial to know the real nature of reason can occur in two different ways. On the one hand, individuals can close themselves off from the knowledge the doctrine of science provides by a total disavowal of the will to true philosophical knowledge. On the other, they can remain in the contemplation of the abstract concept of reason, namely in the conviction that reason is only the pure absolute unity of certainty and truth without its manifestation in the appearance.[31]

This last point makes evident that Fichte does not consider the second part of his *1804 Wissenschaftslehre*, the so-called theory of phenomenality, as an addendum to its first part, the theory of truth. Rather, the second part is the demonstration (i.e., the genetical deduction) of the unity of truth and certainty the first part has explained. In this regard, it must be said that the "ought" or "should" (*Soll*) that appears in the second part of the *1804 Wissenschaftslehre* is not a "new leading category,"[32] a kind of principle that Fichte applies only to this part of *1804 Wissenschaftslehre*, but rather, as Fichte himself remarks, it has been from the very beginning of the lectures the principle of his investigation.[33] Moreover, the leading-back of the total multiplicity to the absolute unity, which is according to Fichte the task of philosophy,[34] is only accomplished when the quintuplicity of forms of (self-)consciousness has been genetically deduced. Fichte considers this fivefoldness the condition of possibility of the effective realization (*wirkliche Realisierung*) of the doctrine of science[35] or, in other words, of the "absolute genesis" that the "genesis of the doctrine of science" represents.[36] So the solution to the "enigma of world and consciousness," namely to the "absolute fundamental disjunction in S [sc. being, thus: world] and D [sc. thinking, thus: consciousness],"[37] consists, as Fichte says in his first 1804 Berliner course, of the demonstration that knowledge necessarily produces the quintuplicity of forms of (self-)consciousness as the phenomenal manifestation of the original split of the absolute unity of certainty and truth in "world and consciousness (object and subject)."[38]

Therefore, the first part of the *1804 Wissenschaftslehre* (i.e., the "pure theory of truth" or "theory of reason") merely consists of the presentation of the main elements of reason in its facticity, which in this context means nothing but: not-genetically deduced. According to the *1804 Wissenschaftslehre*, philosophy must not only establish principles but also, or rather first, be able to connect reason-multiplicity and reason-unity with each other.[39] Only by means of this connection, which is nothing but the quintuplicity of quintuplicities of I-forms, one can totally comprehend what is the absolute unity of truth and certainty, since the genetical deduction of the phenomenal realm as the appearance of this absolute unity shows that this unity is the foundation of facticity.[40]

According to Fichte, the imperative to know itself reveals that reason's being consists of its knowing-acting and this being/acting accomplishes itself in a passage from steady unity to variable and inconstant multiplicity. Reason's self-knowledge develops firstly into the original duplicity of world and consciousness and secondly in the repetition of this act of self-knowledge on the phenomenal level.[41] This reproduction of the act of self-knowledge corresponds with the phenomenally existent self-consciousness: the multiplicity of free and self-conscious rational beings. Hence, that the absolute knowledge knows itself means that there ought to be a multiplicity of rational beings that spontaneously and constantly understand themselves and their world.

Since the emergence of rational (free and self-conscious) life in the realm of phenomenality results in a fivefold specification of the general concept of the I, the one and universal I as genus (Fichte's transcendental concept of the I-hood) does not exist. The I only exists as a multiplicity that can be systematized in five elementary specifications. The phenomenal I is, like Fichte's scholar, always a *differentia specifica* of its own concept, conditioned not only by time and space but also, as mentioned, by the particular freedom of each existent rational being. Absolute knowledge materializes *necessarily* in one of the five elementary forms of (self-)consciousness. The universal necessarily appears in the particular and the systematization of all particularities, the concept of the fivefoldness of fivefold forms of (self-)consciousness, is the return to the universality of reason.[42] This return means that the fivefold classification of I-forms encompasses all possible particular existential forms of consciousness.

Fichte makes a clear distinction between the philosophical (self-)consciousness and the other four I-forms and establishes a hierarchy among them. Only the first one has an accurate knowledge of reason: the doctrine of science represents, as already said, the absolute genesis of reason in the phenomenal realm. What characterizes the other four forms is precisely the lack of the insight in the very nature reason, namely of that knowledge the doctrine of science presents and discusses. This not-knowing is not contingent but inherent to these four I-forms. As it will be shown in the next section, without this not-knowing, these forms of (self-)consciousness would not develop into a quintuplicity.

Each of these nonscientific or a-philosophical I-forms can be considered as specifications of this not-knowing and at the same time as misinterpretations of the quintuplicity of the philosophical (self-)consciousness. They are not *for themselves*, namely they do not identify with reason's unity of act and being and of subject and object, but conceive themselves as manifestation of a different principle. In each of these I-forms, the principle results of a misreading of one of the elements of the quintuplicity of the philosophical I. Each of these I-forms absolutizes one of the first four elements of the quintuplicity of the philosophical (self-)consciousness: the principle of the sensualist I, for instance, is the sensible object conceived as absolute.

Nevertheless, all five quintuplicities, the right and the wrong ones, are according to Fichte "effects of reason."[43] They all are in fact objectivizations of the intern essence of certainty in the existential form.[44] Being an effect of reason does not mean, however, being absolutely passive. An effect of reason is according to Fichte the realm wherein absolute knowledge appears. In this regard, it conserves and reproduces some main characters of reason as such. Hence, an effect of reason is "internal life and causality" and it is free, although, as already mentioned, this freedom is arbitrary freedom.[45]

Hence, not only the philosophical I but also the other forms of (self-)consciousness are spontaneous and form-giving activity. They all, accordingly, construct the world in which they dwell. In doing so, each of the four forms of non-philosophical (self-)consciousness develops into a new quintuplicity that reproduces the elements of the main quintuplicity. The religious consciousness, for instance, develops its own conceptions of nature, legality, morality, and philosophy, and so it gives form to its own world, although without being aware of its own agency in this process of creating meaning and reality.

The autonomy of all forms of absolute knowledge in the appearance implies a lack of internal connection of these forms with each other.[46] The systematic connection is a product of external reflection. The philosophical I is the only (self-)consciousness to which all I-forms appear as a unity, a quintuplicity of quintuplicities. Whereas the doctrine of science knows that the other four forms are necessary conditions for its own possibility of existing, the other four I-forms necessarily have to ignore the existence of the others as such in order to autonomously exist.

So, within the quintuplicity of quintuplicities it is not possible for the I to immanently develop from one form to the other. Nevertheless, the quintuplicity of forms of (self-)consciousness consists in fact of the concept's return to itself from its dispersion in multiplicity, but this coming back to the origin that happens in and through a positive appropriation of the particularity inherent to multiplicity is executed by only one of the five I-forms, the philosophical (self-)consciousness, namely the doctrine of science *in actu*.

The Concrete Realization of the Quintuplicity of Forms of (Self-)Consciousness

According to Fichte, the appearance of the absolute unity of certainty and truth in the phenomenal realm develops into a quintuplicity of quintuplicities: twenty-five main determinations of absolute knowledge. However, none of the three 1804 manuscripts explicitly mentions all the determinations. In the *1804 Wissenschaftslehre*, which is the most exhaustive presentation of the quintuplicity of quintuplicities, Fichte affirms that the fivefoldness in the first four forms of (self-)consciousness consist of four own and autonomous determinations and one external element common to all I-forms. The lack of an own fifth element, which is the lack of the insight in the real nature of reason that characterizes the first four I-forms, is solved by adding the unifying principle of the philosophical (self-)consciousness (i.e., the doctrine of science) as the fifth element.[47] Hence it seems that only the form of (self-)consciousness represented by the doctrine of science has five elements. The philosophical I shares one of its determinations with the other I-forms. As a result, the *1804 Wissenschaftslehre* does not present twenty-five but actually twenty-one elements (see table 10.1).

Table 10.1. Initial Description of the Fivefold Quintuplicity (21 Elements)

	Philosophy (insight given only by the doctrine of science)			
The genetic concept of the noumenal object of Philosophy of religion	Religion as genuine manifestation of the absolute	Morality as genuine manifestation of the absolute	Positive law as genuine manifestation of the absolute	Nature as genuine manifestation of the absolute
The genetic concept of the noumenal subject of the System of Ethics	Religious morality	Moral religion	Legal concept of religion	Nature-religion
The genetic concept of the phenomenal subject of the Philosophy of natural law	Religious system of law	Moral concept of positive law	Legal concept of morality	Sensualist morality
The genetic concept of the phenomenal object of a Philosophy of Nature	Religious concept of nature	Moral concept of nature	Legal concept of nature	Sensualist system of law

Source: Author provided.

Nevertheless, in explaining the first four forms of (self-)consciousness, Fichte suggests that they have their own unifying principle. This principle is, as it will be shown, essentially a kind of belief that replaces the lacking philosophical insight (belief in nature or in legal equality, for instance). Besides, in the description of the first I-form, the sensualist one, Fichte mentions materialism as the philosophy of this form of consciousness.[48] Hence it has to be presupposed that each form must have its own philosophy. Each I-form ought actually to structure itself as an independent fivefoldness if they all have to be conceived as reason. It seems that in the last lecture of the *1804 Wissenschaftslehre*, Fichte is factually aware of this, but he is not able to genetically deduce the positive content of what appears to him as merely an empty place, the not-knowing constitutive for the non-philosophical I-forms (i.e., the absence of the true insight in the nature of reason). However, this kind of lacuna can be filled up by considering other passages of the 1804 courses on the doctrine of science and of other writings of Fichte. As a result, a quintuplicity of quintuplicities, as presented in table 10.2, can be reconstructed.

The non-philosophical determinations of the main quintuplicity—religion, morality, legality, and nature—must be read in two directions and, therefore, counted twice. When vertically read, they correspond with four moments of the philosophical (self-)consciousness, whereas when horizontally read, they correspond with the principle and main determination of the non-philosophical forms of (self-)consciousness. In the following sections, a reconstruction of the five moments of each non-philosophical form of (self-)consciousness will be attempted. This reconstruction is needed to not only obtain a clear notion of the twenty-five fundamental determinations

Table 10.2. Structure of Fichte's Fivefold Quintuplicity (25 Elements)

	Main quintuplicity: Philosophy			
4 non-authentic philosophies as positive forms of the lack of the insight of the *Wissenschaftslehre*	**Religion**	Morality	Legality	Nature
	Morality	Religion	Legality	Nature
	Legality	Religion	Morality	Nature
	Nature	Religion	Legality	Morality

Source: Author provided.

The Quintuple Quintuplicity of Forms of (Self-)Consciousness | 205

of absolute knowledge but also to show that each I-form is an autonomous quintuplicity, which is what Fichte is actually suggesting when he refers to all the five I-forms as effects of reason.

THE QUINTUPLICITY OF THE SENSUALIST (SELF-)CONSCIOUSNESS

The first form of consciousness is sensualism, a consciousness that absolutizes the factual object (i.e., nature) and recognizes it as its principle. This consciousness is convinced that everything it experiences was earlier in the senses. The I of sensualism understands reality as the appearance or manifestation of the sensibility-principle: being means appearing to the senses. Everything, even subjectivity, is regarded by this consciousness as essentially matter. The notion this consciousness has about itself consists of the subject's identification with the observed empirical reality. So the highest knowledge the sensualist consciousness obtains of itself is that the I is essentially matter: a material thing among material things.

The certainty the sensualist consciousness has of the existence of an external world adopts the form of a belief in nature (*Glaube an die Natur*). This belief occupies the place of the insight in the real nature of reason the sensualist I is not able to achieve. Therefore, the unifying principle is the belief in nature. This is the fundamental insight of the sensualist I. As such it determines the kind of philosophy, religion, morality, and legal order the sensualist consciousness develops in its attempt at systematizing and interpreting reality.

As already said, Fichte calls the philosophy of the sensualist I "materialism."[49] Following the principle of sensibility, this philosophy reflects on the experience of internal and external world as basically matter without any awareness of the spontaneity this reflection presupposes. In 1804^3 lectures, Fichte identifies this materialism with Schelling's philosophy. According to Fichte, Schelling's Absolute "is the object of perception considered as unity."[50]

Within the meaning-horizon opened by the belief in nature, the sensualist I develops a concept of God as food-giver (*Speisegebender*).[51] God's love to humanity is revealed in the fact that he will not allow humanity to starve. God appears as the personification of the wisdom and generosity of nature. There is only one commandment: thou shalt not abuse of God's liberality. Accordingly, piety consists of nothing but self-discipline in eating and drinking.

The self-discipline the Nature-God expects of human beings connects the religious realm with morality, since morality is for the sensualist I a set of rules for a wise enjoyment of nature. A wise man has learned to manage alimentary enjoyment in order to have at all times alimentary sustenance. So moral wisdom consists of knowing how to assure future alimentary enjoyment. The morality of the sensualist I seems to be a very poor form of Epicureanism: it is restricted to bring order and rationality only in alimentary enjoyment.

The sensualist I is aware of the need of positive law for social order. This is basically conceived as a supporting instrument for sensualist morality. By establishing rules that compels individuals to properly and carefully enjoy the gifts provided by the Nature-God, positive law aims at guaranteeing the future alimentary enjoyment, which is according to the sensualist morality the last goal of the individual's actions.

THE QUINTUPLICITY OF THE LEGAL (SELF-)CONSCIOUSNESS

The second form of (self-)consciousness produces, conceives, and experiences reality from an absolutely legal point of view. It absolutizes the subject as it appears in the legal dimension of life. Legal or juridical life means living in a free and egalitarian society under the rule of law. The legal or juridical (self-)consciousness finds in this realm of existence the authentic nature of both the rational being and its world. This consciousness interprets everything essentially in legal terms. Being means for the legal consciousness being subjected to external laws that guarantee equality among all rational beings. The juridical I knows itself as legal person among legal persons. The I appears to itself as essentially citizen; its world is the civil society.

Constitutive for this consciousness is also the lack of that insight on the nature and the last goal of reason the doctrine of science provides. But instead of a belief in nature, what replaces this insight is a belief in the equality of all persons before the law. This juridical equality now plays the function of the unifying principle. It homogenizes the multiplicity of rational beings by bringing them under the unity of the law. It functions at the same time as the element that makes differences among them possible, since rational beings become individuals only through reciprocal recognition as juridical persons. The universality and unifying power of the law creates the world all individuals experience as the same and share.

Although Fichte does not mention what kind of philosophy is appropriate for the juridical consciousness, there are at least two philosophical views that represent the main features of the legal I and its world. The first one is the factual idealism Fichte discusses in the Thirteenth Lecture of *1804 Wissenschaftslehre*. This can be considered as the philosophy of the legal subject, namely of the subject conceived in its facticity, since it remains on the level of the facts of consciousness (*Thatsachen des Bewußtseyns*) and considers consequently pure (self-)consciousness, that is, the absolute I, and the Absolute as facts. The reduction of subjectivity to citizen that characterizes the legal consciousness appears in this idealism as the reduction of (self-)generating activity (*Thathandlung* or *Genesis*) to facts of consciousness.[52] This idealism cannot see the spontaneous activity of the I in thinking and focuses only in "thinking as thinking," namely in the logical laws of the facts of consciousness. In this regard, Reinhold (after 1800) and Bardili can be counted as representatives of the philosophy of the legal I.[53] On the other hand, utilitarianism in its more general conception seems also to be the candidate for a philosophy of the legal consciousness, since not only social and legal equality but also the economic wealth of civil society is fundamental for the legal I. Utilitarianism can be read as the philosophical understanding this consciousness has of the relation between civil society and citizens, namely between the unity of the multiplicity of rational beings in the idea of a common good of society and the affirmation of this multiplicity as such through promoting that each individual pursues its own particular good.

Concerning the religious dimension of the I, the legal consciousness constructs a concept of God mediated by the law: God is conceived as dispensing justice and guaranteeing equality in the universe. God politically administrates the universe, and he is, in this regard, the highest political and juridical authority. The concept of God of this consciousness is a projection of the juridical and political authority of civil society.

The juridical consciousness understands morality as a pre-legal version of the equality positive law establishes and guarantees. A morally good individual serves with its actions to the interest of society. So concerning the content, moral and right-relations do not differ from each other. Morally good is everything that promotes the welfare of civil society. However, for the juridical consciousness, morality is not the foundation of positive law. On the contrary, the truth of morality lies for the legal I in the idea of the equality of citizens before the law.

Like morality, nature appears in this form of consciousness as having its principle in an other. The economic prosperity of civil society is what gives nature a meaning. The physical world exists, as Fichte says, only for the sake of civil industry (*bürgerliche Industrie*).[54]

The Quintuplicity of the Moral (Self-)Consciousness

Whereas the first two forms of consciousness discover their principles in the phenomenal world, respectively, the existent object and subject, the principle of the third I-form, the moral (self-)consciousness, refers to a noumenal entity: the subject's free acting conceived in its realization in the infinity of time. In the short description Fichte offers in the *1804 Wissenschaftslehre* of this form of consciousness, it is not difficult to note that Fichte identifies it with his own reading of the Kantian philosophy.[55]

"Free" means for the moral I being liberated from both the heteronomy of the individual actions in civil life that the second form of consciousness promoted and the belief of nature that determines and guides the first one. The subject's free activity remains a noumenon only accessible to the subject of the action and can only be indirectly thematized in its reference to the existent subject. The principle of the moral (self-)consciousness homogenizes the multiplicity of the subjects by reducing them to executers of the same action, which is the never-ending attempt at acting according to maxims that formally coincide with the categorical imperative. The autonomous validity of all individual differences disappears as soon as it is confronted with the unity of the moral subject all rational beings are when they freely act.[56] The multiplicity is to be found in the principle itself, which is not merely freedom or free action but rather the idea of an infinite series of supra-individual free actions. From the point of view of moral consciousness, it is impossible for these actions, what actually *is*, to be theoretically objectivized. Being means freely and/or autonomously acting (in the sense of the Kantian second critique). The moral consciousness finds its truth, its own nature, in this freedom and comprehends itself essentially as free being, a noumenon.

Fichte does not say explicitly what is the belief that serves as unifying principle and allows this form of consciousness access to a knowledge of itself and the external world. However, the implicit reference to Kant permits stating that this belief coincides with what Kant calls in his first critique the "practical interest"[57] of the rational being. It consists basically of the belief in the absolute freedom as criterion to interpret oneself and the world. Indeed, this belief brings on the existential level of the rational being a solution to the antinomy between determinism and free will and makes possible that the moral I experiences reality as an ordered totality.

The philosophy of the moral (self-)consciousness is the Kantian philosophy, more specifically, Kant's transcendental philosophy as presented in his first two critiques, as Fichte remarks in his doctrine of religion of 1806. This philosophy is according to Fichte the "most consequent example"[58] of this form of consciousness. As it is well-known, Fichte put together the moral and the legal I in the second of his 1806 five of worldviews. Nevertheless, when comparing the explanation of this worldview with the moral I of the *1804 Wissenschaftslehre*, it becomes evident that they share the same principle and describe the I and its world in the same terms.[59]

The God of the moral consciousness is the God Kant presents in his second critique. It does not exist autonomously but in function of the moral law. If there were no moral law, there would be for this (self-)consciousness no need for a God. God's existence is reduced to what Kant calls a postulate of practical reason: a plus of meaning externally inserted in the categoricity of the moral duty.[60]

The moral consciousness conceives civil society, the realm of legality, as an instrument for the moral law. According to the moral I, human beings exist and interact only "in order to be or become moral beings."[61] The same can be said about nature, understood as the external world in general: this is "nothing but the sphere of compulsory acting" (*pflichtmäßiges Handeln*).[62]

The Quintuplicity of the Religious (Self-)Consciousness

As the moral I, the religious (self-)consciousness discovers its principle in the noumenal dimension of reality, but unlike the moral I, this (self-)consciousness finds its principle in the absolute shaping activity and life of the absolute object, God. As in the case of the third I-form, the religious (self-)consciousness conceives the unity of the principle in terms of a multiplicity—the manifestations of a living God in the interior man—and the multiplicity of human beings as a unity, the devoted man described in Fichte's philosophy of religion.[63] The religious I knows itself as a living image of this God, whereas it interprets the world of this consciousness as his dead image.[64] What *is*, is actually only God.

This consciousness finds the unity of certainty and truth in its belief in a God that lives and acts in the devoted individual. Lacking the insight of the doctrine of science about the absolute freedom of reason, the religious I interprets its own creative freedom as the agency of God in the individual rational being. According to Fichte, religion represents the "absolute disappearing and dissolution [of the pure will] in the absolute."[65]

The philosophy of the religious I is not mentioned in the 1804 manuscripts. However, the philosophy this consciousness develops cannot be far from Jacobi's notion of philosophy as a "knowledge of the nothingness."[66] The devoted consciousness knows that God lives in its heart and considers not only that this knowledge is sufficient but also that any conceptual addition to this religious experience, based either on scientific or philosophical research, is nothing but non-sense, illusions the human being creates in order to organize the ignorance inherent to humanity.[67] A philosophy that attempts at a concept of God is not only nihilism but also and necessarily atheism.[68] In this condemnation of not-devoted philosophy, Fichte sees nothing but dogmatism. Moreover, it reveals that the religious consciousness is not prepared for philosophical discussions.[69]

The content of the morality of the religious I does not differ much from the morality of the moral (self-)consciousness. The difference lies in the interpretation of the moral action. Whereas the moral I considers it "as its own work," the religious I sees in its morally good actions the "divine work."[70] For the religious consciousness, God is actively present even in its will, appetites, and happiness. The total disappearance of this consciousness in God reveals in its disinterest or indifference toward political matters. Civil society is nothing but an efflux of God. The same can be said about the way the religious consciousness conceives nature. As such, nature represents in fact the death-being, being outside God. Nevertheless, considered as God's efflux, it lives. Nature's life, however, is God's life.[71]

According to this reconstruction of the four non-philosophical forms of (self-)consciousness, it is possible to obtain a complete view of all twenty-five determinations of the quintuplicity of quintuplicities of the *1804 Wissenschaftslehre* (see table 10.3).

The analysis of Fichte's 1804 quintuplicity of quintuplicities shows that this concept is a genetical deduction not only of the correct form of phenomenal existence of absolute knowledge but also of the defective ways of understanding the self and its world. Hence, the quintuplicity of quintuplicities represents the accomplishment of the task of the doctrine of science since it exhausts the a priori realm of possible forms of existent (self-)consciousness and reconstructs the genesis of consciousness and world in all their possible configurations. In this regard, it can be considered as the "solution to the enigma of world of consciousness"[72] Fichte promised to his audience in 1804.

Table 10.3. Proposed Reconstruction of Fichte's Fivefold Quintuplicity (25 Elements)

	Sensualist I	Legal I	Moral I	Religious I	Philosophical I
Philosophy	Materialism (Schelling)	Factual idealism (Reinhold, Bardili) and utilitarianism	Kantian philosophy according to his first two critiques	Jacobi's notion of philosophy as nihilism	**Principe of the Doctrine of Science: insight instead of belief (Doctrine of Science as philosophia prima)**
Religion	Nature-religion: revelation of God in nature's generosity	God dispensing justice in the universe	God as postulate of practical reason	**Religion-Principle: Belief in the revelation of God in consciousness**	Scientific concept of religion (doctrine of religion as part of the system of the WL)
Morality	Poor epicureanism	Moral translation of legal intersubjectivity	**Moral principle: belief in the moral autonomy of the subject**	God's grace influencing moral actions	Scientific concept of morality (doctrine of customs as part of the system of the WL)
Legality	Law administrating enjoyment	**Legality Principle: belief in Personhood**	Law as means for the subject's moral development	Society as God's efflux (creation)	Scientific concept of rights and law (doctrine of law as part of the system of the WL)
Sense	**Sensibility Principle: belief in nature**	Nature as material for civil industry	Material for moral action	Nature as God's efflux (creation)	Scientific concept of nature (doctrine of nature as part of the system of the WL)

Source: Author provided.

Notes

1. *WL*-1804², 200; *GA*, II/8, 419. All translations are my own.
2. *WL*-1804², 28; *GA*, II/8, 21.
3. *WLnm[K]*, *GA*, IV/3, 500–02.
4. *WL*-1804², 28; *GA*, II/8, 21.
5. *GA*, II/8, XXXVI.
6. *WL*-1804¹, 117–18; *GA*, II/7, 232–35; and *WL*-1804², 199–200; *GA*, II/8, 417–21.
7. *WL*-1804³, 170; *GA*, II/7, 354–68.
8. *WLnm[K]*, *GA*, IV/3, 502.
9. On the quintuplicity of the Erlangen doctrine of science of 1805 see my "Down by Law: On the Structure of Fichte's 1805 *Wissenschaftslehre*," in *The Bloomsbury Handbook of Fichte*, ed. M. Bykova (London: Bloomsbury, 2020), 217–33.
10. *GA*, I/8, 111–15.
11. *GA*, I/8, 198–201.
12. *GA*, I/9, 106–12.
13. KrV B94.
14. *GA*, I/9, 112–13.
15. *GA*, I/9, 106.
16. *GA*, I/8, 64–65.
17. G. W. F. Hegel, *Werke in 20 Bänden* (Frankfurt AM: Suhrkamp, 1979), bd. 8, 198.
18. *WL*-1804¹, 117; *GA*, II/7, 233.
19. *GA*, I/8, 201.
20. *WL-nm[K]*, *GA*, IV/3, 508. See also *WLnm[H]*, *GA*, IV/2, 241.
21. *SS*, *GA*, I/5, 229–30. See also *WL*-1804², *GA*, II/8, 417.
22. *WL*-1804², 33; *GA*, II/8, 35.
23. *WL*-1804², 198; *GA*, II/8, 415.
24. This idea of a more originary categorical imperative than the Kantian one as the fundamental law of reason can be found already in the first published version of the doctrine of science (*GWL*, *GA*, I/2, 396 n.). Furthermore, it seems to have been one of the first insights Fichte had in the time he was trying to develop his own philosophical system by critically analyzing and improving Reinhold's elementary philosophy (*Own Meditations on Elementary Philosophy*, 1793/1794; *GA*, II/3, 48, 233).
25. *WL*-1804², 196; *GA*, II/8, 411.
26. *WL*-1804², 120–21; *GA*, II/8, 241–43.
27. *WL*-1804², 196; *GA*, II/8, 411.
28. *WL*-1804², 194; *GA*, II/8, 407.
29. *WL*-1804², 198; *GA*, II/8, 415. See also *WL*-1804¹; *GA*, II/7, 150; and *WL*-1804³, *GA*, I/7, 360.

30. *WL*-1804², 27–28; *GA*, II/8, 19–21. See also *GA*, I/3, 83 (*Ueber Belebung und Erhöhung des reinen Interesse für die Wahrheit*, 1795).
31. *WL*-1804², 198; *GA*, II/8, 415.
32. George Di Giovanni, "Fichte's Transcendental Spinozism (1804)," in *The Bloomsbury Handbook of Fichte*, 208.
33. *WL*-1804², 126; *GA*, II/8, 255.
34. *WL*-1804², 23; *GA*, II/8, 9.
35. *WL*-1804², 34; *GA*, II/8, 37.
36. *WL*-1804², 51; *GA*, II/8, 77.
37. *WL*-1804², 30; *GA*, II/8, 27.
38. *WL*-1804¹; *GA*, II/7, 70.
39. *WL*-1804², 121; *GA*, II/8, 243.
40. *WL*-1804¹; *GA*, II/7, 197.
41. *WL*-1804², 196; *GA*, II/8, 411.
42. *WL*-1804², 200; *GA*, II/8, 421.
43. *WL*-1804², 199; *GA*, II/8, 417.
44. *WL*-1804¹; *GA*, II/7, 232.
45. *WL*-1804¹; *GA*, I/7, 150.
46. *WL*-1804², 199; *GA*, II/8, 417.
47. *WL*-1804², 200; *GA*, II/8, 419.
48. *WL*-1804²; *GA*, II/8, 417.
49. *WL*-1804², 199; *GA*, II/8, 417.
50. *WL*-1804³; *GA*, II/7, 366–67.
51. *WL*-1804², 200; *GA*, II/8, 419.
52. *WL*-1804², 105; *GA*, II/8, 201–3. See also 1804², 98–99; *GA*, II/8, 187–89.
53. *WL*-1804², 104; *GA*, II/8, 197. See also Fichte's review of Bardili's *Grundriss der Ersten Logik*, 1800, *GA*, I/6, 433–50, esp. 436–42; and his *Antwortschreiben an Herrn Professor Reinhold* (1801), *GA*, I/7, 291–24, esp. 295.
54. *WL*-1804², 200; *GA*, II/8, 419.
55. *WL*-1804², 31–33; *GA*, II/8, 29–33.
56. *WL*-1804¹; *GA*, II/7, 233.
57. KrV B 503–04. See on Kantian "practical interest" my "Was vernünftig ist, das ist widersprüchlich und was widersprüchlich ist, das ist vernünftig: Widerspruch und Wirklichkeit der Vernunft in Kants Philosophie," in *Zirkel-Widerspruch-Paradoxon: Das Denken des Selbst in der Klassischen Deutschen Philosophie und in der Gegenwart*, eds. Chr. Asmuth and W. Ehrmann (Würzburg: Königshausen & Neumann, 2015), 111–26.
58. *GA*, I/9, 108 (*Die Anweisung zum seligen Leben*, Fifth Lecture).
59. *GA*, I/9, 107–8.
60. KpV, AA 05, 126.
61. *WL*-1804², 200; *GA*, II/8, 419.
62. *WL*-1804², 200; *GA*, II/8, 419; see also *GA*, I/9, 107.

63. *GA*, I/9, 111–12 (*Die Anweisung zum seligen Leben*, Fifth Lecture).
64. *GA*, I/9, 111.
65. WL-1804³; *GA*, II/7, 368.
66. *GA*, III/3, 245 (*Jacobi an Fichte*).
67. *GA*, III/3, 238 (*Jacobi an Fichte*).
68. *GA*, III/3, 249 (*Jacobi an Fichte*).
69. *GA*, I/7, 323 (*Antwortschreiben an Herrn Professor Reinhold*, 1801).
70. WL-1804², 200; *GA*, II/8, 419.
71. *GA*, I/9, 111 (*Die Anweisung zum seligen Leben*).
72. *GA*, I/8, 17.

Chapter 11

Immanent Thinking and the Activity of Philosophizing in Fichte's *1804 Wissenschaftslehre*

Angelica Nuzzo

Fichte's 1804 series of lectures on yet another version of the *Wissenschaftslehre* offers a unique insight not only into his project of a philosophical science to follow and indeed complete Kant's transcendental enterprise but also into his peculiar conception of the method or procedure of philosophizing that is constitutive of such a science. It is often underscored, in the aftermath of Fichte's own occasional proclamations, that for him the act of thinking with and within the *Wissenschaftslehre* is a performative, fundamentally practical gesture. In this way, the action or *Thathandlung* that informs from early on his idea of thinking actually shapes the way in which philosophical thinking itself is to construct the Doctrine of Science. Beyond restating this general point, however, the 1804 lectures offer a further, more concrete sense of what the activity of philosophizing in Fichte's sense looks like.[1] And this is so much more remarkable since at stake herein is not the act of an isolated "I" (the philosopher Fichte's I or even the "absolute" I)[2] but rather the activity of a "we"—the collective subject that is setting out to enter the path of the *Wissenschaftslehre* thereby, at the same time, expounding the nature and essence of this (version of the) new science. Week after week, in his 1804 lectures Fichte addresses the audience he teaches, leading them—and now leading us, modern readers—to the insight into the new proposed *Wissenschaftslehre*. He guides us first into the prolegomena, then leads us to the threshold of the actual science, then within the science itself up to its point of absolute origin or genesis, then down again to the level of appearance. Reading these lectures, we ourselves are engaged (or are summoned to engage) in the very activity that the *Wissenschaftslehre* purports to be—thinking (or rather acting) and being are indeed one in the way the Doctrine of Science comes to life in our own activity. We understand what the *Wissenschaftslehre* is by actively making or constructing it, allegedly step by step, in our own self, in our own thought, and in our own life. And Fichte reminds us often, at the beginning of each lecture, of what our psychological state needs to be in order for us to be up to the task he is setting for us, the task that is the *Wissenschaftslehre* itself. It is not just a question of understanding (and not mis-understanding) the principles of the Doctrine of Science but it is also, more fundamentally, a matter of the quality of our participation. Thus, Fichte requires from us "full, complete attention," thereby underscoring that at stake in the science of knowing is our self-awareness and self-observation. After all, *we* are the ones who are mobilized in the intellectual construction that the new *Wissenschaftslehre* purports to be. Accordingly, at each step of the way, we are encouraged to check back on our spiritual and intellectual powers and progress. Indeed, Fichte's insistence on having our "full, complete attention as distinct from that partial attention which hears with half an ear and thinks with half its thinking power" is a healthy reminder of how philosophy should be done. This is the case for his audience in 1804 but even more so for us today, for us who are so prone to distraction, interruption, multitasking, and half thoughts (or even a lesser fraction of a thought).[3] To be sure, despite Fichte's rootedness in the immediate post-Kantian aftermath, there is something very ancient to this method—or indeed style—of philosophizing, something reminiscent of the conversational mode of Plato (at least, the not fully dialogical style of the later Plato)[4] or, at times, something of the loftiness of Plotinus's enterprise, an initiation or an "ascent,"[5] as it were, to the highest One—or to the utterly pure light—open only to selected few.[6] We should, indeed, be willing to lend him our full, complete attention.

And yet, as much as this performative embrace of thinking's own personal living activity is offered as the general requirement of the program laid out by the new *Wissenschaftslehre* and is further underscored, in 1804, by Fichte's lecture style at each step of the way, it is hard to admit that after the programmatic commitment made at the beginning we are in fact still in the flow of that thinking activity once the *Wissenschaftslehre* starts laying out its formulae (starting with the simple):

$$A \bullet \text{---B--T---} \text{ and } A \text{ x, y, z} \bullet \text{B--T}).^7$$

We have, then, most likely lost that flow when Fichte abruptly discloses the reality of the Pure Light, the Absolute, the Divine Life, insisting that we are now ourselves placed in that absolute point of origin. How did we get there? Did "we" really ever get there *in our own thinking*? It is indeed hard to answer in the positive. I, for one (this time I should humbly use the first-person pronoun here and speak for myself), must confess that my spiritual "eye" may have indeed "remained factical" time and again, hence "entirely closed to the higher world of the conceptual beyond."[8] On the other hand, the opposite danger may also undermine our progress, namely the danger of falling into "speculative fantasy" instead of following "pure, ever serene reason." Indeed, the tendency of falling prey of the illusion of a too easy grasp of the absolute is an error, Fichte warns us, as bad as the "stubbornness of empiricism."[9]

In this chapter, I shall address the general question of the method endorsed or rather actually performed by Fichte along with the "we" made up by his audience and readers of then and now in the 1804 lectures on the *Wissenschaftslehre*. At stake is the way in which we do indeed move up or rather back, transcendentally, to the highest point of origin, to the very genesis of the oneness of thinking and being while retaining the facticity and empirical phenomenality proper to all thinking process as such. In particular, I am interested in what I call the issue of *immanence*, namely in whether the act of *thinking within the Wissenschaftslehre* does suffice to constitute the very form and content of this science without recurring to external, reflective intervention, or whether instead a position outside thinking's own activity must be appealed to at some point (this could be, perhaps, Fichte himself as the teacher).[10] Now, crucial to the very idea of philosophy (or, rather, to the activity of philosophizing) as *Wissenschaftslehre* is the claim that "there is a truth which alone is true and everything apart from this is unconditionally false." This is the most general presupposition that Fichte advances, "in all seriousness," he insists, right at the beginning of the First Lecture.[11] At stake, then, in the project of the *Wissenschaftslehre*, is the immanent process whereby such an unconditional absolute truth is achieved by (our) thinking. This, however, is the process in which thinking finds itself always already engaged once the initial decision to think with and within the *Wissenschaftslehre* is made. This means that at no point we should in fact meet the falsity that the presupposition of the First Lecture places right outside of the *Wissenschaftslehre*, thoroughly excluding it from philosophy as such. The point of blindness, then (the spiritual "eye" utterly "shut closed" at the level of facticity of which Fichte warns us), which may occur in the process (to the distracted audience, that is), is only a failure to really think with the immanent flow of the *Wissenschaftslehre*. It represents the audience drifting away from Fichte's lecture. It does not, however, seem to be itself part of the Doctrine of Science. It is not an immanent (let alone necessary) stage of its action. And yet, there is a sense in which the constitutive separation of consciousness and truth brings the possibility of error (or the illusion of truth for consciousness) right at the heart of the movement of thinking in the science.[12]

To put this point differently, I am interested in the role that negativity and the possibility of "refutation"[13] plays in the act of philosophizing presented in the *1804 Wissenschaftslehre*. I am interested in the possible point of convergence between immanence and negativity. I should say, at the outset, that I understand negativity broadly on a spectrum that covers the position of interruption of the flux of scientific thinking, the failure to grant full attention, existential doubt, and skepticism toward truth in its absoluteness.

I begin this chapter by sketching out some moments of the historical constellation in which Fichte's *1804 Wissenschaftslehre* is inscribed, dwelling in particular on one point of Kant's *Critique of Pure Reason*. In the second part of the chapter, I move on to the discussion of the procedure employed by Fichte's presentation in the 1804 lectures, addressing, in particular, the issue of immanence. I shall use some relevant methodological ideas of Hegel's 1807 *Phenomenology of Spirit* in order to highlight Fichte's position. I employ these references in a systematic rather than historical way.[14] The broader focus of my argument is the way in which, in the period 1804–1807, Fichte and Hegel while embracing analogous ideas concerning the nature and task of philosophizing in Kant's aftermath end up crystallizing such ideas in works that display a very different form and structure. The point is that this difference is due to the method—alternatively transcendental and dialectical—that gives these sciences their distinctive shape. Ultimately at stake is the different way in which these philosophical methods respectively address the negativity or falsity encountered by thinking on its way to the highest truth. Ultimately at issue is philosophy's stance toward methodological skepticism.

The Art of Philosophizing and Its Conditions—After Kant

In the first two lectures of the 1804 cycle, Fichte dwells on the philosophical scene on which the *Wissenschaftslehre* is announced as making its unique innovations. Herein, Kant is the overwhelming presence, overshadowing by far any other player. Opening one's lectures on philosophy with a more or less detailed sketch of the history of philosophy up to that point should be recognized as a custom of the time, a custom that is famously echoed in the opening pages of the first preface to the *Critique of Pure Reason* (1781).[15] Fichte follows Kant, but explicitly abbreviates the history of philosophy in declaring it all enclosed in the turning point of Kantianism. What is left to do is to improve on Kant's transcendental philosophy, but doing so means to thread the utterly new path of the *Wissenschaftslehre*.[16] Indeed, Fichte considers it useful to historically characterize the Doctrine of Science only in relation to "the sole neighbor against which it is immediately juxtaposed and to which it can be compared: Kantian philosophy." He is adamant in claiming his right to ignore the history of philosophy before Kant. Historically as well as systematically, he maintains that the new "science of knowing" can be directly compared neither to any of the pre-Kantian philosophies nor to any of the "recent afterbirths, since it shares nothing with them." The only comparison is Kant's philosophy with which Fichte's *Wissenschaftslehre* "shares the common genus of transcendentalism." The transcendental *method*, then, is the ground on which Fichte locates the task of "demarcating" his own philosophy from Kant's.[17]

On Fichte's view, the turning point of Kant's philosophy against his predecessors consists in positing the absolute neither in "being," that is, in "the dead thing as thing"[18] (as all pre-Kantians have done), nor in subjective consciousness or knowing but "in the oneness of both,"[19] that is, in the "indivisible union of being and thinking." And yet, it is Fichte's considered view of Kant's transcendental philosophy throughout the three *Critiques* that he has been unable to grasp the most original root—the truth or the absolute—to which the transcendental inquiry should instead have led. From this account one may infer that Fichte addresses Kant's transcendentalism by turning the question of method into a metaphysical question, that is, into the question of the absolute as the point of origin to which the transcendental regress should lead. Kant's issue of the conditions of possibility of experience becomes Fichte's issue of the metaphysical origin or genesis of experiential facticity. As a consequence, Fichte suggests that Kant has posited three distinct "absolutes" that remain unfortunately distinct thereby blocking the ascent of the transcendental method, that is, ultimately, leaving the promise of Kant's philosophy unfulfilled. For Kant, "there are actually three absolutes and the true unitary absolute fades to their common property."[20] This seems, in fact, a strange account of Kant's critical project. In the *Critique of Pure Reason*, Fichte argues, the "absolute (x)" is *sensible experience*—its absoluteness being measured in relation to the disappointing way in which Kant accounts for the value of reason's Ideas and, more generally, of the "higher, spiritual world."[21] The second absolute is the "moral world = z" of the *Critique of Practical Reason* (in which "the high inner morality of the man [Kant] corrected the philosopher").[22] The moral world discloses the supersensible, higher dimension inaccessible to the merely empirical knowing of the first *Critique* as well as the true dimension of subjectivity. Finally, in the *Critique of Judgment*, Kant reaches his "third absolute = y." This is, Fichte argues, the "confession" that the sensible and the supersensible worlds must somehow come together "in a common but wholly unknown root"[23]—this latter formulation being Fichte's adaptation of the expression used by Kant in the first *Critique* to indicate the possible common root of the two branches of the human cognitive faculty, namely sensibility and understanding.[24] In Fichte's rendition, instead, at stake is the "common root" of Kant's three absolutes, that is, ultimately, that one and unique absolute that stands at the convergence of all forms of human experience (perhaps, still with Kant, as their condition of possibility). On this basis, the immanent, performative action staged by thinking in the science of knowing purports to exhibit that higher absolute in our own experience.

Set against this reconstruction of Kant's critical "transcendentalism," Fichte sees the task of the Doctrine of Science as that of disclosing the true point of origin that has remained hidden to Kant himself—the One in which all manifoldness is ultimately and necessarily unified. The absolute "A is divided into B and T and into x, y, z; all at one stroke,"[25] promises Fichte at the beginning of the Third Lecture. And we are supposed to produce this movement ourselves and in ourselves. What follows from the fact that Kant's philosophy has remained "trapped" in the "three absolutes"[26] without being able to indicate their point of convergence is not only the incompleteness of his transcendental philosophy, which has not dared to be transcendental enough as to discover the one common root of all knowledge and being or, in another Fichtean formulation, has only offered a "synthesis *post factum*" but not a truly "*genetic* synthesis."[27] What follows from Kant's incomplete transcendentalism is also a fundamental skepticism toward philosophy's capacity to reach the truth—a skepticism that has become, historically, a widespread phenomenon of the age. To be sure, Kant had already contended with the opposition of dogmatists and skeptics as he presented the *Critique of Pure Reason* as the only way out of their stalemate, hence as the only way of saving knowledge in its truth against the skeptic's attacks.[28]

Fichte opens the First Lecture by locating his philosophy in the present time in a way that not only echoes the beginning of Kant's preface to the 1781 edition of the first *Critique* but reminds, perhaps even more closely, of Hegel's 1807 preface to the *Phenomenology of Spirit* (as well as of positions of his earlier Jena years). The "chief characteristic of the present time," Fichte maintains, "is that in it life has become merely *historical* and *symbolic*, while *real living* is scarcely ever found." Countering what Hegel calls around the same period the dead "positivity" that stiffens the spontaneity of life—and in particular thinking's life—Fichte's enterprise is to bring thinking (and in particular *philosophical* thinking) to rejoin the immediacy of life. This is the first "decision" he asks us to make: to undertake the *living* thought process again for ourselves. Herein lies the foundational *practical* moment of these lectures. This is also the condition of the *Wissenschaftslehre*, which is set against the "historical superficiality" of the age, the "dispersion into the most multifarious and contradictory opinions, indecisiveness about everything altogether, and absolute indifference to truth."[29] Dogmatism and skepticism (along with what Kant had already called in the 1781 preface "indifferentism") are opposite, all-too-easy answers to the climate of the time.[30] The foundational decision to embrace truth should be seen as Fichte's first and foremost argument against the skeptic. Her position is checked at the door.[31]

Fichte's most general twofold "presupposition" of all philosophizing is set directly against this intellectual scene, and in particular against modern skepticism. He claims that "there is a truth which alone is true and everything apart from this is unconditionally false; further, that this truth can actually be found and be immediately evident as unconditionally true." The methodological claim follows. "Not even the least spark" of such truth, Fichte contends, "can be grasped or communicated historically, as an appropriation from someone else's mind," that is, merely empirically or "factically." Rather, "whomever would have it must produce it entirely out of himself."[32] Alternatively, Fichte warns that the "essence of the science" of knowing can be disclosed only by "its originator" in the form of the present lectures (and not by any other indirect report).[33] In sum, there is truth; such truth is absolute to the extent that it excludes all else as false. The access to this truth is not an act of "appropriation" of something foreign—and given (historically and externally) from and by a foreign mind. It is, instead, the living, creative act of self-production in which each person or mind should be engaged. There seems to be, properly, no confrontation with anything foreign or other—factical or historical—let alone false in this path of the *Wissenschaftslehre*. The skeptic remains utterly outside of the act of philosophizing. Or, to put this point differently, outside of the position of immanence is only nihilism: "Whoever does not do this will never obtain the object about which we speak here. And since our whole discourse will be about this object, he will have no object at all; for him our entire discourse will be words about pure, bare nothingness."[34] The skeptic seems to be doubting and denying something else entirely than what the philosopher is after. On the other hand, however, this means that the self-production of truth taking place in the philosophizing activity of Fichte's lectures is a fundamentally closed action that may well engage a collective "we" (and not a solipsistic I), but this is a collective "we" that is always already of likeminded, of minds in agreement about that unique truth to be pursued against the skeptic. Indeed, Fichte sees a "categorical decisiveness between truth and error" as the condition of (all) science. Now, such a categorical separation is precisely what shuts out once and for all the "skeptical paralysis" of all contemporary philosophies.[35] This, I suggest, is a position that fundamentally distinguishes Fichte's *Wissenschaftslehre* from Hegel's phenomenological dialectic. In the latter, skepticism is coopted as an immanent force within the phenomenological movement of consciousness. Indeed, from the position of immanence, that is, within consciousness, the *Phenomenology* is, in a famous formulation, the "way of doubt, or, more properly, the way of despair."[36] The *Phenomenology* is itself the movement of a complete skepticism that in its completeness refutes itself. I shall suggest, in the final part of the chapter, that despite his programmatic distance from Hegel's project, Fichte does in fact embrace a similar idea at a more advanced stage of his 1804 lectures.

In the Doctrine of Method of the first *Critique*, Kant establishes an idea of philosophy that constitutes the background for the notion of philosophizing as active, immanent doing characterizing, among others, Fichte's *1804 Wissenschaftslehre* and Hegel 1807 *Phenomenology*. Pleading for the unification of all our cognitions into a "system" "under the government of reason," Kant famously defines the "system" as "the unity of the manifold cognitions under one idea." Is philosophy a system—or ought it to be?[37] This is a crucial question for all the post-Kantians. Kant explains that the "architectonic unity" of the system (as opposed to the "technical" unity) is the unity provided by reason's a priori ends, not by empirical contingent aims.[38] At this advanced point of the *Critique*, Kant indicates the task of this work as that of "outlining the architectonic of all cognitions from pure reason"—reason, he reiterates, being the second branch of our cognitive faculty next to the empirical.[39] With regard to the form of cognition ("subjectively"), Kant opposes "historical" to "rational" cognition. The former is obtained and learned according to a "*fremde[r] Vernunft*"—to an alien reason that merely imitates, does not create ("*das nachbildende Vermögen ist nicht das erzeugende*"). The latter is cognition originating "*from* reason itself (*aus Vernunft*)."[40] Philosophical cognition is of this kind insofar as it is "cognition from concepts" and not "from the construction of concepts," which is instead mathematical cognition. Philosophical reason is (or rather ought to be) creative, not imitative; in its creation, it does not harken to "alien reason" but only to itself. Fichte's 1804 lectures pick up faithfully and programmatically this Kantian thought.[41]

In this framework, Kant draws a set of important distinctions. First is the distinction between philosophy (as a discipline and "idea") and philosophizing (as an ongoing activity). He claims that one cannot learn philosophy ("except historically") because there is no actual philosophy to be learned (hence the creativity required in this pursuit). Philosophy is the "mere idea of a possible science" never given *in concreto*. Indeed, Kant asks, "Where is it?"—where is philosophy in actuality? "Who has possession of it?"[42] Philosophy—let alone the "system" of philosophy—is nowhere to be found *in concreto*. In its ideality, philosophy seems to be out of time and out of place—out of the world, as it were. On the other hand, however, one can learn the *activity of philosophizing*, which is the exercise of the "talent of reason" in following its general principles. Unlike (the idea of) philosophy, philosophizing is the open-ended process taking place in the world and aiming at the idea of that possible science (aiming at being congruent with that idea). It is the activity practiced by philosophers (or by aspiring philosophers) in the world. This is the point that becomes relevant in the post-Kantian discussion. While it is often repeated that many post-Kantians consider the task of philosophy to provide the "system" that Kant's transcendentalism has promised but not actually given, I want to shift the focus to the distinction between the *idea of philosophy* and the *activity of philosophizing*. The latter, in its worldly reality and worldly embeddedness, is at the basis of Fichte's performative idea of the method of the science of knowing—the method that we see concretely at work in the 1804 lectures. But it is also the ground on which Hegel develops his own idea of the phenomenological path leading consciousness to the standpoint of science.

After having separated the idea of philosophy and the activity of philosophizing—the former merely ideal, the latter eminently real and concrete—Kant introduces the second distinction, that between *Schulbegriff* and *Weltbegriff* of philosophy. Importantly, such a distinction is placed in the specific time frame of the present, setting to the present a specific task. "*Until now*," Kant maintains, "the concept of philosophy has only been a *Schulbegriff*, namely, that of a system of cognition" the end of which is nothing more than "the systematic unity of this knowledge, hence only the logical perfection" and completeness of cognition. "But there is also a *Weltbegriff* (*conceptus cosmicus*) of philosophy that has always grounded this term, especially when it is, as it were, personified and represented as an archetype in the ideal of the philosopher."[43] The *Weltbegriff* of philosophy is somehow more original and grounding than the *Schulbegriff* and shows this originality "especially" in the personification and individualization that the idea of philosophy receives in the "ideal of the philosopher." Somehow, in the philosopher (as ideal), philosophy comes closer to the world joining its *conceptus cosmicus*, which needs now to be retrieved by the critical and transcendental standpoint beyond its dominant scholastic notion. The *Weltbegriff*, Kant argues, sets "all cognition in relation to the essential ends of human reason." In this perspective, the philosopher is not a "*Vernunftkünstler*" occupied with building a logically consistent system (as the mathematician, the natural scientist, the logician are). In referring all cognition to the "essential ends" of reason, the philosopher is rather "the legislator of human reason."[44] Now Fichte's conception of the activity of philosophizing crystallized in the Doctrine of Science harkens back to Kant's cosmical-cosmopolitan concept of philosophy that lies, transcendentally, at the root of the historical and scholastic concept of philosophy. Kant insists that the concept of the world is related to reason's highest and most essential ends (not to mere logical systematicity). It is related to ends in which everyone has a necessary interest. These practical ends shape the activity of philosophizing in the world. Accordingly, the world is the expanded sphere of a rationality that is fundamentally intersubjective or collective. Ultimately, the *Weltbegriff* of philosophy accounts for the world in which reason exercises its legislative activity with regard to its most essential ends.

Transcendental and Phenomenological Immanence: Fichte and Hegel

While in the passage of the Architectonic Kant underscores the moral-practical import of philosophy in its cosmopolitical concept, in the 1804 lectures Fichte's focus is chiefly metaphysical. Transcendentally, reason connects not so much with its highest moral ends but with its first absolute origin or point of genesis. Ultimately, however, the two coincide for Fichte in the unity (and systematicity) pursued by the science of knowing. Embracing a method that is no longer transcendental but rather dialectical and speculative, Hegel expands on the worldly dimension of Kant's proposed *Weltbegriff* of philosophy. Historicity and the phenomenological, experiential aspects of philosophy's rootedness in the world are the points he develops in the first decade of the new century. My suggestion here is that the Kantian passage of the Architectonic should be seen as the background and inspiration of both Fichte's and Hegel's idea of "philosophizing" as the immanent, living thought-activity constitutive of the philosophical science—respectively, the transcendental Doctrine of Science and the dialectic-speculative *Phenomenology of Spirit*. Importantly, the different, perhaps irreconcilable strands at play in Kant's *Weltbegriff*—which is at the basis of reason's insoluble antinomies but also at the basis of the very idea of philosophy (beyond its merely scholastic practice)[45]—surface again, albeit transformed, in his followers. For Kant, speculative reason's pretension with regard to a (scholastic) *Weltbegriff* that is fundamentally antinomic or insolubly dialectical is to grasp an absolute origin truly impenetrable to it, but also to impossibly prove (or to just as impossibly deny) that freedom has a place in the world-whole. Kant already recognizes that speculative reason's defeat in this cognitive endeavor may leave the door open to skepticism. And yet, being itself rooted in a *Weltbegriff*—this time, however, not a scholastic but a cosmopolitical concept of the world—reason practically engages in the activity of philosophizing in this world pursuing ends that are themselves the living proof of freedom's actuality. This tension, I suggest, is at play in the very method shaping Fichte's philosophizing in the *1804 Wissenschaftslehre*—itself a proof of freedom and of worldly engagement on the part of the philosopher. It is revealed, at the most general level, in the opposition—or rather in the "disjunction"—that separates the claim of the absolute point of origin and truth from the immanent, factical, and experiential thought-activity that is supposedly constructing and producing that absolute point of origin and truth. In contrast to Fichte, Hegel's choice is to sacrifice the absoluteness of the first principle or origin of the science, insisting, rather, on the immanent, experiential, and historical self-making of science's own path. The absolute, for him, can only be result. As a result, however, the Absolute is no longer the metaphysical absolute.[46] With this latter turn, the transcendental method is abandoned once and for all.

In discussing the performative, immanent way of philosophizing mobilized in the 1804 lectures, it is useful to distinguish two stages. The first stage concerns Fichte's act of preparing the audience to enter the thematic circle of the science as well as our own setting out to think with him. What we are offered herein are the "prolegomena" to the *Wissenschaftslehre*. The prolegomena are followed by the activity of philosophizing *within* the actual science itself. This unfolds through the "ascent" (to absolute oneness) and then through the "descent" (to the level of appearance and facticity) that are constitutively built into such an activity.[47] In the previous section, I have discussed some of the necessary conditions of the former, introductory stage (among them, the decision to assume the truth in its absoluteness checking the "skeptical paralysis" at the door; the willingness to think freely and immanently and creatively and not historically or from alien authority; our own psychological preparedness to such an endeavor). I should add that the main issue this introductory stage raises is already at the heart of Kant's first *Critique* precisely on the ground of its transcendental and critical function. Indeed, this is a work that "oscillates" (to use a Fichtean word) between offering the preparation to the system of science (and metaphysics) and being itself the first part of the science.[48] To be sure, the same ambiguity is to be found in Hegel's 1807 *Phenomenology*—presented, at once, as the path leading consciousness up to the "standpoint of science" and as the very first part of the system of philosophy.[49]

Moving now "from the prolegomenon . . . into the science" itself, Fichte underscores the seamlessness of the transition—a transition of which we, who are practicing the thinking (and while we are practicing it), are barely aware.[50] Fichte's claim is that just by enacting the thinking proper of the science (even at the level of the prolegomenon) we reach the point in which we have already, at least "formally," proceeded beyond the level of facticity proper of the prolegomenon. For the living thinking that we have been practicing up to that point is the creation of "insights in ourselves," which have the power of "transposing us into the entirely new world belonging to the science of knowing."[51] This is, to be sure, a persuasive way of rendering the chief methodological implication of the position of immanence: by practicing immanent thinking (within experience and life) we are, ipso facto, installed in a dimension that is beyond that experience—and, Fichte argues, beyond our life, namely, in "a divine life."[52] We are projected into "an entirely new world." Thereby Fichte's Doctrine of Science can be seen as entailing his own *Weltbegriff* of philosophy.

At the beginning of this chapter, I expressed my doubt about whether the thinking process of the audience/reader is actually ever able to find itself (or rather to place itself) in such a high position of truth. However, there can most likely be no proof of either this claim or its opposite beyond the very act of producing such a position in ourselves—this being precisely the act Fichte is summoning us to perform. And yet, there is also no doubt that the consciousness of such an act (and the consciousness of truth) is integral to science and to the truth science pursues. Now, it is at the level of consciousness that the tension—the disjunction and even the contradiction—I mentioned above emerges in a prominent way. At stake is the tension between the absoluteness of the point of origin and the phenomenological, indeed worldly, context of thinking's ongoing experience. The task herein is to ascertain whether and how Fichte accommodates this moment of negativity—or this disjunction, as it were—within the science (or, maintaining, with Kant, the cosmological validity of the concept of philosophy proposed here, in the "entirely new world" of the science of knowing). Significantly, this is the point in which Fichte's 1804 lectures come closest to Hegel's phenomenological project.

On the other hand, however, it seems that the further implication of the claim of immanence should go in the opposite direction, namely to the outright elimination of the thinking subject as such. It seems that the "we" practicing the thinking must eventually disappear; that the disjunction separating consciousness and truth must be overcome; hence that the "idealism" of this position must be left behind in a higher "realism" (I am tempted to use here Hegel's expression and say: they must all be *aufgehoben*). As Fichte puts it, "*We* did not construct the in-itself . . . , it constructed itself."[53] This claim brings Fichte very close to Hegel's position. The endpoint of the *Phenomenology* is "absolute knowing"—a level of absoluteness that is immediately overcome or *aufgehoben* in the non-phenomenological beginning of the Logic. This latter represents the systematic place in which thinking has lost all subjectivity (it has become, as it were, "objective thinking"),[54] and consciousness is no longer at stake. Significantly, for Hegel, the final *Aufhebung* of the position of consciousness that itself has constructed the phenomenological science up to its conclusion in "absolute knowing" is the work of what he calls "*sich vollbringender Skeptizismus*" (complete or "thoroughgoing skepticism")[55]—an expression used by Fichte himself in a context that comes close to Hegel's.

In the remainder of this chapter, I shall briefly address these two interconnected points, namely, on the one hand, the seemingly disruptive (and negative) function that consciousness plays on the way to truth—the "contradiction" of consciousness or its "opposition"[56]—and on the other hand, the need for consciousness (and its idealism) to be eventually overcome, or itself, somehow, skeptically refuted.

There is a "dialectical" tension—or rather, in Fichte's terminology, a "disjunction" or even a "contradiction"—in the claim that philosophy should hinge on thinking's performative action. At issue is the tension between that which thinking actually *does* and that which thinking reflectively *claims it is doing* (and claims it has done). Ultimately, and most generally, this is the opposition between thinking's acting and living in its immediacy and our consciousness of such thinking; between facticity and (self-) production, life and the concept, realism and idealism. To be sure, the position of immanence is both the source of such a tension and that which allows us to discover or become aware of it. This is how Fichte puts the point at the beginning of the Nineteenth lecture: "In all derivative knowing, or in appearance, a pure absolute contradiction exists between enactment [*Thun*] and saying [*Sagen*]: *propositio facto contraria*." To be sure, *propositio* is contrary to the *factum* as *actum*—an *actum* that is always crystallized in a *factum*. Parenthetically, Fichte adds to this a crucial claim: "A thoroughgoing skepticism must base itself on just this and give voice to this ineradicable contradiction in mere consciousness."[57] The contradiction between the actual doing—the *Thathandlung*—and the claim that reflectively objectifies such a doing is the basis of a refutation proper of a complete, all-sided, and all-consuming skepticism—a skepticism that in its thoroughness and completeness is very different from the superficial negation of truth pervading the contemporary world. Taking up a Kantian distinction, we can say that this is, in fact, a *methodological* skepticism.[58] Its final result, precisely on the "basis" on which, in Fichte's view, it must be established, seems to be the overcoming or the negation of consciousness itself as the unavoidable origin of that absolute contradiction.

Thus, as much as the *Wissenschaftslehre* advocates from its listeners and readers—from the "we" that makes the science—the actual, living enactment of thinking as the way of philosophizing proper to the science itself, such "doing" is always in opposition with that which consciousness (hence the "we" aware of that thinking) claims it is doing. If truth is in the former, then the latter is simply false (and vice versa). On this basis, skepticism seems justified in raising its doubt. However, once skepticism has permeated consciousness as such or consciousness taken in the entirety of its claims, the disjunction separating thinking's immanent doing (and being) from truth is overcome or brought to a higher level. This, it then seems, is the true position of science—a position of higher "realism." Again, as Fichte maintains, "*We* did not construct the in-itself in its immediately true and clear concept, instead, . . . it constructed itself just as it was in the constructive process, as denying thinking."[59] And yet, this realism is not the end-result of Fichte's exposition. It is, instead, the springboard of a new "dialectic" between realism and idealism.[60] The ongoing process necessarily linking these positions signals, perhaps, that skepticism has not been thorough enough. For, ultimately, Fichte suggests that a truly "thoroughgoing skepticism" produces the definitive "refutation of all systems that do not elevate themselves to pure reason."[61] In these systems, the contradiction regards the principles claimed for philosophy and what these principles actually bring about. The conflict of idealism and realism is the target of this skeptical refutation on the basis of which the *Wissenschaftslehre* establishes its higher truth—a truth, it seems, that lies beyond that disjunction.

The question, however, remains: What happens to the immanent thinking that is impugned as the true performative method of philosophizing after the skeptical refutation of consciousness? In Hegel's *Phenomenology*, the overcoming of the "opposition of consciousness" is precisely the condition for the beginning of the Logic as the first, foundational part of the system of philosophy.[62] In Fichte's 1804 lectures, however, the answer to this question is less clear and less definitive. As the lectures remain open ended, the philosophizing "we" is harder to abandon, especially if the facticity that lies outside of thinking's own action should not be given the last word. This means, perhaps, that the thinking of the audience seamlessly merges with that of the *Wissenschaftslehre*'s "originator." Or it may mean, alternatively, that in Fichte's *Wissenschaftslehre* phenomenology is the highest, insurmountable path thinking will take.[63]

Conclusion

In the argument of this chapter I have discussed some implications and difficulties of what I consider the fascinating methodological idea of thinking's performative immanence that is at work, in different ways, in Fichte's *1804 Wissenschaftslehre* and in Hegel's 1807 *Phenomenology of Spirit*. While I have indicated the inspiration of this idea in Kant's distinction between the idea of philosophy and the activity of philosophizing presented in the Architectonic of the first *Critique*—a distinction that rooted the latter in the concreteness of the world—I have focused my attention on the moments of tension, the disjunctions and contradictions, encountered by immanent thinking in its way to and within the science. Ultimately, I have indicated in the methodological use of skepticism (in the figure of "thoroughgoing skepticism") the force that both Fichte and Hegel mobilize in order to advance the science (or properly immanent thinking itself) to a position in which the opposition or disjunction separating consciousness from truth is left behind once and for all. I have ended, however, with an open question to the Doctrine of Science. What happens to the immanent thinking that has gone through a complete skeptical refutation? The true answer to this question should be found, perhaps, in our own thinking activity—in (what remains of) our own consciousness.

Notes

1. See 1804^2, 106; *GA*, II/8, 202–3 for a semi-Platonic remark on the better conduciveness of listening to the lectures live in order to understand their meaning in contrast to having them written down.

2. See Fichte's announcement in the First Lecture: "From now on, honorable guests, I wish to be considered silenced and erased, and you yourself must come forward and stand in my place." 1804^2, 22; *GA*, II/8, 4–5.

3. See, extensively, the beginning of the Fifth Lecture, 1804^2, 47; *GA*, II/8, 66–67.

4. The conversational tone emerges, for example, in the Ninth Lecture where Fichte directly addresses the "higher idealism" in "personified form." 1804^2, 102; *GA*, II/8, 192–93. But the second part of the 1800 *Bestimmung des Menschen* already offers a relevant example of this style.

5. See 1804^2, 101; *GA*, II/8, 190–91.

6. See how Fichte characterizes his "introductory remarks" in the First Lecture: they "are designed to *initiate* you to the art . . . of philosophy"—the art "practiced" in the following lectures. 1804^2, 22–23; *GA*, II/8, 6–7, my emphasis.

7. Respectively, 1804^2, 30; *GA*, II/8, 24–25 and 1804^2, 40; *GA*, II/8, 52–53. Fichte's formulae in these lectures are not as clear as he seems to assume they are (i.e., given the scant amount of explanation he thinks they deserve). This is precisely my point in referencing the formula here. Generally, it seems that A indicates the position of the Absolute, while B and T express the positions of Being and Thinking as attributes or modifications of the Absolute (in Spinozistic fashion: "Everything together," Fichte explains in the same passage, "is only just a modification of A"). B and T are that into which the Absolute immanently and organically divides itself or, alternatively, they are appearances of the Absolute. Following the same pattern, x, y, z are seen as "primordial modes" of the Absolute's division. 1804^2, 30; *GA*, II/8, 26–27.

8. 1804^2, 58; *GA*, II/8, 92–93.

9. 1804^2, 102; *GA*, II/8, 190–91.

10. This is, clearly, another way to put the doubt I raised above: Did I really achieve the thought of the Absolute in my own thinking? How did that happen?

11. 1804², 22; *GA*, II/8, 4–5.
12. See 1804², 107; *GA*, II/8, 204–5.
13. See in the First Lecture 1804², 24, 25; *GA*, II/8, 8–9, 10–11.
14. In what follows, I shall not expound on Hegel's position at any length. My aim is to use Hegel as a counterpoint in the 1804 lectures and with regard to the limited issue of the method of immanent thinking—the *Mit-Denken*, as it were, at stake both in the lectures and the *Phenomenology*.
15. Kant, *Critique of Pure Reason*, Aixf.
16. See 1804², 25; *GA*, II/8, 10–11: The *WL*, Fichte declares, "resembles no system but is completely distinct from them all, new, and self-sufficient."
17. 1804², 32; *GA*, II/8, 34–35. In the course of these lectures, however, Fichte does occasionally dwell on some moments of the post-Kantian contemporary scene, see for example the discussion of Reinhold's and Jacobi's positions in the Ninth Lecture, 1804², 104f; *GA*, II/8, 196–201.
18. 1804², 25; *GA*, II/8, 10–11.
19. 1804², 26; *GA*, II/8, 14–15.
20. 1804², 31; *GA*, II/8, 26–27.
21. 1804², 31; *GA*, II/8, 26–29.
22. 1804², 31; *GA*, II/8, 28–29.
23. 1804², 32; *GA*, II/8, 30–31.
24. KrV B29/A15.
25. 1804², 34; *GA*, II/8, 36–37. See note 7 above.
26. 1804², 32; *GA*, II/8, 32–33.
27. 1804², 76; *GA*, II/8: 132–33.
28. Famously, KrV Aix, the preface to the 1781 edition.
29. 1804², 21; *GA*, II/8: 2–3.
30. 1804², 22; *GA*, II/8: 4–5.
31. This is the argument that Dan Breazeale impugns against Paul Franks's reconstruction of Fichte's position against skepticism in the Jena *Wissenschaftslehre* in *All or Nothing: Systematicity, Transcendental Arguments, and Skepticism in German Idealism* (Cambridge, MA: Harvard University Press, 2005). I think that the *practical* argument (the argument from a practical conviction and decision to enter the path of the *WL*) is valid in the 1804 lectures as well. Dan Breazeale, "Fichte, Skepticism, and the 'Agrippan Trilemma,'" *Fichte-Studien* 44 (2016): 1–16, see 13f.
32. 1804², 22; *GA*, II/8, 4–5.
33. 1804², 106; *GA*, II/8, 202–3.
34. 1804², 22; *GA*, II/8, 4–5.
35. 1804², 68; *GA*, II/8, 112–13.
36. *Phenomenology of Spirit*, in *Werke in zwanzig Bände*, eds. E. Moldenhauer and H. M. Michel (Frankfurt, a.M.: Suhrkamp, 1986), (= TW), TW 3, 72.
37. KrV B860/A833.
38. KrV B861/A833.
39. KrV B863/A835.

40. KrV B864/A836.

41. Different is Fichte's position on the relation between philosophical and mathematical cognition and construction.

42. KrV B866/A838.

43. KrV B866f./A838f.

44. KrV B867/A839.

45. See, for this, Norbert Hinske, "Kants Verankerung der Kritik im Weltbegriff," in *Kant and Philosophy in a Cosmopolitical Sense*, Akten des XI Kant-Kongress, eds. S. Bacin, A. Ferrarin, and M. Ruffing (Berlin: DeGruyter, 2013), 263–75.

46. See Hegel's polemic against Fichte and Schelling on the beginning of philosophy with the "absolute" or "absolute knowing." *Phenomenology*, TW 3, 31. See in general, Angelica Nuzzo, "The 'Absoluteness' of Hegel's Absolute Spirit," in *Hegel's Philosophy of Spirit: A Critical Guide*, eds. M. Bykova and K. Westphal (Cambridge: Cambridge University Press, 2019), 207–24.

47. See respectively 1804^2, 101; *GA*, II/8, 190–91; 1804^2, 141; *GA*, II/8, 288–89.

48. See KrV section VII of the introduction (B25-28/A11-14).

49. *Phenomenology*, TW 3, 29f; and see the subtitle of the book: "first part" of the "system of science." The ambiguity is entirely resolved in the very different "phenomenology" of the *Philosophy of Subjective Spirit*.

50. 1804^2, 73; *GA*, II/8, 126–27.

51. 1804^2, 73; *GA*, II/8, 126–27.

52. 1804^2, 72; *GA*, II/8, 124–25.

53. 1804^2, 102; *GA*, II/8, 192–93.

54. Enz. §25.

55. *Phenomenology*, TW 3, 72. See Angelica Nuzzo, "The Truth of '*absolutes Wissen*' in Hegel's *Phenomenology*," in *Hegel's "Phenomenology of Spirit*," ed. A. Denker (Amherst, NY: Humanities Press, 2003), 265–94. For the role that skepticism as a method plays in Hegel, see Michael N. Forster, *Hegel's Idea of a "Phenomenology of Spirit"* (Chicago: University of Chicago Press, 1998). See also Dan Breazeale, "Putting Doubt in Its Place: K. L. Reinhold on the Relationship between Philosophical Skepticism and Transcendental Idealism," in *Skepticism Around 1800: Skeptical Tradition in Philosophy, Science, and Society*, eds. Johann van der Zande and Richard Popkin (Dordrecht: Kluwer, 1998), 119–32.

56. Respectively, 1804^2, 141; *GA*, II/8, 288–89; *Science of Logic*, TW 5, 43.

57. 1804^2, 141; *GA*, II/8, 288–89.

58. In the first *Critique*, Kant had drawn the distinction between the phenomenon of "skepticism" and the "skeptical method" (KrV B451f./A423f.)—the latter is entailed in the very idea of a transcendental "dialectic." See Michael N. Forster, *Kant and Skepticism* (Princeton, NJ: Princeton University Press, 2010).

59. 1804^2, 102; *GA*, II/8, 192–93.

60. This dialectic occupies the entire Thirteenth Lecture.

61. 1804², 141; *GA*, II/8, 288–89. For the role that skepticism plays in Fichte's earlier philosophy, see Dan Breazeale, "Fichte, Skepticism."
62. See *Science of Logic*, TW 5, 43.
63. Perhaps a suggestion at 1804², 107; *GA*, II/8, 206–7.

Chapter 12

Fichte's *1804 Wissenschaftslehre*
A Possible Reply to Schelling's *Bruno*

MICHAEL VATER

Many aspects of Fichte's second series of house seminars in 1804 inspire admiration and some provoke perplexity. Chief among the latter are the differences in principle, style, and reasoning between this presentation and both published and unpublished Jena versions of the *Wissenschaftslehre*. The Berlin *Wissenschaftslehre* offers a two-part system, with both idealistic and realistic aspects. Idealism obviously explores *being* or the absolute, although it also extends to a *phenomenology* that investigates reason's appearance in practical or active contexts; realism functions as a brake on the idealistic account and imposes a restriction of philosophy's scope to the cognition and agency of embodied beings. In the 1804 lectures Fichte requires his auditors to form their own versions of philosophy, which implies that student and teacher will have different versions of philosophy, none the canonical one but none a mere copy. Both features—the combination of realism and idealism and the opening to alternative formulations of *Wissenschaftslehre*—lack precedent in Fichte's earlier systems, but they seem explicable if one reads the text as a draft response to Schelling's *Bruno*. That dialogue introduced the idea that though philosophy is one, different versions of it are possible—realistic, idealistic, materialistic, and religious—if there is a fundamental theory such as the *identity of identity and difference* capable of supporting the various directional variants.¹ I suggest that Fichte is at least exploring the idea of a comparable philosophical pluralism in this iteration of *Wissenschaftslehre*, provided his version of fundamental theory—a transcendental and genetic account of reason's self-construction in our knowing—replaces Schelling's static identity theory.

Unlike the plainly idealistic early *Wissenschaftslehre* where transcendental thinking posited a primal activity and its check as the platform for explaining cognition and agency, Fichte's 1804^2 lectures stage a meta-level combat between idealism and realism whose outcome is not a conquest but territorial division. The force that directs the combat is philosophical reflection, a narrative (re)construction of a first knowing that juxtaposes simple *seeing* with thinking—or the opposition of unity and multiplicity inherent in the concept. *Disjunction* is a principle for thinking multiplicity into unity or deriving the former from the latter. In this context, Fichte invokes a disjunctive logic he names *genesis* (and we in hindsight might call dialectic) that both forges manifolds into unities or genera and stages a contest between being and thinking that turns singulars into plurals, and vice versa. It is this disjunctive thinking that Fichte finds at the basis of Kant's unfinished transcendental philosophy, and whose defects he sets out to remedy.² As the genetic self-presentation of this reflection unfolds, an unintuitable ideal principle, *seeing*, effects a stepwise overcoming of realism, the philosophical position that takes brute fact as its principle and gestures to an inexpressible facticity at the basis of things. What philosophical reconstruction depicts is the process of an energetic seeing evolving into functional intelligence and, at once self-made reason and intelligence constrained to appear under factical conditions, creating for itself a dual reality as reason-in-itself and understanding in us. In the multiple voices and vocabularies Fichte uses to prompt his students to construct their own accounts of knowing, Fichte meets Schelling's challenge to discover a fundamental theory capable of supporting variant ontic interpretations—in Fichte's case, philosophy of consciousness, a dualistic variant of realism, Platonism or spiritualism, and a version of Christianity. Considering the ugly denouement of the Fichte-Schelling dispute in the mutual public denunciations of their 1805–1806 essays, I can only claim that Fichte's unpublished moves toward reconciliation with a realistic version of transcendental philosophy in this single text from 1804 are *exploratory*, and, like Schelling's arguments in *Bruno*, as much eristic as pacific.³ But such a reading helps explain the otherwise bewildering plethora of philosophical voices in the 1804^2 lectures, and also the demand that the auditor not just accept the professor's philosophical reconstruction of consciousness as such but instead construct her personal *Wissenschaftslehre*.

This essay will first consider the backstory of the Fichte-Schelling disputes as documented in the *Correspondence* and the semi-conciliatory moves Schelling made in *Bruno*. This account will not review the entire history but focus on the major claims the philosophers made about the systematic and unitary nature of fundamental theory, given the diverse, directional, or geographical character of their differing interpretations. Each deeply influenced by Spinoza, Fichte, and Schelling share a taste for geometric construction. Schelling translates Spinoza's single substance expressed in contrasting attributes into a three-dimensional or geocentric model, where a single planetary entity is the basis of the four chief directional descriptors, while Fichte uses two-factor kinetic, mathematical, and optical models to depict the origin of being-plus-phenomena as a juxtaposition of active and limiting elements, similar to Spinoza's *conatus* and determination. In a second section I explore the disjunctive logic that defines *Wissenschaftslehre*'s account of genesis. Fichte conceptualized the unity of opposites as a principle of movement, the resolution of conflicting forces into a single vector, while Schelling conceived their unification in dynamical terms as a suspension of opposites in state of nondifference prior to differentiation, a crystallization of opposites into an "idea" or hyperconceptual thought-entity. One thinker offers motion or activity as the basic category, the other, rest. In a third section, I look to Fichte's text more closely to discover echoes of Kant and Spinoza in the 1804 lectures. While a naive reading might try to localize idealistic elements in the deduction of being in the lectures' first part, and realism in the account of practical reason billed as "phenomenology" in its second part, it is the progressive refinement of seeing into active reason that is the sole story of this text, or the contrast between intuition (*seeing* into) and brute fact that motivates the story. Idealistic thinking devours facticity on the way to articulating the absolute fact, living reason. Thinking is everywhere challenged by fact—the projection of an image in the absence of rational light—and so prompted to move beyond it to offer the alternate story of *genesis*, which is what I/We are. Since Fichte stages its movement as a repeated or potentiated encounter between various sorts of idealism and realism, we might regard the lectures as a series of matches in an extended arm-wrestling contest. The upshot is pretty much a draw, a real-idealism closer to Schelling's claimed subject-objectivity than the "subjective idealism" Schelling and Hegel charged Fichte with in 1801.[4]

Disagreements between Fichte and Schelling— and Conciliatory Moves

Fichte's self-exile from Jena to Berlin because of the 1798/1799 atheism controversy occasioned deep changes in his philosophical orientation. During the same period Schelling was experimenting with fashioning a philosophy of nature and integrating it with the core of transcendental philosophy already articulated by Kant, Reinhold, and Fichte. Physical distance forced the two thinkers to exchange their ideas on the future of transcendental philosophy on paper. The *Correspondence* of 1799–1802 gave way to essays and books addressing their differences—Schelling's *Presentation of My System* and Hegel's *Difference between Fichte's and Schelling's System of Philosophy* in 1801, Schelling's *Bruno* in 1802, Fichte's *Wesen des Gelehrten* (1805), *Characteristics of the Present Age* and *The Way towards the Blessed Life* (both 1806), and Schelling's 1806 reply, *Statement on the True Relationship of the Philosophy of Nature to the Revised Fichtean Doctrine*. With regret at enlarging the list, I suggest that Fichte's 1804[2] *Science of Knowing* lectures explore a conciliatory response to Schelling's somewhat conciliatory *Bruno*, though they were published only after Fichte's death.

Although the dispute focuses on whether systematic transcendental philosophy will be inflected toward the phenomena of conscious knowing and human agency or toward nature as an objective embodiment of philosophy's self-originated constructive activity, with the parties hurling epithets like "subjectivism" or "naturalism" at one another, two sharp comments by Fichte in the *Correspondence* set the parameters for future debates.

- Fichte contends that the intelligence in Schelling's nature is *found*, not intuited. Philosophy must originate in *seeing*, not *being*.[5]

- To Schelling's query whether a philosophy other than *Wissenschaftslehre* is possible, tangentially related to it, and eventually returning to it (evolutionary biology's account of intelligence would be a contemporary example), Fichte replies that every philosophy must be *Wissenschaftslehre* or be tacitly based on principles borrowed from it.[6]

At the time of their private dispute, Fichte and Schelling agree that transcendental philosophy or *Wissenschaftslehre* is the sole comprehensive theoretical foundation for all specific branches of philosophy, that their differences rest in part on the choice of starting points for explanation and in part on terminology.[7] On this basis, Schelling is able to claim in *Bruno* that identity philosophy underlies all disciplinary branches, the same claim that Fichte makes for his reworked transcendental idealism in the 1804[2] lectures. A careful reading of the four-phase contest between realism and idealism in the latter shows that Fichte has softened the strong contrast between *seeing* and *being* that drove his earlier criticism of Schelling and is now content to accept an idealism whose seeing abrogates the "not" that distinguishes *seeing* and *being*, a move whereby in fact "seeing becomes substance."[8]

When Schelling labors in 1800/1801 to put life and organic phenomena at the basis of his *Naturphilosophie* and to elaborate a transcendental version of Spinozism that includes God, nature, and humankind together in one fundamental account, his effort is to put a kind of seeing—*intellectual intuition* or reason's identification of difference—at the basis of his account. In the same period, Fichte seeks to enlarge his descriptive accounts of knowing and social existence (law, economy, morals) to a theory of a "supersensible world" where the interactions of persons would find a spiritual or metaphysical basis. Schelling seems to come around on Fichte's first point, then, while Fichte himself wants to explore expanding *Wissenschaftslehre* toward exploring spiritual or religious possibilities. Both still regard their common endeavor as the systematization of the viewpoint Kant announced in saying that mind could only understand what mind constructs, and they both still think that their private differences are reconcilable.

Space does not permit a review of the break that the publication of *My System* and Hegel's *Difference* essay precipitated. And there is no need to comb the *Correspondence* in detail, as Hartmut Traub has done. I turn to the *Bruno*'s fourfold elaboration of identity philosophy in different historical and systematic guises, and especially to the claims of its concluding section that only identity philosophy as a core theory can coherently ground the alternative positions then current—intellectualism (Leibniz) and materialism (Spinoza), and idealism and realism. Schelling's claim that only his identity philosophy can provide the logical space for these alternative ontologies is his direct response to Fichte's claim that all transcendental philosophy must be his theory or based upon it. It is difficult to see this response in all its directness, however, since Schelling chose to embed identity philosophy's presentation in Neoplatonic and indeed hermetic garb. Talk of the three levels or powers of being as "the eternal," "the infinite," and "the finite" is a rhetorically elevated way of talking of Spinoza's "God or Nature" as the single substance that supports the attributes of thinking and extension and their modal appearances as discrete ideas and finite bodies. The hermetical geology of a Platonic living Earth—with its four directions and four noble metals—populated with "ideas" imagined as natural species, may seem like science fiction or the logical train wreck to be expected at the end of the research program called "speculative physics." If its historical garb is removed, its symbolic meaning is that different specific metaphysics or ontic theories can coexist on a common ontological foundation, as East and West designate different directions on the one globe. *Bruno*'s basic claim is that transcendental thinking can accommodate different specific or disciplinary articulations if its logic is sufficiently clear and basic or grounded in the absolute propositions (1) that reason is and effects the identity of identity and difference; (2) that its essence is form or expressivity, or an identity of being and knowing; and (3) that its expression is the ground of phenomena. In Schelling's words:

1. "We must define this supreme identity as the identity of identity and opposition, or the unity of the self-identical and the nonidentical."[9]

2. "Absolute cognition stands in a relation of pure indifference to the essential reality of the absolute. . . . Since form comprehends both thought and being as subordinates, it will be impossible for us to make thought or being into an immediate attribute of the absolute itself, in its essential reality."[10]

3. "The essence of all things is one, and considered by itself there is no ground of the particular: that whereby they are separated and distinguished is form, which is the difference of the universal and particular in them and is expressed in them through their existence."[11]

The language may be confusingly abstract, but all phenomena can appear, and none fail to appear, on the transcendental stage the logic of identity provides. Tom Rockmore claims that transcendental thinking and Kantian philosophy in particular, with its Copernican revolution, returns to Parmenides's axiom: "The same is for being and for knowing," or logic is ontological, not just propositional.[12] This allows for philosophical pluralism, grounded in our perceptions of different aspects of phenomena and various attitudes we adopt toward them.

My contention is that Fichte's 1804 lectures—despite their philosophical pluralism, mention of the idea of a "specific *Wissenschaftslehre*," and the push to get the individual student to formulate her own philosophy on the basis of the lectures—return to his demand in *Correspondence* that all philosophies take their origin and principles from *Wissenschaftslehre*.[13] At the same time, they reflect *Bruno*'s attempt to find a fundamental theory that will ground opposing regional or ontic theories, not in this case Schelling's logic of identity but the disjunctive logic of the *Wissenschaftslehre*.

The question of whether Schelling's and Fichte's fundamental theories—reason or the absolute viewed either as the *identity of identity and difference* or as *disjunctive unity*—are the same or different, and if different, whether one is superior to the other, can be answered only indirectly here and in summary fashion. Schelling seems, with Hegel's help, to have gone from "indifference" as the identity of difference in 1801 (which would put a negation as the first item in being) to the formula "identity of identity and difference." Schelling explained this as identity in essence, difference in form or expression. Manfred Frank has glossed this as a logical item that is equally present in different forms, but neither contained in them, or characterizable in terms of them.[14] Earth is earth, not east or west, but east and west are the east and west of earth. Logical space is expansive, and all determination occurs within it as limitation, specification, or negation. For his part, Fichte does not offer much explanation of the operator [●] that signifies disjunction,[15] but it seems to indicate that items joined or separated by it may both be the focus of consideration, or one without the other. Its logical equivalence to "not neither/nor" makes it the mirror opposite of Schelling's indifference (the Sheffer stroke or Quine's dagger). In substantive form, Fichte makes disjunction the negation of the infinite judgment—the denial of all predicates of a subject—making it, like Kant's ideal of reason, the epitome of all concepts.

Seeing or Being? Disjunction or Indifference?

Fichte offers no plan or outline for his lectures; they unfold in short bursts of intense reasoning and end in a suspenseful manner, since the larger problem always outruns the answer presented. There is a preliminary consideration of transcendental philosophy, Kant's peculiar achievement, and a proposal for adopting a fundamental logic of disjunctive unity to remedy Kant's failure to achieve systematicity (First through Fourth Lectures). This is followed by a construction of a theory of being as a series of dramatic confrontations between various forms of realism and idealism (Fifth through Fifteenth Lectures), culminating in an inward idealism that sees being as active, living, and surpassing all objectification.[16] Fichte clearly marks this conclusion as the peak that speculation can achieve, and its genetic (i.e., self-achieved) construction shows that, despite the apparent objectivity clinging to the noun *being*, its assertion as basic verb (*be-ing*) makes it quite of a piece with the self-positing or intellectual intuition that was the core principle of earlier versions of *Wissenschaftslehre*. Once the absolute character of be-ing as light or reason has been discovered, philosophy proceeds to explore "truth in appearance" or the rational foundation of appearances (Sixteenth through Twenty-Fifth Lectures). Hypothetical necessitation or command provides the logic of appearances, and its elaboration introduces two points of contraction in its depiction of agency, the collapse of knowing into certainty, and its situation as existence. The three concluding lectures (Twenty-Sixth through Twenty-Eighth) refer practical thinking to various domains of human activity and their spiritual or religious significance.

Fichte's course of reflection is labyrinthine. Each sentence is considered and precisely crafted, and the movement of genetic thinking soon consumes each proposition like leaves caught in a vortex of draining water. If one attends to what he calls the "outer history of *Wissenschaftlehre*" and records the flaws of competing theories, one can approximate to an understanding of the *inward seeing of being* that is Fichte's improvement on Kant's transcendental philosophy. This outer history can be represented spatially as a fourfold or geographical deviation from the center, as Schelling does with identity philosophy and its kindred elaborations in the *Bruno*. The diagram below displays light or intuition horizontally and thought vertically. Kant's view of cognition as the *union of thought and intuition* is the core of Fichte's vision of philosophy as life or genesis, discussed below as "performative rationality." Four defective positions are arrayed around lifelike intuition: ready-made reason, externalized thought (Spinozism/Reinhold), finite *thought* incapable of reaching the absolute (Jacobi), reason grasped as intuition but lacking systematic focus (Kant), and performative intuition grasped as external formula (Schelling) (see table 12.1).

A similar tetrad of deficient, one-sided variations of the central disjunctive principle emerges in the deduction of consciousness that concludes the second, phenomenological part of this system. Under conditions of hypothetical manifestation, seeing is negated as seeing and is concretized as life and externality; under these conditions, intuition sees itself only derivatively, as dependent on externality. But there is yet a union of living intuition and externality as knowing, whence intuition takes it energetic life or genesis as persisting in appearances: the fivefold synthesis that is consciousness.[17] These static characteristics attain dynamic display as five functions or life-modalities

Table 12.1. Philosophical Alternatives to the *Wissenschaftslehre*

	(1) Reinhold thinking = the principle of being; all seeing is eliminated (crypto-Spinozism)*	
(2) Kant abstract, a-systematic but inward reason†	(5) *Wissenschaftslehre* construction: genetic seeing erases difference between seeing and being → seeing is substance	(3) Schelling Reason externalized as the indifferent of subject and object‡
	(4) Jacobi thought unable to reconstruct what exists → non-philosophy§	

Source: Author provided.
*1804², 90, 104; GA, II/8, 167–68, 198–99.
†1804², 25–26; GA, II/8, 13–16.
‡1804², 109–10; GA, II/8, 116–17.
§1804², 138–40; GA, II/8, 284–86.

of conscious life in a similar pattern: (1) Intuition negated is the function of *sensibility*; (2) its vitality subjected to externality is *legality*; (3) its unity projected as the persisting subject is *moral agency*; (4) objectively intuited as the object of *religion*, it is persistent being posited over against changing consciousness.[18] The 1806 *The Way towards the Blessed Life* lectures add a fifth mindset of personal love to the four, corresponding to *Wissen* on the intellectual. In 1804² Fichte says that each of the four elements can serve as a focus for integrating the other four into a specific constellation so that conscious life can be mapped as array of twenty-five elements.[19] Whatever the predominant focus, the complex or *fivefold synthesis* unifies as it distinguishes. Fichte's fivefold synthesis mirrors the geocentric directional display Schelling uses in *Bruno* because the disjunctive logic modeled in the 1804² lectures, like the procedural model of analysis-synthesis-analysis employed in the second Jena system, involves a presentation of an identity of identity and nonidentity or a unity forged out of the reduplication of the same content in different forms, functions, or guises. If Fichte and Schelling seem to be on convergent courses *in this specific text*, it is because *Bruno* retracts the mistake Schelling made in the 1801 *Presentation* of referring to his efforts as "my system of philosophy," admits that philosophy is one only, while idiosyncrasies are many, and implicitly returns to Fichte's claim that all "branded" theories must take their principle from *Wissenschaftslehre*, or some fundamental theory beyond dispute.[20] Fichte seems, in this exploratory response to *Bruno*, to have conceded Schelling's view that different disciplinary or ontic theories can be overlaid upon a common foundation so that multiple accounts of conscious life can cohabit a common logical ground: materialism or hedonism, personalism (or, in a communal context, legalism), morality, and religion.[21]

All these partial or deficient modes of seeing (or conscious functioning) arise because of an original disjunction or alterity that is at the core of knowing. Internality or externality, unity or multiplicity, and in the intersubjective order individuality or (projected) "other"-personality are not essential characteristics or fundamental features of knowing or of being. They are merely distinctions precipitated out of the limpid flow of reason's light, places where its flow coalesces into concreteness, where (1) awareness shifts from seeing to certainty and (2) practical reason takes the form of free existence. At first these shape-shifting moments might seem to be the interruptions of facticity, the projection of outer existence that disrupts reason by making its flow of light discontinuous, the *gap* that Fichte describes as "death at the root" or "death's lair."[22] But facticity manifests throughout the argument's search for self-sufficient being, not just in these particular points of concretion, and is as much a part of functioning reason as death is part of biological life. Reason and facticity everywhere appear together, which means that a merely factual or dead reading of reason's free activity can stop the pulse of life at any point if thinking ceases to be genetic. Alterity or alteration between disjuncts is the basic character of *Wissenschaftslehre*'s specific manifestation in these 1804 lectures.

To understand Fichte's disjunctive logic more readily and see how it is a reply to the spatialized identity of identity and difference that Schelling asserted in the *Bruno*, we must explore two levels of alterity the text contains, external and internal, for only if there are alternate credible philosophies—or even better, alternate versions of *Wissenschaftslehre*—can Fichte claim his theory is the *Urphilosophie* or philosophy *as such*.[23] Addressing the situated or historical nature of our individual knowing, Fichte at one point speaks of *Wissenschaftslehre in specie*—a specific science of knowing—referring not to this iteration of his theory but its copy in the situated life of an individual auditor. The necessary self-constitution of reason or light that is the essence of knowing will be present but contingently in each student and will require effort to recover.[24] At another point, Fichte refers to the three different versions of *Wissenschaftslehre* he presents in 1804 as a pedagogical help, for it necessitates work on the basic principle he communicated in different terminologies. A student's conception may be blocked if she hangs onto formulae instead of thinking the matter inwardly from her own resources, just as a critic can find advantage in reducing a philosophy to a single proposition in order to dispose of it. Philosophical thinking is not factual or propositional; language carries with it the possibility of falsity and truth, or of a divergence of doing and saying so that trust in a single presentation, or paragraph, or memorized recitation is inherently unphilosophical.[25] For an auditor to follow Fichte, concentrated attention, rehearsal of principles, and exercise with different terms and formulas are necessary so that the inward flame of insight can ignite from its assembled conditions.[26] Between lecture and mastery of *Wissenschaftslehre* must come the student's personal re-creation of the content. Philosophy's whole business is to reconstruct what self-constructs—or pull multiplicity into an original self-articulating unity.

If the external alterity of the science of knowing involves the limits of language, texts, and the psychological processes in a person's comprehending what is, the internal or systematic alterity of *Wissenschaftslehre* is based on the nature of seeing or thinking, on the corelated nature of saying or doing, and on the factual condition that understanding is discursive while reason is integral or systematic. Though Fichte mounted diverse criticisms of Kant's idealism in his many essays and systems, nowhere does he present such a concise introduction to his thinking or a more incisive critique of Kant's than in the first four lectures of this series.[27] To symbolize the systematic intent of Kant's thought, he introduces the following scheme:

$$A$$
$$x \quad y \quad z \bullet B-T\,[28]$$

Each item in the scheme relates to all others disjunctively or dialectically. Transcendental idealism's systematic drive is to portray the domains of *cognition*, moral *action*, and scientific/artistic *creativity*, or otherwise expressed *being* and *thinking* as a disjunction of disjunctions, each of which can be elaborated specifically as further sets of disjunctions if one works downward, or collapsed into a unity if one ascend from lower categories to higher or from higher to ultimate unities of thought that are inexpressible save through negation.[29] The defect of Kant's philosophy is that he succumbed to fear of reason in refusing to ascend from the limited *summa genera* of the three critiques or the interdependence of realism and idealism as epistemic domains. Having reified knowing, mystified moral choice, and simply fudged on reflection, Kant was unable to see the ●-operator as living reason, articulating distinctions within background identity and resolving differences into distinctions—in other words, to grasp reason as *life* or *light* instead of a lifeless proposition. Fichte remedies the abstraction and lack of life by trying to dwell in the ●. Says Fichte:

> I said that the science of knowing stood in the point. I have been asked whether it doesn't rather go in A. The most exact answer is that actually and strictly it doesn't belong in either of these, but rather in the oneness of both. By itself A is objective and therefore inwardly dead; it should not remain so, indeed is should *become* actively genetic. The point, on the other hand, is merely genetic. *Mere* genesis is nothing at all, but this is not just mere genesis, but the *determinate* genesis that is required by the absolute qualitative A: *a point of oneness*.[30]

The discussion suggests that the active nature of philosophic thinking and the restless nature of its object offer many opportunities to stop at half-truths or partially true positions. In the case of Kant, this stopping halfway at dead concepts or abstract principles moves him to acknowledge cognition, action, and reflection as basic functions of reason, but only in the restricted senses of *empirical* cognition, morality as action *under rules*, and *idiosyncratic* or merely personal reflection—reason inflected toward a mechanical world-vision. Fichte also notes that technical forms of realism and idealism originate in natural tendencies in us; it is these natural prompts for thinking, rather than criticism of developed theories, that provoke our efforts into seeing the nature of knowing.[31]

Fichte goes on to note that one can inwardly experience the movement but not express it, or imagine an awkward oscillation between identity and activity, or think of an organic oneness—all of them realizable only in construction, which is precisely the task of conceiving the *inconceivable as inconceivable*.[32] The tension between the static-and-active character of A (*being* in this presentation) and the active-and-static character of ● (light and image [projection]) is what keeps the philosophical account moving forward to the deduction of finite consciousness but inscribes on the conceptual ledger of its qualities and activities an ever-increasing aggregate of opposite characters—which all together shape the equivocal or double nature of the version of *light* we run in our brains. Factually I am self-consciousness projected onto consciousness, *reason and understanding*; "We are the understanding of reason and the reason of understanding."[33] Though we are both, we can account for ourselves only through the self-making of reason and the fortuitous darkening of seeing into existence. If I am reason's self-making, I have no direct insight into that inconceivable situation and carry but a deficient image of it in my limited or situated life and knowing.[34] Underneath all the terminological variation of this version of *Wissenschaftslehre*, the basic categories of the original *Grundlage* endure: activity and limitation. Primal activity remains, in Berlin as in Jena, inaccessible except through philosophical (re)construction.

Performative Reason, Realism, and Idealism

Fichte's daily exposition of his thought in these lectures is complicated and dramatic, its content not segmented or packaged as ready-made philosomemes. In Fichte's writings, thinking is performative activity and has a connective or narrative quality, only occasionally interspersed with preambles, forewarning, exhortations, and summaries. In the two major summaries that he offers of his path of thought, he distinguishes parts or stretches of thinking devoted to *being* and then to the truth of being conveyed in *appearance*.[35] Although we can generally say that it is idealism that is the theoretical force that dominates the first half of the lectures—but ultimately abrogates its own seeing and coalesces into being—while realism, impelled by the hypothetical necessity that is understanding's only tool, leads the discussion down to the phenomenal level where seeing reappears as *consciousness*, these are frail generalizations. Even if they are valid, there's more than a whiff of paradox in a philosophy that employs *idealism to elucidate being, and realism to describe phenomena*. The uncomfortable truth is that there is simply no linear way of reading Fichte, for his method is not analytic nor synthetic, but analytic-synthetic, while the object of his study takes the form of a fivefold synthesis that is always in process, simultaneously unpacking distinctions and reintegrating them.

One way to read Fichte's logic is to look to its inspiration, Kant's tables of judgments and categories in the first *Critique*. The linear logic of the 1794 *Grundlage* used Kant's categories of quality: reality, negation, and limitation in combination with a Spinozistic reading of determination as limitation to derive the parameters of action and cognition ingredient in finite self-consciousness. The *nova methodo* system of 1796/1799 retooled Kant's analytic and synthetic judgment into a reflexive (or feedback-looped) movement of distinction, determination, and integration—the notorious fivefold that describes both philosophy's method and its object. The 1804² *Wisssenschaftslehre* uses Kant's relational judgments but in a way that stands Kant on his head and proposes that truthful judgment starts as *disjunction*, is narrowed or determined as *hypothetical*, and finally crimped into the single line of logical space of the *categorical* judgment. In this empirically upside-down world-picture, the simplest item (*being*) involves the most complicated version of *seeing*, disjunctive thinking. The most complicated item, finite embodied consciousness, escaping philosophical comprehension in its quantitative dimensions and self-referential activity, is where thinking is simplified into the two-function relation handled by standard logic: the categorical proposition. And between the two, the practical deduction of agency from seeing that is the focus of the latter half of the lectures, is a domain signified by *Sollen* (the "should" of Kant's hypothetical imperative) and hypothetical necessity in theoretical contexts. The undergirding of the world of quantifiable objectivity in which finite consciousness locates persons and things is a logical space structured by dyadic, asymmetric, nonreflexive relations; only in such a space could purposive activity, time, space, and individual entities stand out as the conditions for singular minds-or-agents. In this logically upside-down world (that looks much like Spinoza's metaphysics),

- The most evident item is the simplest: *being*, or the self-making of reason. It is apprehended not immediately but dialectically, or through a long process governed by disjunctive thinking.[36]

- At one remove from simplicity are *phenomena*, the framework in which the truth of being appears not simply but discursively, as one feature distinguished from another or related to another, as in the propositional expression or the hypothetical imperative.[37]

- Self-removed from life by a gap or hiatus, a darkening or discontinuity in reason, the individuality of sensible characters and agents' perceptions have only the extra-logical *Evidenz* of bare "thereness" (*Dasein*).[38]

Mention of all these levels is scattered throughout the lectures, though being receives more attention in the Fourth through Fourteenth Lectures, appearance in the Fifteenth through Twenty-Fifth Lectures, and concreteness or *Dasein* in Twenty-Sixth through Twenty-Eighth. These considerations are not sectioned off as separate investigations but form one continuous self-exposition of reason. That being's self-making in reason is relatively inaccessible except through *Wissenschaftslehre*'s (re)construction, while finite consciousness, seemingly so close to us but inexplicable save through logic's sunspots, ranks ontologically last, moves Fichte to compare *Wissenschaftslehre* to Platonism and to the Christian religion. Schelling made similar moves in *Bruno*, recasting the Spinozism of his earlier presentations of identity philosophy in Neoplatonic or Christian trinitarian formulas.[39]

Earlier I stated my intention to explore Kantian and Spinozistic elements of Fichte's 1804 lectures. Kant's influence is pervasive: Fichte sets out to remedy the abstractness and incompleteness of the philosophy Kant left incomplete in the disjunction of the three critiques; only a disjunctive (or reconstructive) thinking deeper than Kant's can pare away the limits of empirical cognition, prescriptive morality, and subjective reflection to get to the fundamental truth that reason constructs itself in these partial genera and the finite agents that embody them. A deeper exploration of the disjunction that views *reality* either as *being* or *thinking* presents a ladder of positions where, as in Kant's partial reconstruction of knowing, idealistic and realistic voices compete and eventually harmonize:

1. Our philosophical reflection moves in a "through" or considers items only in relation. This living "through" is what we call *concept*.[40]

2. On the factical level, either my insight into a fact makes it a knowing or the "evidence" of its content. Neither my reflection nor what is manifest suffices, so a first idealism falls to a first realism. But since the basis is factual, thinking sweeps both away and steps up to conceptual analysis.[41]

3. A second (naturalistic) realism claims that being is light and life, a self-constructing and self-warranting in-itself upon which all claims of insight to be foundational shatter. But idealism counters that it is only in energetic thinking—the scientist of knowing's abstractive reflection—that reason's *Evidenz* can manifest.[42]

4. A third realism—which we are, as embodied reason—counters that the second idealism is nothing but naive trust in the deliverances of immediate consciousness. Only genetic derivation, or dialectical self-construction in the living concept, delivers philosophic truth. So reason is purely in-itself. But idealism, not yet silenced, thinks that this "in-itself" is only relative to a not-in-itself, so not indisputably self-grounded.[43]

5. What is left when reason clears the road of the collision is a pure unity, inconceivable and beyond insight or description. It seems most abstract, but this abstractness is its purity. Its unity is the self-producing infinite judgment of reason, which like the sage in *Brihadaranyaka Upanishad* can only repeat: *not this, not this!* So, a fourth realism comes on the scene and denominates it *being*.[44]

6. But idealism make a further appearance in phenomenological and practical guise when the presupposing of the *through* becomes the self-presupposing of the *from*, which manifests eventually as acting from principles, lawfulness, purpose, and value.[45]

I have represented this course of thinking quite abstractly. Fichte's argument at every stage involves thinking confronting the claims of facticity, for the forward motion of genetic argument comes from nothing other than dialectic, or the negation of facticity. The consistent hearing of the claims of facticity and their consistent rebuttal is what makes his thinking *transcendental idealism*. The same goes for Schelling, although he rarely bothers exploring empiricism or perceptual idealism in detail. What makes *this* ladder of claims and counterclaims by idealism and realism a response to Schelling's *Bruno* is that Fichte takes pains to represent the claims of realism, refine them, and repeatedly introduce them into the argument. In much the same way, the detailed argument of the *Bruno* works toward the meta-principles of identity of identity and nonidentity, reduplication of relative identities, and homology of principles from a Fichtean account of consciousness that originates in Kant's view that cognition is the union of concept and intuition. But just as Schelling's conciliatory discussion eventually tilts toward *Naturphilosophie*, the phenomenological section of Fichte's 1804^2 lectures tilts back (unsurprisingly) toward philosophy of agency—an account of reason as purposive and norm-deploying. What is surprising about Fichte's line of reasoning is that in the end he applies the name "being" to the result of a course of thought that annihilates thinking and comes to rest in the "I don't know what to say." And that, surely, is a conciliatory move toward Schelling and Spinoza's ghost.

If we closely examine Fichte's argument—its genetic methodology and its insistence that the operative element in knowing is *seeing* (light or life)—it seems to be idealistic. If so, it would be fair to call it Kantian and rank it as but a variant of the Jena systems that Schelling and Hegel called *subjective idealism*. Yet it is perplexing that at the break in the deduction where one part is called theory of being and the other phenomenology—or "truth" and "story" (*Darstellung*) in the language of 1805—a realism seems to prevail. A closer consideration of facticity and its role of transforming wooden fact into active self-display (genesis) shows what sort of Spinozist Fichte was in Jena and still is in Berlin, viz., *methodological*, not ontological. Positing and nonpositing, activity and limitation, energy and check, and in this text *factual proposition* and *genetic display* depend on Spinoza's principle: *determination is negation*, voiced in a context where the subject is energetic and self-manifesting. But whereas Spinoza's subject was mute being, a self-enclosed substance uncharacterizable by any or all predicates, Fichte's is *seeing* or self-empowering intuition. At a turn in the 1804^2 argument that we labeled (4) above, the onset of a third realism, thinking as light is blocked by the quotidian facticity of the categorial *is* that is asserted in every isolated proposition:

> This consciousness projects a *true* reality outward, discontinuously, an absolute inconceivability and inexplicability. This discontinuous projection is the same one we . . . call the form of outer existence, which shows itself in every categorical *is*. For what this means, as a projection about which no account can be given, and which thus is discontinuous, is the same as what we have called "death at the root." The gap, the rupture of intellectual activity in it is just death's lair. Now we should not admit the validity of this projection, or form of outer existence, although we can never free ourselves from it factically, we should know that it means nothing.[46]

Though the light of reason does flow freely at this point through death's prison to assert reason's self-making as being (5), later in the Twenty-Sixth through

Twenty-Eighth Lectures a fourth realism seems to stalk phenomenal being's manifestations as agency or norm-governed performance until it coarsens or knots the thread of argument at two points, depicting on the subjective side the coalescence of principled agency into *certainty* (or qualitative oneness), and on the objective, the collapse of active reason into existence (*Dasein*).[47] I said "seems" quite deliberately: *if* there is an expression of reason that turns it into a something rather than a process, the concretization might be the effect of reason's traversing the dark or dead zone—encountering facticity as limitation. Or is there some process of reason that transforms the flow of light into existing singularity? Or did Fichte simply fudge the point, presenting facticity as the ballast of reason only in sections treating theoretical reason (being) and forgetting its presence in appearance? If, in the final handful of lectures, Fichte subjects self-wrought reason not only to practical restrictions (free, i.e., hypothetical, cognition) but to conditions of sensibility, he falls into a sort of Platonism, as Schelling does in talking of a "fall" or self-separation from the absolute as the defining parameter of individual existence.[48]

To settle the issue, let us first look at what Fichte does in the derivation of *certainty* and *existence* to transform genetic reason from reason-in-itself to reason qua understanding. We can then consider how he does it. *Certainty* is the inward version of the self-enclosed being that seeing discovers in the Fourteenth Lecture; here as there, it projects a self-negation and becomes a self-enclosed living entity, a self-description that articulates inner and outer dimensions that collapse into one, producing four interrelated characters: life, externality, their union in knowing, and a liveliness or energy. In this living self-enclosed certainty, which other theories have termed "subjectivity," objectivity and activity (or genetic knowing) merge.[49] The logical character of certainty is that it abolishes the two-function or hypothetical character of the propositional expression previously displayed as lawfulness or principle-providing, and collapses it into one expression. Self-performing reason or agency has become fact. As fact, it takes on the character of *existence*, a concretion of the seeing that is absolute reason as performed or self-enacted. In this self-enactment it simultaneously posits itself and becomes an in-itself.[50]

As fact or existence, reason's seeing establishes the necessity of its self-positing and the impossibility of it being other than self-positing. This *causa sui* or self-constructed aspect of reason emerged in the first half of the lectures as the account of *being*. It also establishes its presence in us as living reason, a self-expression that is *active freedom*. The subject, we might say, or appearing freedom, is inwardly free inasmuch as it is internally necessary or actually existing. With these two features elaborated, Fichte announces "absolute appearance, or genesis, has been presented"—the absolute element as reason's self-construction or *being*, the apparent or phenomenological element as reason's free existence in us.[51] This is as far as a first philosophy can go.

There is no mention here in the second half of the lectures of an encounter with facticity, though absolute genesis is said to become *absolute fact*. The two-place or subjunctive should/would (*sollen/müssen*) expression that characterizes reason's presence in appearance is abrogated when means-end explanation becomes hypothetical command, instruction becomes principle-providing, and the latter is seen to be lawfulness. Does *practical reason* mean in this context that reason becomes active in a free rational subject or that law enacts itself? Evidently, genetic reason requires concretion or embodiment as the reach of its own legislation or the condition of its own activity. In the closing pages of the Twenty-Fourth Lecture, Fichte spells out this line of reasoning:

- Objectivity (facticity) or relativity has no relation to truth. We began our inquiry into knowing not exactly realizing the difference between knowing in-itself and our reconstruction of it.

- Our effort presumed a law linking knowing and our (re)construction. If we just construct the law ourselves, it is fictional and not a law. The same holds for knowing: if it is only we who construct knowing, there is none.

- So there is a disjunction between reason in-itself and reason in us. "It is not the outward disjunction into subject and object, which fell away in the full annulment of the persistent form of projection and objectivity, rather [it is] the inner living difference between both: two forms of life."

- It is not we who constructed absolute law; therefore, "it must be evident that we cannot construct it, rather it constructs itself on us and in us. In short, it is the law itself that posits us, and itself in us."[52]

The performative or self-active aspect of reason entails that it be self-specifying, or both acting and enacted. If it is not the dark gap of mere fact that splits cognition into subject and object and agency into actor and deed, what causes the split? The only answer *Wissenschaftslehre* can offer is its first word: *logic is both active and disjunctive; when you think you see two items, you see one, and when you think you see one, there are two*. Fichte himself explains it in the subsequent and final lecture: "Self-construction on us and in us" involves a projection or production of an image, but the question is, "Whose construction? Reason's or ours?" We cannot account for the presence of reason in us by free or arbitrary thinking, for we cannot construct reason. If we can only be reason by (re)constructing it in us, all questions must end with reason's self-making—in a processive or genetic form whereby reason is the *duplicity* of reason and understanding, or reason in-itself and reason in us. The absolute fact, engendered in reason or genetically self-elaborated, is that reason has "existence" or concreteness (*Dasein*) in itself and this is the ground of its existence (*Existenz*) in us. As existing, it is consciousness or I/We, its unity the appearance of a *subject*, its multiplicity the display of *objectivity*, their unity the reality of *knowing*, and knowing's externalization or projection as absolute *reality*. These four aspects of consciousness dictate the fourfold forms of life that embodied reason deploys as its conditions: sensibility, understanding as law and logic, morality, and religion.[53]

We undertook this detailed analysis of the course of the 1804^2 lectures in order to show Kantian and Spinozistic aspects of Fichte's argument. While our initial suspicion was that the two would show themselves in separate contexts (e.g., with an idealistic construction of being in the first half of the lectures and a realistic construction of the factical limitations of appearance as practical reason in the second half), the upshot is more complicated. The whole of Fichte's argument is idealistic *and* realistic, the genetic (re)construction of being always risking the interruption of "dark" or merely factual explanations but always consuming them as its fuel. The second half of the lectures, far from returning to bare facticity or the given structure of consciousness, involve consciousness and its location only as a *terminus ad quem*, never as a premise. The duplicity of reason in-itself and reason in us, and reason's sole responsibility for the duplicity, is the hallmark of *Wissenschaftslehre*. It is not our capacity as knowers and agents that explains reason, but just the reverse. Reason's self-making and actuation in us is absolute fact; it has and needs no discursive justification. This active, self-constituting, and self-embodying character of reason captured in *Wissenschaftslehre* makes the basic theory capable of grounding multiple specific disciplinary or regional ontologies—idealistic, realist, moral, and religious. The authors of *Bruno* and the 1804^2 *Science of Knowing* seem to agree, however fleetingly, on the fivefold character of reason.

Notes

1. F. W. J. Schelling, *Bruno, or on the Natural and Divine Principle of Things 1802*, trans. Michael Vater (Albany: State University of New York Press, 1984) 205–23; *Bruno, oder Über das göttliche und naturliche Princip der Dinge. Ein Gespräch. Herausgegeben von Schelling*, in *Friedrich Wilhelm Joseph Schelling Historische-kritische Ausgabe im Auftrag der Bayerishen Akademie der Wissenschaften* (HKA), I/11, 1, eds. Manfred Durner and Ives Radrizzani (Stuttgart: Fromann-Holzboog, 2017), 429–48. A preliminary discussion harmonizes ancient "materialism" (Greek physics, pre-Socratic, and Platonic) with recent "spiritualism" (Leibniz's monadology) as prelude to a dialectic reconciliation of identity-theory's realism with idealism—the higher "idealism" of *eternal ideas* that the dialogue advocates, not the lesser idealism that merely provides a practical (i.e., moral) foundation for ordinary consciousness. Hereafter cited as *Bruno*, English, *HKA* pagination.

2. 1804^2, 115–16; *GA*, II/8, 229–30.

3. Fichte's stark denunciation of *Naturphilosophie* as a distorted and limited presentation of the intrinsic life of God in *Über das Wesen des Gelehrten* (1805) also invokes the divide between ontology and phenomenology as conceived in the present text. See Johann Gottlieb Fichte *Über das Wesen des Gelehrten, und seine Erscheinungen im Gebiete der Freiheit*, eds. Alfred Denker, C. Jeffrey Kinlaw, and Holger Zabrowski (Freiberg and München: Verlag Karl Alber, 2020) 25–26, 29–30. Schelling's intemperate reply to this and other provocations in *Characteristics of the Present Age* and *The Way towards the Blessed Life* is found in F. W. J. Schelling, *Statement on the True Relationship of the Philosophy of Nature to the Revised Fichtean Doctrine*, trans. Dale Snow (Albany: State University of New York Press, 2018); *Darlegung des wahren Verhältnisses der Naturphilosophie zu der verbesserten Fichtischen Lehre*, in *Friedrich Wilhelm Joseph Schelling's sämmtlitche Werke*, ed. K. F. A. Schelling, I/7 (Stuttgart: Cotta, 1856–1861), hereafter cited as *SSW*.

4. F. W. J. Schelling, *Presentation of My System of Philosophy (1801)*, in *The Philosophical Rupture between Fichte and Schelling: Selected Correspondence and (Texts 1800–1802)*, eds. and trans. Michael Vater and David W. Wood (Albany: State University of New York Press, 2012), 142; *HKA*, I/10, 110–11.

5. "Fichte to Schelling, May 31–August 7[8?], 1801," in *Correspondence 1800–1802*, in *RFS*, J. G. Fichte/F. W. J. Schelling, 55–56; *Friedrich Wilhelm Joseph Schelling Historisch-kritische Ausgabe*, III/2, eds. Thomas Kisser, Walter Schieche, and Alois Weishuber (Stuttgart: Fromann-Holzboog, 2010), 364–66. Hereafter cited as *HKA*, III/2. Cp. "Fichte to Schelling, November 15, 1800," in *RFS*, 42; *HKA*, III/2, 276.

6. "Schelling to Fichte, November 19, 1800," in *RFS*, 45–46; *HKA*, III/2, 280–82; and "Fichte to Schelling, May 31–August7[8?]," in *RFS*, 55; *HKA*, III/2, 364.

7. Compare "Fichte to Schelling, May 31–August7[8?]," in *RFS*, 55; *HKA*, III/2, 364; and "Schelling to Fichte, October 3, 1801," in *RFS*, 60; *HKA*, III/2, 374. For a more detailed account of how the *Correspondence* serves as background

for Fichte's 1804² lectures, see Hartmut Traub, "*Schellings Einfluß auf die Wissenschaftslehre 1804, oder 'Manche Bücher sind nur zu lang geratene Breife,*'" in *Schelling zwischen Fichte und Hegel*, eds. Christoph Asmuth, Alfred Denker, and Michael Vater (Amsterdam: B. R. Güner, 2000), 77–92.

8. 1804², 115–16; *GA*, II/8, 229–30.

9. *Bruno*, 136, 359. This principle makes opposition just as primary as unity; it depends on a "principle of reduplication" derived from Leibniz's identity of indiscernibles, Kant's concept of being, and Plouquet's concept of judgment. See Manfred Frank, "'Identity of Identity and Non-identity': Schelling's Path to the 'Absolute System of Identity,'" trans. Ian Alexander More, in *Interpreting Schelling*, ed. Lara Ostaric (Cambridge: Cambridge University Press, 2014) 121–30.

10. *Bruno*, 217, 442.

11. "Further Presentations from the System of Philosophy (1802)," in *RFS*, 210; *HKA*, I/12, 1, 108.

12. Tom Rockmore, *German Idealism as Constructivism* (Chicago: University of Chicago Press, 2016) 11–39.

13. Reason's light cannot be seen immediately but must be reconstructed laboriously (through philosophy) by sustained individual attention, linguistic variation undoing rigid ideas about the meaning of specific terms, and repeated attempts to inwardly create the light. The process eventually moves one from factual enumeration to genesis or living reason "like a lightning flash" [*Blitzschlag*]. 1804², 48; *GA*, II/8, 68. Cp. 1804², 44–45, 78–79; *GA*, II/8, 63–64, 138–40.

14. Frank, op. cit., 121–35.

15. Sometimes Fichte places the dot [•] at the apex of double lines of derivation-or-ascent [/ and \], visually suggesting disjunction. Wright employs the simple dot. Compare 1804², 40 with *GA*, II/8, 52.

16. 1804², 113–16; *GA*, II/8, 224–30.

17. 1804², 187; *GA*, II/8, 389–90.

18. 1804², 199–200; *GA*, II/8, 416–19.

19. Johann Gottlieb Fichte, *The Way towards the Blessed Life, or the Doctrine of Religion*, trans. William Smith (London: John Chapman, 1849) 77–94; *Die Anweisung zum seligen Leben*, in *GA*, I/9, 103–14.

20. Hegel remarks a few months after the *Presentation*'s publication "the essence of philosophy . . . is a bottomless abyss for personal idiosyncrasies. In order to reach philosophy, it is necessary to throw oneself into it *à corps perdu*—meaning by 'body' here, the sum of one's idiosyncrasies." *The Difference between Fichte's and Schelling's System of Philosophy*, eds. and trans. H. S. Harris and Walter Cerf (Albany: State University of New York Press, 1977), 88.

21. 1804², 199; *GA*, II/8, 417–18.

22. 1804², 111–12; *GA*, II/8, 221.

23. The phrase *Philosophie schlechthin* comes from Schelling (*Bruno*, 216, 441).

24. 1804², 181; *GA*, II/8, 278.

25. 1804², 77–78; *GA*, II/8, 136–37.

26. 1804², 27–29; *GA*, II/8, 21–25.

27. 1804², 40–44; *GA*, II/8, 53–64.

28. "A" symbolizes the absolute, "B-T" the disjunction of being and thinking, "x, y, z" the role of the transcendental apperception of consciousness, the moral imperative, and the principle of reflection in Kant's three *Critiques*. The •-operator denotes disjunction, the unity in diversity of logical space that makes elaboration and judgment possible.

29. On the nature of negative thinking and its role as the sole opening onto philosophical assertion, see 1804², 71; *GA*, II/8, 122–23.

30. 1804², 40–41; *GA*, II/8, 52.

31. 1804², 95; *GA*, II/8, 179.

32. 1804² 41; *GA*, II/8, 54.

33. 1804², 159; *GA*, II/8, 328.

34. 1804²,196–98; *GA*, II/8, 411–14.

35. 1804², 118–19; *GA*, II/8, 235–36; and 1804², 186; *GA*, II/8, 386–87. Both summaries make the point that the march of argument is genetic or dialectical, involving destruction of the factual, not reliance upon it as would a simple-minded idealism that appeals to facts of immediate consciousness.

36. This argument culminates in the Fourteenth Lecture. After dismissing Schelling's positing of reason as something external to the thinking, Fichte says the task requires abstraction—both from consciousness and from life (which we factually are). That leaves the bare requirement: think the in-itself! But since the in-itself is a relational term, to think it removes both the related not-in-itself and the thinking itself—if it is genetic thinking (1804², 109–14; *GA*, II/8, 216–28).

37. The complex relationships between explanation, prescription, and normativity that evolve in the text's second half originate in the Eleventh Lecture where the "should" (*Sollen*) of life's claim is first introduced as the lively demand thinking makes in the "through" (*Durch*), the reflexive relation among notes in the concept that make it self-supporting (1804², 88–89; *GA*, II/8, 161–62). The self-presupposing character of being revealed in the Fourteenth and Fifteenth Lectures gives way to other-supposing structures of causal explanation, rule, law, and value's pervasive reach throughout being. But *life* is the basic self-supposing item, and Fichte ranks it with being rather than phenomena.

38. In the thumbnail sketch of the 1804² *Wissenschaftslehre* that Fichte offers in the second of the 1805 *Wesen des Gelehrten* lectures, Fichte argues that the factical limitations of truth's appearance as human consciousness can only be noted, not explained. Philosophy can only point to the fact (*Daß*) of truth's exhibition (*Darstellung*) under finite conditions, not its manner or cause (*Wie*), op. cit., 26.

39. The literary and popular appeal of *Bruno* lies in its expression of the Spinozistic triad of substance, idea, and body in Neoplatonic guise as *the eternal, the infinite, and the finite* (200, 423) and their subsequent interpretation in mythological and trinitarian terms (221–23, 446–48).

40. *GA*, II/8, 155–58, 1804², 84–86.

41. *GA*, II/8, 162–68; 1804², 88–91.
42. *GA*, II/8, 177–78; 1804², 94–95.
43. 1804², 106–7; *GA*, II/8, 193–95; and 1804², 112–13; *GA*, II/8, 221–22.
44. 1804², 114–16; *GA*, II/8, 225–30.
45. 1804², 156–57; *GA*, II/8, 322–23.
46. 1804², 111–12; *GA*, II/8, 219–20.
47. 1804², 166–67; *GA*, II/8, 345–47; and 1804², 190–91; *GA*, II/8, 398–88.
48. *Bruno*, 159–60, 381–82, 163–65, 386–88.
49. 1804², 187–89; *GA*, II/8, 388–90.
50. 1804², 191; *GA*, II/8, 399.
51. 1804², 194–95; *GA*, II/8, 407–8.
52. 1804², 176–77; *GA*, II/8, 367–68.
53. 1804², 191, 197–99; *GA*, II/8, 399–400, 414–18.

Chapter 13

Fichte contra Idealism in the *1804 Wissenschaftslehre*

MICHAEL STEINBERG

It is generally accepted that the *Wissenschaftslehre* is some form of idealism. *Transcendental* idealism, Fichte called it, claiming thereby the mantle of Kant. Later scholars have seen it as the founding move in *German* idealism, thus connecting it with Schelling and Hegel. We seem content with the term; the alternative of "classical German philosophy," which Lukács among others preferred, has not found favor. Whatever species Fichte's philosophy falls into, we assume without much additional consideration that it belongs to the genus *idealism*. It begins as transcendental idealism, making no ontological claims, and even those who find a significant break between the Jena writings and those that come afterward see the "late Fichte" as moving toward an absolute idealism, not to any sort of realism.

There are plausible reasons for this classification. In the 1797 and 1798 introductions to the *Wissenschaftslehre* Fichte had written that there were only two types of philosophy possible, idealism and dogmatism, and "according to the former system, the representations accompanied by a feeling of necessity are products of the intellect, which is what this system presupposes in order to explain experience. According to the latter, dogmatic system, such representations are a product of the thing in itself, which is what the system presupposes."[1] His own system is of the first sort, and so it must be idealist in nature. The second, rejected system is self-evidently realist.

It may seem surprising, then, to see that in the *1804 Wissenschaftslehre* Fichte not only critiques idealism but suggests that his philosophy had always tended to realism instead. "Beginners," he warns, "are easily tempted to remain one-sidedly trapped in . . . [the idealist] point of view, since it is the perspective in which their speculative power first develops."[2] It is wrong to assume that this is what he teaches, he adds. "Idealistic stubbornness . . . has long been attributed to the fantasy of the *Wissenschaftslehre* which circulates among the German public,"[3] when, in fact, "All the expressions of the *Wissenschaftslehre* so far show a predilection for the realistic perspective."[4] What it holds to as real is something literally inconceivable, and is not a "thing" at all, but it is real all the same. The text is divided, like Parmenides's poem, into a way of truth and a way of appearances, and it is realism that prevails in the first half. Idealism only comes into its own in the second part, in Fichte's account of the phenomenal world.[5]

In parallel with this apparent shift from idealism to realism is a shift in pedagogy. Fichte's teaching, here as in the early classes described by Henrik Steffens, aimed at redirecting his auditors' attention, leading them to a perspective point from which they could unfold the *Wissenschaftslehre* on their own.[6] There is a striking difference in emphasis, though, between the Jena lectures and the Berlin ones. In Jena the students had been asked to think an object, typically the wall, and then to think that which thinks the wall—again, an object, although this is, of course, the I, which is the sole object that is simultaneously a subject. In 1804, however, the listeners are continually bidden to think a *through* or a *from*, and to do so not passively but energetically. The *Wissenschaftslehre*, Fichte says there, stands in the point from which the innumerable things of the world and the division between being and thought flow out as the activity of the unnameable Absolute.[7] Since the aim of his teaching is for his auditors to *become* the *Wissenschaftslehre* rather than adhere to it as a set of theories, that is where they must place—and discover—themselves.[8] And where both auditors and *Wissenschaftslehre* are grounded is not an objective state of things or an explicit idea but a maelstrom of activity.

It is activity to which these lectures turn us, again and again, and the fundamental shift in conscious awareness that Fichte was always trying to elicit now points through itself or from something else toward a point of genesis. In one passage, in fact, he appears to repudiate what has always been taken as his inescapable foundation, the self as both subject and object. If you have attained the essential insight of the *Wissenschaftslehre*, he writes, you will never again "allow yourself to be deceived by the illusion . . . that you yourself are the very thing that objectively posits the one knowing (that you therefore are the subject with it as your object)."[9] It was all too easy to think that one was thinking that which thinks the wall once one embraces the idea that the I is both subject and object. The Berlin listeners are asked to go *beyond* the I, to think in terms of productive activity, to stand radically open to process and to free themselves of concepts. That which they must think exists only as manifestation and transformation.

How is this realism? Fichte devotes a large part of the Tenth through Fifteenth Lectures to critical reflections on idealism and realism, critiques that are then recapitulated, concisely and clearly, in the Fifteenth Lecture with its "basic proposition" of the *Wissenschaftslehre*. There is something Kantian about this *via negativa*; just as Kant makes way for faith by his critique of pure reason, Fichte brings his students to his original insight by his critiques of idealism and of realism. Yet over and over again it is idealism that is shown to fall short. It can chart out the transformations of experience, but it cannot account for experience itself.

Fichte starts with idealism, and he sets the listener up, as it were, by framing the idealist argument in a way that many of us today might read as the very heart of the *Wissenschaftslehre*: "The concept is . . . the inner immediate life of reason, merely *existing* and never appearing, which appears as energy. . . . This inner life . . . is the principle of concept and intuition at once and in the same stroke:—thus it is the absolute *principle of everything*."[10] Well, yes, one might say. Here are the elements of Fichte's Jena philosophy, the drives through which the absolute I manifests itself as I and Not-I, striving, and an all-encompassing reason that is manifest as self and world.

But no. All life is found in the movement of reason—and yet the idealist stance traces reason back to an absolute that is ungraspable within its terms and indeed within any cognition. The idealist absolute is a kind of philosophical black hole, moribund because it is external and can only be presupposed. "The basic character of the ideal perspective is that it originates from the presupposition of a being which is only hypothetical . . . and it is very natural that it finds just this same being, which it presupposes as absolute, to be absolute again in its genetic deduction."[11] And this mean that it rests on something "inwardly static, motionless, and dead." Idealism is trapped in "the form of outward existence"—by which Fichte presumably refers to that which is a world for us in our conscious experience—and it cannot reach that what it recognizes is the ground for outward existence. As he had said as early as 1794, in his Zurich lectures, the mind cannot escape the circle it draws for itself.[12]

"So much by way of a sharp, penetrating critique of the idealist position," Fichte announces.[13] Idealism is circumscribed by the facts of consciousness, and the hypothetical but inert absolute it asserts cannot rescue it from the standpoint of reflection in which it is trapped.[14] Its facticity leads it into a dead end. "This is idealism's stubbornness," he writes, "not to let one go further, once one has finally arrived at it."[15]

Realism, too, is factical, but unlike idealism it reaches beyond consciousness. It presupposes "an absolute life, grounded in itself." In the same counterintuitive way in which idealism is said to be grounded in external existence, by which Fichte means the facts of consciousness, realism is said to be grounded in an immanence that gives rise to experience in the first place.

From this perspective, though, "intuition itself is obviously negated."[16] Not as empirically given, of course; intuition and consciousness are always available if not immediately present. What follows from the implicitly Parmenidean assertion of an "absolute *immanent*" and self-enclosed life, in which "all reality whatsoever is encompassed,"[17] is that an *objectifying* intuition of that life cannot arise. One cannot step aside from being and take a look at it.

These two standpoints, though, are still partial. Both are undermined by their factical assertions. Realism undermines experience and subjectivity altogether. It cannot explain how inner experience can emerge or exist. Idealism, by contrast, describes the forms of possible experience, but it remains trapped within that charmed circle.

One might think then that the two should be synthetically unified, but this, too, would be a mistake. Nothing truly genetic can arise from yoking together two factically grounded insights. Fichte makes this clear in a brief and vitriolic attack on Schelling, whose much more conventional metaphysics does indeed take these to be philosophical positions demanding a discursive reconciliation. By joining idealism to a realistic *Naturphilosophie* Schelling could achieve only "a synthesis *post factum*,"[18] a useless result, and in his identity philosophy he failed to grasp that the absolute point of indifference must also be an absolute point of differentiation. Worse yet, he had objectified reason. This "is completely the wrong path," says Fichte. "The business of philosophy is not to talk around reason from the outside, but really and in all seriousness to conduct rational existence."[19]

That is what the *Wissenschaftslehre* is about. It is not about having certain ideas; its explicit, discursive content is ultimately superseded by the lived activity that it expresses and to which it points. One does not adhere to it or argue in its favor, one embodies it. But before we "become the *Wissenschaftslehre*," as Fichte calls it, there are additional dialectical twists and turns. Instead of synthesizing the realist and idealist perspectives Fichte sets them in dialogue with one another. It is an excellent example of his mature dialectical method, which has left behind the sometimes mechanical formalism of his early work. It is also deeply integrated with his program of posing intellectual problems and observing the processes whereby we resolve them—the philosophy of seeing at work.

Fichte implies, if he does not assert, that the value of realism is precisely its negation of intuition and thinking. The in-itself negates everything else, and it negates all construction and thinking as well; it is independent of all thinking and thus, surprisingly, the movement implicit within the stance of realism is itself the in-itself. In yielding to the negation of thinking we embody the activity of the Absolute.[20] This reframing of the in-itself as an activity rather than a thing gives us a genetic insight into something that we previously understood only factically.[21]

This is the crucial step in Fichte's critique of idealism. Idealism asserts that intuition exists and insists that we must be able to *think* the in-itself, and think it *energetically.*"[22] From this perspective realism appears to be the embrace of something inert, dead, a commitment to being a piece of lava on the moon. But just the opposite is the case. It is idealism that dies "at the root," because even in its higher forms, where the contents of consciousness and even the fact of consciousness are set aside, and where one proceeds from the mere possibility of consciousness, idealism cannot support a self-understanding that is genuinely genetic. Thinking the in-itself always proceeds from the facticity of "the *objectifying* light."[23] Crucially, Fichte emphasizes the word "objectifying," because it shows how idealism always starts too late. It always begins after the move toward objectification is in process and for that reason it can never come to terms with the source of that objectification. It must always posit something outside that produces its object, and it cannot give an account of that production. Its object is inevitably "a thing that it projected purely and through an absolute gap,"[24] and "the gap, the rupture of intellectual activity in it, is just death's lair."[25]

Realism takes over. Yet the realism that speaks of the in-itself is itself undermined, because its in-itself "is still always qualified by the negation of something opposed to it, thereby as an *in-itself* it is itself something relative" and "is not a true oneness."[26] Behind its putative oneness is duality, the reciprocal interplay of the in-itself and a not-in-itself, much as Hölderlin had argued in *Urteil und Seyn*.[27] The unitary in-itself of this realism, then, fails for the same reason as does the objectifying light of idealism; it, too, is a projection through an irrational gap.

Such a realism is no realism at all, moreover, because it is grounded on at least the possibility of consciousness, on an absolute that we can think. Fichte unmasks it as a concealed idealism; its project "is fundamentally factical and a discontinuous projection, [it] does not stand up to its own criteria, and, according to the rules it itself established, it is to be given up."[28]

At this point in Fichte's argument the critique of idealism is as profound as it can get, and it encompasses the entire realm of discursive thought. All modes of thought are "negations of the in-itself. Not as absolute negations, but as privative ones."[29] This is obvious in the case of idealism, even the transcendental kind, because idealism always starts from consciousness itself. But it is just as true in the case of what we had supposed to be realism, because our assertions about the in-itself are also framed from the standpoint of consciousness. Both are idealism, both fail to escape subject-object dualism, and both are false.

As Fichte puts it in the Fifteenth Lecture, idealism insists that the fact of reflection must be taken as valid, and nothing else, while realism maintains that the content "of the evident proposition is to be taken as valid, and nothing else; and, for that very reason, both are at bottom factical, since indeed even the contents of what is manifest, which alone should be valid for realism, is only a fact."[30] We must move beyond both. "Realism, or more accurately *objectivism* perishes along with that idealism which . . . we might better call *subjectivism*. Reality remains, as *inner* being . . . but in no way does it remain a term of any relation, since a second term for the relation, and indeed all relations in general, have been given up."[31]

This leads us to the basic proposition in the Fifteenth Lecture, the climax of Fichte's way of truth. He is not asserting a realism that is a covert idealism because it asserts a being present to consciousness, but a realism attained by letting go of "being in-itself as a negation and a relational term."[32] What remains is being as self-grounded act, its "inner essence" known only after "the entire outer existential form has perished" in the shape of objectification and projection, and which "we truly work . . . through if we see into it as the genesis for its appearance in the outer existential form."[33] We fall into error and death if we objectify or define the in-itself, but we can stand in and as the in-itself insofar as we surrender discursive thought, and surrender, too, the separations of self and other and subject and object that arise in and as consciousness. "Away with all words and signs!" Fichte exhorted his audience. "Nothing remains except our living thinking and insight, which cannot be shown on a blackboard or be represented in any way but which can only be surrendered to in nature."[34] Only if we stop trying "talk around reason from the outside" can we "really and in all seriousness . . . conduct rational existence." Only through this realism can we avoid the traps into which Schelling fell. And it *is* a realism, not an idealism, because its standpoint lies outside of and before the emergence of consciousness, and because it asserts the reality of that movement that our "words and signs" grasp at but can never fully express.

In a very contemporary way, Fichte recognizes and refuses to subscribe to either the myth of the given or what the late Susan Hurley called the myth of the giving.[35] Realism seems at first blush to assert a separation between subject and object, against which idealism pushes back, and it is essential to Fichte's thought that one see into the illusionary nature of that separation. But idealism is so structured that it cannot transcend that illusion. It always depends on an absolute that it is compelled to posit but which remains external to its workings. Between that absolute and the self there is the projection through an unbridgeable gap, the "death at the root" to which the aporias of the Jena *Wissenschaftslehre* testify. It will indeed not let us go forward, so it can never bring us to oneness—which "cannot in any way consist in what we *see* or *conceive* . . . because that would be something objective."[36]

Idealism, then, must perish in favor of a realism, which is at least structurally compatible with the genetic unity of knower and known. It is a realism without a subject or object, which rests on the reality of the process that manifests as all we can experience, ourselves included. In it being and act are one, as are self and other and percipient and thing perceived. One might consider it a Parmenidean realism as well, for the absence of subjects in what are often translated as Parmenides's assertions about Being suggests that he, too, may have grasped reality as act and as self-manifestation. This is the "basic proposition" of the *Wissenschaftslehre*: "Being exists immediately only in being, or life, and . . . it exists only as whole, undivided oneness."[37]

Fichte is not done, however, and here he departs most decisively from Parmenides, who had framed the second part of his poem as the way of illusion. The remaining lectures in Fichte's course, by contrast, valorize appearance; what one experiences in perception and introspection "is a projection of nothing else but [the in-]itself, wholly and completely as it inwardly is."[38] We are always inescapably moments within the self-revelation of the Absolute. As he says in his sonnets of 1812, once one understands appearance *as* appearance the divine life is revealed, not behind those appearances but as the appearances themselves; the veil—our belief that the appearances are appearances of something else—dissolves.[39] In Hegel's well-known words, "The consummation of the infinite End . . . consists merely in removing the illusion which makes it seem yet unaccomplished."[40]

Idealism had been seen into and abandoned in the ascent, but it reappears now as an elucidation of the necessary forms of experience. It is undermined as an independent philosophical stance, but once it assumes its proper, subordinate role it can show the identity of the unknowable real with the realm of experience. As Fichte argued in the Eleventh Lecture, it is from a realist stance that we see that appearances are the manifestation of the principle-providing life of the in-itself, and this shows us where idealism comes into its own:

> Perhaps a simple misunderstanding underlies the proof, given earlier in the name of realism, that an expressive intuition of absolute life can in no wise arise. In that case, what is proven and needs to be asserted is only that such an intuition, as valid for itself and self-supporting, can never arise. This assertion very conveniently leaves room for an interpolation: this intuition might well arise, and must arise under certain conditions, simply as a phenomenon not grounded in itself. Insight into this interpolation could thus provide the standpoint for the science of knowing and the true unification of idealism and realism;—so that the very intuition, purely as such, which we previously called "*our selves* at root," would be the first appearance and the ground of all other appearances; and because this would not be any error but instead genuine truth, it and all its modifications, which must also be intuited as necessary, would be valid as appearances. On the other side, however, seeming and error enter where appearance is taken for being itself.[41]

Idealism elaborates the system of appearances, which are grounded by the "genuine truth" of "our selves at root," and without its elucidation of the laws of conscious experience we either fall back into common sense realism or lose ourselves in the night where all cows are gray.

Here, I would suggest, is where we might grasp not just the argument of the 1804 lectures but their relationship with the writings of the Jena period. That relationship is not one of repudiation but of contextualization and argumentative strategy. In 1804 he told his listeners that he had consistently held, from as early as the *Anesidemus* review, that "immediate consciousness is in no way sufficient and that . . . it does not suffice in its basic law of *projection per hiatum*."[42]

He had tried at first to lead his students beyond immediate consciousness, guiding them through its structures step by step, showing them how "to divide the illusion, and intellectually to destroy each part one at a time."[43] This strategy dominated his first versions of the *Wissenschaftslehre*.

It may also explain some of the cruxes in the Jena texts. The notion of the summons, for example, demands another and thus external free being, which would seem to substitute a summoner-in-itself for the thing-in-itself, which Fichte had rejected. Worse yet, it leads one into an infinite regress. If one cannot find oneself as a rational subject without a summons from another rational subject, who or what summoned the first rational subject? Fichte has no solution for this but an all-but-literal deus ex machina, the God of Genesis summoning Adam.[44] Nor can the inherent ambiguity of the *Anstoss* be resolved without undermining the theoretical consistency of the *Wissenschaftslehre*. If it is an encounter with an external physical world we are left with common sense realism. If it is produced by something non-physical and outside of experience its source can only be the posited but inert being that Fichte identified as idealism's Achilles' heel. These are destabilizing elements, but they are not bugs; they are features. They are cracks through which the light gets in. They force one toward an internal critique that leads ultimately to grasping being (more accurately, being/thinking) as pure act.

As Fichte indicated in 1804, though, he soon concluded that this indirect teaching technique only deferred the moment when insight truly dawned, and he sought a more explicit route to that same moment. As he reflected, "It is clear that [this path] leads to the goal, although with greater difficulty . . . [but] if one knows the origin of non-genesis in advance, and that it always comes to nothing, although it is unavoidable, than one no longer fights against it, but rather allows it to work peacefully; one simply ignores it and abstains from the results. It is possible in this way alone to gain access to insight immediately."[45] By the *Vocation of Man* of 1800, then, and even more in these lectures, he had decided to demonstrate the inadequacy of idealism head-on rather than construct a system that encompassed its own self-critique.

What he did not do is substitute a theistic absolute idealism for a critical and transcendental one, or slip ontological commitments into an analysis of self-consciousness and its transcendental underpinnings. Fichte's project remained consistent. It was to show where transcendental idealism has validity and where it must be left behind, and to show, as well, that while starting with the act of self-positing the *Wissenschaftslehre* points beyond immediate consciousness and thus beyond the self. The ontological commitments can be found even in the 1794 *Foundations of the Entire Wissenschaftslehre*, where "critical idealism," confronted with the question, "What is the ground of the reciprocal relationship that has been assumed to exist between the I and the Not-I?" concedes its failure; "critical idealism confesses its ignorance and indicates that inquiry into this ground lies beyond the boundaries of theory."[46] The answer thus lies elsewhere; "It is [the] practical part [of the *Wissenschaftslehre*] alone that deals with an original reality,"[47] and the upshot of the practical part is this: "The *Wissenschaftslehre* is . . . *realistic*. It shows that it is purely and simply the case that the consciousness of finite creatures cannot be explained unless one assumes the presence of a force posted utterly in opposition to them, a force that is, with respect to the empirical existence of such finite creatures, completely independent of them."[48] For Fichte to call this a realism all but certainly shows that he was committed from the first to an ontologically real though untheorizable ground, a pure imminence without which the movements of self-consciousness were inexplicable.

A few years later, sketching out an approach to a new presentation of his thinking that he hoped would not be as profoundly misunderstood as the earlier versions had been, he wrote that "if idealism is to be called a system that derives all consciousness from mere ideal activity, then the *Wissenschaftslehre* is not at all idealism."[49] Such a system would be "utterly inconsistent and incapable of *explaining* the consciousness that we all really have."[50] The *Wissenschaftslehre* is "a system in which consciousness is derived from the immanent laws of the intelligence, which for it are neither ideal nor real, but the unity of both."[51] These notes, from 1800, are roughly contemporaneous with the *Vocation of Man*, and that popular text culminates in a section titled "faith" or "belief" (*Glaube*), which is said to encompass and surpass the self-enclosed and self-negating idealism of its second section. It, too, cannot be read as purely or even primarily idealist, and it culminates in a prose hymn to the movement of the incomprehensible divine life that manifests itself in all things.

It cannot be doubted that Fichte *starts* from idealism, but that does not mean that he intended to end up there. His early work begins by deriving and elucidating a system of consciousness, and this cannot be done from the "dogmatic" standpoint, which presumes that conscious activity reflects a system of external objects. Consciousness can be explained only from within, on the basis of its immanent principles. One therefore philosophizes from the I, and philosophy as discourse never departs from the I. But while discursive philosophy can only be carried out within those boundaries, its territory does not extend to the whole of reality, and Fichte's ultimate concern is with that unknowable real which manifests itself as I and Not-I.

Consciousness cannot be understood without recognizing its embeddedness within something else, even though what it is at which consciousness aims or from which it proceeds is utterly incomprehensible; it is "a force that is merely felt but not cognized by the finite being."[52] As he wrote to Schelling, "The Absolute *itself* . . . is neither being, nor cognition, nor identity, nor the indifference of the two; but it is precisely—*the Absolute*—and to say anything else about it is a waste of time."[53] Every act of cognition only pushes it farther way; "As soon as we say 'explain,' we have already entered the domain of finitude."[54] Once we do that we drag the Absolute into the realm of discourse and it becomes an object; as he writes in his *Juridical Defense*, "by comprehending something it ceases to be God; and every supposed concept of God is necessarily that of an idol."[55] Better that this be passed over in silence. But what must be passed over in that silence is, in fact, the heart of Fichte's thought.

It was Fichte's lifelong annoyance that his contemporaries took the *Wissenschaftslehre* to be a straightforward and un-self-critical idealism, something to be learned rather than lived.[56] Much like Wittgenstein in the *Tractatus*, Fichte thought he had provided a comprehensive system of the world of experience, and like Wittgenstein he thought that he had also shown how little was accomplished in doing so. And both philosophers found themselves misunderstood by those who overlooked the second of these two claims, and who failed to recognize either that the unwritten philosophy was more important than the written one or that living rationally was more important than codifying the laws of reason.

Part of Fichte's problem may be that the published writings of the Jena period do not set out the full range of his thought. As he told Schelling, he had not yet presented his system of the intelligible world.[57] He had hinted at that system in his literally ek-static vision of one life, manifest as all of creation, in the third section of the *Vocation of Man*, and this clearly pointed beyond a strict idealism, but this aspect of his thought was not foregrounded in his other work. It was easy to pass the popular text off as edification and overlook the incomplete state of the academic ones.

It may also be that Fichte simply failed to see how much his own understanding and deployment of idealism was shaped by his all but inexpressible original insight. The sonnets portray a visionary experience, in a literal sense; once he had seen into Urania's eye, he wrote, it became *his* eye; the eternal one lived in him and looked out through his seeing.[58] He had come to that moment of clarity through long wrestling with transcendental idealism, which had been his own path to "becoming the *Wissenschaftslehre*," and in 1795 he set out to take his students along that same route—into and through idealism and then outward toward that vision. He found few if any who could stay the course. It was simply too easy to remain within the system of idealism, or to get tangled up in it and assume that one was grappling in a responsible way with difficult problems no different in kind from other philosophical conundrums.

The assault on idealism in the 1804 *Wissenschaftslehre*, then, need not be read as a repudiation of the Jena writings. It is a different way of imparting the same message, one that sidesteps the pitfalls Fichte had come to see in his earlier way of teaching. If we take him seriously when he insists that his philosophy had not changed, as I think we should, it suggests that the Berlin *Wissenschaftslehre* does not supplant the Jena work so much as it completes it and places it in a context that those writings most often merely imply. Instead of reading him forward, taking the early versions of his system as the norm, it might be better to read him backward—seeing the Jena work as sketches of something larger and more commodious, implying what the "late Fichte" makes explicit.

As Fichte says, in an analogy that Wittgenstein was to use as well, his teaching is like the ladder one climbs and must then throw away.[59] The idealism of the Jena years was *always* propaedeutic. It was *always* meant to direct one toward a higher realism, toward that from which experience originated. It was *always* meant to be superseded, to yield to the insight that the process it elaborates, through which the I is generated, cannot itself be the activity of the I. "From the perspective of 'we' or 'I' there is no philosophy," Fichte warns. "There is one only beyond the I,"[60] and idealism is inherently incapable of leading beyond the I.

Few if any of his contemporaries ever grasped that point, and the structure and the rhetoric of the 1804 *Wissenschaftslehre*, and its sustained critique of what almost everyone had taken to be the heart of the Fichtean philosophy, arguably grew out of that failure to be understood. Fichte's frustration, written all over these lectures, is that of the Zen master who points to the moon but whose students, seriously and earnestly, never take their eyes off his finger. Sadly, his decision to teach privately instead of publishing a revised *Wissenschaftslehre* text has made it all too easy for later generations to fall into the same mistake.

Notes

1. *IWL*, 11; *SW*, I, 426.
2. 1804², 90; *GA*, II/8, 166–67.
3. 1804², 90; *GA*, II/8, 166–67.
4. 1804², 92; *GA*, II/8, 172–73.
5. Fichte himself divides the lectures this way, although he does not note the parallel with Parmenides; 1804², 115; *GA*, II/8, 228–29.
6. Henrik Steffens, *The Story of My Career as a Student at Freiberg and Jena, and as Professor at Halle, Breslau and Berlin*, trans. Gage (Boston: Gould and Lincoln, 1863), 64.
7. 1804², 40; *GA*, II/8, 52–53.
8. 1804², 41; *GA*, II/8, 52–53.
9. 1804², 49; *GA*, II/8, 70–71.
10. 1804², 89; *GA*, II/8, 164–65.
11. 1804², 89; *GA*, II/8, 164–65.
12. Fichte, *Foundations of the Entire Wissenschaftslehre and Related Writings (1794–95)*, ed. and trans. Daniel Breazeale (Oxford: Oxford University Press, 2021) (henceforth *FEW*), 448; *GA*, IV/3, 32.
13. 1804², 89; *GA*, II/8, 166–67.
14. 1804², 95; *GA*, II/8, 178–81.
15. 1804², 90; *GA*, II/8, 166–67.
16. 1804², 90; *GA*, II/8, 166–67.
17. 1804², 90; *GA*, II/8, 168–69.
18. 1804², 109; *GA*, II/8, 214–15.
19. 1804², 110; *GA*, II/8, 216–17.
20. The sense of a Hegelianism *avant la lettre* is hard to avoid here.
21. 1804², 97; *GA*, II/8, 184–85.
22. 1804², 98; *GA*, II/8, 186–87.
23. 1804², 99; *GA*, II/8, 188–89.
24. 1804², 111; *GA*, II/8, 218–19.
25. 1804², 111–12; *GA*, II/8, 220–21.
26. 1804², 113; *GA*, II/8, 222–23.
27. Friedrich Hölderlin, "Über Urtheil und Seyn," in *Hegel's Development: Toward the Sunlight, 1770–1801*, by H. S. Harris (Oxford: Clarendon Press, 1972).
28. 1804², 114; *GA*, II/8, 224–25.
29. 1804², 100; *GA*, II/8, 188–89.
30. 1804², 118; *GA*, II/8, 234–35.
31. 1804², 109; *GA*, II/8, 214–15.
32. 1804², 114; *GA*, II/8, 224–25.
33. 1804², 114; *GA*, II/8, 224–25. There are strong parallels between this and the *Sittenlehre*; see, e.g., *SE*, 245; *SW*, IV, 256: "It is precisely by means of . . . [the]

disappearance and annihilation of one's entire individuality that everyone becomes a pure presentation of the moral law in the world of sense."

34. 1804^2, 60; *GA*, II/8, 94–95.
35. S. L. Hurley, *Consciousness in Action* (Cambridge, MA: Harvard University Press, 1998), 240 ff.
36. 1804^2, 56; *GA*, II/8, 86–87.
37. 1804^2, 120; *GA*, II/8, 240–41.
38. 1804^2, 169; *GA*, II/8, 350–51. Here is another clear parallel with *Ch'an*: ordinary mind is Buddha nature.
39. *SW*, VIII, 462.
40. Hegel G. W. F., *Hegel's Logic: Being Part One of the Encyclopedia of the Philosophical Sciences*, trans. William Wallace (Oxford, 1975), § 212, at 274.
41. 1804^2, 92; *GA*, II/8, 172–73.
42. 1804^2, 119; *GA*, II/8, 238–39.
43. 1804^2, 119; *GA*, II/8, 238–39.
44. *FNR*, 38; *SW*, 3, 39–40.
45. 1804^2, 119–20; *GA*, II/8, 239.
46. *FEW*, 267; *SW*, I, 178.
47. *FEW*, 346; *SW*, I, 286.
48. *FEW*, 342; *SW*, I, 280.
49. J. G. Fichte, "New Version of the Wissenschaftslehre [1800]," in *The Philosophical Rupture Between Fichte and Schelling*, J. G. Fichte and F. W. J. Schelling, eds. and trans. Michael Vater and David Wood (Albany: State University of New York Press 2012), 117; *GA*, II/5, 366–67.
50. Fichte, "New Version of the *Wissenschaftslehre* [1800]," 117 (*emphasis added*).
51. Fichte, "New Version of the Wissenschaftslehre [1800]," 117.
52. *FEW*, 342; *SW*, I, 280.
53. Fichte and Schelling, *Philosophical Rupture*, 73, letter of January 15, 1802.
54. *FEW*, 343; *SW*, I, 281.
55. J. G. Fichte, *Fichte and the Atheism Dispute*, trans. Curtis Bowman (Farnham, UK: Ashgate, 2010), 179; *GA*, I/6, 52.
56. See, for example, his complaints about the neglect of the practical sections of the Foundations quoted in the introduction to Breazeale's introduction to that text, *FEW*, 38.
57. Fichte and Schelling, *Philosophical Rupture*, 48–49, draft dated October 8, 1800.
58. *SW*, VIII, 461–62.
59. 1804^2, 182; *GA*, II/8, 379–80.
60. 1804^2, 139; *GA*, II/8, 284–85.

Chapter 14

The Self-Justification of Fichte's Philosophy

JACINTO RIVERA DE ROSALES

The last three lectures on the *Wissenschaftslehre* of 1804 address two interlinked themes: (1) the deduction of the *Wissenschaftslehre* (*Science of Knowledge*) itself as the final standpoint of knowing, or appearance and (2) the presentation of the five worldviews in which the *Wissenschaftslehre* or philosophy as such finds its place as the fifth of those views; this serves as a kind of justification of the *Wissenschaftslehre*. The *Wissenschaftslehre* as such, *in specie*, should represent and validate itself within the theory of appearance as a moment, in the manifestation of the absolute Being or God, namely its last, highest manifestation. At the beginning of the Twenty-Sixth Lecture, Fichte regards the establishment or presentation of the content of absolute knowing as being objectively finished;[1] this is his doctrine of appearance, which encompasses the whole idealistic second part of the *Wissenschaftslehre* Fichte contrasts this with "our first part's preference for realism and for the maxim that ruled there always to orient ourselves realistically."[2]

But in this doctrine of appearance the question of the *Wissenschaftslehre* itself remains, that is, "How *we* have become this knowing, since we have become it, and, if this has further conditions, what are they."[3] The first, subjective question is asked in the Twenty-Sixth Lecture: how we arrived at this knowing, at the *Wissenschaftslehre*. The second question, about objective conditions, is explained in the Twenty-Seventh Lecture. Thus, the *quaestio juris* is raised about the *Wissenschaftslehre* itself, requiring a defense of philosophy as such and its claim to truth. A philosophical system is such that no moment within it should be posited and used arbitrarily and without reason. "The true ϕ [philosophy] must justify itself within itself and can do so. This is the sign of its truth, and its perfection *in specie*."[4] A similar move occurs in the Hegelian system: philosophy is positioned and justified as the supreme mode and manner of knowledge at the end of the system in his *Encyclopedia*. In this way, the circle is closed: the point of view and the starting point, from which the philosopher began, becomes an object itself in the end, and it is exhibited to be correct. This is how this philosophical approach can be confirmed.

I

The Twenty-Seventh Lecture begins with a summary of the result of the previous lecture: seeing (*Sehen*) or knowing (*Wissen*) sees itself in the *Wissenschaftslehre*, and by virtue of that "necessarily surrenders itself as something independent and posits an absolute Being."[5] This was taken as being the description of certainty, a self-contained or enclosed knowing in itself.

Philosophy as such is also a kind of seeing, the seeing of seeing (*ein Sich-Sehen*), a look at itself, precisely the last moment in the development of knowing, the complete seeing-itself of absolute knowing. The whole world of our experience has here genetically emerged from absolute knowing. This life of absolute knowing and its development are what philosophy or *Wissenschaftslehre* communicates and analyzes in its transcendental guidelines and basic moments. Philosophy is a seeing of absolute knowing itself, the ultimate one; if there were no definitive seeing, then there will be only a *regressus ad infinitum* of seeing of seeing, and actually no absolute knowing that could be realized and understood as such. But according to Fichte this should be: "The existence of absolute knowing does not have its ground in itself, but instead in an absolute purpose, and this purpose is that absolute knowing should exist"[6] for the sake of the manifestation of absolute Being. But only when knowing is fully understood in its fundamentals, thanks to the *Wissenschaftslehre*, can the one absolute Being be revealed in knowing through the opposition to appearance, to knowing, as non-image and real ground of the knowing and its world. There is a duality: absolute Being and absolute knowing (*Sein und Wissen*). For this reason, philosophy becomes necessary, since it accomplishes the seeing of absolute knowing itself, without which this could not be fully realized, because the essence of knowing is self-knowing. In the theory of appearance this "Should" (*Soll*) drives the absolute knowing throughout its development.

Philosophy is also a seeing, and therefore it has an image character like every seeing or act of seeing. Since it is the ultimate or final reflection, knowing understands itself completely without being a being itself or absolute reality, but that only happens in the correct philosophical system, the *Wissenschaftslehre*. In this way, knowing destroys its real independence and, in this annihilation, the Other looks on as absolute inner self-contained Being. But what kind of being is referred to here?

1. *First*, "being" refers to the being of absolute knowing as an existing imagining or forming life (*bildendes Leben*), an original and primordial life of knowing from itself and by itself. According to the *Wissenschaftslehre*, this life is the totality of our experience, including our world and we ourselves, because all these are moments in the development of the absolute knowing or God's appearance. Only this being of absolute knowing, as the "ex-istence" of the absolute Being, is discussed in these last lectures, which still fall into the second part of the *Wissenschaftslehre*, that is, into the theory of appearance. For this reason, the *Wissenschaftslehre* understands itself as a doctrine of knowing, as a scientific doctrine (*Wissen-schafts-lehre*) that wants to explain and entirely expound the knowing to its very foundations.

2, Ultimately, absolute Being as such would be discovered or properly presupposed, since from the outset the *Wissenschaftslehre* interprets all knowledge as an image and without a being or reality of its own, and therefore, it is essentially pointing to an absolute Being as its ontological foundation. But this discovery of absolute Being had already happened at the end of the ascending argument in the first part of the *Wissenschaftslehre*. According to Fichte, the *Wissenschaftslehre* remains transcendental because it distinguishes between absolute Being (or God) and knowing, and thanks to that distinction it manages to establish an ontological limit to knowing, in contrast to Spinoza and Schelling, who believe they have the absolute itself in their hands.[7] Very little can be said about absolute Being as such according to Fichte, only that it is absolute reality, by itself, through itself, from itself (*von sich durch sich aus sich*). For Fichte this means that it is not dead, is not an effect, not even a thing in itself, but life. How absolute knowing derives from absolute Being will remain incomprehensible because knowledge cannot penetrate the interior of this absolute Being.[8]

In Lecture Fifteen of the WL-1804² Fichte tells us something more about this absolute Being: it is "a self-enclosed I,"[9] an absolute I or We in such a way that "we live immediately in the act of living itself, therefore we are the one undivided being itself."[10] But soon Fichte realizes that this cannot be so, that the absolute Being cannot be conceptualized as an I or a We, nor can we be placed within its enclosed life, because the I and the We are essentially knowing and require consequently multiplicity and change. Accordingly, after 1805, Fichte locates the I and the We within knowing itself and outside the inner life of the absolute Being. In the *Wissenschaftslehre* of 1805, Fichte writes: the I is "therefore in the true sense the direct *representans* and the representation of God . . . but by no means God himself."[11] In *The Way towards the Blessed Life* (1806) he says:

> In our ineradicable being we are only knowing, image and representation [*Wissen, Bild und Vorstellung*]; and even in that coincidence with the One [with the Absolute, in which our bliss consists] our basic form cannot disappear . . . , [God] does not become . . . our own being itself, but he only hovers before us as something alien [*fremdes*] and that which is outside of us, to which we simply give ourselves and nestle in deep love.[12]

In *1810 Wissenschaftslehre* Fichte explains: "What I am is just a schema."[13] Or in the *1812 Wissenschaftslehre* we read: "In this sense the WL includes the true and fitting propositions of Sp. [Spinoza's] system: the true parallel. One and All is the same. ἐν καὶ πᾶν. All in One, all the same. Certainly, namely in the one appearance. In him [in God] we live and move, in him we are: yes, in his appearance: never in his absolute being."[14]

Since Being is by itself life, knowing must also be life in order to be the true image of Being. Yet its life is not the very *existent life* (*seiendes Leben*) of the Absolute, but rather it is the forming life of knowing from which the world and all of us, even the *Wissenschaftslehre*, arise as moments of its genesis. To think the opposite, to think that we live the same inner life of God (as Fichte seems to say in the *Wissenschaftslehre* 1804²), would be mysticism and enthusiasm (*Schwärmerei*).[15]

Absolute knowing, as the sole appearance or manifestation of absolute Being, has its own forming life. Its fundamental characteristic is to be *self*-knowledge in the sense that it ought to know itself (its being is a task). The manifold of our whole world has emerged from this fundamental characteristic. Knowing ought to recognize and acknowledge itself as knowing. In this way, absolute Being is manifest by means of opposition. In the process of the fulfillment of this task, the world and ourselves and the *Wissenschaftslehre* are born (cf. the absolute Idea in Hegel); that is to say, in the doctrine of appearance idealism is completely carried through.[16]

Self-knowing, forming life is the mode of being of absolute knowing, which is where philosophy and *Wissenschaftslehre* belong as the last moment of its genesis. For this reason, the essence of knowing is not just a dead image of absolute Being, but also, and in order to be a proper image of it, something that relies on itself, "essential, immanent self-enclosure (as absolute Being was previously seen to be)."[17] Therefore, this is not simply human subjective knowledge, but a "cosmogonic" one (again, like Hegel's Idea), and human subjective knowledge, including that of philosophy or *Wissenschaftslehre*, is a moment of its genesis. The *Wissenschaftslehre* describes this wholeness and self-enclosure of knowing, which is not hindered and interfered with by a partially unconditional Not-I, nor by a world as reality in itself, as the ordinary consciousness believes. This is contrary to what Fichte said about how experience arises through the pure I during his Jena period. The *Wissenschaftslehre* is therefore the highest element or moment of this wholeness, where knowing takes full knowledge of oneself. At the same time, this philosophical description should also recognize itself as a moment of this wholeness of knowing in order not to regard itself as the thing described, for the absolute knowing that creates the world. In Fichte's words, the *Wissenschaftslehre* should annihilate itself too, to see itself as seeing, so as to posit the whole knowing that has been described and seen *idealiter*. In this way, the innermost essence of pure seeing as a manifestation of Being is also generally and directly determined and understood, and it appears quite clear as an image in its character. This is the insight into absolute light or knowing as a living inner self-expression.

II

If all of these philosophical reflection had not been created merely through arbitrary freedom, then knowing would thereby be exhausted. But the *Wissenschaftslehre* is "an absolutely evident insight which in general we freely produced."[18] This philosophical insight into the being of knowing as an absolute, self-contained, living and efficacious *esse* was nothing other than *merely factical*, even more, it was only *conditionally* accomplished: if seeing is so and so, then, "Undoubtedly, it was we, scientists of knowing, who created this insight into the essence of seeing."[19] But this freedom alone, and the indicated facticity and conditionality, only give us a ground of possibility, a free ground of this insight and thus of the being or existence of absolute knowing; consequently this insight remains a problematic assertion so that philosophy as *necessary* moment of the whole is not yet elucidated in its necessity. Hence, we and the *Wissenschaftslehre* are only indirectly the factical appearance of reason, but not absolute reason itself, which is necessary. Philosophical insight would be a free reconstruction, objectification, or repetition of a primordial construction on the part of reason that has not yet been shown. But the insight and the existence of absolute knowing should have reality and necessity and be asserted by reason itself. Consequently, there are still gaps to fill in, and there is another insight that we have overlooked. Fichte speaks of a condition that still needs to be sought. That's the topic of the Twenty-Seventh Lecture.

I believe this objective condition is *immediacy* (*Unmittelbarkeit*) in philosophical insight along with the assertion of the existence of absolute knowing, which is no longer just ours but must also be that of absolute reason itself. In other words, the objective condition sought is an identification of both. In the Twenty-Sixth Lecture, seeing penetrated us as something absolutely external, thereby a being of absolute knowing was posited. This being or existence of knowing is therefore posited *in a mediated way* (*mittelbar*) through us, and not *directly*. According to Fichte, in the insight into absolute reason we now acquire the sought after immediacy, which shows the existence of absolute knowing as *real* and no longer problematic. To that aim we have to understand that it is in seeing itself, in the *Wissenschaftslehre*, that the real life of reason lies; it is an act that demonstrates to itself that it is really there, vigorous and active, like being alive, in its *immediate* self-penetration, in its execution. Let us remember that this was also the thinking experience of Descartes, namely, that thought is an activity involving the recognition of one's existence. But this time seeing is not purely *subjective* as is the case in Descartes, it is *absolute,* and that is new. What we did in the *Wissenschaftslehre*, absolute reason did with us. That is so, I would even add, because it was done in a rigorously scientific, systematic, reflexive, and transcendental way. "The insight that we have just completed is now the absolute insight of reason, that is, absolute reason itself. In this insight, we have immediately become absolute reason, and have dissolved into it."[20] That is the claim of the *Wissenschaftslehre* (which is really the pretension of every philosophical system, I would argue): to have found the correct method of thinking and therefore the true philosophy, which would construct reason out of itself, regardless of the individuality of the person that carries out the construction. But this absolute reason-insight leads to the absolute existence of seeing, the existence of absolute knowing, directly through itself because of its self-penetration *Selbst-Durchdringung*,[21] that is to say, absolute reason penetrates itself as such in the effect, in the *Wissenschaftslehre*.[22] Reason posits its absolute existence and penetrates itself. "Reason is intrinsically genetic,"[23] alive, bound to itself with necessary laws, that cannot not be in its act, leading its *necessary* existence in its execution.

Therefore, in the *Wissenschaftslehre*, absolute reason is "absolutely inwardly and secretly what it asserts outwardly about external seeing."[24] Hence, there is an *identification* for both moments: absolute reason and the *Wissenschaftslehre* as its expression because reason is always equal to itself. Absolute reason is the ground of its own active existence, the activity of the *Wissenschaftslehre*. There can be no life outside absolute reason, and it cannot go beyond itself—it is absolute, not merely subjective or merely objective. Consequently, philosophical reason, as the reason of reason, as absolute reason, manifests itself in itself; so the *Wissenschaftslehre* is "a doctrine of reason [*Vernunftlehre*], as the first and highest part of the science of knowing, which does not *become*, but rather *is* unconditionally in itself, and is that which it is,"[25] a foundation of the special sciences. Reason is immediately and absolutely the ground of its existence, and this existence cannot be further justified by any premise, by any higher reason, but only by self-identification in its manifold—thus it is for us "a pure absolute fact."[26] Absolute knowing is a *factum*, that is, incomprehensible, because knowing in its image character is based on the reality of absolute Being, while knowledge cannot penetrate this absolute Being in order to know the how and the why of the emergence of itself. It is for this reason that we have to operate with its facticity. It is because it is, but since it is, it is necessary and cannot not be because there can be no change in absolute Being.[27]

III

However, according to Fichte we are not at the end of our justification of the *Wissenschaftslehre*. Absolute reason posits its existence with total spontaneity, but it has not yet seen itself as positing itself.[28] That can also be expressed in a different way:

> Reason posits its life and existence unconditionally and inseparably from itself. No living and existence are possible apart from this one, and it is impossible to escape it. Now, however, although we say that it cannot be escaped, we ourselves have obviously done so [because we had distinguished ourselves from absolute reason]. Consequently, reason's genetic life, which we have described in positing seeing's absolute existence in case this latter is merely thought, is still not reason's primordial and absolute existence.[29]

"Reason itself must start talking directly."[30] How? In our own speech. We therefore need to look at the aforementioned identification more deeply. Our saying is not only ours, it is at the same time the speech of absolute reason itself. This is so because reason has an *I-character* and expresses itself in an I or self-seeing (in his earlier period Fichte would have called it self-consciousness): "We indeed are reason, because reason is simply the I, and cannot be anything else than I. . . . Thus 'we seem' [*erscheinen*] or 'reason seems' are completely synonymous."[31] Thus, we who philosophize correctly, or the *Wissenschaftslehre* itself in this insight and in this act of understanding, are in fact absolute reason itself; we (the WL) are the place where absolute reason posits and expresses itself, and the insight of absolute reason takes place and realizes itself in us; therefore it sees and points out that it is the positing one. The justification of philosophy runs through the *identification* of the *Wissenschaftslehre* and of our pure I with reason as the true expression of absolute reason: "We ourselves have continually objectified reason, and therefore posited its existence, as existence, in the 'form of outer existence.' Now we are reason. . . . This is a fact from which we cannot ever escape, and that cannot be explained or understood from any further genetic premise."[32] This is the fundamental facticity of absolute knowing. "True absoluteness is not found in what is objectified, nor in the objectifying [agent], but rather in the immediate event of objectifying,"[33] in the act, in the life of absolute knowing and not outside of it. We are the fact of the expression and the life of reason, the insight into this fact, and the knowledge that the fact is equal to genesis.[34] "The characteristic mark of the science of knowing consists purely in this synthesis."[35] Only this insight makes us the *Wissenschaftslehre*. "Therefore, this very insight, or the science of knowing, is reason's immediate expression and life,"[36] and in this way "reason itself lives and appears. In its existence, the insight appears to be possible only by means of freedom"[37] because, first, freedom is the character of the life of reason, and second, its insight is possible only through *our* freedom because of its I-character.

IV

"Here is where we stood: reason is the unconditional ground of its own existence and its own objectivity for itself, and its primordial life consists just in this."[38] But in the insight of the *Wissenschaftslehre*, in reflection, this life splits again into a double appearance: "Numerically reason occurs here twice, once in us and once outside of us,"[39] subjective and objective. We come to the Twenty-Eighth Lecture, the last one of the 1804 *Wissenschaftslehre*.

Absolute Reason makes itself absolutely or necessarily intuiting, and that is its being, a pure, transparent intellection (*Intelligieren*), the ground of all objectivizing intuition, without any partly unconditioned Non-I (unlike the I and reason in the Jena period) and without any gap (*hiatus*) between object and subject. It is an absolute immediate self-making (*Sich-Machen*) object-subject, not one by the other, both in the center, by the same primordial essence-effect (*Wesenseffekt*). This self-making by itself, through itself, and from itself is life, an absolute primal activity (*Urtätigkeit*) in itself, though our reconstruction (in the WL) is an imitation and image of it, but as it has already been said, the same absolute reason in both moments, as object and as subject. Reason is in fact seen in the image we have reconstructed in imitation of the original, immediately in ourselves. We and reason are at the center of the absolutely effective self-making. Reason has become an inner I in the *Wissenschaftslehre*, intellection of itself. However, this self-making splits in reflection and results in (1) a fixed (*stehendes*) object, (2) its objective life, (3) a fixed subject or the comprehending I, and (4) the imaging as imaging (*Bilden als Bilden*). Thus, reason splits the life of this self-making into being and making, both understood as original and as copied in the *Wissenschaftslehre*. This is the primordial disjunction.

Now I can either objectify or not objectify this absoluteness of reason. If I do not objectify it (if I do not distinguish between the subjective and the objective in a new act of reflection), everything is completed, the system is finished, and reason is closed, exhausted, described. But if I do objectify it, then I have and keep the act of absolute reason in its subjective imitation and in the imaging of an objectively finished I (the manifold of empirical I's, humans) as the ground and primal condition of this state, an I in which reason is factical, a consciousness and self-consciousness of an I as primal factum that underlies all other facticity. Let us make a necessary remark here, namely that objectification of reason appears in Fichte's text as an optional reflection. That is so, in my opinion, because this reflection is an act of freedom of the I, but I also believe that it must be understood as a necessary task for freedom in order to achieve the realization of absolute knowing itself. In this reflection, the five points of view adopted by human beings in relation to reality have to appear, and in order to complete the system they must be put into effect, which is in turn a new deduction from the requirement of philosophy, from the *Wissenschaftslehre*. *The Way towards the Blessed Life* explains that the split into five worldviews occurs together with the one in the infinite manifold of things in the world, "that neither of these two divisions can assume the place of the other, . . . but that they are inseparable, and are therefore to be found together wherever reflection, whose unchangeable forms they are, is to be found."[40] If these five worldviews did not happen, human comprehension and consequently the *Wissenschaftslehre in specie* would not be achieved, the knowing would never really see itself as such, and therefore the absolute Being would not properly be manifested. Without them the system would not be completed. The five worldviews belong to the system itself because they are moments of the realization of knowing as such and therefore of the manifestation of absolute Being. This is a subjective process of the objective-subjective knowing itself. Therefore, even though these five worldviews arise from actions of freedom, they are derived as necessary steps for knowing, and also for the manifestation of God. Freedom contains its own specific necessities. The last step in the genesis of knowing is the work of freedom.

The I in itself is the result of the self-making and of the self-knowledge of reason in appearance or in knowing; it is a primordial effect of reason (in the Jena period of Fichte, on the contrary, the pure I was the primal reality and not the reflex, and the empirical I was a synthesis of pure I and Non-I). In this I arises the insight of the *Wissenschaftslehre*, the reconstruction of the self-making of absolute reason. How so? In every emergence the resulting being appears as arising from its opposite according to the law of reflection. But the opposite of the absolute qualitative oneness of reason is manifoldness and changeability. Hence, the consciousness of the factical I must appear as plural and changeable. If it should arrive at *Wissenschaftslehre* (and that is our topic, the last in the WL04^2, now viewed from the other side, that is, in the temporality of the thinking individuals and their subjectivity), then such a consciousness or I, as a primordial reason-effect, must be made to appear.

The path of this changing consciousness, according to Fichte, runs over five stages, and although the act of absolute reason is first and fundamental, it appears in factical insight as a philosophical view (precisely the point of view of the philosophy of Fichte or at most Kant's point of view, not of the other philosophies) as the last and fifth degrees of points of view to emerge even from its opposite, the lower views. This is a similar reversal to the one that occurs in the *Wissenschaftslehre nova methodo* between intellectual intuition and repose (*Ruhe*): although activity, intellectual intuition, is the first action of the I (§ 1), it is seen later by the following reflection (by us) as emerging from the repose or capacity (*Vermögen*) of the I (§ 2). Aristotle also stated that what is first in itself is the last for us.

This changeable insight of the I gives us five conceptions of reality or five worldviews according to the synthetic five-foldness (*Fünffachheit*) peculiar to Fichte's method of thinking.[41] The objects are divided into an infinite variety, but the reflection on the object also necessarily splits into five "different modes of inwardly viewing, apprehending, and understanding the One abiding World,"[42] into five ways or modes to be in the world or, according to Hegel's wording, five forms of the spirit. For Fichte "the five modes of viewing the world, now spoken of, are the same as those progressions which, in the Third Lecture, I named the various possible stages, and grades of development, of the inward spiritual life."[43] The I rises from lower levels, which would be the second ascension to the absolute, a rising not this time for readers or listeners of the *Wissenschaftslehre*, as was the case in the first part of WL04^2, the doctrine of truth, but for the knowing itself in its self-knowledge or appearance.[44]

These worldviews are the following:

(1) In the enduring [*stehenden*] object, and indeed in what is absolutely transient: the principle of sensibility, belief in nature, materialism. (2) In the enduring subject: belief in personality . . . and equality of personality, the principle of legality. (3) Holding to the absolutely real forming of the subject . . . the standpoint of [higher] morality, as an activity that proceeds purely from the enduring I of consciousness. . . . (4) Holding to the absolute imaging and living of the absolute object . . . the standpoint of religion.[45]

The fifth worldview is that of philosophy, in fact of the *Wissenschaftslehre* itself, which should lead us to the correct synthesis of the four previous perspectives and to a different interpretation of them, of their objects and activities. This leads to Fichte's division of the special philosophical sciences: philosophy of nature, of law, of morality, of religion, and the *Wissenschaftslehre* itself. Indeed, it is according to each of these respective views, that is, according to their individual basic principles, that the objects and activities of others are interpreted, because reason is whole and unique and wants to interpret, from where it is, the totality at each level of its reflection. This results in twenty-five main moments "and primordial fundamental determinations of knowing."[46]

This theory about worldviews is expanded and supplemented in *The Way towards the Blessed Life*, with the idea of love as the fundamental affect of our existence (for Kant it is respect and admiration) and with a religious emphasis, according to the meaning of this book. The five worldviews are bound not only as different considerations or understandings of the real but also "as many standpoints of enjoying the world and oneself,"[47] bound with love to what each considers to be the most real and existent, that is, to the principle of each view or interpretation. In the last three levels, higher morality, religion, and philosophy, what is considered to be the most real is in essence the same for Fichte, but only seen in an increasingly clear and adequate way. "Love is the affect of being,"[48] of being as absolute Being; it is a consequence of the feeling of being grounded by the real and unconditional Being, which supports itself and holds itself together because it is sufficient for itself and needs nothing but itself. This love is a feeling or at least an expectation of satisfaction or even of blissful life if this Being were reached: "Wellbeing is union with the beloved; Pain is separation from the beloved."[49] Love is the felt self-assertion and the felt self-holding and self-maintaining of reality that allows us to be. But because the *Wissenschaftslehre* has shown us that there is only an absolute Being, and that everything else, our whole world, is an appearance and image of this Being, we should actually see true love as the bond of pure Being with its existence or ex-istence. This bond connects most intimately to different modes of being, the absolute Being, and its manifestation or image. Expressed in religious terms, it would be the love from God and for God. It is higher than all reflection, it is the source of reason,[50] the most powerful presence of absolute Being in its appearance. "Love is the source of all certainty and all truth and all reality,"[51] of all moral action, just as in the *Foundation* the feeling of limitation and longing was the fundamental consciousness of the primordial reality of the I and the non-I. Here, too, the feeling indicates an assertion of reality and a limitation, the limitation that we have no being of our own, but we are an image (contrary to what the selfish closed I believes) and related to absolute Being. "Love . . . is only there where is clear consciousness."[52] True love is really in the highest understanding, that is, in Christianity and in the *Wissenschaftslehre*. But every worldview will interpret it according to its perspective and will place it in different objects.

In spite of the affect, this fivefold split in the worldviews is carried out through the freedom of reflection, "and being comes, in relation to each individual [standpoint], not to be taken as necessary or as real, but only to be taken as possible,"[53] because they are mutually exclusive and are posited as equally possible. The real "posits through its existence therefore a freedom, that in its essence is completely independent of the real, and independence of its being-taken or of the way in which it is reflected; and now the same thing expressed even more sharply: Absolute being presents itself in this its existence [in its exteriority or appearance] as this absolute freedom and independence to take oneself."[54]

This is because actually all activity, including that of freedom and reflection, is one of existence or the appearance of absolute Being. But in order to be seen as freedom, this freedom must appear as the act of an independent and free I within time, of a human individual, because the form of knowing and reflection is self-knowing and therefore appears as an I. "That freedom and independence is also nothing more than the mere possibility of the standpoints of life: but this possibility is limited in number to the five indicated ways."[55] But when the I has risen to the highest point of view, "this consciousness [of freedom, of one's own being[56] and the drive to self-activity], which would now be deceptive, falls away, and from now on the reality [the appearance of absolute Being or the pure divine existence[57]] flows off quietly in the only remaining and ineradicable form of infinity"[58] with "a far more sacred love."[59]

In *The Way towards the Blessed Life* a point of view is added, so to speak, a point of view "zero," to explain through contrast[60] what it means and implies to maintain a worldview. Every worldview includes spiritual energy and strength, contracting in one point, in a fundamental principle that is believed to be the most real and loved as such. In the standpoint "zero" none of this exists, only distraction does. Nothing is loved or hated, and one is not interested in anything, not even in oneself. One is without inner spiritual life and without affects, only blind nature is at work there. That is a spiritual nonexistence, a being-dead and being-buried alive.[61]

A different spiritual attitude is also placed somewhat higher than this spiritual nullity, but lower than the first worldview. This does not take a fixed standpoint, but it instead is positioned sometimes in one or in the other depending on how the actual reality is considered, or simply in a combination of both. It is a confused and variable worldview that peers at the manifold. It is "cowardly and discouraged."[62]

The first, lowest, and most superficial view of the world takes the *sensible world*, the sensible fixed object, as the highest, the most truthful, and as existing from itself.[63] Sensible enjoyment is predominant, and this is based on the affect of sensible being and on the love for it. Self-love is a "drive for happiness in and through certain objects"[64] and for paradise.[65] Its *philosophy* is materialism. Its *religion*: God only exists to give food. Its *morality* consists of this: "To distribute one's pleasures wisely, so that one always has something more to enjoy, especially not to ruin things with this God who provides."[66] Its *legality* is "something analogous to reason and spirituality and that is also to enjoy these pleasures in the right order and with prudence."[67]

For the second view, what is truly real is "a law of order and equal right in a system of rational beings."[68] That is the standpoint of formal *legality*. "Man from the second worldview is himself the law . . . a living, feeling law, affected by himself . . . an affect of the law . . . an unconditional Ought, a categorical imperative; who, precisely through this categorical [character] of its form, absolutely rejects all love and inclination towards what is commanded"[69] and destroys them. Here freedom is understood as pure, empty, and formal. It specifies a cold and strict Ought, without positive self-respect for people, only with negative contempt if they do not follow the law. It is not possible to go beyond compliance with the commandment and "positively regard and honor oneself as something excellent."[70] All of this depends on the person and his free action: "You don't need anything but yourself; not even a God; you are yourself your God, your Savior and your Redeemer."[71] Its *philosophy*: "Kant, if one pursues his philosophical career no further than the *Critique of Practical Reason*"[72] and stoicism.[73] Its *religion*: God is the higher police here. Its *morality* coincides with the external legal relationships; it is "the usual moral doctrine, which only assumes that nobody does the other injustice."[74] Fichte's right and moral doctrine of Jena also has its place in this low morality. The *objective world* is only there for the sake of bourgeois industry; it is just the sphere of free action.

The third worldview is the standpoint of true and higher morality. With it begin the higher and true views. The highest, the first, and absolutely real aspect for it is a new law that creates supersensible life, a life that is an image, an imprint for the revelation of the absolute Being. "What is truly real and independent for it is what is sacred, good, and beautiful."[75] Its *philosophy*: Plato and Jacobi. Its *religion*: God exists "as principle, but not for his own sake; instead, so that he maintains the moral law. If they had no moral law, they would not need a God."[76] *Morality* is the subject's own work. Its *legality*: people only exist to be moral. The *objective world* is only the means and sphere of dutiful action,[77] the means for true life. It is "the sphere for the outer and inner, lower and higher freedom and morality . . . what it is and remains on all [three] higher points of view."[78]

The fourth view maintains the standpoint of *religion*, "the clear knowledge that the sacred, good and beautiful [thing] is by no means our product . . . but that is the appearance of the inner being of God in us."[79] "God alone is, and apart from him there is nothing."[80] Its *philosophy*: Fichte does not state anything in this respect, but we could probably think of the *Wissenschaftslehre* itself, since Kant, Plato, and Jacobi have already been placed in previous points of view. *Morality* is a divine work in man, it works in him as a determination and as an accomplishment. True *religion* is confirmed in the moral act that takes the form of higher morality.[81] Its *legality*: other people are the outflow of the one divine life. The *objective world* is also the outflow of this one divine life. No enjoyment of the world can grant him real joy, but he grasps his world as an activity, and only in him does he find all the enjoyment of himself.[82]

The fifth worldview is that of philosophy, of the *Wissenschaftslehre*, considered as the finished, perfect, and complete understanding of all reality and of the other four worldviews, which will lead us to the four special sciences of the *Wissenschaftslehre*, to Fichte's philosophy of nature, of law, of morality, and of religion. Its real existence *in specie* is therefore necessary to complete the system of knowledge and absolute knowing itself, which was what had to be deduced and justified.

Notes

1. "Absolute knowing has been presented objectively and in its content, and if that were the only issue, our work would be completed." 1804^2, 184; J. G. Fichte, *The Science of Knowing: J. G. Fichte's 1804 Lectures on the Wissenschaftslehre*, ed. Walter E. Wright (Albany: State University of New York Press, 2005), 184; *GA*, II/8, 383.

2. 1804^2, 130; *GA*, II/8, 264.

3. 1804^2, 184; *GA*, II/8, 383.
4. "The true ϕ must justify itself within itself and can justify. Let this be the sign of its truth and *in specie* its completion." *GA*, II/11, 302.; see also § 14; *GA*, I/10, 345. "Then the concept of philosophy is the most intrinsic and highest result of itself." Heidegger, *DGP*; *GA*, 24, 5.
5. 1804^2, 190; *GA*, II/8, 397.
6. 1804^2, 182; *GA*, II/8, 378.
7. *GA*, II/8, 344–46; GA, II/10, 185. GA, II/13, 52, 68. GA, II/15, 133.
8. *GA*, I/9, 88.
9. 1804^2, 118; *GA*, II/8, 235.
10. 1804^2, 116; *GA*, II/8, 231.
11. GA, I/9, 249.
12. GA, I/9, 103.
13. WL10, *GA*, II/11, 387.
14. WL12, *GA*, II/13, 60. "Only God is. Out of him only his appearance. The only truly real thing in appearance is freedom, in its absolute form, in consciousness; thus as a freedom from I. These and their products of freedom are truly real. A law is directed to this freedom, a realm of ends, the moral law. Therefore, this and its content are the only real objects." *Staatslehre*, *GA*, II/16, 63.
15. "Mysticism: Everything in God . . . a devout enthusiasm [*Schwärmen*]." WL12, *GA*, II/13, 54.
16. *GA*, II/13, 127. *GA*, II/8, 173, 265.
17. 1804^2, 185; *GA*, II/8, 385.
18. 1804^2, 187; *GA*, II/8, 391.
19. 1804^2, 190; *GA*, II/8, 397.
20. 1804^2, 191; *GA*, II/8, 399.
21. 1804^2, 191; *GA*, II/8, 401.
22. 1804^2, 191; *GA*, II/8, 399.
23. 1804^2, 192; *GA*, II/8, 401.
24. 1804^2, 192; *GA*, II/8, 401.
25. 1804^2, 192; *GA*, II/8, 401.
26. 1804^2, 193; *GA*, II/8, 403.
27. *GA*, II/13, 52, 54, 56–58, 61, 66–67, 100. *GA*, II/11, 361. Letter to Jacobi of May 3, 1810 (GA III/6, 328).
28. 1804^2, 191; GA, II/8, 399.
29. 1804^2, 192; *GA*, II/8, 401.
30. 1804^2, 193; *GA*, II/8, 403.
31. 1804^2, 192; *GA*, II/8, 401.
32. 1804^2, 193; *GA*, II/8, 405.
33. 1804^2, 193–94; *GA*, II/8, 405.
34. Factum refers to the fundamental facticity of absolute knowing. Genesis means that absolute knowing is the source of its own life.

35. 1804², 194; *GA*, II/8, 405.
36. 1804², 194; *GA*, II/8, 407.
37. 1804², 194; *GA*, II/8, 407.
38. 1804², 196; *GA*, II/8, 411.
39. 1804², 196; *GA*, II/8, 411.
40. *GA*, I/9, 104.
41. "This reflection on oneness immediately breaks down into five-foldness." 1804², 200; GA, II/8, 421.
42. *GA*, I/9, 104.
43. *GA*, I/9, 105.
44. The first four stages of reflection follow the four links of the primordial reasoning effect in appearance, an inner manifold discussed in the Twenty-Sixth Lecture (GA, II/8, 389, 391).
45. 1804², 199; *GA*, II/8, 417, 419.
46. 1804², 200; *GA*, II/8, 419. A very brief explanation of these five points of view was already included in 1804¹ (*GA*, II/7, 23–34) and in *GA*, II/11, 335–36. See, e.g., the essay by Helmut Girndt, "Die fünffache Sicht der Natur im Denken Fichtes," *Fichte-Studien* 1 (1990): 108–120. But isn't there a lack of aesthetic and historical worldviews? And wouldn't the skeptical mindset be a view of its own?
47. *GA*, I/9, 133.
48. *GA*, I/9, 133.
49. *GA*, I/9, 134.
50. *GA*, I/9, 166–68.
51. *GA*, I/9, 167.
52. *GA*, I/9, 81.
53. *GA*, I/9, 144; 145.
54. *GA*, I/9, 145.
55. *GA*, I/9, 146.
56. *GA*, I/9, 148.
57. *GA*, I/9, 149.
58. GA, I/9, 146.
59. *GA*, I/9, 146. "On the other hand, just as man gives up and loses his own freedom and independence through the highest freedom, he shares in the one true and divine being and all bliss contained in it." *GA*, I/9, 154.
60. "Everywhere the clarity gains through the contrast." AzL, *GA*, I/9, 130.
61. *GA*, I/9, 131–33.
62. *GA*, I/9, 109.
63. *GA*, I/9, 106.
64. *GA*, I/9, 147.
65. *GA*, I/9, 147, 151–52.
66. 1804², 200; *GA*, II/8, 419.
67. 1804², 200; *GA*, II/8, 419.

68. *GA*, I/9, 107.
69. *GA*, I/9, 136.
70. *GA*, I/9, 137.
71. *GA*, I/9, 138.
72. *GA*, I/9, 108.
73. *GA*, I/9, 138–40, 148.
74. *GA*, I/9, 107.
75. *GA*, I/9, 109.
76. 1804^2, 200; *GA*, II/8, 419.
77. 1804^2, 200; *GA*, II/8: 419.
78. *GA*, I/9, 109–110.
79. *GA*, I/9, 110.
80. *GA*, I/9, 110.
81. *GA*, I/9, 113.
82. *GA*, I/9, 114.

Chapter 15

Blockchain as Fichtean Problem

ADAM HANKINS

In the First Lecture of the *1804 Wissenschaftslehre*, Fichte establishes that the task of philosophy is leading all multiplicity to unity.[1] From the beginning, Fichte castigates multiplicity as confused, dead, and deadly; whatever the truth is, it cannot be the bickering mass hurling their various opinions back and forth. So the science of knowing grants priority to unity: truth is the way it has to be, and it can only be one way, and not another. From there, Fichte proceeds to a knowing that is absolute, and a system through which this knowing can be actual, but his original judgment of multiplicity is hasty. Even on Fichte's own evaluation, the multiple is constantly changing, so there is no reason to discount the chance that, through the passing of history, multiplicity could not complexify to the point that it could sustain permanence in the same way that an ideal science does. The conceit of this chapter is that this is the condition in which we actually find ourselves: the potential of the multiple to preserve a permanent truth has finally emerged through the growth of digital technology, and so we have to reconsider how the science of knowing stands with regard to the multiple.

Based on how Fichte arranges his exposition of the science of knowing in the series of lectures from 1804, this reconsideration is best approached through the issue of certainty. Fichte's main indictment of multiplicity, what disqualifies it as a vessel for truth, is that it creates variability: the facts can be "this way or equally well the other."[2] Permitting ambiguity to remain in truth ultimately leads to incompatible worlds and the struggle between competing philosophical systems. Fichte asserts that the essential prerequisite of truth is invariability and that only unity can maintain this invariability; invariability in oneness is how Fichte initially defines certainty.[3] Reviewing his concept of certainty will clarify exactly what Fichte maintains unity, as elaborated through the science of knowing, can alone achieve, and whether or not multiplicity has met that standard in its own way.

I will spend the first part of this chapter discussing blockchain, a digital technology used to record transactions. Blockchain can produce unquestionable ledgers of any kind of exchange or transfer, made impervious to fraud by using encryptions that are so complex that no human could possibly crack them. It eliminates the need for trust because its outcomes are totally certain. I will then follow the development of certainty in the *1804 Wissenschaftslehre*, especially in the two lectures where the concept is most explicitly addressed, the Twenty-Third and Twenty-Sixth, and also the concurrent development of Fichte's concept of projection in its three types. Projection is a key component of how Fichte explains the nature of certainty, and variations in the presence or quality of the gap are relevant for knowing, successfully mitigating the illusions embraced by consciousness. After that, I will argue that blockchain can essentially serve the same purpose as the *Wissenschaftslehre* with regard to securing ordinary certainty. Although the science of knowing devises a number of concepts proprietary to its own operations, the initial form of certainty defined by Fichte is not one of them, and the idealist grounds supplied for its foundation can be replaced by digital ones. Fichte's ideas are nevertheless valuable for thinking about what is occurring inside blockchain and inside other technologies that rely on computations that human beings are unable to perform or predict. I will conclude with a brief theological reflection about the wider relevance of the problem posed by blockchain to the *Wissenschaftslehre*, as a problem also for how faith is modeled today.

The most basic definition of a blockchain is a "distributed ledger." A record of a transaction plus its cryptographic encoding is a block; series of these transactions and their encodings form a chain. That is what makes up the ledger. Anyone attempting to add to the chain needs to repeat the cryptographic processes to ensure that all of the previous recorded transactions really occurred, and this process is checked against numerous copies of the ledger that are held by different participants in a network. Changes to the ledger only occur when supported by the majority of the holders of the ledger. This is why it is described as "distributed."

I

If people have heard of blockchain, they most likely know it as the technology that makes Bitcoin possible. Bitcoin was introduced in 2009 by a person or persons calling themselves Satoshi Nakamoto, who published a white paper describing how a peer-to-peer electronic currency would function without the intervention of a third party.[4] For most current electronic transactions, verification has to be performed by a bank or corporation. When I pay you, the debit from my account and credit to yours is recorded and reconciled by our banks or credit card companies or electronic wallet providers so that the currency that I spend paying you is not used again to pay someone else. Verification requires trust to exist between each of these third parties, and because of that, Nakamoto notes that no transaction is nonreversible; the possibility of errors in reconciliation, unintentional or otherwise, requires that the history of transactions be capable of correction.

Bitcoin replaces trust with cryptography. One does not have to rely on the reputation of the institutions maintaining the ledger to believe their history of the transactions that have or have not occurred. Nakamoto writes: "The only way to confirm the absence of a transaction is to be aware of all transactions."[5] Bitcoin provides this: every coin has a complete history of every time it has been spent. This history has two defenses that prevent attempts to tamper with it: every transaction is encrypted when it is added to the ledger, and the ledger is held by multiple individuals. Whenever a transaction occurs using Bitcoin (or any cryptocurrency) those transactions are verified by other holders of the ledger, who can cryptographically validate that someone has not already spent the same bit of cryptocurrency somewhere else; this transaction is then added to the ledger and encrypted. The people who devote their computational power to verifying and recording Bitcoin transactions are compensated by receiving Bitcoin—they "mine Bitcoin" by validating Bitcoin exchanges. Bitcoin is secure because, first, the cryptographic process used creates vastly different encryptions as a result of even the smallest alteration, so trying to work backward from the encryption to the encrypted is impossible for all practical purposes. But also, second, there are potentially thousands of other people who are checking transactions against their own copies of the ledger; a majority of those working on a transaction must agree that a transaction is legitimate so that someone trying to submit a fraudulent alteration would simply be overruled.[6]

None of the technology involved in this process was new in 2009. What Bitcoin did was demonstrate that it could actually work: you could have a collection of agents cooperate in producing an indisputably trustworthy record despite the fact that no trust existed between any of them.[7] Since then, blockchain has been researched by open-source groups, like Ethereum and the Linux Foundation's Hyperledger, alongside companies like IBM and Microsoft. These have extended the application of blockchain beyond financial transactions or cryptocurrencies; blockchains can be used to create an incontestable record of any kind of transaction or exchange. It is even possible, using what are called "smart contracts" as a part of a blockchain, to automate entire bureaucracies that currently exist solely to review and reconcile organizational decisions. Human approval becomes unnecessary because a blockchain produces inarguably accurate outcomes, so any job that primarily evaluates requests or executes actions according to an established set of rules can be performed instantly by the smart contract, creating what is called a "decentralized automatic organization." One—admittedly infamous—example of a decentralized automatic organization was an automated investment firm built with Ethereum's blockchain and investing its cryptocurrency, the ether. Within a few months this firm was bankrupted by a malicious user, but this attempt was a failure "only from the viewpoint of its investors."[8] The code functioned as intended, and—aside from the tragi-comic loophole in the smart contract that allowed someone to request over $50 million in payment—the program recorded investments, disbursed funds, and tabulated shareholder votes without any managers or directors. With a better designed smart contract, the firm could have perpetuated itself indefinitely—and in any case, it managed to produce an unimpeachable record of its own demise.

As blockchain research has expanded outside of the financial sector, initiatives have started either proposing or actually applying blockchain to a broad number of fields. Blockchain can be used to improve scientific research: implemented in a research project management system, blockchain can help eliminate tampering, redundancy, plagiarism, and misallocation of funds in scientific research. One could design a system where management occurred automatically within the chain, and the various scientific teams that contributed to validation of the blocks would receive funds in exchange for ensuring the accuracy of their contributions.[9] Blockchain can be used to guarantee the authenticity and provenance of works of art by eliminating forgeries;[10] in 2018, a blockchain startup partnered with Christie's, and a blockchain-based auction house for digital art was launched with plans to expand into physical works.[11] Kodak attempted to create a blockchain-based digital rights management platform that, combined with crawler bots, would track images across the internet and establish their connection to the copyright holder so that artists and photographers could be compensated for the use of their work.[12] A number of groups are currently attempting to introduce e-voting systems that use blockchain to record and tally votes, and several trials have been run, from smaller-scale experiments like Massachusetts town hall meetings to support for the general elections in Sierra Leone. More than simply enabling people to vote from their phone without getting out of bed, e-voting advocates claim that blockchain can improve the accuracy of voting totals, enhance the legitimacy of elections, prevent voter suppression, and even reduce the likelihood of violence.[13]

Science, art, and the State are the three Ideas that Fichte lists in the exposition of Higher Morality from his 1806 text *The Way toward the Blessed Life*.[14] The role of philosophy in that text is thwarting the perverse forces of death that would impede us pursuing the calling of God to action in the world: while God guides their genius, the scientist, poet, and politician are freed to transform reality because philosophy defends them against skeptical doubts about their work. But researchers are demonstrating that blockchain can secure the actuality of our Ideas for us as well; if blockchain can serve our vocation as well as the *Wissenschaftslehre*, then it is not evident why the *Wissenschaftslehre* needs to be expounded. What blockchain provides, essentially, is certainty: if the ledger says it, it is undoubtably true. If we can thoroughly examine Fichte's account of certainty, we will have a basis for comparing it with the certainty offered by the blockchain and mark out precisely how we benefit from undertaking the *Wissenschaftslehre*.

II

In the 1804 lectures, certainty serves as the basic link between truth and appearance in the phenomenological division of the system, which begins with the Sixteenth Lecture. The first division, the doctrine of truth, establishes that there is a living oneness of being beyond all disjunction; the second division, the doctrine of appearance, is supposed to sanction ordinary knowledge by demonstrating its connection to that one being. Formulating this arrangement in terms of the history of philosophy, Fichte claims that it was Kant who first saw that being was not "the sum of all possible realities": rather, being, singular and absolute, closed within itself, is the "support" for all other realities.[15] Given, empirical reality—which Fichte calls "absolute multiplicity"[16]—is grounded in the unity of the absolute. Kant, however, simply declared that being must be the condition for possible realities; the task of phenomenology is showing how true appearances can emerge from that singular being. Phenomenology, for Fichte, investigates what in the absolute makes it capable of having an intelligible connection with appearance at all, and certainty is ultimately integral to guaranteeing the validity appropriate to appearance.[17]

The basis for certainty in the *1804 Wissenschaftslehre* is that knowing projects itself, and is the principle for this projecting. Projection can occur *per hiatum*, or "across a gap," and this gap can be either rational or irrational. There is also projection *per transubstantiationem*, or description, which occurs without a gap. Fichte introduces projection *per hiatum*, specifically across an irrational gap, in the last lectures of the first division. Projection through a gap originates in Fichte's review in the Fourteenth Lecture of why Reinhold's idealism fails: consciousness tries to explain its claims that thought is the principle of being and finds itself reduced to asserting that it simply is that way.[18] A similar failure occurs with realism: the gambit to make the in-itself the final unity fails not just because accounting for it necessarily involves a duality—an in-itself by which it is a unity, and a not-in-itself by which it can be thought—but because these explanations never explain how they formed a unity in the first place. The only explanation is that the in-itself just is the unity of this duality, which consciousness can only posit as an immediate fact.[19] Immediacy is an important constituent of the gap because immediate objects do not have explanations; assigning them a genesis or principle would mediate them through our conceptualization and thereby eliminate the gap.[20] In the Fifteenth Lecture, Fichte argues that the *Wissenschaftslehre* only accepts truths that have been genetically justified, and on that basis excludes all contributions from immediate consciousness the "essence" of which is "non-genesis."[21] The gap is a break in the ability of thought to explain why this or that actuality is, or, in more specifically Fichtean language, to provide something with a genesis, principle, or ground, "an absolute inconceivability or inexplicability."[22] Objects that enter our awareness as just there, realities that allegedly inhere in some substance impenetrable to our insight, are said to be projected through a gap. These objects have "the form of outer existence," that is, their mode of appearing is as exterior fact. Fichte designates this gap as a basic illusion in consciousness—consciousness always encounters its objects as though encompassed by a cognitive gap for which it cannot account. He condemns it as "death at the root" and insists that we treat it as a senseless, if incorrigible, flaw in how consciousness encounters objects. If the gap were real, if there were inexplicable entities for which reason could provide no ground, then there could never be a single system of thought, and the project of philosophy to lead all multiplicity back to unity would be doomed. As the *WL*'s exposition unfolds, we discover that the failure of philosophy to express truth ultimately compromises access to what Fichte understands as eternal life. So his militancy regarding the illusory nature of the gap is not dramatic flair: accepting the multiplicity of truth bars us from loving God.

Relevant here is Fichte's attack on the doctrine of creation in *The Way toward the Blessed Life*.[23] Interpreting the prologue to the Gospel of John, Fichte denounces the inability of Judaism or Heathenism to give up the reality of the finite; finitude is instead provided a root of existence in a divine act of arbitrary power. This arbitrary act annuls and dethrones the true, Johannine concept of God, where God and Logos, that is, Being and Reason (and implicitly, the world) are always eternally together and one, so no discrete *fiat lux* is required. The connection between God and the world through creation, although it still makes the world dependent on God, nevertheless inserts a break between them where rational reflection cannot enter, and, Fichte declares, ultimately usurps any true conception of God. A decree to create substantial finite beings would, in fact, depict God establishing his own rivals and leaving creatures with no chance at true unity with him, which strikes Fichte as more like an "expulsion" from God than creation.[24]

Fichte's comments on creation in the Nineteenth Lecture, though without any explicitly religious associations, seem related to his denunciation of any *fiat lux*: he there rejects a "pale and factical" doctrine of creation that allows for beings to just be.[25] To a fictional interlocutor, who asks why something requires a principle—what if I say "it *is*, and that's all"?—Fichte responds that nothing exists without also being thought: there would be existence that just is, and your consciousness, confronted by the deadly gap of inexplicability. "Just being" is an illusion made possible by a thinking that fails to recognize that a creature must express its originator, through and from which it is. Creation does not produce "bare, dead existence." Rather, existents are never understood in abstraction from their principle, a relation abridged by Fichte as a "through," "because-of," or especially "from," for which he then provides a scientific justification that undermines but does not banish the illusion. Science cannot integrate into a unified system of reason beings that just are, that confront consciousness from across a gap its reflection cannot span, that seem to burst spontaneously from nothing. Creation ex nihilo, then, is an irrational gap. But just as Fichte presents

Johannine non-creation in the Logos, Fichte presents forms of projection that avoid the pitfalls of consciousness.

Projection begins to take on a major role at the end of the first division of the *Wissenschaftslehre* because there cannot be anything other than an absolute being-or-I containing all reality; projection becomes decisive for the second division because if something other does seem to arise through the intervention of the objectifying consciousness, we can be certain that this something other is the projection or "empty repetition" of the absolute.[26] Although distinctions may appear in the singular and self-enclosed being or I, these distinctions can never divide the absolutely one so that something remains truly exterior. At most, they will be provisional aspects of the one, which the science of knowing will not permit to stand as independent actualities; independence from the absolute is always an illusion. Fichte presents the addition of a phenomenology as a change in tactics from previous orderings of the *Wissenschaftslehre*, which have systemically hunted down the illusion of consciousness while the illusion fled into the next movement of the antithesis. The strategy now will be to tolerate this chronic illusion, because we know that when consciousness encounters an unaccountable independence of existence, this seeming separation can be overcome.

Fichte implements this strategy in the Sixteenth Lecture: consciousness claims that there is an objectified repetition of being. That is true, Fichte concedes, but this ideal repetition is not an autonomous substance, rather being itself must essentially be connected to its objectified repetition as its own inner construction—being "should" be connected with its repetition. The "should" in Fichte abbreviates conjectural formulas produced by thought of the "If thus-and-such should be/occur, then . . ." type. These kinds of statements, premised on nothing but their own contention, share the self-making and self-sustaining properties of the I that makes them; these statements can build their own conceptual world using only the possibilities of thought.[27] But this liberty is also a severe limit on the efficacy of these statements within science: while the "should" connection makes and sustains itself by virtue of its own hazarding, it remains the purely hypothetical product of thinking. If there were some ground for making the statement, it would be a categorical "must."[28]

This limit in the "should," in fact, plays a major role for its initial analysis in the phenomenological division of the lectures. When Fichte connects being and its repetition through the "should," he states that this is a projection through an irrational gap. Operating purely within the possibilities of thought, the "should" does not provide an actual cause for being's construction, only a model about the conditions under which such a construction should occur. "If this should be, then this will . . ." does not amount to an explanation. Indeed, the essence of a "should" is that it makes and sustains itself; the "should" is not accountable for explaining the reality of its terms, and Fichte understands this to be basically saying that it just would be—so that being's repetition remains "factical" and "external."[29]

III

The major shifts in the phenomenological division of the lectures follow the initial variations on this "should," then move to a discussion of the "from," and then return to the "should" from a new, transcendental vantage.[30] During Fichte's attempts to connect transcendental and ordinary knowledge, knowing's self-genesis is revealed not to be absolute: self-genesis finds a principle in a higher knowing and, since it now has a principle, must let its absoluteness be negated so that as negated self-genesis it becomes "enduring being." At the same time this higher knowing is manifested, paradoxically, through a knowing qua non-genesis, which affirms its own "pure oneness from all appearance." The persisting knowing capitulates to this non-genetic knowing as its superior principle and is aware of it precisely as the refusal of all genesis, which is to say, as through a gap. Fichte makes the significance of this interaction obvious: understanding, or persisting knowing, here recognizes reason, or the non-genetic one, as its unconditional principle, and reason will not explain its independence. From the standpoint that knowing occupies in the Twenty-First Lecture, this discontinuity is inevitable. But the discontinuity is not irrational because the gap opens within the ambit of the singular, self-constructing absolute as an event within knowing, rather than simply arriving as a given outer being.[31] The discontinuity in fact occurs as a transcendental disjunction, rather than one formed from terms discovered in appearance, and, as Fichte will emphasize, in a "should": "Should understanding have a principle, then reason. . . ."[32] This operation—a projection within knowing resulting in terms connected a priori—is one precondition for Fichte introducing certainty in the Twenty-Third Lecture. The other will be identifying exactly what the higher knowing that joins reason and understanding is, namely, the We, which thus far in the science has been able to perceive that the supposed gaps are only illusory.

What Fichte is basically doing in the Twenty-Third Lecture is providing a genesis for the claim that the We is the same as knowing. The We is us, as it were: "scientists of knowing," or those of us engaged in recreating the *Wissenschaftslehre* through our own cognitive acts. This assembly of subjects engaged in transcendental reflection mostly just perform the necessary acts of thinking and observe their consequences, at times observing misrecognitions or illusions that the I whose genesis We are reconstructing cannot itself perceive. But at certain stages of the system, the reality that some individuals are actually thinking these acts of thought is made explicit within the system itself; our "factical selves" take on roles in the science of knowing. We serve this role sometimes dubiously, since we can assert arbitrary propositions that, while they may provide the hint to eventually locating their rational grounds, do not bear the mark of necessity that would make them scientific. But Fichte will also exploit the oneness of knowing ourselves to prove that knowing is capable of some position or configuration because we, or We, actually have that configuration, and so knowing must have it as well—since we are the same as knowing.

Yet the claim "We are knowing" remains factical up until the Twenty-Second Lecture. In the Twenty-First, Fichte had demonstrated that We were the immediate basis of the "should" that transcendentally connected reason and understanding.[33] While the "should" had been discussed in previous lectures, Fichte argues that its return in the Twenty-First signals an advance: whereas previously the terms of the "should" had to be assumed as given facts, the terms have now been apprehended genetically, that is, the conditioning of knowing's being, or understanding, by knowing as non-genesis, or reason.[34] But Fichte had remarked that in both of these terms, self-genesis was genuinely occurring and was their actual source. Indeed, the essences of these faculties could not be really grasped without the interplay that transpires in this disjunction. This self-genesis was in fact We ourselves, joining in our insight the absolute oneness and negated persistent knowing that projects it as untouchable and inviolable. What is at stake in this still-provisional "should" is the relation between the regions of knowing of which these faculties are the principles, the absolute knowing of reason and the ordinary knowing of the understanding; should ordinary knowing relinquish its self-sufficiency, then absolute knowing will become somehow possible. But as a "should," even transcendentally formulated, it remains merely a provisionally true proposal. For the proposal to become scientific, the hypothetical character of the "should" has to be negated. The negative of the hypothetical is the categorical: "It should be this way" becomes "It must." In order to accomplish this transition, Fichte has to put aside the terms of this hypothetical and their absolute relation and ask what remains of the insight, divested of its content.

In this abstracted view of the insight, we uncover pure certainty. Pure certainty is described as the unchanging permanence of a quality, "that it is what it is."[35] Fichte notes that quality, as the negation of changeability, necessarily introduces precisely what it negates, changeability or quantifiability, which together compose the elements of appearance.[36] He also remarks that in this reflection on certainty we find, "for the first time," something about living being or I through which it has an intelligible connection with appearance.[37] Pure certainty is revealed at the core of the "should" joining transcendental and ordinary knowledge and evidences, although emptily and indifferently, the contours of appearance. As presented so far by Fichte, living and self-enclosed being never emerges from itself and permits nothing to exist beyond itself—but nevertheless, there is its objective repetition, its appearance. Pure certainty is the first trace of something within the total self-enclosure of being that suggests that the self-construction of this self-enclosure, as it proceeds within Our scientific reflection, is intrinsically oriented toward making itself amenable to our thinking it.

Permanence of quality, however, is not a sufficient description of what certainty is but rather designates an "externalized and objectivized" certainty; Fichte accordingly sets out looking for absolute certainty. That the quality, or the "what," is one, and that it remains one, can only be grounded on certainty; certainty is therefore its own ground, and its self-grounding is the condition for the oneness of quality. Certainty considered in its self-grounding unity, which dispenses with issues of quality, is absolute certainty. To be self-grounding is to provide oneself as a principle for oneself, and Fichte states that projection is the provision of a principle. Fichte's explanation in the Twenty-Third Lecture involves two types of projection, which we mentioned above but which are implicated with each other here. One is life's own inner projection, projection as transubstantiation. Projecting oneself and intuiting oneself in this projection—this process, for Fichte, is the vivacity of the primordial light, what makes it living rather than inert objectivity. Simultaneously, this immanent projection is everything that the living light is: absolute, enclosed, and unconditioned. The projection as transubstantiation allows life to behold itself in its totality, but it also repeats the dynamic that occurred in the Twenty-First Lecture between reason and understanding. The "higher" transubstantiation is rightly "unintuitable," and yet it results in a persistent knowing and a projection across a rational gap of life's through-itself qua self-enclosed absolute, bound together in life's projecting-and-intuiting process, or "principle-providing." Fichte notes that this is not the same as providing-itself-a-principle; due to the real self-enclosure, life's "principlizing" could only take its own absoluteness as an object.

In the miracle of transubstantiation, ordinary bread and wine have that through which they subsist transformed into the substance of Christ: the bread and wine are Christ, they are no longer bread and wine at all. Fichte seems to prefer an analogy with the Catholic doctrine to the Protestant since, in Lutheran consubstantiation, the bread and wine remain bread and wine—they retain what individuates them alongside the new divine presence. The *Wissenschaftslehre*, in Fichte's elaboration, cannot abide two realities side by side; just as the bread and wine are wholly converted into Christ, so appearance must be utterly nothing apart from being, which it images. Or, again, there can be no creation by arbitrary decree, and trying to hold out a finite being as something for itself leads to the death of God.[38] The objective reality of the projected image manifests itself as an independent world: but after the miracle of transubstantiation, we perceive that this world is the effect of another event transpiring in a more profound reality, being's intuition of itself.

In the Twenty-Fourth and Twenty-Fifth Lectures, the projecting occurring in absolute certainty is integrated into the representation of absolute knowing, preparing for the task of the final lectures, proving the reciprocal determination of transcendental and ordinary knowledge—in other words, the demonstration that ordinary knowing exists so that absolute knowing can come to be. In the Twenty-Fourth Lecture, projection is revealed to operate under a law through which this projection is marked as projection, yet because this law is manifest for consciousness, it may merely be contrived and imposed by consciousness, legislated by the arbitrary liberty of the We. And so in the Twenty-Fifth Lecture, this suspicion is eliminated by making clear that the projected image, specifically as an image, indicates its construction through a law. Even though it remains only an image, then, and not a self-sustaining reality, it represents the truth of its law. Knowing, having found itself in this image, becomes absolute; both we and Fichte attain absolute knowing.[39] We are absolute knowing, the knowing that is life—the same knowing, Fichte notes, that Christ preaches as eternal life: that "they know you and whom you have sent" (John 17:3). The *Wissenschaftslehre*, however, is not completed merely by achieving eternal life. The final task is demonstrating that the *Wissenschaftslehre* is not only absolute knowledge but also a particular knowledge, a knowledge that can be explained through an actually existing science.[40]

The Twenty-Sixth Lecture begins by asking by what right we claim to have absolute knowing as specifically ours, and Fichte answers: we have absolute knowing because we are certain of it.[41] Due to the character of absolute knowing, we can no longer rely on the previously developed concept of pure certainty. Pure certainty meant the permanence of a quality. But absolute knowing surpasses qualities, so pure certainty gives us no guidance for the crossing from eternity to *Wissenschaftslehre*.[42] Fichte intends to navigate this impasse by returning to the description of absolute certainty, certainty as self-enclosure, but first has to justify employing absolute certainty at this level by explaining what it means to perform a description.

Fichte lays out the conditions of a description by calling it a seeing. A description is a projection, but a "projection that recognizes itself as a projection."[43] That is, the projection is immanent, rather than casting before consciousness something that ostensibly transcends its powers of comprehension, in contrast to other times when knowing was confronted with a gap while only Fichte and We scientists could detect the illusion. But a projection aware that it is a projection is an intuition, or a seeing. Indeed, it is the seeing through which We have been "We" this whole time, the *Einsehen* that yields all of our insights. Fichte constructs the dialectic like this: in order to see, seeing must negate itself, that is, it has to see what it looks at, not itself. At the same time, even in its negation, seeing remains—otherwise, no seeing would occur. By virtue of this self-negation, seeing is the expression of the seen, external to the expressed, persisting even in its negative externality, and displacing attention from its expressing to the expressed. But with an inward seeing occurring within absolute knowing, what it sees is this negation, something refusing any outside—self-enclosure or being, as anticipated by the lectures on realism's in-itself. Fichte explicitly refers us back to the Fifteenth Lecture, designating this analysis of seeing as the genesis of the ultimate insight of the first division. Or compare this with Fichte's aside in the Twenty-Seventh Lecture, that his discussion of seeing rectifies traditional flaws in the ontological argument.[44] The negation of unconditioned seeing produces a concept of absolute certainty convertible with the idea of the fullest and most perfect being, because this seeing, interchangeable with intuition, is a projection—intuition projects itself in its negation, becomes expression of its own projected essence.[45]

Having completed the analysis of seeing and thereby the basis for description, Fichte claims that he has actually already performed the description of absolute certainty, since he has outlined the structure of self-enclosure. Two moments transpire in seeing, negation and insistence, matched by two moments occurring within being: the advent of enclosure when seeing withdraws in order to intuit, which results in "dead being," a lifeless in-itself, existing without any reciprocity, projected through a rational gap; and seeing as external expression, announcing an impulse within being to emergence for another, which Fichte designates as its drive.[46] These two moments are united in the living of being: the drive prompts emergence so that being approaches appearance, and enclosure cancels it so that being remains in itself. This living retrieves the contours of ordinary knowing that had been lost in the achievement of absolute knowing: the recurring emergence of the drive generates change, which is the condition for quantity, while enclosure pulls being back into its singularity, the oneness necessary for quality.[47]

This process accomplishes projection as transubstantiation within the *Wissenschaftslehre*. The self-making of certainty in its intuition sustains itself as the substance of living being and the species of that life's expression. The priesthood by which this miracle is performed is We ourselves. Fichte remarks that the life that this being enjoys occurs only within seeing—and how could it not, if this being is nothing other than the essence of seeing negating itself—and Fichte further states that this seeing is how he and his audience have hitherto been able to occupy the place of that "We" who have been integral to the progress of the *Wissenschaftslehre*. The goal of the Twenty-Sixth Lecture was confirming Our possession of absolute knowing. Fichte's conclusion is that the seeing that We perform, operating at the level of absolute knowing, by its own essence arrives at the concept of absolute certainty. Previously, when We were involved directly in spurring the *Wissenschaftslehre* forward, the freedom associated with our acts required that any of the insights derived from our intercessions be revisited and made compulsory. In the Twenty-Sixth Lecture, we receive assurance that through actual *Wissenschaftslehre*—that is, the science of knowing as thought and composed by rational individuals—We can justify our claim to be one with absolute certainty, and the certain qualities that We encounter in reality are in fact our own self-grounding projected into objective being. We can formulate this claim, from this standpoint, without any gap: there is no cognitive break between the scientific system of Our construction and objective certainty that it finds in ordinary knowing. Any pretension to independent substantiality on the part of external existence is unquestionably known to be illusory, and any hiatus representing itself as opaque to cognition is known to Us as the negligible consequence of consciousness, mitigated by Our transcendental insight.

IV

Certainty becomes a major theme in the *1804 Wissenschaftslehre* after the being of knowing is established. Asking how to move beyond the hypothetical "should" relation that obtains between the knowing of being and self-genesis, Fichte reflects on the insight into their relation itself and abstracts from the terms; what remains is certainty. Initially, Fichte defines certainty in the way we normally experience it, as persistence of given qualities, and presents an abstracted pure certainty as a general explanation of our experience. But he quickly assimilates pure certainty to the transcendental self-grounding structure of being he had uncovered in the first part of the lectures. From there, he re-deduces the terms of the "should" categorically, significantly by outlining a projection that occurs both with and without a gap. Later returning to the problem of describing certainty, Fichte elects to analyze the seeing through which We have been investigating the construction of being. This analysis turns out to be exactly the description of absolute certainty's self-grounding enclosure that was required. Now We know that our insights are identical with the manifestation of absolute being and that Our transcendental science really does think the one truth. Having laid out this complex, we can say precisely what we contend blockchain can emulate and what it makes superfluous.

The pure certainty that Fichte uncovers is the same kind of certainty offered by blockchain. Certainty in the Twenty-Third Lecture does not designate a mental event exclusive to the *Wissenschaftslehre*. Fichte does not present certainty there as an insight that grows systematically or organically from insights restricted to fellow scientists: his detection of certainty involves not only "complete abstraction from everything" but specific dispensing with the terms received from the Twenty-First and Twenty-Second Lectures.[48] Fichte re-derives those terms from the structure of absolute certainty by the end of the lecture but arrives at absolute certainty through inquiry into the ground of pure certainty's oneness—he has already moved into transcendental reflection. Fichte arrives at pure certainty, by contrast, through abstraction, careful attention, and thinking about quality, which seem more like reflecting on the common experience of certainty that anyone has in everyday life and abstracting from the various convictions or attributes about which we are certain, which allows him to delineate what precisely to be certain is.

While pure certainty is itself abstracted from particular qualities, it is not thereby removed from ordinary knowing. While Fichte notes that pure certainty is not certainty about something, the "absolute indifference" of that certainty with regard to "what" it is certain about does not mean that it is indifferent to having any "what" at all.[49] This is precisely why the passage to absolute certainty is necessary: pure certainty is indifferent to its quality, but it does require a quality and only evidences itself with regard to qualities. Fichte refers to pure certainty as "externalized and objectivized": objectivized because it is intrinsically linked with the qualitative dimension of the apparent world of objects; externalized because it ostensibly happens outside of the self-enclosure of being. Pure certainty is a concept developed for a discussion at the formal level about the certainty we have within everyday knowing. Any knowing about objects within appearance will involve certainty regarding the qualities they exhibit; conceptualizing pure certainty clarifies what that certainty entails, that the qualities of the object are unchanging.

Blockchain does not create absolute certainty in the sense that phrase is used by Fichte. But the concept of absolute certainty is developed by Fichte partially in order to secure the legitimacy of pure certainty after the elimination of qualities in absolute knowing renders permanency in appearance irrelevant. Certainty qua enclosure, schematized in the Twenty-Sixth Lecture's description of seeing, becomes the ground of pure certainty, established so that quality and quantity can be introduced in the totally enclosed unity of absolute knowing. Only the *Wissenschaftslehre* can disclose absolute certainty as the ground of oneness of quality in objectivized knowing. But is also important only to the *Wissenschaftslehre* that ordinary certainty be compatible with absolute knowing, and it could only be incompatible because Fichte conceives self-enclosed being as a unity to which the immense variety of quality in appearance must be lead back.[50]

If I know some quality to be permanent, that is to say, if I experience a certainty that could, by abstraction, result in pure certainty, absolute certainty will not make that quality somehow more permanent. Absolute certainty is not additional certainty over and beyond pure certainty, nor, if I feel certain, could I also feel absolute certainty as a supplemental sensation. Absolute certainty is a philosophical model for how my ordinary certainty functions. If, feeling certain about the truth of the *Wissenschaftslehre*, I were to be cast about on the throng of philosophical opinions that Fichte mentions in the First Lecture, absolute certainty qua philosophical model may help me put down that bristling mass of guesswork and relieve my consciousness of certainty from being besieged. But I will not feel absolute certainty by wielding that model; I cannot ever experience absolute certainty, unless one associates that with the eternal joy in knowing that Fichte seems to style after the intellectual love of God in Spinoza.[51] But still, satisfaction is not certainty.

Blockchain provides a ground for pure certainty, not by developing a concept through which to thwart the throng but by creating conditions through which more opinions lead to greater certainty: the more distributed the ledger, the less possibility of tampering or fraud. Multiplicity produces invariability. Blockchain performs the same service for pure certainty as absolute certainty does; it provides an exhaustive, unequivocal basis for making claims about the world. Absolute certainty does it through a conceptual framework for energetic thinking, whereas blockchain relies on computational power. In 1804, Fichte is correct, multiplicity of opinion could only create the problem that Nakamoto describes in his white paper: nothing is nonreversible. The only method for wholly excluding skepticism will ultimately rely on unity, since any amount of variety introduces the possibility of doubt. But material changes in the empirical world since that time, decisive shifts that Fichte's version of idealism has difficulty properly conceptualizing, have changed what multiplicity is capable of doing.

Advances in multiplicity, however, should not be taken as invalidating Fichte's insights. As our simplest interactions with the world begin to be filtered through digital technology, a philosophy of how knowledge interacts with itself in the most primordial way is profoundly relevant. Fichte's account of certainty provides us with concepts that we can use to better interpret our relationship with blockchain. We habitually confront digital objects as though they were substantially independent entities, rather than something thoroughly integrated into the being of knowing. Fichte provides a brief comment on this habit in the Twenty-Eighth Lecture: confronted with objects in the world, we tend to surrender to their independence; we want to abandon ourselves to mere appearance.[52] This has been his consistent refrain about consciousness and its illusions: consciousness finds itself among inexplicable objects, cannot bridge this gap of comprehension without gathering its energy for thought, and will opt for any number of heroic or pious dodges rather than suffer the rigor of science. The complexity of contemporary digital technology exacerbates this tendency; it accomplishes tasks that no "factical self" could perform, like big data detecting otherwise unpredictable correlations in behavior, the machine learning happening inside artificial intelligence, or the encryptions involved in Bitcoin mining. Blockchain especially seems to encourage surrender: Ian Bogost writes that "Bitcoin is hard to grasp because it's almost like a technology from an alien civilization."⁵³ But any discourse around digital technology that imbues it with inevitability, uncontrollability, or uncritical incomprehensibility is an expression of the tendency to succumb to appearance, evocations of the irrational gap spoken from the standpoint of a knowing as yet incapable of recognizing its illusory nature.

In this regard, the structure that Fichte gives to certainty is extremely valuable. Certainty is possible because knowing projects and intuits its own self-sufficiency; the enclosure of being, and the permanence of qualities grounded in it, is the result of knowing negating itself before itself. In its transubstantiation, knowing simultaneously sees itself as living singularity and projects itself as external world. This is the same as the situation in which knowing finds itself with regard to digital technology. The actual conceptualization of projection through the *Wissenschaftslehre* supports Fichte's call to conduct rational existence in the face of overwhelming technological development: although a technology like blockchain is totally impenetrable to consciousness in its operation, it is simultaneously solely the effect of the power of reason, and the incontestable certainty of blockchain is nothing but reason's own self-sufficiency translated into objectivity. Digital technology is a manifestation of reason's vibrant life, despite the impulse of reason to abdicate its sovereignty and submit to the apparent. As a commentary on knowing's behavior, the *Wissenschaftslehre* offers a thematic orientation for thinking about technology that can critically reappropriate breaks in its comprehension as acceptable byproducts of consciousness experiencing rational action.

Blockchain, machine learning, and big data are all better understood as meaningful, cognizable processes that require major spheres closed to consciousness in order to operate; they demand concepts of negation that can set unparalleled clarity about the actual conditions of the world in dynamic connection with the inaccessible method for reaching that clarity. The Fichtean reflective standpoint allows for these other possibilities of negation. Projection as an event that accompanies all acts of knowing incorporates a rational gap, and the *Wissenschaftslehre* can both explain this process and mitigate the illusions concomitant with it. The concept of the gap gives us a program for dealing with new technologies based on impossible calculation: the more intense its purported independence, the more fully its attainments signify the repetition of reason in the objective domain.

Contriving an encounter between Fichte and blockchain seems like a mostly idiosyncratic concern, so I would like to end this chapter by connecting this problem with a larger oncoming theological issue. Connecting theology with this text is, I think, not as eccentric: at the end of the *1804 Wissenschaftslehre*, Fichte speculates about future lectures, suggesting that he could apply the discoveries of this series to the topic of religion, and he eventually made good on that suggestion in *The Way toward the Blessed Life*. Fichte's relation to religion is a thoroughly debatable subject, given his personal history with the topic, but the stance of the *Wissenschaftslehre* for this period can be seen from where it places religion on the path to blessedness: right beneath philosophy. Nevertheless, theological topoi are constantly braided into the science of knowing—not that Fichte is a crypto-theologian, he is very clear that Jesus is a crypto-Fichtean—so that without some fluency with transubstantiation, eternal life, and the Trinity, the motivations, if not the ideas themselves, become opaque. And in these lectures, Fichte is sincerely concerned with God, even as he prefers to dispense with that particular title, and the depth of love for God that we can experience through knowing. His comments on contemporary Christianity, although typically huffy, indicate a meaningful religious sense: faith is concerned with knowing the eternal, which knowing is life itself, and religion only becomes an "ethics of prudence" in a state of decay.

Fichte, for appreciable reasons, does not embrace terminology like "faith." But absolute certainty holds a position like, and creates effects similar to, what faith would in a systematic theology. What makes our love for God possible is something parallel to grace, that the absolute is intrinsically self-revelatory, and something parallel to the Incarnation, that we can know that appearance is genuinely grounded in being. Certainty arrives at the joint between the enclosed-yet-manifesting absolute and the evidence for factical subjects to believe that this manifestation concords with our knowing. And Fichte very gently accommodates the vices of consciousness. By its essence consciousness is incapable of thinking the Absolute, and it also prefers to let objects stagger it into passivity. Systematic truth requires tremendous labor to expunge falsehood, but by phenomenologically rendering its illusions benign, consciousness more easily bears the call of science. Fichte's concern about the issue at stake in a theological exposition of faith is genuine, even if he wants to supplant faith's traditional finality, and ultimately the inflection is very Protestant: How do we know that absolute knowing is ours?

I have been arguing that the development of digital technology creates a crisis for the *Wissenschaftslehre*, but naturally this crisis is shared by faith. The significance invested in instances of everyday certainty as the contact of ordinary and absolute knowing is degraded if certainty can be generated by a machine, instead of needing to be shepherded by introspection and energetic thinking. Broadly speaking, mainline theologies think about faith on the model of trust—that is, rather than thinking faith primarily means assent to a set of doctrines, which often do not meet modern criteria of knowledge, faith is confidence that God will fulfill God's promises and so can still be a source of life. Although its applications are currently limited, blockchain poses a concrete threat to faith qua trust because dislocating the place of trust in human life trivializes its value as an image for understanding how we can relate to God. Blockchain makes trust irrelevant. Processing this issue through Fichte and the *Wissenschaftslehre* is useful for theology because Fichte navigates a similar problem in reflecting on how thought confronts thought, which is exactly what occurs, in a manner faster and more direct than in previous technologies, when we try to comprehend the digital.

Notes

1. *GA*, II/8, 8; 1804², 23.
2. *GA*, II/8, 8; 1804², 23.
3. *GA*, II/8, 347; 1804², 167.
4. Satoshi Nakamoto, "Bitcoin: A Peer-to-Peer Electronic Cash System," *Bitcoin*, October 31, 2008, https://bitcoin.org/bitcoin.pdf.
5. Nakamoto, "Bitcoin," 2.
6. Morgen E. Peck, "Blockchains: How They Work and Why They'll Change the World," IEEE Spectrum, IEEE, Sept. 28, 2017, https://spectrum.ieee.org/computing/networks/blockchains-how-they-work-and-why-theyll-change-the-world.
7. Tomaso Aste, Paolo Tasca, and Tiziana Di Matteo, "Blockchain Technologies: The Foreseeable Impact on Society and Industry," *Computer* 50, no. 9 (2017): 25.
8. Aste, Tasca, and Di Matteo, "Blockchain Technologies," 22.
9. Yu Bai, et al., "Researchain: Union Blockchain Based Scientific Research Project Management System," 2018 Chinese Automation Congress (CAC): Proceedings, Xi'an, China, Nov. 30–Dec. 02, IEEE, Piscataway, NJ, 4206.
10. Anneli Botz, "Is Blockchain the Future of Art? Four Experts Weigh In," Art Basel, Art Basel, accessed Sept. 5, 2022, https://www.artbasel.com/news/blockchain-artworld-cryptocurrency-cryptokitties.
11. Zohar Elhanani, "How Blockchain Changed the Art World in 2018," *Forbes*, Dec. 17, 2018, https://www.forbes.com/sites/zoharelhanani/2018/12/17/how-blockchain-changed-the-art-world-in-2018/#d36455130740.
12. Hilary K. Grigonis, "KodakOne Uses Blockchain and Web Crawlers to Spot Stolen Images," *Digital Trends*, May 10, 2018, https://www.digitaltrends.com/photography/kodakone-creates-photo-registry-blockchain-ces2018/.

13. Nir Kshetri and Jeffrey Voas, "Blockchain-Enabled E-Voting," IEEE, *Software* 354, no. 4 (2018): 98.
14. Johann Gottlieb Fichte, *The Popular Works of Johann Gottlieb Fichte*, vol. 2, trans. William Smith (Bristol, UK: Thoemmes Press, 1999), 450.
15. *GA*, II/8, 347; 1804², 167.
16. *GA*, II/8, 84; 1804², 55.
17. *GA*, II/8, 333; 1804², 160.
18. *GA*, II/, 219; 1804², 111.
19. *GA*, II/8, 224; 1804², 113.
20. *GA*, II/8, 249; 1804², 124.
21. *GA*, II/8, 238–39; 1804², 119.
22. *GA*, II/8, 238–39; 1804², 119.
23. Fichte, *The Popular Works*, 2:385.
24. Fichte, *The Popular Works*, 2:387.
25. *GA*, II/8, 295; 1804², 144.
26. *GA*, II/8, 235; 1804², 118.
27. *GA*, II/8, 252; 1804², 125.
28. *GA*, II/8, 252; 1804², 125.
29. *GA*, II/8, 250; 1804², 124.
30. *GA*, II/8, 335–36; 1804², 162.
31. *GA*, II/8, 325; 1804², 158.
32. *GA*, II/8, 337; 1804², 163.
33. *GA*, II/8, 341–42; 1804², 165.
34. *GA*, II/8, 336; 1804², 163.
35. *GA*, II/8, 346; 1804², 167.
36. *GA*, II/8, 348–49; 1804², 168.
37. *GA*, II/8, 347; 1804², 167.
38. Cf. *GA*, II/8, 115; 1804², 69.
39. *GA*, II/8, 372; 1804², 179.
40. *GA*, II/8, 378; 1804², 181.
41. *GA*, II/8, 383; 1804², 184.
42. *GA*, II/8, 385; 1804², 185.
43. *GA*, II/8, 385; 1804², 185.
44. *GA*, II/8, 397; 1804², 191.
45. *GA*, II/8, 389–90; 1804², 187.
46. *GA*, II/8, 389; 1804², 187.
47. *GA*, II/8, 391; 1804², 188.
48. *GA*, II/8, 345; 1804², 166.
49. *GA*, II/8, 346; 1804², 167.
50. *GA*, II/8, 8; 1804², 23.
51. *GA*, II/8, 379; 1804², 182.
52. *GA*, II/8, 415; 1804², 198.

53. Ian Bogost, "Cryptocurrency Might be a Path to Authoritarianism," *Atlantic*, May 30, 2017, https://www.theatlantic.com/technology/archive/2017/05/blockchain-of-command/528543/.

Chapter 16

Is Fichte a Kantian, a German Idealist, Both, or Neither?

Tom Rockmore

As a result of recent discussions, attention has increasingly turned once again to Fichte's relation to Kant. This chapter will focus on clarifying a series of complicated issues concerning Kant and German idealism. I will be arguing that, depending on the interpretation, in different ways and from different perspectives Fichte is both a Kantian and a German idealist as well as arguably neither.

Fichte presents his position as "nothing other than Kantianism properly understood." His claim was rejected by Kant but accepted by the young Schelling and the young Hegel. Though Fichte begins as a kind of self-described Kantian, as his position unfolds he moves steadily away from Kant and from idealism as well. By 1804, relatively early, and depending on the interpretation given to "Kant," "German idealism," and "idealism," he has arguably left Kant, German idealism, and perhaps even idealism behind.

Fichte loudly claims to be a "Kantian" and an "idealist." Yet, since neither term is clear, it is unclear that he is either. Fichte's relation to Kant is difficult to evaluate for at least four reasons. To begin with, Fichte's position is not only unclear as well as difficult but also highly labile, clearly different in different texts. Second, Kant's position is at least unclear since, after several hundred years of intensive study often by talented observers, there is apparently no agreement in the massive Kant debate beyond the obvious but not very helpful point that the critical philosophy is very important. Further, as Fichte's position evolves, its relation to Kant's position, however understood, also evolves. Finally, Fichte's claim to be a Kantian is further specifically transformed by his appeal in the *1804 Wissenschaftslehre* to the obscure concept of a *projectio per hiatum irrationale*.

The present effort to clarify Fichte's claim to be a Kantian will focus on two points. On the one hand, I will argue that Fichte's claim to be a Kantian follows from Fichte's and Kant's shared commitments to German idealism that I will understand as a form of epistemic constructivism. On the other hand, I will argue that Fichte's later turn to irrational projection improves his position while rendering less plausible his claim to be a Kantian.

Leibniz Invents "Idealism"

It will be useful, to start, to say a few words about "idealism" and "German idealism." For reasons that will emerge shortly, I believe that Fichte and Kant are both German idealists. "Idealism" is rarely studied, at least in any detail, and is more often criticized than understood. At least since Kant's critique of Berkeley, idealism has mainly been used as a term of reproach. In part, the rejection of idealism is due to lack of interest in or knowledge about this approach. The rejection of idealism is due to the manifest failure to agree about the reference of the term. When "idealism" is mentioned, it is often understood, for instance in Marxism, as an indefensible counterpart to materialism.[1]

Though there are exceptions, such as Nicholas Rescher, few contemporary philosophers are willing to declare an interest in idealism. References to idealism are mainly negative. Kant, whose view is unclear, both espouses and rejects idealism. In the *Prolegomena*, he briefly rejects but also inconsistently espouses idealism. His intention seems to lie in escaping the possible opprobrium of any possible link between the critical philosophy and the views of either Descartes or Berkeley, especially the latter. At the beginning of the twentieth century the rejection of idealism was one of the founding acts of Anglo-American analytic philosophy. According to G. E. Moore, idealism in all its forms is committed to the denial of the existence of the external world.[2]

In part, unclarity about idealism is due to ignorance about its possible meaning. The initial reference to idealism as a philosophical approach is apparently due to Leibniz in 1702. Ever since Engels, Marxism in all its varieties has always insisted on the incompatibility between idealism and materialism. Leibniz, who is sometimes understood as an idealist, has a different view. He suggests that idealism and materialism are compatible doctrines, which can at least in principle be synthesized in a single position. In responding to Pierre Bayle, he objects to "those who, like Epicurus and Hobbes, believe that the soul is material," adding that in his own position "whatever of good there is in the hypotheses of Epicurus and Plato, of the great materialists and the great idealists, is combined here."[3]

We can take Leibniz as suggesting that idealism and materialism both begin as early as Greek antiquity. Their common origin seems to lie in the view of the pre-Socratic Parmenides. According to Parmenides, thinking and being are the same (or identical).

In retrospect, Parmenides can be read as pointing to two main cognitive approaches either of which satisfies his criterion of cognition as requiring the identity (or unity) of thought and being. On the one hand, there is the cognitive grasp of the real, reality or the world to which Parmenides is apparently committed as the cognitive standard. The view that to know means to know the real echoes through the entire later tradition where over the centuries it has always reigned as the favored approach to knowledge, never more so than at present. The conviction that to know requires knowledge of the real has been popular at least since Parmenides. Plato is an early champion of this view. Yet it has never been shown how to demonstrate this claim. On the other hand, there is the alternative view I will be calling epistemic constructivism that, though we do not and cannot grasp the real, we can avoid epistemic skepticism through the alternative cognitive approach that we know and can only know what we construct.

These alternatives are exemplified in widely known positions. Thus, Plato, a strong Parmenidean, is deeply committed to the view that cognition requires a grasp of the mind-independent real. Platonism can be understood as an effort to show that on grounds of nature or nurture at least some gifted individuals can literally "see" the real. Platonism stands or falls on the demonstration of the claim to intuit the real through the theory of forms. The effort, if not to intuit at least to grasp the real, echoes through the entire tradition, but if Kant is right, there has never been even the least progress in that direction.

Epistemic Constructivism and German Idealism

If the effort to grasp the real fails, an alternative is necessary to avoid epistemic skepticism. Epistemic constructivism is based on ancient Greek mathematics. It comes into the early modern tradition through Hobbes, Bacon, and Vico. It later arises again independently through Kant and other German idealists. German idealism provides the context of an intense struggle among thinkers of the first rank, each of whom is committed to formulating an acceptable version of the constructivist view that, as Kant famously remarks, we only know what we construct.

It is often claimed that German idealism begins after Kant. Yet, if Kant is an epistemic constructivist, and if epistemic constructivism includes German idealism, then four points follow. The first point concerns the relation of Kant to German idealism. If German idealism is concerned with forms of epistemic constructivism, and if Kant is an epistemic constructivist, then, since he writes in German and focuses on the German-language philosophical debate, it is plausible to suggest that he is a German idealist. In short, despite the widespread belief to the contrary, it turns out that Kant is not a predecessor of German idealism but rather a German idealist.

This point is obviously controversial. Many observers think, as the canonical locution "post–German idealism" suggests, that Kant precedes German idealism that only begins in his wake. According to Paul Franks, who is in that respect typical, Reinhold is the initial German idealist.[4] Yet, if Kant is committed to epistemic constructivism, then he is misunderstood as a predecessor of German idealism but correctly understood as belonging to and perhaps even as initiating that specific philosophical tendency. In fact, since there is widespread agreement that Fichte is an idealist, and Fichte claims to be an authentic Kantian, it would be inconsistent to think that Fichte is a post-Kantian German idealist, but, to be consistent, Kant is a pre-Fichtean non-idealist. For it would be an obvious contradiction to claim that Fichte is a Kantian as well as an idealist. Kant could not then be a pre-Fichtean idealist.

Further, Schelling, who is obviously an important thinker but who does not hold a constructivist view, is not, or at least from this perspective is not, a German idealist. Third, if Fichte is a Kantian, then he is also a German idealist, and not, say, as Alexis Philonenko thinks, situated outside this debate.[5] Finally, German idealism and epistemic constructivism are not discontinuous but rather continuous. There are different ways to understand the German idealist tradition. It has recently been suggested that the main theme is nihilism.[6] Other ways to understand this period are possible as well. Suffice it to say that, beginning in the so-called Copernican turn, a term Kant never uses to refer to his own position, epistemic constructivism is a central theme linking together the German idealists, including in my view Kant, Fichte, Hegel, and perhaps Marx. Yet the last point, which lies outside the scope of the current discussion, will have to wait for another discussion.

Kantian Idealism

I have suggested that both Fichte and Kant are both German idealists. Though Kant says he is a critical idealist, his view of idealism is confusing and possibly confused. A number of observers favor a representationalist interpretation of the critical philosophy. According to Béatrice Longuenesse:

> Kant's first formulation of the problem which eventually becomes that of the transcendental deduction of the categories in the *Critique* is to be found in his "Letter to Marcus Herz" of February 21, 1772. The problem of the relation between a priori concepts and given objects is the occasion for a more general inquiry into the relation between a representation and its object, an inquiry taken up again, almost word for word, nine years later in the Transcendental Deduction. However, the two texts differ in a fundamental respect. The "Letter to Herz" presents the relation between a representation and its object as a causal relation between two heterogeneous entities, or the representation that is "within" the mind and the object which is "outside" it, the *Critique* internalizes the relation between the representation and the object within representation itself, so that the problem assumes a new meaning.[7]

Longuenesse usefully distinguishes between the transcendental deduction of the categories, representation or representationalism, and the real. If it were possible to demonstrate the relation between a representation and its object, it would be possible to cognize the mind-independent real or, in Kant's language, the thing in itself. Yet this cannot be Kant's project since several years after the Herz letter he clearly and forcefully denies that epistemic representation is possible.[8]

This view is further supported by Kant's comments on what is often called the Copernican revolution or more informally the Copernican turn. According to Kant, the rise of modern natural science teaches us that "reason has insight only into what it itself produces according to its own design."[9] He further famously suggests a similar epistemic constructivist approach in metaphysics:

> Up to now it has been assumed that all our cognition must conform to the objects; but all attempts to find out something about them a priori through concepts that would extend our cognition have, on this supposition, come to nothing. Hence let us once try whether we do not get farther with the problems of metaphysics by assuming that the objects must conform to our cognition, which would agree better with the requested possibility of an a priori cognition of them, which is to establish something about objects before they are given to us.[10]

Fichtean Epistemic Constructivism in the *Wissenschaftslehre*

I turn now to Fichte's relation to Kant in the initial version of his position in his formulations of two versions of his position in 1794 and again in 1804. The relation of Fichte to Kant changes with each new version of the Jena philosopher's system. Simply speaking, the former text explains experience, hence cognition, on the basis of the subject, and the latter text, which responds to a change in the role of the subject, describes a later model of experience.

In his role as a supposedly faithful Kantian, Fichte follows the spirit if not the letter of Kant, hence of the Copernican turn. According to the early Fichte, the cognitive object is posited and determined by the cognitive faculty and the cognitive faculty is not determined by the object.

Is Fichte a Kantian in 1794? In confronting Fichte and Kant, we have two different perspectives. Kant and then Fichte are centrally concerned with cognition on the basis of very different conceptions of the subject. Here a reference to psychologism will be helpful. According to the dictionary, "psychologism" is the conflation of logical and psychological factors. In rejecting what later was called psychologism,[11] Kant "deduces" the subject that in theory is able to construct and therefore know the cognitive object. Fichte appears to embrace psychologism in his account of the cognitive object starting from a finite human subject. His aim in this and other writings is always to explain what he describes as "the ground of all experience." He explains experience and knowledge through a new view of the subject as constrained in its actions by its surroundings, hence as practically finite but theoretically infinite. Kant sketches a supposedly transcendental account of the interaction of the transcendental subject and reality in a third-person, causal account. As part of his reformulation of the subject that Kant deduces,

Fichte proposes a first-person account of the interaction of subject and object in a statement of the fundamental principles that begin the *Science of Knowledge* (1794).

From Kantian Anti-Psychologism to Fichtean Psychologism

Kant deduces a philosophical conception of the subject that Fichte replaces through an anthropological shift. Kant's transcendental deduction reaches a high point in his conception of the transcendental subject, or original synthetic unity of apperception, which he "deduces," as "the supreme principle of all use of the understanding."[12] With Leibniz in mind, Kant describes the subject as the "I think" that "must be able to accompany all my representations," and as a "pure apperception" that is not "an empirical one."[13] Fichte, on the contrary, approaches the cognitive problem through a post-Kantian conception of finite human being in a social context.

The critical philosophy is speculative, hence concerned with possibility, as well as transcendental, hence supposedly able to isolate the only possibility. Kant begins from the cognitive object in constructing a regressive deduction of the cognitive subject. He understands "deduction" as a retrospective progression from conditioned to condition, hence as regressive. Kant justifies the appeal to a thing in itself about which we can at least in principle know only that it exists on the premise that there cannot be an appearance without anything that appears.[14]

Fichte is routinely but I believe incorrectly described as a transcendental, more correctly characterized as a speculative thinker. The difference is crucial. A speculative argument describes, refers to, or deduces a possibility. A transcendental argument describes, refers to, or deduces the only possibility. Fichte's view, which is not transcendental, is limited to a description rather than a deduction of the conditions of experience and knowledge. Kant claims to demonstrate the necessary existence of the thing in itself about which he can know nothing. Fichte in turn objects that the thing in itself is an arbitrary assumption that explains nothing, but through intellectual intuition, the subject perceives itself as active. Fichtean idealism explains experience through intellectual activity based on his view of the necessary laws of the intellect. If the subject is independent and the object is dependent, then philosophy, which can only strive for but cannot be wholly objective, finally depends on subjective factors, famously including, according to Fichte, the kind of person one is.

Fichte further considers the finite human subject from at least three perspectives: (1) as a finite human being, as a person who is both a theoretical entity, namely as an unlimited subject of consciousness who is unlimited and a practical, or limited moral, being. (2) As a real finite being, the individual is limited through that person's relation to the external world. (3) Fichte finally invokes the concept of absolute being on the philosophical or meta-experiential level, namely as a philosophical concept useful in the explanation of experience.

To the types of finite human being or so-called self (*das Ich*) Fichte associates three kinds of activity. As theoretical a person posits, as practical a person strives, and as absolute a person acts in theoretical independence of the surroundings. The concept of an ideally existent absolute being is justified as a means to understand the experience of the really existent finite being. Forms of activity are theoretically subtended by activity in general. Fichte understands a finite human being as above all a practical being. He further identifies pure activity with the absolute self that is an acknowledged philosophical construct. Since his view of finite human being supposedly follows from the concept of absolute self, Fichte may be said to "deduce" the concept of the individual from that of the absolute. As he notes in a letter: "My absolute self is clearly not the individual. . . . But the individual must be deduced from the absolute self."[15]

As a British empiricist, Hume focuses on human knowledge, not knowledge in general. Fichte depicts himself as a Kantian. Yet his conception of the finite human subject is perhaps closer to Hume's conception of subjectivity than to Kant's abstract subject that is reduced to its epistemic role in the critical philosophy. Fichte's anti-Kantian anthropological reformulation of the subject arguably reinstates the psychologism that Kant in anticipating Husserl seeks to avoid. It further removes the Kantian ambiguity due to a simultaneous commitment to epistemic representationalism, hence to metaphysical realism, as well as to epistemic constructivism and empirical realism.

Consider for a moment the triple distinction between a phenomenon, an appearance, and a representation. In simple terms, a phenomenon is given to consciousness but does not refer beyond itself; an appearance is given to consciousness and further refers beyond itself but does not necessarily represent or correctly depict that to which it refers; and a representation refers to and correctly depicts that to which it refers beyond itself.

Previously I mentioned the interpretive difficulty that arises in the critical philosophy in virtue of Kant's early interest in representation that, during the critical period, he later rejects. Fichte, who is clearly aware of this theme, rejects Kantian representationalism in, like Plato long ago, rejecting a causal approach to knowledge. Fichte, hence, removes the inconsistency in Kant's simultaneous but inconsistent commitment to two rival views of cognition in restating the Kantian epistemic constructivist model on the basis of the subject's activity. In this way, Fichte sets the agenda running throughout post-Kantian German idealism. This agenda consists in an effort to restate the a priori Kantian epistemic constructivist approach to cognition in an acceptable form.

On Fichte's Kantianism in the *1804 Wissenschaftslehre*

It is well said that *Wissenschaftslehre* is not the name of a text but rather of a type of thought. Each version of the *Wissenschaftslehre* presents another system. Fichte's defense of Kant is a constant factor in the different versions of his position. Since the Copernican turn lies at the center of the critical philosophy, in principle Fichte should be understood as presenting one or more post-Kantian version of the Copernican turn.

So far we have been discussing Fichte's early view of Kantianism in the initial formulation of his position. His initial position underwent rapid changes in a short period as he sought to perfect it. It will be sufficient, for present purposes, to consider the relation of Fichte's position in the *1804 Wissenschaftslehre* to Kant's view.

According to the Kantian form of epistemic constructivism, cognition depends on the complex claim that sensory content is worked up into an appearance, more precisely an object of experience and knowledge, through being brought under the categories. Writing in Kant's wake, Fichte is, like the Königsberg thinker, an epistemic constructivist. Kantian and Fichtean forms of epistemic constructivism are very different. We have seen that the first version of the Fichtean system extends but also reformulates Kant's Copernican turn. According to Fichte's initial position, literally everything comes from the subject. This approach, which is inspired by Kant, is clearly non- and even anti-Kantian. At this early point in his evolution Fichte only partially follows Kant in explaining that cognition amounts to explaining experience as the product of an unlimited subject that creates and creates itself without limits.

It is or at least should be obvious that Fichte goes too far in 1794 in explaining experience solely in terms of the subject. Rather than like Kant claiming that the subject and object interact in constructing an appearance, he suggests that the object is wholly and solely explicable through the active subject. Fichte is however not unaware of this difficulty that he rapidly attempts to correct. In the *1804 Wissenschaftslehre* he reduces his cognitive pretentions in reformulating the relation of the subject to the object. At this point he gives up the effort to explain experience in deducing the world, an effort which is neither plausible nor possible. He now rather seeks to explain the given on the basis of the subject.

In 1804, the explanation is no longer directed toward the analysis of experience from the perspective of the subject but on the contrary toward a sort of phenomenology. At this point, the aim to develop the critical philosophy beyond Kant has not changed, but the strategy is different. Fichte, who still understands himself as a Kantian, still says that his aim is to present Kantianism in another manner than Kant, but, as we will see in a moment, now in a different way.

Kant limits cognition to appearances as well as the condition of appearances. He does not claim, in fact he explicitly denies, the possibility of knowing the real. But he allows speculation about the cause of appearances. Fichte, who does not pretend to know the real any more than Kant, is, unlike the latter, further skeptical about appearances. Fichte, like Kant, is an idealist, hence an epistemic constructivist, in short committed a distinction between an unknowable real on the one hand and what we construct and know on the other. Kant carefully distinguishes between the claim to know the real, which he rejects, and the further claim to know appearances, which he accepts. He is, as Maimon among his contemporaries noted, in that respect skeptical. Fichte, who continues to believe Kant fails to explain experience, now ceases his effort to do so in place of Kant. As a result, Fichte, like Kant, but for different reasons, becomes epistemically skeptical. In the Fourteenth Lecture, he affirms that consciousness turns on something actual, true, and present, something that one cannot explain. "Your consciousness of thinking should contain a thinking process *{Denken}*, actual, true and really present, without your being able to give an accounting of it; therefore, this consciousness projects a *true* reality outward, dis-continuously: an absolute inconceivability and inexplicability."[16]

On the Projection *per hiatum irrationale*

In 1797, Fichte thinks that the aim of philosophy is to explain experience. In the Fifteenth Lecture of the *1804 Wissenschaftslehre*, Fichte has changed his mind. He now justifies his newly found cognitive skepticism in affirming that it is not possible to explain experience. In place of an explanation, he now speaks, in inventing a solecism, of the absolute projection of an object and of what is "projected," as he says, as "entirely black and bare." He further says in what he concedes is somewhat scholastic terminology that it is a question of what he describes as "a projection through an irrational hiatus." Here is the passage whose interpretation is crucial but difficult: "What is this consciousness's effect, for the sake of which it is discarded; and therefore what is that which must always be removed from the truth? Answer: the absolute projection of an object whose origin is inexplicable, so that between the projective act and the projected object everything is dark and bare; as I think I can express very accurately, if a little scholastically, a *proiectio per hiatum irrationale* (projection through an irrational gap)."[17]

This obscure statement provides a term that is inexplicable and does not really help us. Clues to its interpretation are lacking. We do not know what Fichte intends to say nor even how he can pretend to know what he says. In adopting this difficult locution, Fichte seems to refer to the limits of cognition. In simple terms, he seems to be conceding that the limits of cognition lead to the conclusion that we cannot explain everything, even that we cannot explain cognition.

There is a distinction between what one can and what one cannot explain. We recall that the initial version of the *Wissenschaftslehre* is directed toward explaining presentation accompanied by a feeling of necessity. In the meantime, Fichte seems to have abandoned this goal in adopting a more modest aim. In 1794 Fichte intends to explain cognition to whose limits he draws attention in 1804. Fichte is interested in establishing the limits of cognition. In colloquial language: his position seems to be that we can only explain what we can explain since we cannot explain the origin of experience.

Lukács and Lask React to Fichte

The change in Fichte's position in 1804 influenced two thinkers early in the twentieth century: Georg Lukács, the Hungarian Marxist, and Emil Lask, the German neo-Kantian. Lukács, who was influenced by Lask, identifies the difference between the mathematical method in the special sciences and the supposed irrationality of matter discussed by Wilhelm Windelband, Heinrich Rickert, and Lask.[18] Lukács draws attention to the distinction between the bourgeoisie and the proletariat in suggesting the former cannot know modern industrial society, which can only be correctly cognized from the proletarian perspective. Lask, whose dissertation was on Fichte's theory of history, directs attention to the problem of irrationality, more specifically to what cannot be rationally explained and, since explanation is rational, surpasses the limits of rationality, surpasses the limits of what we can know.

Plato long ago suggested that on grounds of nature and nurture some selected individuals can see the real. This suggestion now returns in Lukács's implausible claim that it is only from the proletarian perspective that can we grasp the real or, in other words, the thing in itself. Lukács implausibly maintains that the infinite cognitive superiority of the proletarian perspective points to the impossibility of grasping the real or, in other words, grasping the thing in itself.

This claim is obviously implausible for two reasons. First, Lukács is presenting the proletariat as solving or having solved the Kantian problem of the thing in itself. Yet it can only be asserted but cannot be demonstrated that we can know the real. If we could know the real, then we could know the thing in itself that, if Kant is correct, we do not and cannot know. Second, it cannot be shown that one segment of the population, say the proletariat, can know what another segment of the population, say the bourgeoisie, does not and cannot know.

The neo-Kantian Lask, under Fichte's influence, draws the consequences of Fichte's view in 1804 in pointing to irrationality. Irrationality has a twofold function in Lask's position. On the one hand, it points to an epistemological limit through the identification of an uncognizable residue, an ontological surd that, like the Kantian view of the real, since it resists all efforts at cognition, cannot be known. Lask, like Kant, holds that though we cannot know the real, we know that there is a real that we do not know.

Clearly, the concept of irrationality, if not the terminology, long precedes Lask. The Greek fear of the essentially irrational is well known. For Lask, "irrational" does not mean "a-rational," or "non-rational," but rather the "not-rationalizable (*Nicht—Rationalisierbarkeit*)." At stake is a basic change in Fichte's view. In 1794 he strives to explain cognition in explaining what, as he now seems to concede in 1804 in distantly following Kant, simply cannot be explained.

Kant, Fichte, and the Copernican Turn

Fichte and Kant each seek, each in his own way, to resolve the cognitive enigma in invoking a constructivist approach. The mature Kant describes the Copernican turn that Fichte revises in different texts in proposing new versions of the critical philosophy. If the Copernican turn lies at the center of the critical philosophy, and if Fichte is a Kantian, then the Fichtean system should turn on the proposed effort to reformulate Kantianism, hence to reformulate the Kantian version of the Copernican turn after Kant.

At the center of Kantianism, we find the following complex claim: we can neither represent nor otherwise know the real, but we can know appearances since we construct them. As his position evolves, Fichte revises Kant's Copernican turn. We can understand Fichte's positions in 1794 and in 1804 as proposing different versions of the Kantian Copernican turn, or the view that the necessary condition of cognition lies in the construction of the object.

This thesis presents a balanced conception of cognition without in any way explaining what one can neither explain nor know. Since that Copernican turn describes what one knows through what we can neither know nor explain, it necessarily remains mysterious. Fichte is therefore well within his rights in saying that the Kantians do not understand the way in which Kant overturns the philosophy of his period, that is, the representationalism dominant in the modern tradition, in both its rationalist and its empiricist formulations. To put the same point otherwise: according to Fichte the Copernican turn is literally as well as figuratively intended to reverse the philosophical tendency dominant at the end of the eighteenth century. Yet the mystery that is not dissipated in Fichte's view remains.

When all is said and done, one must ask what remains of Fichte's version of the Copernican turn. If, as Fichte pretends, he agrees with Kant whose position he faithfully describes in another way, then we can expect to find another form of the Copernican turn in his position, a revised and corrected form of the basic affirmation: we know only what we construct. Now it is not at all clear that Fichte, as he says, presents a new form, either in the first version of his system or again in a later version of 1804. What is not clear in 1794 becomes clearer in 1804 when he seems to abandon his early effort to explain experience, that is, one must say, what in 1804 seems to become impossible.

Conclusion: Is Fichte a Kantian, an Idealist, Neither, or Both?

There is a basic difference between the early Fichte in 1794 and the more mature Fichte ten years later. In 1794 Fichte intends to explain experience and knowledge on the generous assumption that Kant has already done so but failed to be understood. Ten years later he comes to the very different conclusion that, as he says, consciousness contains something of which we cannot give an account, which hence remains inexplicable.

This new version of Fichte's position contains an important retreat that brings him closer to Kant, closer to the suggestion that we paradoxically know there is a real about which we can know nothing. It follows that a deduction, or a complete deduction, is not possible. If this is the cognitive criterion, then we must concede that, if judged by its result, at least in this respect Fichte's theory, which we can infer was supposed to be a deduction, fails.

In replacing the dualism of subjectivity and objectivity by the single theme of subjectivity, Fichte improves on the Kantian description of the relation of subject to object in adopting the first-person perspective. But at the same time, he makes it possible to perceive the limits of an approach to subjectivity through objectivity in reducing the latter to the former. The modern tradition underlines the idea, correctly I believe, that the road to objectivity necessarily runs through subjectivity. The main difficulty lies in grasping subjectivity and objectivity in a single epistemic theory. Though Fichte improves on Kant, at the end of the day neither Fichte nor Kant resolves the ancient Parmenidean problem of the epistemic relation of subjectivity to objectivity, which remains to be resolved. And because we cannot decide how to interpret either Fichte or Kant, it further remains unclear whether Fichte is a Kantian, a German idealist, both, or neither. It follows that the question cannot be answered.

Notes

1. See Diego Fusaro, *Marx, Epicurus and the Origins of Historical Materialism* (Partinent Press, 2018).

2. G. E. Moore, "The Refutation of Idealism," *Mind* 12, no. 48 (Oct. 1903): 433–53.

3. G. W. Leibniz, *Philosophische Schriften*, vol. 4, ed. C. I. Gerhardt (Berlin: Weidmann, 1875–1890), 559–60.

4. Paul Franks, *All or Nothing: Systematicity, Transcendental Arguments, and Skepticism in German Idealism* (Cambridge, MA: Harvard University Press, 2005).

5. See Alexis Philonenko, *La Liberté humaine dans la philosophie de Fichte* (Paris: Vrin, 1967).

6. Karin Nisenbaum, *For the Love of Metaphysics: Nihilism and the Conflict of Reason from Kant to Rosenzweig* (Oxford: Oxford University Press, 2018).

7. Béatrice Longuenesse, *Kant and the Capacity to Judge* (Princeton, NJ: Princeton University Press, 1998), 17.

8. In the *Dohna-Wundlacken Logic*, presumably based on lectures given in the 1790s, hence in the critical period, he states representation "cannot be explained at all." Immanuel Kant, *Lectures on Logic* (New York: Cambridge University Press, 1992), 440.

9. Kant, *Critique of Pure Reason*, B xiii, 109.

10. Kant, B xvi, 110.

11. See Martin Kusch, *Psychologism: The Sociology of Philosophical Knowledge* (London: Routledge, 1995).

12. Kant, *Critique of Pure Reason*, B 136.

13. Kant, B 132.

14. See Kant, B xxvi–xxvii.

15. *GA*, III/2, 391–92.

16. *GA*, II/8, 219; 1804^2, 111.

17. *GA*, II/8, 236; 1804^2, 118.

18. "Where philosophy has recourse to the structural assumptions lying behind the form-content relationship it either exalts the 'mathematicising' method of the special sciences, elevating it into the method proper to philosophy (as in the Marburg School), or else it establishes the irrationality of matter, as logically, the 'ultimate' fact (as do Windelband, Rickert and Lask)." Georg Lukács, *History and Class Consciousness*, trans. Rodney Livingstone (Cambridge, MA: MIT Press, 1971), 120.

Contributors

Emiliano Acosta is associate professor of philosophy at the Vrije Universiteit Brussel and visiting professor at Ghent University and at the University of Catania.

Daniel Breazeale is professor emeritus of philosophy at the University of Kentucky.

M. Jorge de Carvalho is associate professor of philosophy at the New University of Lisbon and researcher at the Institute for Philosophical Studies (University of Coimbra).

Benjamin D. Crowe is lecturer in philosophy at Boston University.

Gabriel Gottlieb is associate professor of philosophy at Xavier University.

Adam Hankins is an independent scholar and teacher in Roanoke, Virginia.

C. Jeffery Kinlaw is professor of philosophy and religion at McMurry University and adjunct professor of philosophy at the University of North Carolina, Pembroke.

Michael Lewin is senior researcher at the Academia Kantiana, Immanuel Kant Baltic Federal University, Kaliningrad.

Andrew J. Mitchell is professor of philosophy at Emory University.

Matthew Nini is postdoctoral research fellow at Albert Ludwigs Universität Freiburg.

Angelica Nuzzo is professor of philosophy at the Graduate Center and Brooklyn College, CUNY.

Jacinto Rivera de Rosales was professor of philosophy at Universidad Nacional de Educatión a Distancia in Madrid.

Tom Rockmore is distinguished professor emeritus at Duquesne University and distinguished humanities chair professor at Peking University.

F. Scott Scribner is professor of philosophy at the University of Hartford.

Kit Slover is a tutor at St. John's College, New Mexico.

Michael Steinberg is an independent scholar and attorney in Rochester, New York.

Michael Vater is associate professor emeritus of philosophy at Marquette University.

Index

absolute, 15, 18, 20, 22–27, 29, 41–43, 62–63, 69–71, 97, 99, 104, 138–139, 220
  knowing, 54, 182, 227, 232
  knowledge, 193–194, 200–202, 205, 210, 302
  oneness, 2–3, 21, 36–37, 45, 86, 158, 163–164, 193, 198, 200, 202
  reason, 252, 278–283
  self-determination, 12–13, 19–20, 22–23, 25, 27–29, 63
act, 13–15, 18–20, 22–25, 27–30, 38–40, 43, 53–54, 64–67, 69–71, 80–83, 89–90, 120–121, 126, 180, 208–209, 227, 265, 268–269, 275–276, 278–280
  of absolute reason, 281, 283
  pure, 12, 19, 64, 106, 120, 267
  self-constituting, 12, 15, 19, 21, 23–24, 27, 30–31, 51, 254
activity, 19–20, 28, 65, 71, 121, 125, 174–175, 251–252, 263, 270, 278–279, 285, 320
art of philosophizing, 41, 219
attention, 38–39, 91–92, 97–98, 100, 102–103, 105, 107, 109–112, 114, 145, 152–153, 303, 305

Begriff, 77, 149, 159–160, 171

being, 45, 57–58, 70–71, 87–89, 104–107, 115–117, 125–128, 132–133, 135–136, 138–143, 180–181, 237–241, 243–246, 248–251, 260–262, 265–267, 275–278, 284–285, 295–296, 300–309
  thinking and, 36, 65, 70–71, 86–87, 94, 132–137, 141–143, 217, 219, 230, 236

cognition, 49–50, 71–74, 101, 222–224, 235–236, 242, 245–246, 250, 252, 269, 315, 318, 321, 323–325
concept, 4, 20–23, 43, 46, 62–64, 71–73, 133–136, 138–143, 159–160, 163–164, 184–186, 193–197, 201, 203, 207, 223–224, 261, 303–304, 306–308, 320
  pure, 38, 62–63, 71, 73, 141, 198
consciousness, 2, 11–14, 17–20, 45–48, 51–54, 57–58, 62–64, 98–101, 103–107, 109–112, 114–117, 121, 193–213, 226–230, 262–265, 268–269, 282–283, 296–298, 302–304, 306–309
  collective, 180, 184, 187
finite, 14, 119, 247–249

consciousness *(continued)*
  immediate, 66, 123, 127, 179, 250, 257, 267–268, 296
  standpoint of, 46, 264
construction, 2, 87–90, 92, 100–102, 117, 136, 138, 180–181, 241–243, 246–247, 249, 253–254, 299, 302, 304
Copernican turn, 317–318, 321, 324–325
critical philosophy, 45–46, 53, 121, 124, 127, 131, 142, 314, 317, 319–322, 325

death, 105, 107, 115, 124–125, 132, 141–142, 244, 264, 295, 302
dialectic, 35, 42, 76, 137, 229, 232, 236, 250, 303
disjunction, 2, 19, 21–22, 25, 104, 119–120, 122, 124, 161–163, 165, 227–230, 241, 245, 248–249, 256–257
doctrine of appearance, 5, 114, 273, 295
  and illusion, 35, 114
doctrine of science, 193–195, 197–204, 206, 209–212, 215–216, 218–220, 224, 230

epistemic constructivism, 314–316, 320–321
epistemic standpoint, 13, 20–21, 25
Evidenz, 14, 20, 40, 87, 99–101, 107–108, 110–113, 248–249
existence, 44–45, 54, 57, 105–106, 114, 116–117, 126, 194, 197–198, 205–206, 252, 254, 278–281, 284–285, 297–298
expression, 70, 72, 74, 88–89, 97, 100, 139–141, 240–241, 252–253, 257, 260, 279–280, 303

fact-act. *See* Tathandlung
factical, 34, 37–38, 105, 117, 119, 126, 131–132, 134, 170, 222, 225, 262, 264, 282, 299–300
facticity, 4, 7, 200, 207, 226, 228–229, 244, 250–253, 262–263, 279, 282
facts of consciousness, 67, 207, 262
faith, 6, 85, 261, 268, 292, 309–310
Fichte
  and Hegel, 218, 224
  and Jacobi, 51, 76, 115, 174–176, 179, 183, 187–188, 210–211, 214, 242, 287–288
  and Kant, 142, 313–314, 317–318, 324
  and Schelling, 3, 7, 30, 232, 236–238, 243, 255, 272
first principle, 37–38, 61–77, 82, 121, 179, 225
freedom, 14, 29–30, 49–50, 55, 59, 83–85, 80–91, 117, 198–199, 202, 208, 225, 277–278, 281–282, 285–286, 288–289
  self-determination, 16, 19–20, 23, 27–30
  system of, 55–56, 90

gap
  cognitive. *See* hiatus
  irrational. *See* hiatus
genetic unity, 132, 135, 137, 140, 142, 265
God, 61–63, 68–74, 77, 178, 205, 207, 209–211, 269, 273, 275–276, 282, 284, 286–288, 297, 309–310

hiatus, vi, 5–6, 21–22, 97–101, 103–105, 109, 111–114, 119–121, 124–128, 151–159, 167–169,

176, 248, 263–264, 281, 296–299, 303–305, 307–308, 322–323

idealism, 6, 42, 65, 67–69, 76–77, 120–124, 178–179, 207, 227–229, 235, 239, 246–247, 249–250, 255, 259–266, 268–270, 313–315
  absolute, 3, 55, 259, 267
  and materialism, 315
  and realism, 24, 67–68, 121–124, 228–229, 235–237, 239, 241, 246, 250, 261, 266
  subjective, 179, 251
identity, 11, 157, 162, 235, 240–241, 243–244, 246, 250, 256, 266, 269
  of identity and difference, 235, 240–241
  identity of, 235, 240–241, 243, 250, 256
identity philosophy, 7, 239, 242, 249, 262
I-hood, 12–19, 22, 24, 26–30, 36, 38, 46, 50–51, 56, 201
indifference, 170, 210, 241, 262, 269
insight, 20–21, 23–24, 26–27, 29, 38–42, 44–45, 47–48, 55–56, 87–88, 117, 131–133, 163–167, 177–178, 181–184, 203–206, 249–250, 265–267, 277–282, 300–301, 303–305
  clear, 53, 55, 183
  fundamental, 147–148, 162, 165, 205
  genetic, 132, 180, 182, 263
  immediate, 51, 110
intellectual intuition, 19, 30, 39–40, 64, 66, 239, 242, 283, 319
intuition, 41, 63, 70, 81–82, 133–134, 140–142, 237, 242–243, 250, 261–263, 266, 302–304

Kant, I., 63–64, 72, 74, 78, 109, 133, 196, 198, 208–209, 220, 223–226, 242, 295
  Critique of Practical Reason, 220, 286
  Critique of Pure Reason, 63, 78, 115, 119, 218–221, 231, 261, 327
Kantianism, 62, 64, 101, 104, 133, 208, 211–213, 219–220, 223, 240, 242, 251, 254, 313–327
knowing, 2–4, 38, 48, 86–87, 99–103, 131–140, 177–179, 181, 219–221, 225–227, 236, 238–240, 244–247, 249, 251–254, 273–280, 282–285, 291–292, 298–300, 302–309
knowledge, 34, 44, 48–49, 65–66, 86–87, 89–100, 102–103, 134–136, 153–154, 175, 177–178, 193–195, 199–201, 273–277, 279–280, 314–315, 318–321
  pure, 66–67, 69–71, 198

language, 51, 64, 76–77, 80, 105, 109, 141, 150, 240, 245, 251
life, 25, 36, 43, 57, 89, 97–98, 104–107, 109–110, 114, 123, 180, 182–184, 198–199, 221, 226, 242, 251–254, 275–276, 279–281, 301–302
  of absolute knowing, 274, 280
  conscious, 243–244
  forming, 275–277
  inner, 26, 261, 276
  moral, 176, 182–184
light, 20–23, 26, 44–45, 48, 64, 87–89, 101–102, 110, 142, 147–148, 160–162, 164–165, 177–178, 242, 245–247, 251–252
  pure, vi, 5–6, 26, 36, 48, 88, 131–135, 137–143, 159, 161, 216–217

334 | Index

logic, 227, 229, 232–233, 240, 242, 254, 327
Lukács, G, 7, 259, 323–324

manifestness, 20–21, 28, 87–88, 114, 142
materialism, 85, 204–205, 211, 239, 244, 255, 283, 286, 314–315
Mittelpunkt, 146–148, 161

Naturphilosophie, 3, 7, 85, 203, 238–239, 250, 255, 262, 284
negation, 23, 138–142, 228, 241, 246, 248, 250–251, 263–264, 301, 303, 308
  first, 138–140
  second, 139–140
non-philosophy, 175, 243

objectivity, 12–16, 19, 22, 26, 44–45, 86, 198, 252–254, 281, 308, 326
oneness, pure, 124–125, 299

perspective, 19, 54, 173–175, 178–179, 181–184, 186–187, 260, 262, 284–285, 316, 318, 320, 322
philosophical systems, 2, 22, 42, 79, 82–83, 177, 181, 212, 274, 279
philosophizing, vi, 27, 46, 215–233
Plato, 149, 168, 216, 287, 315, 321, 324
Platonism, 61, 236, 249, 252, 315
posit, 17–18, 47, 89, 98–99, 112, 117, 133–134, 141–142, 165, 263, 265
practical reason, 50, 209, 211, 220, 237, 244, 253–254, 286
  pure, 62, 183
pure reason, 62–63, 71–72, 74–75, 77–78, 115, 119, 175, 218–221, 229, 231, 327

quintuplicity, 5, 117, 193, 195–198, 200–202, 204–206, 208–212
  of quintuplicities, 193, 200, 202, 204, 210

realism, 6, 42, 65, 67–69, 76–77, 120–123, 227–229, 236–237, 239, 247, 250–252, 259–266, 268
  higher, 68–69, 74, 122, 178, 270
reconstruction, 11, 13, 19–22, 28, 102, 105, 111, 125, 139, 175–176, 204, 210, 281–282
reflection, 24, 26, 38–40, 68, 70, 97, 100, 173, 176–177, 246, 249, 262, 264, 281–285, 289
Reinhold, K. L., 56, 58, 63–64, 75–76, 82, 121, 174, 207, 211, 231–232, 238
religion, 68–70, 183, 186, 193, 196, 203–205, 209, 211, 243–244, 254, 256, 283–284, 286–287, 309
representation, 36, 62–64, 103, 133, 135, 138–139, 141, 156, 161, 259, 276, 317, 319–320

Schelling, F. W. J., 3, 7, 16, 29–30, 76, 85, 232, 235–239, 241–244, 249–252, 255–256, 259, 262, 269, 272
seeing, 16–18, 106, 157, 180, 184, 236–239, 241–248, 251–252, 263, 270, 274–275, 277–279, 303–306
self-consciousness, 61, 63, 83, 196, 247, 267–268, 280, 282
  embodied, 197
  finite, 248
  free, 196
  individual, 199
self-constitution, 14–15, 22, 24–25, 108
self-determination, 16, 19–20, 24, 26, 28, 30

self-knowledge, 12, 194, 200, 282–283
self-positing, 27, 30, 38, 43, 62, 64–67, 69–70, 74, 77, 242, 252
skepticism, 49, 53, 176, 218, 220–222, 225, 228–229, 231–233, 307
 thoroughgoing, 227–229
space, 81, 87–88, 99, 103–107, 110, 188, 201, 239, 248
Spinoza, B., 71, 106, 115, 237, 239, 275–276, 307
standpoint, 21, 25, 27, 31, 44, 65–69, 71, 73–74, 196, 262, 265–266, 283–287, 304
subject, 63–68, 70, 86, 106, 108, 142, 177–180, 199–200, 206–208, 211, 251–252, 260–261, 265, 281, 318–322
 finite human, 318, 320
 free, 91, 112
 rational, 267
 self-forming, 66
subjectivism, 3, 7, 67–68, 76, 238, 264
subjectivity, 103, 106, 177, 181, 205, 207, 220, 227, 252, 320, 326
subject-object, 38, 51, 65–66, 69–70, 74, 198
substance, 87, 136–138, 243, 257, 296, 302, 304

Tathandlung, 38, 46–47, 51, 55, 57, 64, 120–121, 123
technologies, digital, 291–292, 307–309
theology, 68–70, 77, 309–310 theory
 of appearance, 98, 273, 275
 of being, 241, 251
transcendental
 argument, 108–109, 113, 116, 231, 319, 326
 deduction, 132–133, 141, 317
 insight, 182, 304
 philosophy, xi, 4, 13–14, 36, 39, 44, 50–51, 62–63, 71, 104, 236, 238–239, 241
 standpoint, 14, 224
 subject, 104, 121, 318–319

Wissenschaftslehre, vi–7, 11–31, 33–44, 50–58, 61–71, 79–85, 87–93, 119–122, 145–149, 154–156, 168–170, 173–179, 181–184, 198–200, 207–212, 215–219, 235–245, 259–285, 302–306, 308–310
 nova methodo, xii–1, 6, 43, 51, 76–78, 212, 283
worldviews, five, 66, 196, 209, 273, 282–285, 287

www.ingramcontent.com/pod-product-compliance
Lightning Source LLC
Chambersburg PA
CBHW020121240426
43673CB00038B/549